COMMON PRAYER

COMMON PRAYER

A LITURGY FOR ORDINARY RADICALS

SHANE CLAIBORNE
JONATHAN WILSON-HARTGROVE
ENUMA OKORO

ZONDERVAN

Common Prayer
Copyright © 2010 by The Simple Way and School for Conversion

ISBN 978-0-310-32620-5 (audio)

ISBN 978-0-310-32621-2 (ebook)

Requests for information should be addressed to:
Zondervan, 3900 *Sparks Dr. SE, Grand Rapids, Michigan* 49546

Library of Congress Cataloging-in-Publication Data

Claiborne, Shane, 1975-
    Common prayer : a liturgy for ordinary radicals / Shane Claiborne, Jonathan Wilson-Hartgrove, and Enuma Okoro.
      p. cm.
    ISBN 978-0-310-32619-9 (hardcover)
    1. Worship programs. 2. Prayers. I. Wilson-Hartgrove, Jonathan, 1980- II. Okoro, Enuma, 1973- III. Title.
    BV198.C56 2010
    264'.15—dc22
                                                                                     2010034213

Scripture quotations marked TNIV, other than those from the book of Psalms, are taken from the Holy Bible, *Today's New International Version*® *TNIV*®. Copyright © 2001, 2005 by International Bible Society.® Used by permission of International Bible Society®. All rights reserved worldwide. "TNIV" and "Today's New International Version" are trademarks registered in the United States Patent and Trademark Office by International Bible Society®.

All quotations from the book of Psalms are taken from *The Book of Common Prayer.*

Any Internet addresses (websites, blogs, etc.) and telephone numbers in this book are offered as a resource. They are not intended in any way to be or imply an endorsement by Zondervan, nor does Zondervan vouch for the content of these sites and numbers for the life of this book.

All rights reserved. No part of this publication may be reproduced, stored in a retrieval system, or transmitted in any form or by any means—electronic, mechanical, photocopy, recording, or any other—except for brief quotations in printed reviews, without the prior permission of the publisher.

Published in association with the literary agency of Daniel Literary Group, LLC, 1701 Kingsbury Drive, Suite 100, Nashville, TN 37215.

Woodblock prints for February, Holy Week, July, October, and December are by Rick Beerhorst (www.studiobeerhorst.com).

Linoleum block prints for January, March, April, May, June, August, September, and November are by Joel Klepac (www.joelklepac.com).

Woodblock prints for Evening, Morning, and Midday, and art for the Lord's Prayer borders are by Jesce Walz (www.jesce.net).

Cover image: Shutterstock®
Interior design: Beth Shagene

First printing November 2011 / Printed in the United States of America

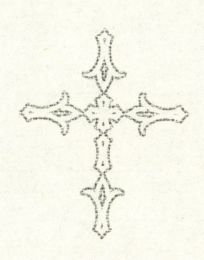

CONTENTS

List of Sidebars | 008

Introduction | 009

Evening Prayer | 027

Sunday | 028

Monday | 030

Tuesday | 033

Wednesday | 035

Thursday | 038

Friday | 040

Saturday | 042

Morning Prayer | 045

December | 047

January | 087

February | 127

March | 165

Holy Week | 205

April | 219

May | 259

June | 301

July | 341

August | 381

September | 423

October | 461

November | 501

Midday Prayer | 541

Occasional Prayers | 545

House Blessing | 546

Prayers for a Workplace | 551

Major Life Transition | 552

Before or After a Meal | 553

Prayer to Welcome the Sabbath | 554

Death of Someone Killed in the Neighborhood | 555

For Healing | 555

A Prayer for Adoption | 556

Baby Dedication | 557

Commissioning/Sending Out | 559

Celibacy Commitment | 560

Blessing of the Land or a Garden | 561

A Litany to Honor Women | 562

Sanctus | 563

Prayer for Communion/Eucharist | 564

Songbook | 565

Credits | 589

LIST OF SIDEBARS

A Note on Advent | 050

Reading Scripture | 068

A Note on Christmas | 078

A Note on Lent | 139

Sacred Space: Thinking About Where We Pray | 159

Order and Spontaneity | 175

Taking Liturgy to the Streets | 213

Eucharist and Communion | 224

Liturgy Is Magical, but Not Magic | 245

Smells and Bells | 266

Prayer Beads | 292

Prayer Bowl | 313

The Celebration of Yahweh's Kingship | 347

Whole Body Prayer | 361

Offering a Sacrifice of Praise | 404

Confession | 411

Note for Columbus Day: We Need New Heroes | 477

Alleluia | 505

A Note on Christ the King Sunday | 538

Passing the Peace | 543

INTRODUCTION

If you love liturgy, this book is for you.

If you don't know what liturgy is, this book is also for you.

Whether you are over-churched or under-churched, a proud evangelical, a recovering evangelical, or not an evangelical at all; whether you are high church, low church, or no church, a skeptic or a Pentecostal; whether you have found a community or have burned out on community; this book is for you.

This is a different kind of book. It's not a book you pick up and read straight through. In fact, this book is not designed to be read alone. It is a book filled with songs, prayers, ideas, and memories that are meant to be spoken aloud and shared together in some form of community. That community may be your biological family or a small group of friends. It could be a gathering of folks in your public housing unit or dorm room, in your village or cul-de-sac. The early church met in homes and as congregations in local assemblies. Whatever form your community takes, this is a book about "we," not "me."

Common Prayer

There are so many different divisions of Christianity — Greek, Russian, and Serbian Orthodox, Roman Catholic, Anglican, Reformed, Presbyterian, Baptist and Anabaptist, African Methodist Episcopal, Pentecostal, nondenominational, Mennonite and Quaker. By one count, there are more than thirty-eight thousand Christian denominations. Many people have said that the greatest barrier to becoming a Christian is all the division they see in the church.

God's deepest longing is for the church to be united as one body. In Jesus' longest recorded prayer, he prayed that we would be "one as God is one." As one old preacher said, "We gotta get it together, because Jesus is coming back, and he's coming for a bride, not a harem."

God has only one church.

This prayer book is the result of a collaboration of people from many different branches of Christianity, all of which come from one trunk — if you trace the branches all the way back.

Folks are bound to ask if this prayer book is for Catholics or for Protestants. Our answer is, "Yes, it is." We want the fire of the Pentecostals, the imagination of the Mennonites, the Lutheran's love of Scripture, the Benedictines' discipline, the wonder of the Orthodox and Catholics. We've mined the fields of church history for treasures and celebrated them wherever we've found them. We've drawn on some of the oldest and richest traditions of Christian prayer. And we've tried to make them dance.

Our prayer lives connect us to the rest of the body of Christ around the world; at any hour of any day, many of the prayers in this book are being prayed in some corner of the earth. Using these prayers is also a way of connecting ourselves to the past; we're talking about the greatest hits not just from the 1960s, '70s, and '80s but also from the 1800s and the 300s. Many of these prayers and songs are more than a thousand years old.

A Word about Liturgy

Liturgy comes from the Greek word *leitourgia*, meaning "public worship." When we hear the phrase *public worship*, many of us think of large meetings, like Sunday morning services, and while public worship *can* mean that, it doesn't have to take place in a big group. After all, *public* shares the same root word as *pub*, and it really just refers to a gathering of people to share life (and maybe a drink), a get-together that's always open to strangers joining in. Jesus promised that wherever two or three of us gather in his name, he'll be there with us. Jesus will be with us at the "pub" whether there's wine or not (and if not, he might conjure some up, or conjure up grape juice for the Baptists).

For those of us who are new to liturgy, it's noteworthy that, though there are some variations among different traditions, a majority of Christian liturgies around the world share an overall structure — especially the liturgies of Catholics, Anglicans, Lutherans, Presbyterians, and Methodists.* It has been said that if the covers were removed from the major worship books of the late twentieth century, it would be difficult to tell which book belongs to which church body. The major traditions follow pretty much the same script.

When we first experience the organized cycle of readings that is a part of liturgical worship — a lectionary, as it's often called — it can seem like magic

---

*And although charismatic movements are not yet among the majority in the global church, these movements represent the fastest growing parts of the church today. Even in these movements, many people are reestablishing the fundamental value of common prayer and liturgy, just with a little more oomph. In fact, charismatic Christians can offer a refreshing surge of fiery passion to enliven a tradition that may have grown stale or cold.

or a conspiracy. We may hear a pastor preach from the same text we read in morning prayer and think, "How in the world? The Spirit must be moving!" And, in fact, the Spirit is moving, just in a more organized way than we would have guessed. Some liturgical types smile when evangelicals discover the "miracle" of the liturgy. But it is a miracle nonetheless. So lean in and listen as you pray these prayers. Sometimes it may feel like you can hear the church's heart beat as you pray in a way you never have before.

The readings of the church are arranged in a three-year cycle so that we hear the entire biblical story — creation and fall, the exodus, captivity and return, the promise and advent of the Messiah, the coming of the Holy Spirit, and the promise of the coming kingdom. These cycles are used all over the world, so that on the same day, Christians in Africa are reading the same texts as Christians in Latin America. Since *Common Prayer* is designed to be repeated each year, we have done our best to honor these cycles, though we've squeezed them into only one year of readings.

Participating in the liturgy of the worldwide Christian community, whether on a Sunday morning or at another time, is more than attending a service or a prayer meeting. It is about entering a story. It is about orienting our lives around what God has been doing throughout history. And it is about being sent forth into the world to help write the next chapter of that story. Wandering the world in search of meaning and purpose, we may not even realize how desperately we need a story. But we know we've found something priceless when we find ourselves in God's narrative.

Liturgy is not about getting indoctrinated. Doctrines are hard things to love.

It's not even really about education. Liturgy at its core is not about learning facts and memorizing phrases.

Liturgy is soul food. It nourishes our souls just as breakfast strengthens our bodies. It's sort of like family dinner. Hopefully you get some nutritious food, but more than nutrition, family dinner is about family, love, community. Liturgy is kind of like family dinner with God. Liturgical theologian Aidan Kavanaugh says it well: "The liturgy, like the feast, exists not to educate but to seduce people into participating in common activity of the highest order, where one is freed to learn things which cannot be taught."

While liturgy is a party, it's also about disciplining our spirits like we exercise our muscles. Certainly we are learning as we pray, as we listen to Scripture, as we learn the songs and stories. But we are also participating in the work of God — active prayer, active worship. As we will see, liturgy offers us an invitation not just to observe but to participate. "O Lord, let my soul rise up to meet you" invites us to respond, "As the day rises to meet the sun." When we hear, "God is good," we want to call back, "All the time." Liturgy is a dialogue, a divine drama in which we are invited to be the actors. We become a part of God's story. We sing God's songs. We discover lost ancestors. And their story becomes our story.

Welcome to a Whole New World

Liturgy is a workout for the imagination, because we are invited to see the reality of the universe through a new lens. Liturgy offers us another way of seeing the world. The liturgical imagination is different from the imagination of films or video games, though every once in a while you catch a film that gives you a hint of another world (like when Neo takes the red pill in *The Matrix*).

In *Common Prayer* we enter a counterintuitive story. *Common Prayer* helps us to see ourselves as part of a holy counterculture, a people being "set apart" from the world around us (and the world inside us) to bear witness that another world is possible. We're invited to become a peculiar people, living into a different story, and orienting our lives around a different set of values than those we are taught by the empires and markets around us. In an individualistic culture, liturgy helps us live a communal life. In an ever-changing world, liturgy roots us in the eternal — something that was around long before us and will live long after us, a God who is the same yesterday and today and tomorrow, no matter what happens on Wall Street.

Liturgy's counterintuitive nature may feel a little culturally strange at first. It is weird enough in our culture just to get together to sing songs (unless you are going to a concert or playing Rock Band on the Wii). Singing and praying together can feel awkward, especially if it is not Thanksgiving or Christmas. But liturgy is meant to be an interruption. It disrupts our reality and refocuses it on God. It reshapes our perceptions and lives with new rhythms, new holy days, a whole new story.

What we discover is not just a poetic genius behind the words but a community in, with, and under the words. Just as people of the world pledge allegiance to flags or sing national anthems with pride and adoration, these creeds, songs, and prayers are ways that we proclaim our allegiance and sing our adoration not to a nation but to another kingdom altogether. That may sound a little esoteric or ethereal, like heaven is less real than the stuff of earth. But liturgy actually draws us out of the world of counterfeit power and splendor and into another reality. As we pray, this world, with its billboards and neon signs and false promises, becomes ghostlike. We are invited into an ancient and eternal place and time that transcends all that is around us.

Worship is not about God needing us, as if our love and admiration were necessary for God to feel complete. God is not codependent. The beauty of it is not that God needs us but that God wants us. The love of God is so big that it spilled over into the creation of man and woman. The love of the Trinity is so big that we were created to share in the community of God. And we are the image of that love. If loving communion is at the core of the Trinity, then it is also the core of who we are. "Who am I?" cannot be answered without asking "Who are we?" We cannot properly know ourselves until we properly conceive of God and our neighbor.

Liturgy invites us into a new "we." The church reflects the most diverse community in the world — white, black, and all shades in-between, rich and poor, all walks of life. We are called to bring our lives and our cultures together to become a new community.

The world the liturgy reveals may not seem relevant at first glance, but it turns out that the world the liturgy reveals is more real than the one we inhabit day by day. It outlasts McDonald's and Walmart, America and South Africa. The songs and readings and prayers of the liturgy are more ancient and true than any culture or empire.

The liturgy presents a form of worship that transcends our time and place. It does not negate culture but creates a new one. Certainly we can see the fingerprints of the cultures from which it has come — Mediterranean, Greco-Roman, North African, German, Frankish, Anglo-Saxon. But we are formed into a people who are singing songs and prayers that transcend place and nation. Though its forms may vary, the liturgy will never grow old. It has been meaningfully prayed by bakers, housewives, tailors, teachers, philosophers, priests, monks, kings, slaves, and revolutionaries for centuries.

This is the story of the Israelites. Their story is our story. The God who saved the Hebrew children saves us today. When we say "Father Abraham," it does not need to feel like artificial words on paper; it can feel like we are discovering lost relatives. Abraham and Sarah are our grandparents. And their God is our God. God is the same yesterday, today, and forevermore. When we say in the Apostles' Creed (one of the oldest declarations of our faith) that we believe in "the communion of saints," we are saying that we are in community with those who have gone before and with those who will come after. We are one in Christ, a union so strong and eternal that nothing can separate us, not even death, and certainly not time or space.

In prayer and worship, we can feel like we are transported to another place, taken into another world. When we say, "O Lord, let my soul rise up to meet you," we are ascending beyond this world and all that is temporary. It is not an escape. Just the opposite — it is a warning not to escape from the eternal into the stuff of earth. In liturgical prayer, we are never alone, because we are surrounded by the thousands of folks who are singing and praying with us around the world. And as we pray, we are lifted up into a place beyond the building or city we are in. We are living in the "city of God," which isn't something you can find with a GPS.

Welcome to a New Time Zone

Every sturdy society has created its own calendar according to its own values. For some time now, Western civilization has used the Julian and Gregorian calendars, which are influenced largely by the Roman Empire's traditions ("August" referring to Caesar Augustus and "January" referring to the god Janus, etc.). The United States' civil religion uses this calendar, mixing in its own set of holy days, most notably its date of inception (July 4) and its remembrances of human sacrifice (Memorial Day and Veterans Day). Consumer culture always threatens to monopolize the feast days on which the church remembers saints like Nicholas, Valentine, and Patrick, turning them into little more than days to buy stuff in the name of cultural idols such as Santa, the Easter bunny, and green leprechauns. Too often we have forgotten the lives of the people for whom these days are named.

But if we in the church are going to take our citizenship in heaven seriously, we must reshape our minds by marking our calendars differently. We must remember the holidays of the biblical narrative rather than the festivals of the Caesars, and celebrate feast days to remember saints rather than war heroes and presidents. Our inception as the church was on Pentecost, not on July 4. Our fireworks should go off a few months earlier than America's. And instead of commemorating people who sacrifice themselves in order to kill for their country, we find a deeper and more powerful observance on Good Friday, when we remember that Jesus willingly died for everyone in the world, even his enemies, instead of killing them to "change the world."

Or consider our holy season of Epiphany, when the church celebrates the civil disobedience of the magi, who, coming from outside of Caesar's realm, honored a different kind of king and sneaked away from the violent Herod. One of our lesser-known holidays is the Feast of the Holy Innocents (December 28), when the church remembers Herod's genocide of children in his attempt to root out any would-be incumbents. On such a day, we take in the harsh truth that there was and still is a political cost to the incarnation of God's peaceable love. Such a holy feast day of mourning provokes our own political memory and prompts us to communally and publicly remember the Iraqis (around one million) who have died since the US invasion in 2003. On such a day, we don't consider those deaths to be the necessary sacrifice of "collateral damage"; we lament their deaths as acts of our contemporary Herods.

Many of us have learned history by studying wars and violence; we organize it by the reigns of kings and presidents. But in Jesus, we reorder history. We date it from his visit to earth and examine it through a new lens — identifying with the tortured, the displaced, the refugee, and remembering the nonviolent revolutions on the margins of empires.

We enter a new time zone, where it can feel like there is a "cloud of witnesses" surrounding us, praying for us, cheering us on from eternity. It should feel like we are singing "Holy, Holy, Holy" with all of the people of God who have come before us. And our own pasts become bigger than ourselves. The day the "world changed" was not September 11 but way back in 33 AD. The most significant event in our pasts is not our most shameful transgressions but the death and resurrection of Jesus. Our pasts are defined not by our sins but by Christ's victory. God's story is the lens through which we understand our current world. It affects how we interact with evil and how we hold our possessions. The future, like the past, is no longer held hostage. We are no longer defined by the anxieties of our age. We know how the story ends, and it is beautiful. This is the good news that transcends the nightly news. Even more certain than who the next president will be is the reality that Christ will come again.

Our lives are filled with overlapping calendars and dates. For some folks, football season is the favorite time of year, and everything must give way for *Monday Night Football*. Football has its holy days and landmark moments, its hall of fame (and hall of shame). For those of us who are following the way of Jesus, part of what we do is orient our lives around a different calendar and history. (That's not to say you can't watch a good football game from time to time.)

The worldwide church has its holy days, as you will see in the morning prayers — days such as the Presentation, the Annunciation, the Visitation, and the Transfiguration. These are our holidays. We also have our own hall of fame (and hall of shame).* There will be days when we highlight different women and men throughout church history (often on the days they died). They are exemplary models of Christian discipleship from around the world and across the centuries, and they're just really fascinating people who have lived well. It is our hope that their lives and courage will inspire us, and rub off on us, as they point us to Christ. In their imperfect but beautiful lives, we can see our own possibilities and potential. More on that later.

The church's calendar weaves in and out of the world around us. It is not that we need a "Christian" calendar because we want to separate ourselves from the "secular" world, similar to the way that some Christians adamantly listen only to "Christian" music or have "Christian" T-shirts or bumper stickers or even iPods shaped like a cross. (There really is such a thing as a cross-shaped iPod, by the way!) The point is not to be sectarian or to try to put ourselves at odds with non-Christians. The point is to keep God's story at the center of our lives and calendar. And it is through the lens of Jesus that we read history and interpret whether an event is good or bad. It is important to note that many of the dates on the Christian calendar have their basis in the world's calendar. For instance, the date of Easter has little to do with the actual day

---

*Because of space limitations, we were not able to include a complete list of saints from every tradition, but we did our best to celebrate the women and men who beautifully represent the faith and global church by their witness. Besides, there are many saints who have not yet been recognized as such and others just being born. Feel free to add your own saints and heroes to the list, and let's keep sharing their stories with one another.

on which Jesus rose from the grave, but it is the first Sunday after the first full moon on or after the spring equinox. It's interesting to note too that the natural seasons also teach us about God, even though in Australia it's summer during Advent. (So they go to the beach on Christmas rather than sit by the fire.) But as we build our lives around God's story, we are reminded that this story is the center of the universe.

Much of the church has created a life with common prayer at the center. Our days begin in the evening as we light the Christ candle in darkness, then continue when we greet the morning with resurrection praise and later come back to prayer at noon to center ourselves in the midst of our activity. (And by doing so, we proclaim, "Christ has died. Christ is risen. Christ will come again.") Morning and evening prayer are the touchstones of common prayer, going all the way back to ancient Judaism. The *Didache*, a collection of practical instructions for the early church, instructs believers to say the Lord's Prayer three times a day. We've stuck with the three times of prayer in this book. But it's worth noting that some monastic communities have taken quite literally the psalm that says "seven times a day do I praise thee." They even get up once in the middle of the night to pray together.

The daily cycle of evening, morning, and midday prayer is like a heartbeat for the global church, passing from one time zone to the next each day, so that we as a people can, as the apostle Paul taught us, pray without ceasing. But this daily rhythm is but a "wheel within a wheel" of the weekly cycle, which begins on Sunday (Resurrection Day), remembers Jesus' gathering the twelve disciples on Thursday, suffers with Christ symbolically on Friday (hence many Christians fast), and makes preparation on Saturday for the great feast after the resurrection. And that brings us back to "do," a deer, a female deer. Then we do it all again, and again. *Common Prayer* honors this weekly rhythm in its seven-day cycle of evening prayers.

But the weekly cycle also happens within an annual rhythm of seasons — Advent to prepare for Christ's coming, Christmas to celebrate the Prince of Peace, Epiphany to remember the Light (a light outsiders often recognize before we do), Lent to confess our resistance to the Light, Holy Week to remember Christ's suffering, Easter to celebrate resurrection's power, the birthday of the church at Pentecost (a good time for pyrotechnics — be careful), and Ordinary Time to bring us back to the beginning again. These are our seasons in the church.

This peculiar way of counting time teaches us to look at our days differently. No longer do we see dates simply as August 29 or October 4. Now they are John the Baptist's day and St. Francis of Assisi's day. No longer are our seasons simply fall and spring; they are also Advent and Lent. Our history is different from the history told by nations and empires; our heroes are not pioneers of colonialism and capitalism like Columbus and Rockefeller but pioneers of compassion like Mother Teresa and Oscar Romero. And our holy days are different from the holidays of pop culture and the dominatrix of power.

The rhythms of the liturgy are not so much something that has been created as they are something that has been discovered over the centuries. Many of our current patterns of prayer and worship began to take shape as early as the second century. Especially in ancient oral cultures, they were ways of remembering the story. And in a world of Twitter and blogs and text messages, these words and songs and prayers feel more rooted and eternal than the virtual truth that is here today and gone tomorrow.

The church calendar begins not on January 1 but with Advent, four weeks before Christmas (*Advent* means "the coming"), as the world waits, pregnant with hope. So you'll notice our morning prayers begin at the end of the world's calendar year (in December) because we begin with the birth of our Savior Jesus, around whom the entire calendar and world revolve. Everything in the kingdom of God is upside down and backward — the last are first and the first are last; the poor are blessed and the peacemakers are the children of God; and the year begins with Advent rather than with New Year's Day.

The church calendar does not help us remember our meetings, but it aims at nothing less than changing the way we experience time and perceive reality. The church calendar does not help us remember sports events or weather cycles, but it is about the movement of history toward a glorious goal — God's kingdom on earth as it is in heaven.

Select any day of the year and you can find its liturgical significance. In fact, one of the cool things about the Christian calendar is that every day is a holy day. Holidays are not just days you get off work but days you remember God's redemptive work in the world.

We also realize that we are not called to be so heavenly minded that we are of no earthly good. We are not to ignore the calendar that the rest of the world lives by, but we are to hold our calendar alongside it and to realize that all of history hinges on the death and resurrection of Jesus two thousand years ago. For this reason, just as we begin morning prayer remembering saints and holy days, this book will also remember significant dates in world history — dates that mark great strides for freedom or grave injustices we dare not forget.

As we look at the Christian calendar, we are reminded that we are in the world but not of it. We are citizens of the kingdom that transcends time, but we sojourn on a time-bound earth. Without liturgical time, we can easily forget our eternal identity. We can get lost in the hustle and bustle of business and efficiency that shapes our culture and society. Likewise, without the cosmic calendar, we can become so heaven-bound that we ignore the hells of the world around us. And the glorious goal we are headed toward is not just going up when we die but bringing God's kingdom down — on earth as it is in heaven.

Why *Common* Prayer?

No doubt, we can pray to God by ourselves; for centuries both monks and evangelicals (and lots of people in between) have prayed solitarily. There is something beautiful about a God who is personal, who talks face to face with Moses, wrestles with Jacob, and becomes fully human in Jesus, a God who needs no mediation, with whom we can speak as a Friend and Lover at any moment and in any place, in a cathedral or an alleyway.

The point of this book is certainly not to take away from the intimacy each of us can have with God. Personal or devotional prayer and communal prayer are not at odds with each other. In fact, they must go together. Just as God is communal, God is also deeply personal and intimate.

Certainly one of the unique and beautiful things about Jesus is his intimacy with God as he runs off to the mountaintop or hides away in the garden. Jesus daringly invites us to approach the God of the universe as Abba (Daddy) or as a mother caring for her little chicks. Our God is personal and wildly in love with each of us.

Some friends who have experienced only liturgical worship and prayer are moved to tears by the childlike winsomeness of charismatics and Pentecostals as they pray with such sincerity and honesty, with tears and holy laughter. That kind of prayer is a gift to the church and has much to offer liturgical types, just as liturgy has much to offer Pentecostals.

Just because our prayer lives are personal does not mean they are private. Many of us have grown up in a culture where rampant individualism has affected our prayer lives. When we think about prayer, our imaginations may be limited to evening devotions or a daily "quiet time" with God. As wonderful as these times of solitude can be, prayer moves us beyond what we can do on our own.

It's certainly possible for people to customize their religion, sort of like the "create your own pizza" menu at a restaurant. Ironically, both conservative evangelicals and liberal New Agers often fall to the same temptation to create a religion that is very self-centered — and very lonely. You can be religious and still be lonely. But part of the good news is that we are not alone. If we see prayer only as a private affair, we miss out. To talk with God is to get caught up in conversation with brothers and sisters we didn't know we had.

There is something to this idea that "when two or three of you gather in my name, I will be with you." Prayer is a communal practice.

There is a reason the Lord's Prayer is a communal prayer to "our" Father, asking for "our" daily bread and asking God to forgive us "our" sins as we forgive others. Our God is a communal God. It is not enough to pray for "my" daily bread alone.

The gift of liturgy is that it helps us hear less of our own little voices and more of God's still, small voice (Psalm 46). It leads away from self and points us toward the community of God. God is a plurality of oneness. God has "lived in community" from eternity as Father, Son, and Holy Spirit. God as Trinity is the core reality of the universe, and that means that the core of reality is community. We often live as if the essence of our being is the "I," and as if the "we" of community is a nice add-on or an "intentional" choice. But the truth is we are made for community, and if we live outside of community, we are selling ourselves short. We are made in the image of community.

Praying with the Saints

To be sure, there is a history in the church of monastic* folks who live in caves and monasteries and seek God in solitude. The funny thing is that these holy hermits pray the same prayers, read the same cycles of readings, and sing the same chants as everyone else. Like birds in the forest, monks all sing the same song. In fact, there was an old saying: "If the monks stop praying, the world will collapse."

Even when they pray by themselves, they know they are not really alone.

We never pray alone, even when praying by ourselves. The prayers and songs in this book are designed to be prayed together, but if you are not physically with others, rest assured that there are others praying with you around the world. It is impossible to feel alone when we pray these prayers, even when we pray them by ourselves. We are praying prayers crafted not by our lonely piety but by the entire body of Christ throughout her history. We are praying prayers whose origin is in another time and place, going all the way back to the early church, and thus we are mysteriously connected with believers who have gone before us. So while we hope *Common Prayer* is fresh and alive for you, it is not new. It may only seem new because of how much of our history we have lost or misplaced. In this book, we discover lost memories and treasures from the past, digging up amid all the clutter of Christendom old pictures and keepsakes from our ancestors and wiping the dust away.

There is a new "we." If our citizenship is in heaven, this truth should change the way we talk. The word *we*, if a person is truly born again, will refer to the new people into whom a Christian has been born — the church. Christians

---

*Monasticism comes from the Greek word *monazein*, meaning "to live alone," and often we think of monastics as folks who live in seclusion from the rest of the world in a pious monastery or convent. But correctly understood, monastics are not fleeing the word so much as they are trying to save the world from itself, beginning with what they can change — themselves. The *mono-* at the beginning of *monastic* means "one," and we can think of monastics as folks who have committed their lives to "one thing" — the single-minded pursuit of God, like the person in Jesus' parable who gives everything for the most precious pearl ever seen. That is what it means to be monastic — to will one thing, and to run after Jesus as our Lover, saying no to everything that might divide our attention or take our eyes off the Pearl.

can no longer refer to "our troops" or "our history" as other people do because of our new identity. Fabricated boundaries and walls are removed for the Christian. Our neighbor is not only from Chicago but also from Baghdad. Our brother or sister in the church could be from Iran or California — no difference! Our family is transnational and borderless; we are in Iraq, and we are in Palestine. And if we are indeed to become born again, we will have to begin talking like it, changing the meaning of *we*, *us*, *my*, and *our*.

We must connect our prayers to the rest of God's children throughout the world and through all time and space, people who are reading the same Scriptures, singing the same songs, praying the same prayers, and grafting their lines into the same old story of a God who is forming a people who are set apart from the world to be God's light and to show the world what a society of love looks like. Today, more than ever before in history, we have a keen sense of what it means to be a part of a global neighborhood. We are aware of how beautifully diverse and terribly dysfunctional the human family is. As we pray through this book together, we are reminded that we have friends in Sudan and China, Afghanistan and Iraq, Palestine and Israel, whether they are our Facebook friends or not. They are praying with us. And the bond we have in Christ is more real than any virtual social network. This is what it means to be born again. We are a part of a global neighborhood and a beautifully diverse family of God's children.

What about When You're Not Feeling It?

Sometimes all you have to do is show up. You may not feel like praying. Others will pray, and perhaps their prayers will welcome yours. It is not that others pray for us or that their voices replace our voices, but there is something that can spark in us when we are surrounded by others whose hearts are on fire. Hot coals build a better fire when they are together. There is a harmony that cannot exist when we go solo. To be sure, there is a place for solos and for *a capella*, but there is also something about a mass choir or mass prayer that gets our spirits soaring.

Liturgy is public worship, but it is also, more literally, the "work of the people." *Common Prayer* isn't so much an "inspirational" text as it is a workout guide. Liturgy is active. It takes patience (part of the fruit of the Spirit, by the way). And patience is very countercultural. Sometimes we don't feel like working out our bodies, but after the first few steps, we feel our bodies start to breathe, and we can feel our heartbeat, which had grown quiet and lethargic. Liturgy is not simply about watching or listening; it's about participating. You can sit back with a bowl of popcorn and watch all the exercise videos you want, but nothing will happen until you get off the couch and start sweatin' to the oldies.

In many ways, the "official" liturgy can't work for each of us if we're not doing things to stay in shape outside of the fixed hours for prayer. Study, discipleship, the works of mercy, and contemplation are the homework assignments that prepare us for the experience of worship and prayer together. Otherwise, it can feel like we are being invited to laugh at a joke we haven't even heard yet. How can you worship unless you have spent some time falling in love? If *Common Prayer* doesn't work for you right away, hang in there and give the divine romance a chance.

But also, a disclaimer: the liturgy is not a magic formula. And you can have liturgy without life in it, just as you can have a nice-looking car that doesn't run. Some of the dreariest services on the planet are rich with liturgy and traditions.

Liturgy is one of the most powerful places to meet and be transformed by God. It is also one of the best places to hide — from God and from others. So may it be a doorway into deeper relationship with God and with others. If it's not, may you keep knocking until you find a door that opens.

About This Book

Creating this book has been a little like directing a symphony — or a circus. We wanted it to be simple enough to captivate the young, but intricate enough that someone more familiar with liturgy can appreciate its reliance on the tradition. To hang with the analogy, we wanted it to work for folks who have never seen a circus and for those who have seen hundreds of them. So we had to get a little creative in places. For instance, we wanted those who are unfamiliar with the Lord's Prayer to feel very welcome and free, so you will find the words of the prayer framing the pages of the evening prayers, and we hope that this is both practical and beautiful for you as you learn it. You will also see the Lord's Prayer in seven of the languages of the world that are spoken by the most people, reminding us that we are part of a global family with many tongues and tribes. And you might find these borders helpful if Mandarin is your first language or you are looking to learn Arabic.

Many prayer books require a lot of tedious and confusing page-turning to find the different prayers and songs you need for a specific day, and we've done our best to minimize that. We have also provided a ribbon, which you can use as you wish. When you reach the end of the day's morning prayers, for example, you may want to use it to mark the page of the next day's prayers. Or you might find it helpful to mark the page of the song that will be used during the day's morning prayers so you can find it quickly.

Like compilers of a good cookbook, we have not just created a book of recipes but also included pictures, comments, tips, and suggestions for taking action that we hope will be useful as you go along. You'll find the pictures at the beginning of each month in the morning prayers section. The comments, tips, and suggestions are set off in boxes throughout the prayer offices. Some of these are designed for folks who are new to liturgical prayer, and others are to get prayer veterans to think outside the box (or outside the cathedral). Many of them are stolen from the wisdom of the centuries past, and we hope they help us become better chefs of holiness.

Evening Prayer

There are seven evening prayers, one for each evening of the week, to be repeated each week throughout the year. We created these evening prayers in the hope that, just as the morning prayers allow us to greet the morning together, the evening prayers will allow us to retire from the day together. They are simple prayers that you should be able to pray in fifteen to twenty minutes. The evenings have a focus on confession — the confession of our sins to one another, and the confession of our faith together. And we have grafted into them some of the core creeds and scriptural songs that are hundreds and even thousands of years old.

Morning Prayer

There are morning prayers for each morning of the year, and eight special morning prayers to be used during Holy Week, the week leading up to Easter. Morning prayers are designed to help us wake up and greet the day, and you should be able to pray them in less than half an hour. The morning prayers invite participation through responsorial psalms to read together and songs to sing. If you do pray by yourself, we hope you'll hear the echoes of others' voices and remember you are not alone.

As is the case with most prayer books, the prayers are designed to have one person lead. Feel free to rotate who that person is, but it is usually helpful to have one person get things rolling. Prayers in normal type are to be said by the leader; prayers in bold type can be said by everyone together. Words in italic type are headings or instructions and are not meant to be read aloud. Also, a colon with a space before and after it (:) indicates a pause. Here's a visual key for future reference:

> Normal type = to be read by single voice/leader
> **Bold type** = to be read by community
> *Italic type* = instructions/headings, not to be read
> A colon (:) = pause

Each month has a little "month at a glance" introduction to kick it off, featuring a lovely piece of art, reflections on one of the twelve "Marks of New Monasticism," and a list of suggested reading (and sometimes viewing or listening) for the month. Several years ago, we held a little "ecclesial council" of sorts, a gathering of dozens of communities, old and young, to try to identify the DNA of the current renewal we see in the church. As we tried to listen to the Spirit together, twelve distinctive marks of that renewal jumped out at us. As we worked on this book, those twelve marks seemed to flow well with the months of the year.

And at the end of each month, we list a few practical ideas for becoming the answer to our prayers. Too often we use prayer as a substitute for action. But it seems that much of the time when we ask God to do something about pain and suffering, we hear God say back to us, "I already *did* do something — I made you." Our little lists are meant to provoke the imagination with ideas on how we might put our prayers into action and our faith into practice. They're meant as brainstorms to get the gears going, so feel free to add to those lists your own recipes for holy mischief.

Many of the morning prayers begin with a glance back into the past — an "On This Day in History" type of story to remind us of significant moments that have occurred in the pursuit of peace and justice over the centuries. We will greet those days with remembrances, for example, that on this day, Nagasaki was bombed, or Rosa Parks went to jail, or Martin Luther King Jr. was killed, or Nelson Mandela was released from prison. One of the unique contributions of this prayer book is to weave into our prayer lives the ongoing struggle for peace and justice, to help us pray with the Bible in one hand and the newspaper in the other. The list of events we commemorate in this book is nowhere near exhaustive, but we did our best, with a very diverse group of friends, to identify global events, both magnificent and terrible, that have been landmark moments, especially as we pray for God's kingdom to come on earth.

Throughout the morning prayers, we also remember different saints who have exemplified what our faith is about. Usually we recognize them on their birthdays or on the days of their deaths (which are really only another kind of birthday, especially for those who were martyred). We have been careful to celebrate the legacy both of Saints with a big *S* (people who are recognized by the Roman Catholic Church and/or the Eastern Orthodox Church) and of saints with a little *S* (people who are not recognized by Catholics and Orthodox, but who give us incredible glimpses of faithful discipleship). It has been said that saints are God's aroma in the world; they leave behind the fragrance of God. Author Frederick Buechner said, "In the holy flirtation with the world, God occasionally drops a handkerchief. These handkerchiefs are called saints."

Selecting the readings was a little tricky, since the traditional liturgy of the church follows a three-year cycle of Scripture readings. We've done our best to honor this cycle with selected readings. We've also tried to honor the cycle of readings from the book of Psalms. You will notice that each month, we move through the sequence of the one hundred and fifty psalms, skipping quite a few, of course, but reading at least a little bit of every psalm by the time we end the year. The Old and New Testament readings for each day also move consecutively through biblical books, with the occasional interruption for a special holiday with a fixed date. For those who use *Common Prayer* year after year, you might choose to read through other books of Scripture some years.

One of the other tricky things we had to resolve is how to merge the world calendar with the church calendar, since many holy days, such as Easter, do not fall on the same calendar day each year. For ease of use, we chose to use calendar dates as our skeleton, but we also created a few additional prayers to use as supplements during these holy days and holy seasons. In the special case of Holy Week (the week before Easter Sunday), instead of using the dated morning prayers in the months of March or April, you will use the morning prayers for Palm Sunday, Monday, Tuesday, Wednesday, Maundy Thursday, Good Friday, Holy Saturday, and Easter in the Holy Week section of the book.

Finally, each morning prayer features a quotation — little nuggets of wisdom for each day. Just as we chose saints from different times and places and traditions, we also selected quotes that represent a diverse chorus of wise voices. Undoubtedly, some of these quotes will be familiar and some will be new. Not all of these quotes are from Christians, nor was it our intention to endorse everyone we quoted, but we do believe that anything true belongs to God, no matter whose mouth it comes from. The quotes we chose to remember in the context of prayer are words that inspire us to shout the gospel with our whole lives.

Midday Prayer

Midday prayer is meant to be a way of carving out space in the busyness of our days to center us on Christ. It is a simple office of prayer put together from various ancient sources and monastic traditions, and can be prayed in about ten minutes. Midday prayer is a great way to gather coworkers and colleagues to be refreshed for the rest of the day. We crafted it in a simple and beautiful form that would continue to "dance" despite the fact that it's repeated each day of the year. If your life prohibits you from taking a noontime break for prayer, you could try integrating elements of this office into your day, even praying in a bathroom stall if you have to. We hope that it is also easy to memorize.

Occasional Prayers

In the back of the book, you will find some prayers and rituals for special occasions which can be used any time of the year. There are prayers for house blessings, for healing, for births and for deaths, for sending people out on adventures, and for gathering folks for meals. A few of them we created. Others we gathered from church history, sometimes even adding a little contemporary flair to make them dance for us today as well.

Songbook

We asked folks from many different traditions to give us their list of "greatest hits," the songs they sing in the shower and have written on their hearts. We've collected those classics and compiled them into a songbook in the back of the book, with words, melodies, and chords — everything from African-American spirituals and freedom songs to Taize chants and old hymns. All of these songs are used in the morning prayers, but this collection of music has all sorts of possibilities — grill some food and plan a night of hymn-singing, or do some caroling in the streets. The songbook could stand alone, but we think singing and prayer should go together. Besides, we're not trying to get more money out of your wallets; we are just trying to get these songs into your hands. So have fun — sing while working, cleaning, or walking in the street. Let these songs be a reminder that we are made to sing of God's goodness, and that new songs are always being written, all over the world.

Website

As big as this book is, we could not fit in everything we wanted to include (and that's not even counting the gems we overlooked or haven't yet discovered). What is more, some songs have to be heard, not just seen on paper. We also recognize, even with its limitations and liabilities, that the internet can help people to connect across time and space. So we have created a website to supplement *Common Prayer*. Here we will be able to more exhaustively include saints, dates, songs, prayers, and ideas that couldn't fit in this book. We hope you'll check out the website and add your ideas to the mix: *www.commonprayer.net*.

Circle of Hope

Truth is not simply imparted by a preacher or a teacher; it is lived together in the context of community prayer, gathered around Jesus. Praying in a circle or around a table can help us to be mindful of this fact, enabling us to see each other's faces and remember that the center of our worship is Christ, not a pulpit. Each day, all across the globe, circles of Christians gather — in basements and in living rooms, on street corners and in slums, in prisons and in palaces — holding hands and praying to the God of the universe to be with us.

So let us pray, and let us become the answer to our prayers.

Acknowledgments

Sometimes it has felt like this book took centuries to create — and really it has.

There are lots of fingerprints on this book. Some of them are ancient, and there are far too many people to name. But there are some more contemporary collaborators we do want to recognize. We have had a brilliant advisory team that gave us wisdom and counsel along the way. Thanks to Phyllis Tickle, Sr. Karen Mohan, Richard Rohr, Eliacin Rosario-Cruz, and Andy Raine. We are especially grateful to Phyllis for her tremendous work on the four-volume manual of prayer *The Divine Hours*, from which we benefited immensely. And we are grateful to Andy and the Northumbria Community for creating *Celtic Daily Prayer*, and for their enthusiasm for our project. Both Phyllis and Andy allowed us to raid and pillage their wisdom and work.

As we sensed the Spirit's motion in creating this book, we gathered a dozen or so folks in North Carolina from different traditions, many of them liturgy and prayer experts (if there is such a thing). We put our hands together and said, "Let's do it." That set things in motion. Thanks to Scott Bass and Roberta Mothershead, who hosted that original gathering at Nazareth House, and Catherine and Pete Askew, Karen Sloan, Monica Klepac, Melanie Baffes, Katie Piche, Richard and Diana Twiss, Christine Sine, Scott Krueger, Mark Van Steenwyck, Chris Haw, Martin Shannon, and the many others who contributed the songs and prayers that are written on their walls and in their hearts. Their fingerprints are on this book.

Joel Klepac, Jesce Walz, and Rick Beerhorst were our fantastic woodcut artists. Katie Jo Brotherton and Brian Gorman poured in countless hours along the way editing, notating, praying, and researching. We are grateful for our tremendous friends Angela Scheff, Brian Phipps, and all the folks at Zondervan who have plotted with us and published this book.

And we have been your compilers. It has been an honor.

Now, add your fingerprints.

— Shane Claiborne, Jonathan Wilson-Hartgrove, and Enuma Okoro

EVENING PRAYER

Sunday

Naked I came from my mother's womb, and naked will I return.
The Lord gives, and the Lord takes away. Blessed be the name of the Lord.

O God, come to my assistance : **O Lord, make haste to help me.**

Glory to the Father, and to the Son, and to the Holy Spirit, as it was in the beginning, is now, and will be forever. Amen.

Kneeling Lord, have mercy. Christ, have mercy. Lord, have mercy.

I confess to almighty God,
and to you, my brothers and sisters,
that I have sinned through my own fault,
in my thoughts and in my words,
in what I have done,
and in what I have failed to do;
and I ask you, my brothers and sisters,
to pray for me to the Lord our God.

Silence (or time to confess to God or to one another)

Rebuke me, O Lord, but not in your anger, lest I come to nothing.

Rising Lord, have mercy. Christ, have mercy. Lord, have mercy. Amen.

A candle is lit during the following song
**Walk in the light, the beautiful light.
Come where the dewdrops of mercy shine bright.
Shine all around us by day and by night.
Jesus, the light of the world.**

O gracious Light,
pure brightness of the ever-living Father in heaven,
O Jesus Christ, holy and blessed!

Now as we come to the setting of the sun,
and our eyes behold the evening light,
we sing your praises, O God: Father, Son, and Holy Spirit.

You are worthy at all times to be praised by happy voices,
O Son of God, O Giver of life,
your glory fills the whole world.

In word or song
Praise God from whom all blessings flow.
Praise God, all creatures here below.
Praise God above, ye heavenly host.
Praise Father, Son, and Holy Ghost. Amen.

Declaration of Faith
We believe and trust in God the Father Almighty.
We believe and trust in Jesus Christ, his Son.
We believe and trust in the Holy Spirit.
We believe and trust in the Three in One.

Prayers for Others
(following each request): **Lord, hear our prayer.**

Our Father

Magnificat (Mary's Song)
My soul glorifies the Lord,
my spirit rejoices in God my Savior.
The Lord looks on me, a lowly servant; henceforth all ages will call me blessed.
The Almighty works marvels for me. Holy is God's name!
God's mercy is from age to age, on those who are faithful.
God puts forth an arm in strength and scatters the proud-hearted —
casts the mighty from their thrones and raises the lowly.

God fills the hungry with good things and sends the rich
	away empty,
protecting Israel, God's servant, remembering mercy,
the mercy promised to our ancestors,
to Abraham, Sarah, and their children forever.

Lord Jesus Christ, you have triumphed over the powers of death and prepared for us a place in the New Jerusalem. Grant that we, who have this day given thanks for your resurrection, may praise you in that city of which you are the light and where you live and reign forever and ever. Amen.

May the Lord bless us and keep us from all harm, and may God lead us to eternal life. Amen.

Monday

Naked I came from my mother's womb, and naked will I
	return.
**The Lord gives, and the Lord takes away. Blessed be the
	name of the Lord.**

O God, come to my assistance : **O Lord, make haste to help
	me.**

Glory to the Father, and to the Son, and to the Holy Spirit,
as it was in the beginning, is now, and will be forever. Amen.

Kneeling Lord, have mercy. Christ, have mercy. Lord, have
	mercy.

I confess to almighty God,
and to you, my brothers and sisters,
that I have sinned through my own fault,
in my thoughts and in my words,
in what I have done,
and in what I have failed to do;
and I ask you, my brothers and sisters,
to pray for me to the Lord our God.

Silence (or time to confess to God or to one another)

Rebuke me, O Lord, but not in your anger, lest I come to nothing.

Rising **Lord, have mercy. Christ, have mercy. Lord, have mercy. Amen.**

A candle is lit during the following song
**Walk in the light, the beautiful light.
Come where the dewdrops of mercy shine bright.
Shine all around us by day and by night.
Jesus, the light of the world.**

O gracious Light,
pure brightness of the ever-living Father in heaven,
O Jesus Christ, holy and blessed!

Now as we come to the setting of the sun,
and our eyes behold the evening light,
we sing your praises, O God: Father, Son, and Holy Spirit.

You are worthy at all times to be praised by happy voices,
O Son of God, O Giver of life,
your glory fills the whole world.

In word or song
**Praise God from whom all blessings flow.
Praise God, all creatures here below.
Praise God above, ye heavenly host.
Praise Father, Son, and Holy Ghost. Amen.**

Declaration of Faith
**We believe and trust in God the Father Almighty.
We believe and trust in Jesus Christ, his Son.
We believe and trust in the Holy Spirit.
We believe and trust in the Three in One.**

*Prayers for Others
(following each request):* **Lord, hear our prayer.**

Our Father

Az Yashir Moshe (Song of the Sea)
I will sing to the Lord,
for God has triumphed gloriously!
The horse and its rider he has thrown into the sea!
The Lord is my strength and song,
God has become my salvation;
Pharaoh's chariots and his army God cast into the sea;
the depths have covered them;
they sank to the bottom like a stone.
In the greatness of your majesty
you have overthrown those who rose against you.
You sent forth your wrath;
it consumed them like stubble.
And with the blast of your nostrils
the waters were piled up.
The surging waters stood firm like a wall;
the deep waters congealed in the heart of the sea.
The enemy boasted, but you blew your breath,
and the sea covered them.
They sank like lead in the mighty waters.
Who among the gods is like you, O Lord?
Who is like you, majestic in holiness,
awesome in glory, working wonders?
You stretched out your right hand;
the earth swallowed them.
In your unfailing love
you will lead the people you have redeemed.
In your strength you will guide them
to your holy dwelling.

Lighten our darkness, we beg you, O Lord; and by your great mercy defend us from all perils and dangers of this night, for the love of your only Son, our Savior, Jesus Christ.

May the Lord bless us and keep us from all harm, and may God lead us to eternal life. Amen.

Tuesday

Naked I came from my mother's womb, and naked will I return.
The Lord gives, and the Lord takes away. Blessed be the name of the Lord.

O God, come to my assistance : **O Lord, make haste to help me.**

Glory to the Father, and to the Son, and to the Holy Spirit, as it was in the beginning, is now, and will be forever. Amen.

Kneeling Lord, have mercy. Christ, have mercy. Lord, have mercy.

**I confess to almighty God,
and to you, my brothers and sisters,
that I have sinned through my own fault,
in my thoughts and in my words,
in what I have done,
and in what I have failed to do;
and I ask you, my brothers and sisters,
to pray for me to the Lord our God.**

Silence (or time to confess to God or to one another)

Rebuke me, O Lord, but not in your anger, lest I come to nothing.

Rising Lord, have mercy. Christ, have mercy. Lord, have mercy. Amen.

A candle is lit during the following song
Walk in the light, the beautiful light.
Come where the dewdrops of mercy shine bright.
Shine all around us by day and by night.
Jesus, the light of the world.

O gracious Light,
pure brightness of the ever-living Father in heaven,
O Jesus Christ, holy and blessed!

Now as we come to the setting of the sun,
and our eyes behold the evening light,
we sing your praises, O God: Father, Son, and Holy Spirit.

You are worthy at all times to be praised by happy voices,
O Son of God, O Giver of life,
your glory fills the whole world.

In word or song
Praise God from whom all blessings flow.
Praise God, all creatures here below.
Praise God above, ye heavenly host.
Praise Father, Son, and Holy Ghost. Amen.

Declaration of Faith
We believe and trust in God the Father Almighty.
We believe and trust in Jesus Christ, his Son.
We believe and trust in the Holy Spirit.
We believe and trust in the Three in One.

Prayers for Others
(following each request): **Lord, hear our prayer.**

Our Father

Magnificat (Mary's Song)
My soul glorifies the Lord,
my spirit rejoices in God my Savior.
The Lord looks on me, a lowly servant; henceforth all ages will call me blessed.
The Almighty works marvels for me. Holy is God's name!
God's mercy is from age to age, on those who are faithful.
God puts forth an arm in strength and scatters the proud-hearted —
casts the mighty from their thrones and raises the lowly.

God fills the hungry with good things and sends the rich away empty,
protecting Israel, God's servant, remembering mercy,
the mercy promised to our ancestors,
to Abraham, Sarah, and their children forever.

Almighty God, we give you thanks for surrounding us as daylight fades with the brightness of the evening light; and we ask of your great mercy that as you enfold us with the radiance of your light, you would also shine into our hearts the brightness of your Holy Spirit.

May the Lord bless us and keep us from all harm, and may God lead us to eternal life. Amen.

Wednesday

Naked I came from my mother's womb, and naked will I return.
The Lord gives, and the Lord takes away. Blessed be the name of the Lord.

O God, come to my assistance : **O Lord, make haste to help me.**

Glory to the Father, and to the Son, and to the Holy Spirit,
as it was in the beginning, is now, and will be forever. Amen.

Kneeling   Lord, have mercy. Christ, have mercy. Lord, have mercy.

I confess to almighty God,
and to you, my brothers and sisters,
that I have sinned through my own fault,
in my thoughts and in my words,
in what I have done,
and in what I have failed to do;
and I ask you, my brothers and sisters,
to pray for me to the Lord our God.

Silence (or time to confess to God or to one another)

Rebuke me, O Lord, but not in your anger, lest I come to nothing.

Rising **Lord, have mercy. Christ, have mercy. Lord, have mercy. Amen.**

A candle is lit during the following song
**Walk in the light, the beautiful light.
Come where the dewdrops of mercy shine bright.
Shine all around us by day and by night.
Jesus, the light of the world.**

**O gracious Light,
pure brightness of the ever-living Father in heaven,
O Jesus Christ, holy and blessed!**

**Now as we come to the setting of the sun,
and our eyes behold the evening light,
we sing your praises, O God: Father, Son, and Holy Spirit.**

**You are worthy at all times to be praised by happy voices,
O Son of God, O Giver of life,
your glory fills the whole world.**

In word or song
**Praise God from whom all blessings flow.
Praise God, all creatures here below.
Praise God above, ye heavenly host.
Praise Father, Son, and Holy Ghost. Amen.**

Declaration of Faith
**We believe and trust in God the Father Almighty.
We believe and trust in Jesus Christ, his Son.
We believe and trust in the Holy Spirit.
We believe and trust in the Three in One.**

*Prayers for Others
(following each request)*: **Lord, hear our prayer.**

Our Father

Benedictus (Zechariah's Song)
Praise the Lord, the God of Israel,
who shepherds the people and sets them free.
God raises from David's house
a child with power to save.
Through the holy prophets
God promised in ages past
to save us from enemy hands,
from the grip of all who hate us.
The Lord favored our ancestors,
recalling the sacred covenant,
the pledge to our ancestor Abraham
to free us from our enemies
so we might worship without fear
and be holy and just all our days.
And you, child, will be called
prophet of the Most High,
for you will come to prepare
a pathway for the Lord
by teaching the people salvation
through forgiveness of their sin.
Out of God's deepest mercy
a dawn will come from on high,
light for those shadowed by death,
a guide for our feet on the way to peace.

O Lord, you have taught us to call the evening, the morning, and the midday one, and you have made the sun to know its going down. Dispel now the darkness of our hearts, that by your brightness we may know you to be the true God and eternal light, living and reigning forever and ever.

May the Lord bless us and keep us from all harm, and may God lead us to eternal life. Amen.

Thursday

Naked I came from my mother's womb, and naked will I return.
The Lord gives, and the Lord takes away. Blessed be the name of the Lord.

O God, come to my assistance : **O Lord, make haste to help me.**

Glory to the Father, and to the Son, and to the Holy Spirit, as it was in the beginning, is now, and will be forever. Amen.

Kneeling **Lord, have mercy. Christ, have mercy. Lord, have mercy.**

**I confess to almighty God,
and to you, my brothers and sisters,
that I have sinned through my own fault,
in my thoughts and in my words,
in what I have done,
and in what I have failed to do;
and I ask you, my brothers and sisters,
to pray for me to the Lord our God.**

Silence (or time to confess to God or to one another)

Rebuke me, O Lord, but not in your anger, lest I come to nothing.

Rising **Lord, have mercy. Christ, have mercy. Lord, have mercy. Amen.**

A candle is lit during the following song
**Walk in the light, the beautiful light.
Come where the dewdrops of mercy shine bright.
Shine all around us by day and by night.
Jesus, the light of the world.**

O gracious Light,
pure brightness of the ever-living Father in heaven,
O Jesus Christ, holy and blessed!

Now as we come to the setting of the sun,
and our eyes behold the evening light,
we sing your praises, O God: Father, Son, and Holy Spirit.

You are worthy at all times to be praised by happy voices,
O Son of God, O Giver of life,
your glory fills the whole world.

In word or song
Praise God from whom all blessings flow.
Praise God, all creatures here below.
Praise God above, ye heavenly host.
Praise Father, Son, and Holy Ghost. Amen.

Declaration of Faith
We believe and trust in God the Father Almighty.
We believe and trust in Jesus Christ, his Son.
We believe and trust in the Holy Spirit.
We believe and trust in the Three in One.

Prayers for Others
(following each request): **Lord, hear our prayer.**

Our Father

Christ Hymn
May our minds be like that of Christ Jesus,
who, though he was in the form of God,
did not regard equality with God
as something to be exploited,
but emptied himself,
taking the form of a slave,
being born in human likeness.
And being found in human form,
he humbled himself

and became obedient to the point of death,
even death on a cross.
Therefore, God also highly exalted him
and gave him the name that is above every name,
so that at the name of Jesus every knee should bend,
in heaven and on earth and under the earth,
and every tongue confess that Jesus Christ is Lord,
to the glory of God the Father. Amen.

God, give us the lamp of love which never fails, that it may burn in us and shed its light on those around us. By its brightness give us a vision of that holy city where the true and never-failing Light, Jesus Christ, lives and reigns with you and the Holy Spirit, now and forever.

May the Lord bless us and keep us from all harm, and may God lead us to eternal life. Amen.

Friday

Naked I came from my mother's womb, and naked will I return.
The Lord gives, and the Lord takes away. Blessed be the name of the Lord.

O God, come to my assistance : **O Lord, make haste to help me.**

Glory to the Father, and to the Son, and to the Holy Spirit,
as it was in the beginning, is now, and will be forever. Amen.

Kneeling   Lord, have mercy. Christ, have mercy. Lord, have mercy.

I confess to almighty God,
and to you, my brothers and sisters,
that I have sinned through my own fault,
in my thoughts and in my words,
in what I have done,

and in what I have failed to do;
and I ask you, my brothers and sisters,
to pray for me to the Lord our God.

Silence (or time to confess to God or to one another)

Rebuke me, O Lord, but not in your anger, lest I come to nothing.

Rising   Lord, have mercy. Christ, have mercy. Lord, have mercy. Amen.

A candle is lit during the following song
**Walk in the light, the beautiful light.
Come where the dewdrops of mercy shine bright.
Shine all around us by day and by night.
Jesus, the light of the world.**

O gracious Light,
pure brightness of the ever-living Father in heaven,
O Jesus Christ, holy and blessed!

Now as we come to the setting of the sun,
and our eyes behold the evening light,
we sing your praises, O God: Father, Son, and Holy Spirit.

You are worthy at all times to be praised by happy voices,
O Son of God, O Giver of life,
your glory fills the whole world.

In word or song
**Praise God from whom all blessings flow.
Praise God, all creatures here below.
Praise God above, ye heavenly host.
Praise Father, Son, and Holy Ghost. Amen.**

Declaration of Faith
**We believe and trust in God the Father Almighty.
We believe and trust in Jesus Christ, his Son.
We believe and trust in the Holy Spirit.
We believe and trust in the Three in One.**

Prayers for Others
(following each request): **Lord, hear our prayer.**

Our Father

Magnificat (Mary's Song)
My soul glorifies the Lord,
my spirit rejoices in God my Savior.
The Lord looks on me, a lowly servant; henceforth all ages
    will call me blessed.
The Almighty works marvels for me. Holy is God's name!
God's mercy is from age to age, on those who are faithful.
God puts forth an arm in strength and scatters the
    proud-hearted —
casts the mighty from their thrones and raises the lowly.
God fills the hungry with good things and sends the rich
    away empty,
protecting Israel, God's servant, remembering mercy,
the mercy promised to our ancestors,
to Abraham, Sarah, and their children forever.

O Jesus, by your death you took away the sting of death. Give us faith to follow the way you have shown us, that we may fall asleep peacefully in you, and rise again in you, for your mercy's sake.

May the Lord bless us and keep us from all harm, and may God lead us to eternal life. Amen.

Saturday

Naked I came from my mother's womb, and naked will I
    return.
**The Lord gives, and the Lord takes away. Blessed be the
    name of the Lord.**

O God, come to my assistance : **O Lord, make haste to help me.**

Glory to the Father, and to the Son, and to the Holy Spirit,
as it was in the beginning, is now, and will be forever. Amen.

Kneeling   Lord, have mercy. Christ, have mercy. Lord, have mercy.

I confess to almighty God,
and to you, my brothers and sisters,
that I have sinned through my own fault,
in my thoughts and in my words,
in what I have done,
and in what I have failed to do;
and I ask you, my brothers and sisters,
to pray for me to the Lord our God.

Silence (or time to confess to God or to one another)

Rebuke me, O Lord, but not in your anger, lest I come to nothing.

Rising   Lord, have mercy. Christ, have mercy. Lord, have mercy. Amen.

A candle is lit during the following song
Walk in the light, the beautiful light.
Come where the dewdrops of mercy shine bright.
Shine all around us by day and by night.
Jesus, the light of the world.

O gracious Light,
pure brightness of the ever-living Father in heaven,
O Jesus Christ, holy and blessed!

Now as we come to the setting of the sun,
and our eyes behold the evening light,
we sing your praises, O God: Father, Son, and Holy Spirit.

You are worthy at all times to be praised by happy voices,
O Son of God, O Giver of life,
your glory fills the whole world.

In word or song
Praise God from whom all blessings flow.
Praise God, all creatures here below.
Praise God above, ye heavenly host.
Praise Father, Son, and Holy Ghost. Amen.

Declaration of Faith
We believe and trust in God the Father Almighty.
We believe and trust in Jesus Christ, his Son.
We believe and trust in the Holy Spirit.
We believe and trust in the Three in One.

Prayers for Others
(following each request): **Lord, hear our prayer.**

Our Father

Nunc Dimittis (Simeon's Song)
Lord, let your servant
now rest in peace,
for you have kept your promise.
With my own eyes
I see the salvation
you prepared for all peoples,
a light of revelation for the Gentiles
and glory to your people, Israel.

Visit this place, O Lord, and drive far from it all snares of the enemy. Send your holy angels to dwell with us and preserve us in peace. And let your blessing be upon us always, through Jesus Christ our Lord.

May the Lord bless us and keep us from all harm, and may God lead us to eternal life. Amen.

MORNING PRAYER

DECEMBER — NATIVITY

DECEMBER

Marks of New Monasticism
Locating Our Lives in the Abandoned Places of the Empire

Everything in our society teaches us to move away from suffering, to move out of neighborhoods where there is high crime, to move away from people who don't look like us. But the gospel calls us to something altogether different. We are to laugh at fear, to lean into suffering, to open ourselves to the stranger. Advent is the season when we remember how Jesus put on flesh and moved into the neighborhood. God getting born in a barn reminds us that God shows up in the most forsaken corners of the earth.

Movements throughout church history have gone to the desert, to the slums, to the most difficult places on earth to follow Jesus. For some of us that means remaining in difficult neighborhoods that we were born into even though folks may think we are crazy for not moving out. For others it means returning to a difficult neighborhood after heading off to college or job training to acquire skills — choosing to bring those skills back to where we came from to help restore the broken streets. And for others it may mean relocating our lives from places of so-called privilege to an abandoned place to offer our gifts for God's kingdom.

Wherever we come from, Jesus teaches us that good can happen where we are, even if real-estate agents and politicians aren't interested in our neighborhoods. Jesus comes from Nazareth, a town from which folks said nothing good could come. He knew suffering from the moment he entered the world as a baby refugee born in the middle of a genocide. Jesus knew poverty and pain until he was tortured and executed on a Roman cross. This is the Jesus we are called to follow. With his coming we learn that the most dangerous place for Christians to be is in comfort and safety, detached from the suffering of others. Places that are physically safe can be spiritually deadly.

> **Suggested Reading for the Month**
> *Sayings of the Desert Mothers and Fathers*
> *Jesus and the Disinherited* by Howard Thurman
> *The Beloved Community* by Charles Marsh

One of the best stories of community in the United States comes from the backwoods of Georgia. In the 1940s, long before the civil rights movement had begun to question the racial divisions in the South, white folks and black folks came together to start Koinonia Farm — a "demonstration plot" for the kingdom of God, as they called it. Koinonia survived attacks from the Ku Klux Klan in the '50s and '60s, tilling the soil and sowing seeds for God's movement in the least likely of places.

December 1

Charles de Foucauld (1858–1916)

While working in the North African desert after a dishonorable discharge from military service, Charles de Foucauld was impressed by the piety of Muslims and experienced a dramatic recovery of his Christian faith. He spent a number of years in a Trappist monastery before hearing the call to a new monasticism among the working poor. "I no longer want a monastery which is too secure," he wrote. "I want a small monastery, like the house of a poor workman who is not sure if tomorrow he will find work and bread, who with all his being shares the suffering of the world." Though Foucauld died in solitude, the Little Brothers and Sisters of Jesus, inspired by his life and witness, have started communities of service among the poor and outcast around the world.

O Lord, let my soul rise up to meet you
as the day rises to meet the sun.

**Glory to the Father, and to the Son, and to the Holy Spirit,
as it was in the beginning, is now, and will be forever. Amen.**

Come, let us bow down and bend the knee : let us kneel before the LORD our Maker.

Song "Servant Song"

May we cry the gospel from the rooftops : both with our words and with our lives.

Psalm 8:4–7
When I consider your heavens, the work of your fingers : **the moon and the stars you have set in their courses,**
what is man that you should be mindful of him? : **the son of man that you should seek him out?**
You have made him but little lower than the angels : **you adorn him with glory and honor;**
you give him mastery over the works of your hands : **you put all things under his feet.**

May we cry the gospel from the rooftops : both with our words and with our lives.

Isaiah 1:1–9   Luke 20:1–8

May we cry the gospel from the rooftops : both with our words and with our lives.

Morning Prayer

Charles de Foucauld prayed, "Father, I abandon myself into your hands, do with me what you will. For whatever you may do, I thank you. I am ready for all, I accept all, let only your will be done in me, as in all your creatures."

Prayers for Others

Our Father

Sometimes, Lord, it takes witnessing another person's commitment for us to realize our own lack of faith. Open our eyes to learn, even from strangers who inhabit other faith traditions, what it means to be committed to you. Amen.

May the peace of the Lord Christ go with you : wherever he may send you; may he guide you through the wilderness : protect you through the storm; may he bring you home rejoicing : at the wonders he has shown you; may he bring you home rejoicing : once again into our doors.

A Note on Advent

Advent, meaning "the coming," is a time when we wait expectantly. Christians began to celebrate it as a season during the fourth and fifth centuries. Like Mary, we celebrate the coming of the Christ child, what God has already done. And we wait in expectation of the full coming of God's reign on earth and for the return of Christ, what God will yet do. But this waiting is not a passive waiting. It is an active waiting. As any expectant mother knows, this waiting also involves preparation, exercise, nutrition, care, prayer, work; and birth involves pain, blood, tears, joy, release, community. It is called labor for a reason. Likewise, we are in a world pregnant with hope, and we live in the expectation of the coming of God's kingdom on earth. As we wait, we also work, cry, pray, ache; we are the midwives of another world.

Just as red, white, and blue have meaning in the world (as in "These colors don't run"), colors also have meaning in the church (though a different sort of meaning, needless to say).

Advent is often marked with purple, signifying royalty; in earlier times, purple often marked the coming of a king or Caesar. (Often, members of the royal family were the only people allowed to wear it.) Many Christians celebrate advent by lighting a purple candle each week for the four weeks leading up to Christmas, and then lighting a "Christ candle" (usually white or red) on Christmas Eve.

As you will note in the morning prayers, many Christians also remember St. Nicholas, who was a faithful man of God before he was a cultural icon. Today, the season between Thanksgiving and Christmas that many of us recognize as Advent is the biggest frenzy of retail spending. More than half of it, hundreds of billions of dollars a year, is spent as we celebrate the birth of the homeless Son of God in that stinky manger. (And he got only three measly presents. One of them was myrrh. What baby wants myrrh?) Hundreds of Christian congregations are now rethinking the Advent season as a time for compassion rather than consumption. (Check out *www.adventconspiracy.org*.)

✦ December 2

In 1980 Maura Clarke, Ita Ford, Dorothy Kazel, and Jean Donovan were murdered by officers of the Salvadoran military. Missionaries serving among the poor during El Salvador's civil war, these women knew, as Ita Ford said the night before she died, that "one who is committed to the poor must risk the same fate as the poor." Their deaths affected the North American church deeply, galvanizing opposition to US support for the Salvadoran government's repression of its people.

O Lord, let my soul rise up to meet you
as the day rises to meet the sun.

**Glory to the Father, and to the Son, and to the Holy Spirit,
as it was in the beginning, is now, and will be forever. Amen.**

Come, let us bow down and bend the knee : let us kneel before the LORD our Maker.

Song   "Were You There?"

O Lord, listen to the song : of your saints who cry, "How long?"

Psalm 12:1–5
Help me, LORD, for there is no godly one left : **the faithful have vanished from among us.**
Everyone speaks falsely with his neighbor : **with a smooth tongue they speak from a double heart.**
Oh, that the LORD would cut off all smooth tongues : **and close the lips that utter proud boasts!**
Those who say, "With our tongue will we prevail : **our lips are our own; who is lord over us?"**
"Because the needy are oppressed, and the poor cry out in misery : **I will rise up," says the LORD, "and give them the help they long for."**

O Lord, listen to the song : of your saints who cry, "How long?"

Isaiah 1:10–20   Luke 20:9–18

O Lord, listen to the song : of your saints who cry, "How long?"

Ita Ford wrote, "The reasons why so many people are being killed are quite complicated, yet there are some clear, simple strands. One is that people have found a meaning to live, to sacrifice, struggle, and even die. And whether their life spans sixteen years, sixty, or ninety, for them their life has had a purpose. In many ways, they are fortunate people."

Prayers for Others

Our Father

Lord, it was not enough for you to care for the poor. You chose to become one of them by descending as you did. Keep us free from fear and selfish preoccupations that we may walk as you walked among the poor, sick, and dying in body and spirit. Amen.

May the peace of the Lord Christ go with you : wherever he may send you;
may he guide you through the wilderness : protect you through the storm;
may he bring you home rejoicing : at the wonders he has shown you;
may he bring you home rejoicing : once again into our doors.

December 3

O Lord, let my soul rise up to meet you
as the day rises to meet the sun.

**Glory to the Father, and to the Son, and to the Holy Spirit,
as it was in the beginning, is now, and will be forever. Amen.**

Come, let us bow down and bend the knee : let us kneel before the LORD our Maker.

Song "Swing Low, Sweet Chariot"

O come, O come, Emmanuel : and ransom captive Israel.

Psalm 18:3–7
I will call upon the LORD : **and so shall I be saved from my enemies.**
The breakers of death rolled over me : **and the torrents of oblivion made me afraid.**
The cords of hell entangled me : **and the snares of death were set for me.**
I called upon the LORD in my distress : **and cried out to my God for help.**
He heard my voice from his heavenly dwelling : **my cry of anguish came to his ears.**

O come, O come, Emmanuel : and ransom captive Israel.

Isaiah 1:21–31   Luke 20:19–26

O come, O come, Emmanuel : and ransom captive Israel.

Justin the Martyr wrote in the second century, "He called Abraham and commanded him to go out from the country where he was living. With this call he has roused us all, and now we have renounced all the things the world offers, even unto death."

Prayers for Others

Our Father

Hound us, Lord, with affection and conviction until we renounce all lesser things to follow you. Help us see that in giving up the fool's gold of the world, we open ourselves to heavenly treasure that lasts forever. Amen.

May the peace of the Lord Christ go with you : wherever he may send you;
may he guide you through the wilderness : protect you through the storm;
may he bring you home rejoicing : at the wonders he has shown you;
may he bring you home rejoicing : once again into our doors.

December 4

O Lord, let my soul rise up to meet you
as the day rises to meet the sun.

Glory to the Father, and to the Son, and to the Holy Spirit,
as it was in the beginning, is now, and will be forever. Amen.

Come, let us sing to the LORD : let us shout for joy to the Rock of our salvation.

Song "Magnificat"

Praise to you who lift up the poor : and fill the hungry with good things.

Psalm 22:22–25
Praise the LORD, you that fear him : **stand in awe of him, O offspring of Israel; all you of Jacob's line, give glory.**
For he does not despise nor abhor the poor in their poverty; neither does he hide his face from them : **but when they cry to him he hears them.**
My praise is of him in the great assembly : **I will perform my vows in the presence of those who worship him.**
The poor shall eat and be satisfied, and those who seek the LORD shall praise him : **"May your heart live for ever!"**

Praise to you who lift up the poor : and fill the hungry with good things.

Isaiah 2:1–11   Luke 20:27–40

Praise to you who lift up the poor : and fill the hungry with good things.

Commenting on the activities of the early church, Roman Emperor Julian said, "The godless Galileans feed our poor in addition to their own."

Prayers for Others

Our Father

Lord, keep us from trying to distinguish between the deserving and the undeserving poor. Help us work to alleviate suffering and injustice wherever we find it, trusting that the rest is up to you. Amen.

May the peace of the Lord Christ go with you : wherever he may send you; may he guide you through the wilderness : protect you through the storm; may he bring you home rejoicing : at the wonders he has shown you; may he bring you home rejoicing : once again into our doors.

✠ December 5

O Lord, let my soul rise up to meet you
as the day rises to meet the sun.

Glory to the Father, and to the Son, and to the Holy Spirit,
as it was in the beginning, is now, and will be forever. Amen.

Come, let us sing to the LORD : let us shout for joy to the Rock of our salvation.

Song "We Shall Overcome"

You speak in my heart and say, "Seek my face" : your face, LORD, will I seek.

Psalm 27:1–4
The LORD is my light and my salvation; whom then shall I fear? : **the LORD is the strength of my life; of whom then shall I be afraid?**
When evildoers came upon me to eat up my flesh : **it was they, my foes and my adversaries, who stumbled and fell.**
Though an army should encamp against me : **yet my heart shall not be afraid;**
and though war should rise up against me : **yet will I put my trust in him.**

You speak in my heart and say, "Seek my face" : your face, LORD, will I seek.

Isaiah 2:12–22   Luke 20:41–21:4

You speak in my heart and say, "Seek my face" : your face, LORD, will I seek.

Nineteenth-century abolitionist Sojourner Truth said, "I'm not going to die, honey. I'm going home like a shooting star."

Prayers for Others

Our Father

Lord, when we strive after healing in the world and nourishment for those who hunger, we find you at our side. Whenever we long to see your face, help us not to avoid the corners of our communities where you most often dwell. Stir our hearts that we might seek and find you today in those places where you have promised to be. Amen.

May the peace of the Lord Christ go with you : wherever he may send you; may he guide you through the wilderness : protect you through the storm; may he bring you home rejoicing : at the wonders he has shown you; may he bring you home rejoicing : once again into our doors.

 # December 6

Nicholas of Myra (Fourth Century)

The original "Old St. Nick" who inspired the tradition of Santa Claus, Nicholas was bishop of Myra in fourth-century Turkey. Little is known about his life except that he entrusted himself to Jesus at an early age and, when his parents died, gave all of their possessions to the poor. While serving as bishop, Nicholas learned of three girls who were going to be sold into slavery by their father. Moved to use the church's wealth to ransom the lives of these little ones, he tossed three bags of gold through the family's window. We recall this ancient Christmas gift, even as we remember that 1.2 million children are trafficked each year in the global sex trade today.

O Lord, let my soul rise up to meet you
as the day rises to meet the sun.

Glory to the Father, and to the Son, and to the Holy Spirit, as it was in the beginning, is now, and will be forever. Amen.

Come, let us bow down and bend the knee : let us kneel before the Lord our Maker.

Song "The Kingdom of God"

Remember your little ones, Lord : and give us courage to stand for them.

Psalm 33:18–21
Behold, the eye of the Lord is upon those who fear him : **on those who wait upon his love,**
to pluck their lives from death : **and to feed them in time of famine.**
Our soul waits for the Lord : **he is our help and our shield.**
Indeed, our heart rejoices in him : **for in his holy name we put our trust.**

Remember your little ones, Lord : and give us courage to stand for them.

Isaiah 3:8–15   Luke 21:5–19

Remember your little ones, Lord : and give us courage to stand for them.

Catherine Booth, co-founder of the Salvation Army and a passionate advocate for children, said, "There is no improving the future without disturbing the present."

Prayers for Others

Our Father

Lord Jesus Christ, you welcomed the little children to come unto you and invited us to come like them. Help us see how we can welcome children as you have welcomed us into your body. Amen.

May the peace of the Lord Christ go with you : wherever he may send you; may he guide you through the wilderness : protect you through the storm; may he bring you home rejoicing : at the wonders he has shown you; may he bring you home rejoicing : once again into our doors.

✺ December 7

Ambrose of Milan (339–397)

A provincial governor in fourth-century Italy, Ambrose was drafted to serve as bishop before he was even baptized. Reluctant to serve the church at first, he took the task seriously when he finally accepted the call. Ambrose gave away all of his possessions, took up a strict schedule of daily prayer, and committed himself to the study of Scripture. Called from the world of politics to serve the church, Ambrose was a leader who spoke truth to power and did not back down, insisting that "the emperor is in the church, not over it."

O Lord, let my soul rise up to meet you
as the day rises to meet the sun.

Glory to the Father, and to the Son, and to the Holy Spirit,
as it was in the beginning, is now, and will be forever. Amen.

Come, let us sing to the LORD : let us shout for joy to the Rock of our salvation.

Song   "I Will Trust in the Lord"

You, O Lord, are king of all : ruler of every nation.

Psalm 37:1–4
Do not fret yourself because of evildoers : **do not be jealous of those who do wrong.**
For they shall soon wither like the grass : **and like the green grass fade away.**
Put your trust in the Lord and do good : **dwell in the land and feed on its riches.**
Take delight in the Lord : **and he shall give you your heart's desire.**

You, O Lord, are king of all : ruler of every nation.

Isaiah 4:2–6   Luke 7:28–35

You, O Lord, are king of all : ruler of every nation.

Addressing Roman Emperor Theodosius about a massacre he had authorized at Thessalonica, Ambrose of Milan wrote, "You are human, and temptation has overtaken you. Overcome it. I counsel, I beseech, I implore you to repentance. You, who have so often been merciful and pardoned the guilty, have now caused many innocents to perish. The devil wished to wrest from you the crown of piety which was your chiefest glory. Drive him from you while you can."

Prayers for Others

Our Father

Lord, we do not always rush to do your will. Often we tiptoe our way into obedience, dragging old habits and mindsets with us. Help us to delight at your voice and to trust that your calling is always good news. Amen.

**May the peace of the Lord Christ go with you : wherever he may send you;
may he guide you through the wilderness : protect you through the storm;
may he bring you home rejoicing : at the wonders he has shown you;
may he bring you home rejoicing : once again into our doors.**

❋ December 8

O Lord, let my soul rise up to meet you
as the day rises to meet the sun.

Glory to the Father, and to the Son, and to the Holy Spirit,
as it was in the beginning, is now, and will be forever. Amen.

Come, let us sing to the Lord : let us shout for joy to the Rock of our salvation.

Song   "Ubi Caritas"

Your glory, Lord, lights up the world : where love is real, it shines.

Psalm 41:1–3, 13
Happy are they who consider the poor and needy! : **the LORD will deliver them in the time of trouble.**
The LORD preserves them and keeps them alive, so that they may be happy in the land : **he does not hand them over to the will of their enemies.**
The LORD sustains them on their sickbed : **and ministers to them in their illness.**
Blessed be the LORD God of Israel : **from age to age. Amen. Amen.**

Your glory, Lord, lights up the world : where love is real, it shines.

Isaiah 5:1–7   Luke 21:20–28

Your glory, Lord, lights up the world : where love is real, it shines.

Jean Vanier, founder of the L'Arche communities, has written, "To love someone is not first of all to do things for them, but to reveal to them their beauty and value, to say to them through our attitude: 'You are beautiful. You are important. I trust you. You can trust yourself.' We all know well that we can do things for others and in the process crush them, making them feel that they are incapable of doing things by themselves. To love someone is to reveal to them their capacities for life, the light that is shining in them."

Prayers for Others

Our Father

Lord, help us minister to others in ways that validate and authenticate them as fellow children of God. Keep us from daring to assume that our good fortune is of our own doing or that our ability to serve is anything other than a gift. Amen.

**May the peace of the Lord Christ go with you : wherever he may send you;
may he guide you through the wilderness : protect you through the storm;
may he bring you home rejoicing : at the wonders he has shown you;
may he bring you home rejoicing : once again into our doors.**

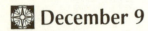 # December 9

Martin de Porres (1579–1639)
Martin de Porres was a Dominican brother who is often celebrated by mixed-race people and those committed to ending racism and segregation. He was born in Lima, Peru, the son of a Spanish nobleman and a former slave from Panama. Having grown up familiar with poverty and prejudice, he became a

passionate advocate for those on the margins, establishing an orphanage and hospital for children, and becoming well known for his compassion. Martin is often depicted with a broom because he considered all work to be sacred and was committed to service and sacrifice.

O Lord, let my soul rise up to meet you
as the day rises to meet the sun.

**Glory to the Father, and to the Son, and to the Holy Spirit,
as it was in the beginning, is now, and will be forever. Amen.**

Come, let us sing to the LORD : let us shout for joy to the Rock of our salvation.

Song "Servant Song"

Great is the LORD, and greatly to be praised : in the city of our God is his holy hill.

Psalm 48:2–7
Beautiful and lofty, the joy of all the earth, is the hill of Zion : **the very center of the world and the city of the great King.**
God is in her citadels : **he is known to be her sure refuge.**
Behold, the kings of the earth assembled : **and marched forward together.**
They looked and were astounded : **they retreated and fled in terror.**
Trembling seized them there : **they writhed like a woman in childbirth, like ships of the sea when the east wind shatters them.**
As we have heard, so have we seen, in the city of the LORD of hosts, in the city of our God : **God has established her for ever.**

Great is the LORD, and greatly to be praised : in the city of our God is his holy hill.

Isaiah 5:8–12, 18–23   Luke 21:29–38

Great is the LORD, and greatly to be praised : in the city of our God is his holy hill.

Cyprian of Carthage, a third-century North African bishop, said, "The Lord Christ did not want us to pray by ourselves in private or for ourselves alone. We do not say '*My* Father, who art in heaven,' nor 'Give *me* this day *my* daily bread.' It is not for oneself alone that each person asks to be forgiven, not to be led into temptation or to be delivered from evil. Rather, we pray in public as a community, and not for one individual but for all."

Prayers for Others

Our Father

Lord, you have woven the threads of creation too finely together for any of us to exist as islands unto ourselves. Teach us to delight in your web of life and to know ourselves in community. Amen.

May the peace of the Lord Christ go with you : wherever he may send you;
may he guide you through the wilderness : protect you through the storm;
may he bring you home rejoicing : at the wonders he has shown you;
may he bring you home rejoicing : once again into our doors.

 ## December 10

Thomas Merton (1915 – 1968)

Thomas Merton pursued the ideals of pleasure and freedom in early adulthood only to reject them as an illusion and embrace a life of prayer and silence as a Trappist monk. His 1949 conversion story, *The Seven Storey Mountain*, was a surprise bestseller, introducing millions of modern people to the gifts of monasticism. A mentor to many activists in the Catholic peace movement, Merton became a prophetic voice for peace and nonviolence in the twentieth century, despite the fact that his "political" writings were censored by his order. Convinced that contemplative life must engage the world, he prepared the way for a new monasticism.

O Lord, let my soul rise up to meet you
as the day rises to meet the sun.

**Glory to the Father, and to the Son, and to the Holy Spirit,
as it was in the beginning, is now, and will be forever. Amen.**

Come, let us sing to the LORD : let us shout for joy to the Rock of our salvation.

Song "Be Thou My Vision"

Behold, God is my helper : it is the Lord who sustains my life.

Psalm 54:1–6
Save me, O God, by your name : **in your might, defend my cause.**
Hear my prayer, O God : **give ear to the words of my mouth.**
For the arrogant have risen up against me, and the ruthless have sought my life : **those who have no regard for God.**
Behold, God is my helper : **it is the Lord who sustains my life.**
Render evil to those who spy on me : **in your faithfulness, destroy them.**
I will offer you a freewill sacrifice : **and praise your name, O LORD, for it is good.**

Behold, God is my helper : it is the Lord who sustains my life.

Isaiah 5:13–17, 24–25   Luke 22:1–13

Behold, God is my helper : it is the Lord who sustains my life.

Thomas Merton wrote, "The monk does not come to the monastery to 'get' something which the ordinary Christian cannot have. On the contrary, he comes there in order to realize and to appreciate all that any good Christian already has. He comes to live his Christian life, and thus to appreciate to the full his heritage as a son of God. He comes in order that he might see and understand that *he already possesses everything.*"

Prayers for Others

Our Father

Lord, teach us to live as contemplative activists, trusting that your Spirit and your word provide all we need to dance with the angels on Jacob's ladder between heaven and earth. Amen.

**May the peace of the Lord Christ go with you : wherever he may send you;
may he guide you through the wilderness : protect you through the storm;
may he bring you home rejoicing : at the wonders he has shown you;
may he bring you home rejoicing : once again into our doors.**

 December 11

In 1981 scores of Salvadoran troops from the US-trained Atlacatl Battalion occupied the town of El Mozote in rural El Salvador, interrogating its citizens about the whereabouts of guerilla troops suspected to be in the area. Though the residents of El Mozote, many of them born-again evangelicals, were known to be neutral in the conflict between the Salvadoran government and the FMLN resistance, nearly one thousand men, women, and children were systematically killed in the largest massacre of modern Latin American history.

O Lord, let my soul rise up to meet you
as the day rises to meet the sun.

Glory to the Father, and to the Son, and to the Holy Spirit,
as it was in the beginning, is now, and will be forever. Amen.

Come, let us bow down and bend the knee : let us kneel before the LORD our Maker.

Song   "I Want Jesus to Walk with Me"

Rouse yourself! Come and see! : Save us, God, from the enemy.

Morning Prayer   61

Psalm 59:1–5
Rescue me from my enemies, O God : **protect me from those who rise up against me.**
Rescue me from evildoers : **and save me from those who thirst for my blood.**
See how they lie in wait for my life, how the mighty gather together against me : **not for any offense or fault of mine, O Lord.**
Not because of any guilt of mine : **they run and prepare themselves for battle.**
Rouse yourself, come to my side, and see : **for you, Lord God of hosts, are Israel's God.**

Rouse yourself! Come and see! : Save us, God, from the enemy.

Isaiah 6:1–13   Luke 22:14–30

Rouse yourself! Come and see! : Save us, God, from the enemy.

The inscription on a memorial in El Mozote's town square reads, "They did not die, they are with us, with you, and with all humanity."

Prayers for Others

Our Father

Lord, we give thanks for the faithful who have gone before us. Strengthen us by their witness of courage and help us live lives that might encourage those who long for the gift of faith. Amen.

May the peace of the Lord Christ go with you : wherever he may send you; may he guide you through the wilderness : protect you through the storm; may he bring you home rejoicing : at the wonders he has shown you; may he bring you home rejoicing : once again into our doors.

✶ December 12

O Lord, let my soul rise up to meet you
as the day rises to meet the sun.

Glory to the Father, and to the Son, and to the Holy Spirit, as it was in the beginning, is now, and will be forever. Amen.

Come, let us sing to the Lord : let us shout for joy to the Rock of our salvation.

Song   "Great Is Thy Faithfulness"

In the light of the morning, Lord : tune our hearts to sing your praise.

Psalm 65:5–8

Awesome things will you show us in your righteousness, O God of our salvation : **O Hope of all the ends of the earth and of the seas that are far away.**

You make fast the mountains by your power : **they are girded about with might.**

You still the roaring of the seas : **the roaring of their waves, and the clamor of the peoples.**

Those who dwell at the ends of the earth will tremble at your marvelous signs : **you make the dawn and the dusk to sing for joy.**

In the light of the morning, Lord : tune our hearts to sing your praise.

Isaiah 7:1–9   Luke 22:31–38

In the light of the morning, Lord : tune our hearts to sing your praise.

Paschasius Radbertus, a ninth-century Benedictine, wrote, "The apostles took every care not to be drawn from the right path. They kept watch, observing the universal precepts their master had given to his disciples so as to be ready when he came again. Consequently we must always be on the lookout for Christ's twofold coming, the one when he comes day after day to stir our consciences, and the other when we shall have to give an account of everything we have done. He comes to us now in order that his future coming may find us prepared."

Prayers for Others

Our Father

With each new day, help us, Lord, to make our lives a hymn of constant praise to you. Teach us that the sweetest song is stirred when our hands are open in generosity and our feet are quick to bring the good news of your reconciling love to rich and poor alike. Amen.

May the peace of the Lord Christ go with you : wherever he may send you; may he guide you through the wilderness : protect you through the storm; may he bring you home rejoicing : at the wonders he has shown you; may he bring you home rejoicing : once again into our doors.

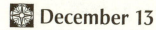
December 13

O Lord, let my soul rise up to meet you
as the day rises to meet the sun.

Glory to the Father, and to the Son, and to the Holy Spirit, as it was in the beginning, is now, and will be forever. Amen.

Come, let us bow down and bend the knee : let us kneel before the LORD our Maker.

Song "O Lord, Have Mercy"

Lord Jesus Christ, Son of God : have mercy on me, a sinner.

Psalm 69:6–7, 14–15
O God, you know my foolishness : **and my faults are not hidden from you.**
Let not those who hope in you be put to shame through me, Lord GOD of hosts : **let not those who seek you be disgraced because of me, O God of Israel.**
But as for me, this is my prayer to you : **at the time you have set, O LORD:**
"In your great mercy, O God : **answer me with your unfailing help."**

Lord Jesus Christ, Son of God : have mercy on me, a sinner.

Isaiah 7:10–25   Luke 22:39–53

Lord Jesus Christ, Son of God : have mercy on me, a sinner.

Fourth-century poet Ephrem the Syrian wrote, "The word of God is a tree of life that offers us blessed fruit from each of its branches. It is like that rock which was struck open in the wilderness, from which all were offered spiritual drink. Be glad then that you are overwhelmed, and do not be saddened because he has overcome you. A thirsty person is happy when drinking, and not depressed, because the spring is inexhaustible. You can satisfy your thirst without exhausting the spring; then when you thirst again, you can drink from it once more."

Prayers for Others

Our Father

God of abundance, help us live today trusting that there will be enough for tomorrow. Your sources have no end. Teach us to share our resources, believing that the more we give, the more you will provide for all. Amen.

May the peace of the Lord Christ go with you : wherever he may send you; may he guide you through the wilderness : protect you through the storm; may he bring you home rejoicing : at the wonders he has shown you; may he bring you home rejoicing : once again into our doors.

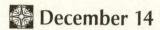 **December 14**

John of the Cross (1542–1591)

Born into poverty in sixteenth-century Spain, Juan de la Cruz joined the Carmelite order at the age of twenty-one. Four years later, he met Teresa of Avila, who was impressed by the young friar and recruited him to help her restore a spirit of radical simplicity to the Carmelites. Their reforms were not welcomed in the days of Spain's Inquisition, and Juan suffered a great deal of persecution at the hands of his religious brothers. One of the great mystics of the Christian tradition, he teaches us how to draw closer to God during the "dark night of the soul."

O Lord, let my soul rise up to meet you
as the day rises to meet the sun.

**Glory to the Father, and to the Son, and to the Holy Spirit,
as it was in the beginning, is now, and will be forever. Amen.**

Come, let us bow down and bend the knee : let us kneel before the LORD our Maker.

Song "Let All Mortal Flesh Keep Silence"

Where there is no love, let us put love : and so, by your power, draw love out.

Psalm 73:14–18
I have been afflicted all day long : **and punished every morning.**
Had I gone on speaking this way : **I should have betrayed the generation of your children.**
When I tried to understand these things : **it was too hard for me;**
until I entered the sanctuary of God : **and discerned the end of the wicked.**
Surely, you set them in slippery places : **you cast them down in ruin.**

Where there is no love, let us put love : and so, by your power, draw love out.

Isaiah 8:1–15   Luke 22:54–69

Where there is no love, let us put love : and so, by your power, draw love out.

John of the Cross wrote, "The soul that is attached to anything, however much good there may be in it, will not arrive at the liberty of divine union. For whether it be a strong wire rope or a slender and delicate thread that holds the bird, it matters not, if it really holds it fast; for until the cord be broken, the bird cannot fly."

Prayers for Others

Our Father

Lord, help us not to despair when you seem far away or when our walk with you proves treacherous. Give us grace to trust your presence even when we feel your absence. Amen.

May the peace of the Lord Christ go with you : wherever he may send you;
may he guide you through the wilderness : protect you through the storm;
may he bring you home rejoicing : at the wonders he has shown you;
may he bring you home rejoicing : once again into our doors.

December 15

O Lord, let my soul rise up to meet you
as the day rises to meet the sun.

**Glory to the Father, and to the Son, and to the Holy Spirit,
as it was in the beginning, is now, and will be forever. Amen.**

Come, let us bow down and bend the knee : let us kneel before the LORD our Maker.

Song "Come, Ye Sinners"

Shepherd us, Lord, with your faithful hand : and guide us gently into your land.

Psalm 78:40–43
How often the people disobeyed him in the wilderness : **and offended him in the desert!**
Again and again they tempted God : **and provoked the Holy One of Israel.**
They did not remember his power : **in the day when he ransomed them from the enemy;**
how he wrought his signs in Egypt : **and his omens in the field of Zoan.**

Shepherd us, Lord, with your faithful hand : and guide us gently into your land.

Isaiah 8:16–9:1   Matthew 3:1–12

Shepherd us, Lord, with your faithful hand : and guide us gently into your land.

Twentieth-century Jesuit Anthony de Mello said, "In the land of the spirit, you cannot walk by the light of someone else's lamp. You want to borrow mine. I'd rather teach you how to make your own."

Prayers for Others

Our Father

Try as we might, Lord, we cannot carry the full load of another's burden. Only you can take on our burdens in a way that frees us to walk upright and confident in our future. Help us learn to trust you even as we continue to lend a hand to others. Amen.

May the peace of the Lord Christ go with you : wherever he may send you;
may he guide you through the wilderness : protect you through the storm;
may he bring you home rejoicing : at the wonders he has shown you;
may he bring you home rejoicing : once again into our doors.

❊ December 16

O Lord, let my soul rise up to meet you
as the day rises to meet the sun.

**Glory to the Father, and to the Son, and to the Holy Spirit,
as it was in the beginning, is now, and will be forever. Amen.**

Come, let us sing to the LORD : let us shout for joy to the Rock of our salvation.

Song "Fairest Lord Jesus"

Rise up, O Lord, and rule the earth : every inch of it is yours.

Psalm 82:1–5
God takes his stand in the council of heaven : **he gives judgment in the midst of the gods:**
"How long will you judge unjustly : **and show favor to the wicked?**
Save the weak and the orphan : **defend the humble and needy;**
rescue the weak and the poor : **deliver them from the power of the wicked.**
They do not know, neither do they understand; they go about in darkness : **all the foundations of the earth are shaken."**

Rise up, O Lord, and rule the earth : every inch of it is yours.

Isaiah 9:1–7   Matthew 11:2–15

Rise up, O Lord, and rule the earth : every inch of it is yours.

Seattle, chief of the Suquamish, asked, "How can you buy or sell the sky, the warmth of the land? The idea is strange to us. Every part of this earth is sacred to my people. Every shining pine needle, every sandy shore, every mist in the dark woods, every clearing and humming insect is holy in the memory and experience of my people. We are part of the earth and it is part of us."

Prayers for Others

Our Father

Lord, we forget that we do not create our world. Help us remember creation as a gift we are called to serve and watch over. Free us from habits that dishonor the land, and teach us to revel in its bounty with gratitude. Amen.

May the peace of the Lord Christ go with you : wherever he may send you; may he guide you through the wilderness : protect you through the storm; may he bring you home rejoicing : at the wonders he has shown you; may he bring you home rejoicing : once again into our doors.

> **Reading Scripture**
>
> With Bibles everywhere, we can lose the sense that Scripture readings are precious words dripped from God's mouth. Jewish rabbis used to put a drop of honey on the holy books held by young Jewish students to remind them of how sweet the word of God is, like honey on our lips. Muslim friends wash their hands before they touch the Koran. There is something to be said for remembering how precious the Story is. As you read the gospel aloud this year (in morning prayer, before a meal), consider standing on your feet and recognizing that this is not just someone reading a newspaper headline or a poem; this is God's word, speaking directly to us. Another practice might be to sing an Alleluia chorus before and after you read aloud a passage of the gospel. (*Alleluia* is the Latin version of the Greek word *allelouia*, an expression of praise and joy that, in turn, comes from the Hebrew *Hallelujah* for "praise the Lord.") Maybe even consider putting a drop of honey on your children's Bible as you read to them.

❈ December 17

O Lord, let my soul rise up to meet you
as the day rises to meet the sun.

Glory to the Father, and to the Son, and to the Holy Spirit, as it was in the beginning, is now, and will be forever. Amen.

Come, let us bow down and bend the knee : let us kneel before the LORD our Maker.

Song "What Wondrous Love"

We bow before your throne, O Lord : to rise and see your face.

Psalm 89:14–18
Righteousness and justice are the foundations of your throne : **love and truth go before your face.**

Happy are the people who know the festal shout! : **they walk, O Lord, in the light of your presence.**
They rejoice daily in your name : **they are jubilant in your righteousness.**
For you are the glory of their strength : **and by your favor our might is exalted.**
Truly, the Lord is our ruler : **the Holy One of Israel is our King.**

We bow before your throne, O Lord : to rise and see your face.

Isaiah 9:8–17   John 3:16–21

We bow before your throne, O Lord : to rise and see your face.

Clement, one of Peter's early successors as bishop of Rome, prayed, "O Lord, who brings to naught the designs of the nations, O Ruler, who raises the lowly and humbles the lofty, have mercy on those who are disheartened! Raise us who have fallen, show thyself to those who entreat thee, and heal those who are sick. Feed the hungry, free our captives, strengthen the weak, encourage those who lose heart! All nations shall know that thou alone art God."

Prayers for Others

Our Father

Lord, we cannot dwell in both light and darkness. Each day we have a choice. Help us choose light, and when we fail in faithful decision-making, have mercy on us. Amen.

May the peace of the Lord Christ go with you : wherever he may send you; may he guide you through the wilderness : protect you through the storm; may he bring you home rejoicing : at the wonders he has shown you; may he bring you home rejoicing : once again into our doors.

December 18

With the passing of the thirteenth amendment to the Constitution of the United States of America, slavery was abolished in the United States on December 18, 1865.

O Lord, let my soul rise up to meet you
as the day rises to meet the sun.

Glory to the Father, and to the Son, and to the Holy Spirit, as it was in the beginning, is now, and will be forever. Amen.

Come, let us sing to the Lord : let us shout for joy to the Rock of our salvation.

Song "Go, Tell It on the Mountain"

The Lord is King! Let freedom ring! : Let freedom ring! The Lord is King.

Psalm 96:9–13
Worship the LORD in the beauty of holiness : **let the whole earth tremble before him.**
Tell it out among the nations: "The LORD is King! : **he has made the world so firm that it cannot be moved; he will judge the peoples with equity."**
Let the heavens rejoice, and let the earth be glad; let the sea thunder and all that is in it : **let the field be joyful and all that is therein.**
Then shall all the trees of the wood shout for joy before the LORD when he comes : **when he comes to judge the earth.**
He will judge the world with righteousness : **and the peoples with his truth.**

The Lord is King! Let freedom ring! : Let freedom ring! The Lord is King.

Isaiah 9:18–10:4   John 5:30–47

The Lord is King! Let freedom ring! : Let freedom ring! The Lord is King.

Speaking as a former slave, Austin Steward said, "The more we knew of freedom, the more we desired it."

Prayers for Others

Our Father

Thank you, Lord, for the signs that confirm you are indeed sovereign and your kingdom will always prevail. May these signs encourage us to persevere in working toward justice for all who have reason to question its possibility in this world. Amen.

May the peace of the Lord Christ go with you : wherever he may send you; may he guide you through the wilderness : protect you through the storm; may he bring you home rejoicing : at the wonders he has shown you; may he bring you home rejoicing : once again into our doors.

❄ December 19

O Lord, let my soul rise up to meet you
as the day rises to meet the sun.

**Glory to the Father, and to the Son, and to the Holy Spirit,
as it was in the beginning, is now, and will be forever. Amen.**

Come, let us sing to the LORD : let us shout for joy to the Rock of our salvation.

Song "We Are Marching in the Light of God"

May your justice be a light to guide us : and your mercy a help on the way.

Psalm 101:1–4
I will sing of mercy and justice : **to you, O Lord, will I sing praises.**
I will strive to follow a blameless course; oh, when will you come to me? : **I will walk with sincerity of heart within my house.**
I will set no worthless thing before my eyes : **I hate the doers of evil deeds; they shall not remain with me.**
A crooked heart shall be far from me : **I will not know evil.**

May your justice be a light to guide us : and your mercy a help on the way.

Isaiah 10:5–19   Luke 1:5–25

May your justice be a light to guide us : and your mercy a help on the way.

Desmond Tutu, a South African bishop and leader in the movement to end apartheid, said, "I don't preach a social gospel; I preach the gospel, period. The gospel of our Lord Jesus Christ is concerned for the whole person. When people were hungry, Jesus didn't say, 'Now is that political or social?' He said, 'I feed you.' Because the good news to a hungry person is bread."

Prayers for Others

Our Father

Lord, we pray that rather than picking apart your gospel to suit ourselves, we would pick apart the twisted assumption that bread is only for the fortunate, water only for the lucky, and freedom only for the strong. Amen.

**May the peace of the Lord Christ go with you : wherever he may send you;
may he guide you through the wilderness : protect you through the storm;
may he bring you home rejoicing : at the wonders he has shown you;
may he bring you home rejoicing : once again into our doors.**

December 20

O Lord, let my soul rise up to meet you
as the day rises to meet the sun.

Glory to the Father, and to the Son, and to the Holy Spirit,
as it was in the beginning, is now, and will be forever. Amen.

Come, let us sing to the Lord : let us shout for joy to the Rock of our salvation.

Song "Sing and Rejoice"

Christ is coming. Christ has come : Christ will come again.

Psalm 104:32–37
May the glory of the LORD endure for ever : **may the LORD rejoice in all his works.**
He looks at the earth and it trembles : **he touches the mountains and they smoke.**
I will sing to the LORD as long as I live : **I will praise my God while I have my being.**
May these words of mine please him : **I will rejoice in the LORD.**
Let sinners be consumed out of the earth : **and the wicked be no more.**
Bless the LORD, O my soul : **Hallelujah!**

Christ is coming. Christ has come : Christ will come again.

Isaiah 10:20–27   Luke 1:26–38

Christ is coming. Christ has come : Christ will come again.

Bishop N. T. Wright of Durham has written, "The whole point of what Jesus was up to was that he was doing close up, in the present, what he was promising long-term in the future. And what he was promising for that future and doing in the present was not saving souls for a disembodied eternity but rescuing people from the corruption and decay of the way the world presently is so they could enjoy, already in the present, that renewal of creation which is God's ultimate purpose — and so they could thus become colleagues and partners in that large project."

Prayers for Others

Our Father

Thank you, Lord, that your promises are not for some distant future but are to be claimed right now, today. Teach us what we must do and say in our local communities and in our larger world to participate in your promise. Amen.

May the peace of the Lord Christ go with you : wherever he may send you;
may he guide you through the wilderness : protect you through the storm;
may he bring you home rejoicing : at the wonders he has shown you;
may he bring you home rejoicing : once again into our doors.

❋ December 21

O Lord, let my soul rise up to meet you
as the day rises to meet the sun.

Glory to the Father, and to the Son, and to the Holy Spirit,
as it was in the beginning, is now, and will be forever. Amen.

Come, let us sing to the LORD : let us shout for joy to the Rock of our salvation.

Song "Vamos Todos al Banquete"

Come now and join the feast : right here in the belly of the beast!

Psalm 106:1–5
Hallelujah! Give thanks to the LORD, for he is good : **for his mercy endures for ever.**
Who can declare the mighty acts of the LORD : **or show forth all his praise?**
Happy are those who act with justice : **and always do what is right!**
Remember me, O LORD, with the favor you have for your people : **and visit me with your saving help;**
that I may see the prosperity of your elect and be glad with the gladness of your people : **that I may glory with your inheritance.**

Come now and join the feast : right here in the belly of the beast!

Isaiah 11:1–9   Luke 1:39–56

Come now and join the feast : right here in the belly of the beast!

Contemporary theologian Harvey Cox has written, "Like the jester, Christ defies custom and scorns crowned heads. Like a wandering troubadour, he has no place to lay his head. Like the clown in the circus parade, he satirises existing authority by riding into town replete with regal pageantry when he has no earthly power. Like a minstrel, he frequents dinners and parties. At the end, he is consumed by his enemies in a mocking caricature of royal paraphernalia. He is crucified amidst snickers and taunts with a sign over his head that lampoons his laughable claim."

Prayers for Others

Our Father

Lord, help us live so foolishly for you that we draw onlookers and those who would deride us. And while they watch and mock, change all our hearts that we might learn to laugh at the foolishness this world calls normal and run away with the circus that is real life. Amen.

May the peace of the Lord Christ go with you : wherever he may send you;
may he guide you through the wilderness : protect you through the storm;
may he bring you home rejoicing : at the wonders he has shown you;
may he bring you home rejoicing : once again into our doors.

✦ December 22

O Lord, let my soul rise up to meet you
as the day rises to meet the sun.

**Glory to the Father, and to the Son, and to the Holy Spirit,
as it was in the beginning, is now, and will be forever. Amen.**

Come, let us bow down and bend the knee : let us kneel before the Lord our Maker.

Song "Lamb of God"

In your mercy, help us, Lord : to prepare the way for your coming.

Psalm 109:20–25
But you, O Lord my God, oh, deal with me according to your name : **for your tender mercy's sake, deliver me.**
For I am poor and needy : **and my heart is wounded within me.**
I have faded away like a shadow when it lengthens : **I am shaken off like a locust.**
My knees are weak through fasting : **and my flesh is wasted and gaunt.**
I have become a reproach to them : **they see and shake their heads.**
Help me, O Lord my God : **save me for your mercy's sake.**

In your mercy, help us, Lord : to prepare the way for your coming.

Isaiah 11:10–16   Luke 1:57–66

In your mercy, help us, Lord : to prepare the way for your coming.

It is written in the *Didache*, "There are two ways, one of life and one of death, but a great difference between the two ways. The way of life, then, is this: first, you shall love God who made you; second, love your neighbor as yourself, and do not do to another what you would not want done to you."

Prayers for Others

Our Father

Lord, it sounds so easy to follow you because you only call us to love. But love is too much for us! Overwhelm us with your love so that our song of praise might continue in patient kindness and generous support of our neighbors throughout the day. Amen.

**May the peace of the Lord Christ go with you : wherever he may send you;
may he guide you through the wilderness : protect you through the storm;
may he bring you home rejoicing : at the wonders he has shown you;
may he bring you home rejoicing : once again into our doors.**

December 23

O Lord, let my soul rise up to meet you
as the day rises to meet the sun.

**Glory to the Father, and to the Son, and to the Holy Spirit,
as it was in the beginning, is now, and will be forever. Amen.**

Come, let us sing to the Lord : let us shout for joy to the Rock of our salvation.

Song "Solid Rock"

Come now, bless the Lord : he is our help and our shield.

Psalm 115:9–13
O Israel, trust in the Lord : **he is your help and your shield.**
O house of Aaron, trust in the Lord : **he is your help and your shield.**
You who fear the Lord, trust in the Lord : **he is your help and your shield.**
The Lord has been mindful of us, and he will bless us : **he will bless the
 house of Israel; he will bless the house of Aaron;**
he will bless those who fear the Lord : **both small and great together.**

Come now, bless the Lord : he is our help and our shield.

Isaiah 28:9–22   Luke 1:67–80

Come now, bless the Lord : he is our help and our shield.
Church father Augustine of Hippo wrote, "No man has a right to lead such a life of contemplation as to forget in his own ease the service due his neighbor; nor has any man a right to be so immersed in active life as to neglect the contemplation of God."

Prayers for Others

Our Father

O Lord whose patience is beyond comprehension, we pray that you may never tire of helping us grow in faithfulness. Though we fail more than we succeed, raise us up each morning to follow after you again. Guide us today for your glory's sake. Amen.

**May the peace of the Lord Christ go with you : wherever he may send you;
may he guide you through the wilderness : protect you through the storm;
may he bring you home rejoicing : at the wonders he has shown you;
may he bring you home rejoicing : once again into our doors.**

December 24

Christmas Eve

O Lord, let my soul rise up to meet you
as the day rises to meet the sun.

**Glory to the Father, and to the Son, and to the Holy Spirit,
as it was in the beginning, is now, and will be forever. Amen.**

Come, let us bow down and bend the knee : let us kneel before the Lord our Maker.

Song "Amazing Grace"

O Light that shines in our darkness : come and free us from our sin.

Psalm 118:19–24
Open for me the gates of righteousness : **I will enter them; I will offer thanks to the Lord.**
"This is the gate of the Lord : **he who is righteous may enter."**
I will give thanks to you, for you answered me : **and have become my salvation.**
The same stone which the builders rejected : **has become the chief cornerstone.**
This is the Lord's doing : **and it is marvelous in our eyes.**
On this day the Lord has acted : **we will rejoice and be glad in it.**

O Light that shines in our darkness : come and free us from our sin.

Isaiah 59:15b–21   Philippians 2:5–11

O Light that shines in our darkness : come and free us from our sin.

Early church father Epiphanius wrote, "The righteous person will shine a hundred times more brightly than the sun, and once saved, even the smallest among you will shine a hundred times more brightly than the moon."

Prayers for Others

Our Father

We await your coming, Lord, with eagerness and thanksgiving and a fair amount of fear. Shine your true light in the corners of our hearts and in the vast wastelands of our society that we might see more clearly the glory of the creation you have come to redeem. Amen.

May the peace of the Lord Christ go with you : wherever he may send you;
may he guide you through the wilderness : protect you through the storm;
may he bring you home rejoicing : at the wonders he has shown you;
may he bring you home rejoicing : once again into our doors.

December 25

Christmas

O Lord, let my soul rise up to meet you
as the day rises to meet the sun.

**Glory to the Father, and to the Son, and to the Holy Spirit,
as it was in the beginning, is now, and will be forever. Amen.**

Come, let us sing to the LORD : let us shout for joy to the Rock of our salvation.

Song "Go, Tell It on the Mountain"

O Word, now wrapped in human skin : speak peace on earth through your children.

Psalm 119:89–93
O LORD, your word is everlasting : **it stands firm in the heavens.**
Your faithfulness remains from one generation to another : **you established the earth, and it abides.**
By your decree these continue to this day : **for all things are your servants.**
If my delight had not been in your law : **I should have perished in my affliction.**
I will never forget your commandments : **because by them you give me life.**

O Word, now wrapped in human skin : speak peace on earth through your children.

Zechariah 2:10–13   Luke 2:1–14

O Word, now wrapped in human skin : speak peace on earth through your children.

Leo the Great preached, "Truly wondrous is the whole chronicle of the incarnation. From the time when Christ came, the ancient slavery is ended, the devil confounded, demons take to flight, the power of death is broken, paradise is unlocked, the curse is taken away, sin is removed from us, error driven out, truth has been brought back, and the speech of kindliness diffused. A heavenly way of life has been implanted on the earth."

Prayers for Others

Our Father

Lord God, we adore you as the infant Christ. Teach us how to tend to you in your self-imposed vulnerability with us. Prepare us in these tender moments to see what incarnation means in our world. Amen.

May the peace of the Lord Christ go with you : wherever he may send you;
may he guide you through the wilderness : protect you through the storm;
may he bring you home rejoicing : at the wonders he has shown you;
may he bring you home rejoicing : once again into our doors.

> **A Note on Christmas**
>
> "The Twelve Days of Christmas" is not just the title of a fun song but also refers to the twelve-day celebration of the coming of Christ, from his birth, which is observed on December 25, until Epiphany, on January 6. This twelve-day celebration is often marked with the colors gold and white, and dates back to the fourth century. *Christmas* is short for "Christ's Mass," referring to the worship service that marks the birth of Christ. Celebrations during the season include the Feast of the Holy Innocents (December 28), when we remember that the joy of Christ's coming was marked by genocide as Herod fearfully massacred other children in Bethlehem. We can remember that the coming of Christ is about God entering the mess of this world, from the stinky manger to the torturous cross.

December 26

Stephen of Jerusalem (? – 35)

Stephen was the first in a long line of Christian martyrs. He looked on those who were about to kill him and asked the Lord to forgive them (Acts 7:60). His courageous nonviolence in the face of death resembled that of Christ. It is said that Jesus sat at the Father's side after his ascension into heaven, but rose to greet Stephen when he arrived.

O Lord, let my soul rise up to meet you
as the day rises to meet the sun.

**Glory to the Father, and to the Son, and to the Holy Spirit,
as it was in the beginning, is now, and will be forever. Amen.**

Come, let us sing to the LORD : let us shout for joy to the Rock of our salvation.

Song "Woke Up This Mornin'"

In the morning when we rise : may your image shine in us.

Psalm 119:164–68
Seven times a day do I praise you : **because of your righteous judgments.**
Great peace have they who love your law : **for them there is no stumbling block.**
I have hoped for your salvation, O LORD : **and I have fulfilled your commandments.**
I have kept your decrees : **and I have loved them deeply.**
I have kept your commandments and decrees : **for all my ways are before you.**

In the morning when we rise : may your image shine in us.

Isaiah 62:6–7, 10–12   John 3:31–36

In the morning when we rise : may your image shine in us.

Fourth-century church father Gregory of Nazianzus wrote, "God became human and poor for our sake, to raise up our flesh, to recover our divine image, to recreate humanity. We no longer observe distinctions arriving from the flesh, but are to bear within ourselves only the seal of God, by whom and for whom we were created. We are to be so formed and molded by Jesus that we are recognized as belonging to his one family. If only we could be what we hope to be, by the great kindness of our generous God!"

Prayers for Others

Our Father

Lord, your coming is still miraculous. Your joining the family of the poor and displaced still baffles and convicts us. Keep us by your manger until we learn the way of love. Amen.

May the peace of the Lord Christ go with you : wherever he may send you; may he guide you through the wilderness : protect you through the storm; may he bring you home rejoicing : at the wonders he has shown you; may he bring you home rejoicing : once again into our doors.

December 27

O Lord, let my soul rise up to meet you
as the day rises to meet the sun.

**Glory to the Father, and to the Son, and to the Holy Spirit,
as it was in the beginning, is now, and will be forever. Amen.**

Come, let us sing to the LORD : let us shout for joy to the Rock of our salvation.

Song "All Creatures of Our God and King"

Overwhelm us, Lord : with the weight of your glory.

Psalm 128
Happy are they all who fear the LORD : **and who follow in his ways!**
You shall eat the fruit of your labor : **happiness and prosperity shall be yours.**
Your wife shall be like a fruitful vine within your house : **your children like olive shoots round about your table.**
The man who fears the LORD : **shall thus indeed be blessed.**
The LORD bless you from Zion : **and may you see the prosperity of Jerusalem all the days of your life.**
May you live to see your children's children : **may peace be upon Israel.**

Overwhelm us, Lord : with the weight of your glory.

Isaiah 65:15b–25   Luke 4:14–21

Overwhelm us, Lord : with the weight of your glory.

Twentieth-century Quaker Thomas Kelly wrote, "Over the margins of life comes a whisper, a faint call, a premonition of richer living which we know we are passing by. We have hints that there is a way of life vastly richer and deeper than all this hurried existence, a life of unhurried serenity and peace and power. If only we could slip over into that Center! If only we could find the Silence which is the source of sound!"

Prayers for Others

Our Father

Lord, with your coming, our lives have a greater demand placed upon them. Help us learn the art of active, consistent service while maintaining enough silent spaces to hear your call. Amen.

May the peace of the Lord Christ go with you : wherever he may send you;
may he guide you through the wilderness : protect you through the storm;
may he bring you home rejoicing : at the wonders he has shown you;
may he bring you home rejoicing : once again into our doors.

December 28

Holy Innocents
After Jesus was born, Matthew's gospel records that King Herod was so disturbed by the news of a potential contender for the throne that he ordered a preemptive strike, executing all boys in Bethlehem under two years of age. Since its earliest centuries, the church has remembered these "holy innocents" who died because Jesus' coming posed a threat to those in power. Today we

remember all the little ones, born and unborn, who are sacrificed in a culture of death that has not yet welcomed the good news of Jesus. And we recall that Herod's kingdom is now long gone, but the kingdom of God goes on.

O Lord, let my soul rise up to meet you
as the day rises to meet the sun.

**Glory to the Father, and to the Son, and to the Holy Spirit,
as it was in the beginning, is now, and will be forever. Amen.**

Come, let us bow down and bend the knee : let us kneel before the LORD our Maker.

Song "O Mary, Don't You Weep"

Remember the lives of your little ones, Lord : and break the sword of the oppressor.

Psalm 136:1–3, 23–25
Give thanks to the LORD, for he is good : **for his mercy endures for ever.**
Give thanks to the God of gods : **for his mercy endures for ever.**
Give thanks to the Lord of lords : **for his mercy endures for ever.**
Who remembered us in our low estate : **for his mercy endures for ever;**
and delivered us from our enemies : **for his mercy endures for ever;**
who gives food to all creatures : **for his mercy endures for ever.**

Remember the lives of your little ones, Lord : and break the sword of the oppressor.

Jeremiah 31:15–17   Matthew 2:13–18

Remember the lives of your little ones, Lord : and break the sword of the oppressor.

Francis Schaeffer, founder of L'Abri, wrote, "Our conscious relationship with God is enhanced if we treat all the things he has made in the same way as he treats them."

Prayers for Others

Our Father

Lord, receive our prayer of tears and sorrow over those children consumed by a world that holds no regard for them. We pray for children left hungry and thirsty, left to fend for themselves on the streets, left to be abused by poor, twisted souls. Lord, in your mercy receive our prayers of intercession for children around the world. Amen.

May the peace of the Lord Christ go with you : wherever he may send you;
may he guide you through the wilderness : protect you through the storm;
may he bring you home rejoicing : at the wonders he has shown you;
may he bring you home rejoicing : once again into our doors.

✦ December 29

O Lord, let my soul rise up to meet you
as the day rises to meet the sun.

**Glory to the Father, and to the Son, and to the Holy Spirit,
as it was in the beginning, is now, and will be forever. Amen.**

Come, let us bow down and bend the knee : let us kneel before the Lord our Maker.

Song "O Lord, Hear My Prayer"

Listen, Lord; listen, Lord : not to our words but to our prayers.

Psalm 143:7–11
O Lord, make haste to answer me; my spirit fails me : **do not hide your face from me or I shall be like those who go down to the Pit.**
Let me hear of your loving-kindness in the morning, for I put my trust in you : **show me the road that I must walk, for I lift up my soul to you.**
Deliver me from my enemies, O Lord : **for I flee to you for refuge.**
Teach me to do what pleases you, for you are my God : **let your good Spirit lead me on level ground.**
Revive me, O Lord, for your name's sake : **for your righteousness' sake, bring me out of trouble.**

Listen, Lord; listen, Lord : not to our words but to our prayers.

Isaiah 12:1–6   John 7:37–52

Listen, Lord; listen, Lord : not to our words but to our prayers.

Origen of Alexandria, a third-century Bible scholar, wrote that "as we — by our prayers — vanquish all the demons that stir up war, and lead to the violation of oaths, and disturb the peace, we in this service are much more helpful to the kings than those who go into the field to fight for them. None fight better for the king than we do. We do not indeed fight under him, although he demands it; but we fight on his behalf, forming a special army of piety by offering our prayers to God."

Prayers for Others

Our Father

Lord, what you call compassion, others call weakness. What you call conviction, others call dissidence. What you call love, others call mixing with sinners. We pray that we too might be found weak, dissident, and in bad company, especially if it means we are closer to you. Amen.

May the peace of the Lord Christ go with you : wherever he may send you;
may he guide you through the wilderness : protect you through the storm;
may he bring you home rejoicing : at the wonders he has shown you;
may he bring you home rejoicing : once again into our doors.

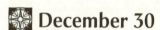 December 30

O Lord, let my soul rise up to meet you
as the day rises to meet the sun.

**Glory to the Father, and to the Son, and to the Holy Spirit,
as it was in the beginning, is now, and will be forever. Amen.**

Come, let us sing to the LORD : let us shout for joy to the Rock of our salvation.

Song "Praise to the Lord, the Almighty"

The Lord lifts up the lowly : but casts the wicked to the ground.

Psalm 147:1–5
Hallelujah! How good it is to sing praises to our God! : **how pleasant it is to honor him with praise!**
The LORD rebuilds Jerusalem : **he gathers the exiles of Israel.**
He heals the brokenhearted : **and binds up their wounds.**
He counts the number of the stars : **and calls them all by their names.**
Great is our LORD and mighty in power : **there is no limit to his wisdom.**

The Lord lifts up the lowly : but casts the wicked to the ground.

Isaiah 25:1–9   John 7:53–8:11

The Lord lifts up the lowly : but casts the wicked to the ground.

Fourth-century preacher John Chrysostom said, "This is the rule of most perfect Christianity, its most exact definition, its highest point, namely, the seeking of the common good. For nothing can so make a person an imitator of Christ as caring for his neighbors."

Prayers for Others

Our Father

Lord, make us a refuge to the poor. Help us prepare a feast for the hungry. Teach us to wipe away the tears of those who mourn, even as you shelter us, feed us, and wipe away our tears. Amen.

**May the peace of the Lord Christ go with you : wherever he may send you;
may he guide you through the wilderness : protect you through the storm;
may he bring you home rejoicing : at the wonders he has shown you;
may he bring you home rejoicing : once again into our doors.**

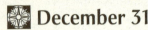 December 31

Watch Night

Established in African-American communities on December 31, 1862, Watch Night is a gathering to celebrate the Emancipation Proclamation becoming law. When the clock struck midnight on January 1, 1863, all slaves in the Confederate States were proclaimed free. Since that date 146 years ago, African-Americans have celebrated the good news of freedom in local churches on New Year's Eve. Like the slaves who first gathered while the Civil War raged on, we proclaim freedom for all captives in Jesus' name, knowing that for millions, freedom is not a reality. Our celebration is a commitment to join modern-day slaves and undocumented workers in their struggle for justice.

O Lord, let my soul rise up to meet you
as the day rises to meet the sun.

**Glory to the Father, and to the Son, and to the Holy Spirit,
as it was in the beginning, is now, and will be forever. Amen.**

Come, let us sing to the LORD : let us shout for joy to the Rock of our salvation.

Song "Glory, Glory, Hallelujah"

Shout the glad tidings o'er Egypt's dark sea : Jehovah has triumphed; his people are free!

Psalm 150
Hallelujah! Praise God in his holy temple : **praise him in the firmament of his power.**
Praise him for his mighty acts : **praise him for his excellent greatness.**
Praise him with the blast of the ram's horn : **praise him with lyre and harp.**
Praise him with timbrel and dance : **praise him with strings and pipe.**
Praise him with resounding cymbals : **praise him with loud clanging cymbals.**
Let everything that has breath : **praise the LORD. Hallelujah!**

Shout the glad tidings o'er Egypt's dark sea : Jehovah has triumphed; his people are free!

Isaiah 26:1–9   John 8:12–19

Shout the glad tidings o'er Egypt's dark sea : Jehovah has triumphed; his people are free!

Writing about the first Watch Night, Booker T. Washington said, "As the great day grew nearer, there was more singing in the slave quarters than usual. It was bolder, had more ring, and lasted later into the night. True, they had sung those same verses before, but they had been careful to explain that the 'freedom' in these songs referred to the next world, and had no connection with life in this world. Now they gradually threw off the mask; and were not afraid to let it be known that the 'freedom' in their songs meant freedom of the body in this world."

Prayers for Others

Our Father

Lord, we know that freedom will prevail because you are already victorious. Help us never lose hope, never stop celebrating your victory, and never stop walking alongside those who struggle to see this freedom come on earth as it is in heaven. Amen.

May the peace of the Lord Christ go with you : wherever he may send you; may he guide you through the wilderness : protect you through the storm; may he bring you home rejoicing : at the wonders he has shown you; may he bring you home rejoicing : once again into our doors.

Becoming the Answer to Our Prayers: A Few Ideas

1. Throw a banquet, a really good one with lots of nice food. Invite folks who struggle with homelessness, mental illness, or addiction. Give everyone a chance to share a gift.
2. Do a creative witness outside a shopping mall. And be nice. Invite folks to see that the best things in life are free. Maybe give out free coffee or cookies.
3. Dismantle a bomb. Or dismantle a theological argument that justifies bombs. Or dismantle an ideology of security and consumption that requires bombs.
4. Experiment in creation care by going fuel-free for a week – bike, carpool, or walk.
5. Start a business whose goal is to provide living-wage jobs to persons from economically disinvested neighborhoods.

JANUARY — THE BAPTISM OF CHRIST

JANUARY

Marks of New Monasticism
Shared Economics

Throughout Scripture we are given a vision of an economy different from the empire's economy. One of the first stories in Scripture is God's rescuing the Hebrew slaves from Egypt. God gives them new patterns of Sabbath as well as the practice of gleaning to make sure that they care for the most vulnerable among them (widows, orphans, immigrants). God also sets in place Jubilee — God's systemic plan for dismantling inequality, relinquishing debts, redistributing property, setting slaves free, and allowing the land to rest and restore itself. There is the promise throughout Scripture that God has created an economy in which there is enough, that God has not created a world of scarcity with too many people or too little stuff. As Gandhi said, "There is enough for everyone's need but not enough for everyone's greed."

We are to pray this day for our daily bread — nothing more and nothing less. Prophets like John the Baptist call us to repentance but then also say things like, "And if you have two tunics, give one away to the person who has none." Rebirth and redistribution must go together. Just as Jesus came preaching repentance, he also invited followers to sell everything they have and give it to the poor. The early Christians went so far as to say that if we have two coats, we have stolen one from the poor, and that when we give to a beggar, we should get on our knees and ask for forgiveness because we are returning what was wrongfully stolen from that person.

Economic sharing was a mark of the early church. Scripture says, "No one claimed that any of their possessions was their own, but they shared everything they had.... There were no needy persons among them" (Acts 4:32, 34). One of the signs of the birthday of the church is that they ended poverty. But it was not just a systemic thing; it was a love thing. The Scriptures say

> **Suggested Reading for the Month**
> *Sabbath Economics* by Ched Myers
> *Rich Christians in an Age of Hunger* by Ron Sider
> *God's Economy* by Jonathan Wilson-Hartgrove
> *Economy of Love* by Relational Tithe

that we can sell everything we have and give it to the poor, but if we have not love, our actions are empty. For Christians, redistribution comes out of a love of neighbor; to love our neighbor as ourselves means we hold our possessions loosely, for the suffering of another is our suffering, and their burden is our burden.

Creative experiments in economic sharing are happening all over the world. One group of Christians in the US started putting out a newsletter listing everyone in the group who was hospitalized and unable to cover their medical bills, so that everyone could be praying for each other and then put their money together to meet the bills. Over the past few decades, that group has paid more than five hundred million dollars in medical bills. Another fascinating experiment is the Relational Tithe, an international group of Christians who tithe (give 10 percent of their income) into a common fund to meet one another's needs and the needs of people they are friends with. One hundred percent of their tithe goes directly to meet needs and is a witness of a community that bears each other's burdens. The reality of rebirth comes with responsibility, for we are reborn into a terribly dysfunctional family. And redistribution, most meaningfully, comes not through guilt or coercion or force but through compassion, solidarity, and love.

January 1

In 1788 Quakers in Pennsylvania freed their slaves, anticipating the emancipation of chattel slaves in the United States some seventy-five years later. Together with free blacks, abolitionist evangelicals, and slaves who were willing to risk their lives, Quakers led one of America's most vibrant faith-based justice movements — the Underground Railroad. Committed to simplicity, religious freedom, and nonviolence, Quakers have contributed to movements for peace and justice throughout US history.

O Lord, let my soul rise up to meet you
as the day rises to meet the sun.

**Glory to the Father, and to the Son, and to the Holy Spirit,
as it was in the beginning, is now, and will be forever. Amen.**

Come, let us sing to the Lord : let us shout for joy to the Rock of our salvation.

Song "This Little Light of Mine"

Jesus, teach us not to shun : what is of God in everyone.

Psalm 7:7–12
Awake, O my God, decree justice : **let the assembly of the peoples gather round you.**
Be seated on your lofty throne, O Most High : **O Lord, judge the nations.**
Give judgment for me according to my righteousness, O Lord : **and according to my innocence, O Most High.**
Let the malice of the wicked come to an end, but establish the righteous : **for you test the mind and heart, O righteous God.**
God is my shield and defense : **he is the savior of the true in heart.**
God is a righteous judge : **God sits in judgment every day.**

Jesus, teach us not to shun : what is of God in everyone.

Genesis 12:1–7   John 16:23b–30

Jesus, teach us not to shun : what is of God in everyone.

George Fox, founder of the Religious Society of Friends, wrote, "People must be led out of captivity up to God. Be patterns, be examples that your carriage and life may preach among all sorts of people, and to them. Then you will come to walk cheerfully over the world, answering that of God in everyone."

Prayers for Others

Our Father

Lord, help us answer your call as readily as our father Abram, that we might extend your blessing throughout our community. Remind us that the places where we find you become altars in our world. Amen.

May the peace of the Lord Christ go with you : wherever he may send you;
may he guide you through the wilderness : protect you through the storm;
may he bring you home rejoicing : at the wonders he has shown you;
may he bring you home rejoicing : once again into our doors.

 January 2

Basil of Caesarea (330–379)

Basil was born in modern-day Turkey. His grandfather was martyred, and his brother, Gregory of Nyssa, became a very influential bishop. In an age marked by doctrinal battles within the church, Basil was a tireless defender of orthodoxy. He is known as an early developer of Christian monasticism, and an incredible preacher and writer. Among his many writings are some of the church's earliest prayers. Basil first left the world to join the monastery, but eventually brought the monastery to the world through the city of Basiliad, also called "The New City." This was a giant community of monastic men and women working with doctors and other laypeople to provide food, clothing, shelter, and medical assistance to the poor of Caesarea. He later went on to become a priest and a bishop, but he always kept his vision of a monastic life not cut off from the world but embracing the pain and sorrow of the world.

O Lord, let my soul rise up to meet you
as the day rises to meet the sun.

**Glory to the Father, and to the Son, and to the Holy Spirit,
as it was in the beginning, is now, and will be forever. Amen.**

Come, let us bow down and bend the knee : let us kneel before the LORD our Maker.

Song "Steal Away to Jesus"

Lord, help us believe : that we might see you come.

Psalm 14:1–4
The fool has said in his heart, "There is no God." : **All are corrupt and commit abominable acts; there is none who does any good.**
The LORD looks down from heaven upon us all : **to see if there is any who is wise, if there is one who seeks after God.**
Every one has proved faithless; all alike have turned bad : **there is none who does good; no, not one.**

Have they no knowledge, all those evildoers : **who eat up my people like bread and do not call upon the LORD?**

Lord, help us believe : that we might see you come.

Genesis 28:10–22   John 6:41–47

Lord, help us believe : that we might see you come.

Basil of Caesarea wrote, "When someone steals a person's clothes, we call him a thief. Should we not give the same name to one who could clothe the naked and does not? The bread in your cupboard belongs to the hungry; the coat hanging unused in your closet belongs to those who need it; the shoes rotting in your closet to the one who has no shoes. The money which you hoard up belongs to the poor."

Prayers for Others

Our Father

Lord, you are always weaving the things of heaven with the things of earth. You dwell among us, above us, and within us. Make us expectant of angels tarrying to do your work. Form us into eager messengers, ready to speak peace in broken communities. Amen.

May the peace of the Lord Christ go with you : wherever he may send you; may he guide you through the wilderness : protect you through the storm; may he bring you home rejoicing : at the wonders he has shown you; may he bring you home rejoicing : once again into our doors.

January 3

Martin Luther, an Augustinian monk and biblical scholar, wrote against the church's use of indulgences and insisted that salvation is a free gift from God, not achieved through good works. Luther refused to recant his criticism of the church, saying, "Here I stand. I cannot do otherwise." He was excommunicated by Pope Leo X on January 3, 1521, unwittingly becoming the leader of a movement that would later be named the Great Reformation.

O Lord, let my soul rise up to meet you
as the day rises to meet the sun.

**Glory to the Father, and to the Son, and to the Holy Spirit,
as it was in the beginning, is now, and will be forever. Amen.**

Come, let us sing to the LORD : let us shout for joy to the Rock of our salvation.

Song "We Shall Not Be Moved"

The LORD lives! Blessed is my Rock! : Exalted is the God of my salvation!

Psalm 18:29–32
You, O LORD, are my lamp : **my God, you make my darkness bright.**
With you I will break down an enclosure : **with the help of my God I will scale any wall.**
As for God, his ways are perfect; the words of the LORD are tried in the fire : **he is a shield to all who trust in him.**
For who is God, but the LORD? : **who is the Rock, except our God?**

The LORD lives! Blessed is my Rock! : Exalted is the God of my salvation!

Exodus 3:1–12   John 6:35–42, 48–51

The LORD lives! Blessed is my Rock! : Exalted is the God of my salvation!

Martin Luther wrote, "When it comes to faith, what a living, creative, active, powerful thing it is. It cannot do other than good at all times. It never waits to ask whether there is some good work to do, rather, before the question is raised, it has done the deed, and keeps on doing it."

Prayers for Others

Our Father

Lord, from Martin Luther in sixteenth-century Germany to Martin Luther King Jr. in twentieth-century Alabama, your disciples have witnessed to a law that is higher than the laws of human institutions. Make us such witnesses, Lord. Amen.

**May the peace of the Lord Christ go with you : wherever he may send you;
may he guide you through the wilderness : protect you through the storm;
may he bring you home rejoicing : at the wonders he has shown you;
may he bring you home rejoicing : once again into our doors.**

✠ January 4

O Lord, let my soul rise up to meet you
as the day rises to meet the sun.

**Glory to the Father, and to the Son, and to the Holy Spirit,
as it was in the beginning, is now, and will be forever. Amen.**

Come, let us sing to the LORD : let us shout for joy to the Rock of our salvation.

Song "It Is Well with My Soul"

When I walk in darkness : Lord, carry me through.

Psalm 23
The LORD is my shepherd : **I shall not be in want.**
He makes me lie down in green pastures : **and leads me beside still waters.**
He revives my soul : **and guides me along right pathways for his name's sake.**
Though I walk through the valley of the shadow of death, I shall fear no evil :
   for you are with me; your rod and your staff, they comfort me.
You spread a table before me in the presence of those who trouble me : **you have anointed my head with oil, and my cup is running over.**
Surely your goodness and mercy shall follow me all the days of my life : **and I will dwell in the house of the LORD for ever.**

When I walk in darkness : Lord, carry me through.

Joshua 1:1–9   John 10:7–17

When I walk in darkness : Lord, carry me through.

Contemporary American author Frederick Buechner has written, "A Christian is one who points at Christ and says, 'I can't prove a thing, but there's something about his eyes and his voice. There's something about the way he carries his head, his hands, the way he carries his cross — the way he carries me.'"

Prayers for Others

Our Father

God, your word instructs us to be ready to give an answer for the faith that is within us. When that time comes, Lord, make us bold to proclaim that your love surpasses human knowledge. Let our answer be actions that mirror your love. Amen.

May the peace of the Lord Christ go with you : wherever he may send you; may he guide you through the wilderness : protect you through the storm; may he bring you home rejoicing : at the wonders he has shown you; may he bring you home rejoicing : once again into our doors.

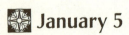 # January 5

O Lord, let my soul rise up to meet you
as the day rises to meet the sun.

Glory to the Father, and to the Son, and to the Holy Spirit, as it was in the beginning, is now, and will be forever. Amen.

Come, let us sing to the LORD : let us shout for joy to the Rock of our salvation.

Song "Come, Thou Fount"

Good Shepherd, we are yours : you know our every care.

Psalm 28:6–9
Blessed is the LORD! : **for he has heard the voice of my prayer.**
The LORD is my strength and my shield : **my heart trusts in him, and I have been helped;**
therefore my heart dances for joy : **and in my song will I praise him.**
The LORD is the strength of his people : **a safe refuge for his anointed.**
Save your people and bless your inheritance : **shepherd them and carry them for ever.**

Good Shepherd, we are yours : you know our every care.

Isaiah 66:18–23   John 14:6–14

Good Shepherd, we are yours : you know our every care.

In the sayings of the desert fathers, this story is recorded: "One day Abba Arsenius consulted an old Egyptian monk about his own thoughts. Someone noticed this and said to him, 'Abba Arsenius, how is it that you with such good Latin and Greek education ask this peasant about your thoughts?' He replied, 'I have indeed been taught Latin and Greek, but I do not know even the alphabet of this peasant.'"

Prayers for Others

Our Father

Lord God, keep us from mumbling on and on in our prayers when all we ought to say is, "Thank you, Lord." Amen.

**May the peace of the Lord Christ go with you : wherever he may send you;
may he guide you through the wilderness : protect you through the storm;
may he bring you home rejoicing : at the wonders he has shown you;
may he bring you home rejoicing : once again into our doors.**

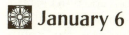 # January 6

Epiphany

Epiphany means "to make manifest." By the fourth century, Epiphany was a major annual celebration for the church. It is a season when we see Jesus' divine mission revealed when the magi visit him, and then we remember his baptism, miracles, ministry, and his call for us to follow.

O Lord, let my soul rise up to meet you
as the day rises to meet the sun.

**Glory to the Father, and to the Son, and to the Holy Spirit,
as it was in the beginning, is now, and will be forever. Amen.**

Come, let us sing to the LORD : let us shout for joy to the Rock of our salvation.

Song "Sing, O Sky (Gaao Re)"

The heavens shine with your glory : as you wrap yourself in skin.

Psalm 33:1–6
Rejoice in the LORD, you righteous : **it is good for the just to sing praises.**
Praise the LORD with the harp : **play to him upon the psaltery and lyre.**
Sing for him a new song: **sound a fanfare with all your skill upon the trumpet.**
For the word of the LORD is right : **and all his works are sure.**
He loves righteousness and justice : **the loving-kindness of the LORD fills the whole earth.**
By the word of the LORD were the heavens made : **by the breath of his mouth all the heavenly hosts.**

The heavens shine with your glory : as you wrap yourself in skin.

Isaiah 60:1–6, 9   Matthew 2:1–12

The heavens shine with your glory : as you wrap yourself in skin.

Fifth-century monk and bishop Paulinus of Nola wrote, "We have no right to our possessions; they have been entrusted to us for the good of all. Let us then invest with the Lord what he has given us, for we have nothing that does not come from him: we are dependent upon him for our very existence. And we ourselves particularly, who have a special and a greater debt, since God not only created us but purchased us as well; what can we regard as our own when we do not possess even ourselves?"

Prayers for Others

Our Father

Lord Jesus Christ, you have shown yourself to the nations and transformed many by your radiant light. Your ongoing revelations bring a continual rebirth, recreating each of us in your likeness. May today's rising sun remind us that your light is for the healing of the nations. Amen.

**May the peace of the Lord Christ go with you : wherever he may send you;
may he guide you through the wilderness : protect you through the storm;
may he bring you home rejoicing : at the wonders he has shown you;
may he bring you home rejoicing : once again into our doors.**

✹ January 7

O Lord, let my soul rise up to meet you
as the day rises to meet the sun.

**Glory to the Father, and to the Son, and to the Holy Spirit,
as it was in the beginning, is now, and will be forever. Amen.**

Come, let us bow down and bend the knee : let us kneel before the Lord our Maker.

Song "Guide My Feet"

Light of the world, shine in our darkness : illuminate the way of peace.

Psalm 37:36–39
Wait upon the Lord and keep his way : **he will raise you up to possess the land, and when the wicked are cut off, you will see it.**
I have seen the wicked in their arrogance : **flourishing like a tree in full leaf.**
I went by, and behold, they were not there : **I searched for them, but they could not be found.**
Mark those who are honest; observe the upright : **for there is a future for the peaceable.**

Light of the world, shine in our darkness : illuminate the way of peace.

Genesis 1:1–2:3   Galatians 1:1–17

Light of the world, shine in our darkness : illuminate the way of peace.

Twentieth-century Jesuit Alfred Delp wrote, "If through one man's life there is a little more love and kindness, a little more light and truth in the world, then he will not have lived in vain."

Prayers for Others

Our Father

Lord, it is hard to live by your patience. Your timing is not our timing, and your ways are not our ways. Keep us from trying to rush peace, and prepare us for the peace that comes only by sacrifice and discipline. Amen.

**May the peace of the Lord Christ go with you : wherever he may send you;
may he guide you through the wilderness : protect you through the storm;
may he bring you home rejoicing : at the wonders he has shown you;
may he bring you home rejoicing : once again into our doors.**

January 8

O Lord, let my soul rise up to meet you
as the day rises to meet the sun.

**Glory to the Father, and to the Son, and to the Holy Spirit,
as it was in the beginning, is now, and will be forever. Amen.**

Come, let us bow down and bend the knee : let us kneel before the LORD our Maker.

Song "Oh the Deep, Deep Love of Jesus"

Though the darkness covers me : I will remember your light.

Psalm 42:1–3, 6–7
As the deer longs for the water brooks : **so longs my soul for you, O God.**
My soul is athirst for God, athirst for the living God : **when shall I come to appear before the presence of God?**
My tears have been my food day and night : **while all day long they say to me, "Where now is your God?"**
Why are you so full of heaviness, O my soul? : **and why are you so disquieted within me?**
Put your trust in God : **for I will yet give thanks to him, who is the help of my countenance, and my God.**

Though the darkness covers me : I will remember your light.

Genesis 2:4–25   Galatians 1:18–2:10

Though the darkness covers me : I will remember your light.

In the sayings of the desert fathers, this story is recorded: "A brother came to see Abba Poemen and said to him, 'Abba, I have many thoughts and they put me in danger.' The old man led him outside and said to him, 'Expand your chest and do not breathe in.' He said, 'I cannot do that.' Then the old man said to him, 'If you cannot do that, no more can you prevent thoughts from arising, but you can resist them.'"

Prayers for Others

Our Father

Lord, we pray not to get lost in the reality of our own depravity, but rather to find ourselves morning by morning in the light of your mercy and redemption. Amen.

May the peace of the Lord Christ go with you : wherever he may send you;
may he guide you through the wilderness : protect you through the storm;
may he bring you home rejoicing : at the wonders he has shown you;
may he bring you home rejoicing : once again into our doors.

✺ January 9

O Lord, let my soul rise up to meet you
as the day rises to meet the sun.

Glory to the Father, and to the Son, and to the Holy Spirit,
as it was in the beginning, is now, and will be forever. Amen.

Come, let us sing to the LORD : let us shout for joy to the Rock of our salvation.

Song "Fairest Lord Jesus"

Clap your hands, all you people : shout to God with a cry of joy!

Psalm 47:5 – 8
God has gone up with a shout : **the LORD with the sound of the ram's horn.**
Sing praises to God, sing praises : **sing praises to our King, sing praises.**
For God is King of all the earth : **sing praises with all your skill.**
God reigns over the nations : **God sits upon his holy throne.**

Clap your hands, all you people : shout to God with a cry of joy!

Genesis 3:1 – 24   Galatians 2:11 – 21

Clap your hands, all you people : shout to God with a cry of joy!

Cyprian of Carthage, a third-century North African bishop, wrote, "The Lord has given us a pattern of prayer, instructing us on how we are to pray. He has made it easy for us to be heard as we pray to the Father in the words taught us by the Son. What prayer could be more a prayer in the truth than the one spoken by the lips of the Son, who is truth himself? To ask the Father in words his Son has given us, to let him hear the prayer of Christ ringing in his ears, is to make our prayer one of friendship, a family prayer. Let the Father recognize the words of his Son."

Prayers for Others

Our Father

Lord Jesus Christ, as we go about our day, we pray that you would recognize not only your word on our lips but also your actions in our deeds. Amen.

May the peace of the Lord Christ go with you : wherever he may send you;
may he guide you through the wilderness : protect you through the storm;
may he bring you home rejoicing : at the wonders he has shown you;
may he bring you home rejoicing : once again into our doors.

✺ January 10

O Lord, let my soul rise up to meet you
as the day rises to meet the sun.

**Glory to the Father, and to the Son, and to the Holy Spirit,
as it was in the beginning, is now, and will be forever. Amen.**

Come, let us bow down and bend the knee : let us kneel before the L ORD our Maker.

Song "Be Thou My Vision"

Against the devil's every wile : protect me, Lord, in times of trial.

Psalm 55:1–6
Hear my prayer, O God : **do not hide yourself from my petition.**
Listen to me and answer me : **I have no peace, because of my cares.**
I am shaken by the noise of the enemy : **and by the pressure of the wicked;**
for they have cast an evil spell upon me : **and are set against me in fury.**
My heart quakes within me : **and the terrors of death have fallen upon me.**
Fear and trembling have come over me : **and horror overwhelms me.**

Against the devil's every wile : protect me, Lord, in times of trial.

Genesis 4:1–16   Galatians 3:1–14

Against the devil's every wile : protect me, Lord, in times of trial.

Desert mother Amma Theodora wrote, "Let us strive to enter by the narrow gate. Just as the trees if they have not stood before the winter's storms cannot bear fruit, so it is with us; this present age is a storm and it is only through many trials and temptations that we can obtain an inheritance in the kingdom of heaven."

Prayers for Others

Our Father

Lord, you have conquered death. You have gone down to the depths of Sheol and risen again to life. Help us to remember as we suffer with you that we will also rise with you to a life that never ends. Amen.

May the peace of the Lord Christ go with you : wherever he may send you;
may he guide you through the wilderness : protect you through the storm;
may he bring you home rejoicing : at the wonders he has shown you;
may he bring you home rejoicing : once again into our doors.

January 11

Brother Lawrence (1611 – 1691)

Born Nicholas Herman in Lorraine, France, Brother Lawrence received little formal education and, as a young man, served briefly in the army. One day, he had an experience that set the course of his life in a new direction. Gazing at a barren tree in winter, Lawrence saw for the first time the majesty of God's grace and the constancy of God's providence. He imagined himself like the tree, waiting for the life that God would inevitably bring in season. Shortly after this experience, he became a lay brother in the Carmelite monastery in Paris. There he worked in the kitchen and, in the repetition of his daily chores, found a way to integrate spirituality and work, which he called the "practice of the presence of God." By learning to perform his daily, mundane tasks for the sake of God, Brother Lawrence turned every moment into an opportunity for prayer.

O Lord, let my soul rise up to meet you
as the day rises to meet the sun.

**Glory to the Father, and to the Son, and to the Holy Spirit,
as it was in the beginning, is now, and will be forever. Amen.**

Come, let us sing to the LORD : let us shout for joy to the Rock of our salvation.

Song "What Is This Place?"

May I sense you every moment : and make my whole life a prayer.

Psalm 61:4–8
I will dwell in your house for ever : **I will take refuge under the cover of your wings.**
For you, O God, have heard my vows : **you have granted me the heritage of those who fear your name.**
Add length of days to the king's life : **let his years extend over many generations.**
Let him sit enthroned before God for ever : **bid love and faithfulness watch over him.**
So will I always sing the praise of your name : **and day by day I will fulfill my vows.**

Morning Prayer

May I sense you every moment : and make my whole life a prayer.

Genesis 4:17–26   Galatians 3:15–22

May I sense you every moment : and make my whole life a prayer.

Brother Lawrence wrote, "Men invent means and methods of coming at God's love, they learn rules and set up devices to remind them of that love, and it seems like a world of trouble to bring oneself into the consciousness of God's presence. Yet it might be so simple. Is it not quicker and easier just to do our common business wholly for the love of him?"

Prayers for Others

Our Father

Though you are worthy of trumpets and the song of angels, you graciously receive our daily prayers of whispered words and mundane habits. Enable us, Lord, to love you with all that we are and in all that we do. Teach us how we might truly pray without ceasing. Amen.

**May the peace of the Lord Christ go with you : wherever he may send you;
may he guide you through the wilderness : protect you through the storm;
may he bring you home rejoicing : at the wonders he has shown you;
may he bring you home rejoicing : once again into our doors.**

✹ January 12

On January 12, 1948, Mohandas Gandhi began his last successful fast in New Delhi to convince Hindus and Muslims in the city to work toward peace. Six days later, convinced that harmony was achieved, he ended the fast. For most of his adult life, Gandhi read Jesus' Sermon on the Mount every morning, convinced that it contained a truth more powerful than the empire that occupied his native India or the enmity that divided Hindus and Muslims. Through "experiments in truth" like the public fast, he sought to put Jesus' teachings into practice for the sake of peace.

O Lord, let my soul rise up to meet you
as the day rises to meet the sun.

**Glory to the Father, and to the Son, and to the Holy Spirit,
as it was in the beginning, is now, and will be forever. Amen.**

Come, let us bow down and bend the knee : let us kneel before the Lord our Maker.

Song   "Jesus, Help Us Live in Peace"

Lord, give us strength: to pray against the powers.

Psalm 67:1–4
May God be merciful to us and bless us : **show us the light of his countenance and come to us.**
Let your ways be known upon earth : **your saving health among all nations.**
Let the peoples praise you, O God : **let all the peoples praise you.**
Let the nations be glad and sing for joy : **for you judge the peoples with equity and guide all the nations upon earth.**

Lord, give us strength: to pray against the powers.

Genesis 6:1–8   Galatians 3:23–29

Lord, give us strength: to pray against the powers.

Gandhi said, "Prayer is not an old woman's idle amusement. Properly understood and applied, it is the most potent instrument of action."

Prayers for Others

Our Father

Lord, as we wait for you, teach us how self-denial might open our spirits to receive your instruction and strength. Amen.

**May the peace of the Lord Christ go with you : wherever he may send you;
may he guide you through the wilderness : protect you through the storm;
may he bring you home rejoicing : at the wonders he has shown you;
may he bring you home rejoicing : once again into our doors.**

✸ January 13

In 2003, George Ryan, Republican governor of Illinois, called for a moratorium on the death penalty. Persuaded by the work of law students exposing race and class discrimination, he called for a halt on executions. Though his political career was tainted by scandal, the 2003 moratorium affirmed and fueled the fire of many Christians and other abolitionists who are working for restorative justice and for an end to the death penalty.

O Lord, let my soul rise up to meet you
as the day rises to meet the sun.

Glory to the Father, and to the Son, and to the Holy Spirit,
as it was in the beginning, is now, and will be forever. Amen.

Come, let us bow down and bend the knee : let us kneel before the LORD our Maker.

Song "Lamb of God"

Christ our Lord is sacrificed for us : therefore, let us keep the feast.

Psalm 70
Be pleased, O God, to deliver me : **O LORD, make haste to help me.**
Let those who seek my life be ashamed and altogether dismayed : **let those who take pleasure in my misfortune draw back and be disgraced.**
Let those who say to me "Aha!" and gloat over me turn back : **because they are ashamed.**
Let all who seek you rejoice and be glad in you : **let those who love your salvation say for ever, "Great is the LORD!"**
But as for me, I am poor and needy : **come to me speedily, O God.**
You are my helper and my deliverer : **O LORD, do not tarry.**

Christ our Lord is sacrificed for us : therefore, let us keep the feast.

Genesis 6:9–22   Galatians 4:1–11

Christ our Lord is sacrificed for us : therefore, let us keep the feast.

Contemporary theologian Mark L. Taylor has written, "Jesus died the victim of executioners with imperial power. There is an inescapable opposition between the life and death of Jesus, and imperial power. To embrace and love the executed God is to be in resistance to empire. To be a follower of the executed Jesus of Nazareth is to venture down a road without having a place in the system of imperial control."

Prayers for Others

Our Father

Lord, even though you have conquered the grave, death is still an enemy that robs creation of your intent for life. Make us offended by death wherever we find it. Help us to advocate for life, from our communities to our capitols. Amen.

May the peace of the Lord Christ go with you : wherever he may send you;
may he guide you through the wilderness : protect you through the storm;
may he bring you home rejoicing : at the wonders he has shown you;
may he bring you home rejoicing : once again into our doors.

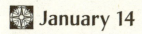 **January 14**

O Lord, let my soul rise up to meet you
as the day rises to meet the sun.

**Glory to the Father, and to the Son, and to the Holy Spirit,
as it was in the beginning, is now, and will be forever. Amen.**

Come, let us sing to the LORD : let us shout for joy to the Rock of our salvation.

Song "Nothin' but the Blood"

I'm so glad, oh I'm so glad : that the blood done signed my name.

Psalm 73:24–29
You will guide me by your counsel : **and afterwards receive me with glory.**
Whom have I in heaven but you? : **and having you I desire nothing upon earth.**
Though my flesh and my heart should waste away : **God is the strength of my heart and my portion for ever.**
Truly, those who forsake you will perish : **you destroy all who are unfaithful.**
But it is good for me to be near God : **I have made the Lord GOD my refuge.**
I will speak of all your works : **in the gates of the city of Zion.**

I'm so glad, oh I'm so glad : that the blood done signed my name.

Genesis 7:1–10, 17–23   Galatians 4:12–20

I'm so glad, oh I'm so glad : that the blood done signed my name.

Twentieth-century Maryknoll sister Mollie Rogers wrote, "Love, work, prayer, and suffering will sustain us in the future as they have in the past. All who are here now, all who will come after us, will have no other tools than these with which to build."

Prayers for Others

Our Father

Lord Jesus Christ, your blood washes away our sins and reconciles us to you. May we never get used to the wonder of a God who gives his own life for those who are killing him. Amen.

**May the peace of the Lord Christ go with you : wherever he may send you;
may he guide you through the wilderness : protect you through the storm;
may he bring you home rejoicing : at the wonders he has shown you;
may he bring you home rejoicing : once again into our doors.**

✺ January 15

On January 15, 1929, Martin Luther King Jr. was born in Atlanta, Georgia. In celebration of his contribution to the civil rights movement, the United States Congress made the third Monday in January a national holiday in 1983. While we celebrate Dr. King's contribution to America, we also remember his insistence that the church exist as the "conscience of the state," speaking prophetically to those in power. We honor Dr. King with all Americans, but we also remember that the sermon he intended to preach the Sunday after his assassination was titled "Why America May Go to Hell."

O Lord, let my soul rise up to meet you
as the day rises to meet the sun.

**Glory to the Father, and to the Son, and to the Holy Spirit,
as it was in the beginning, is now, and will be forever. Amen.**

Come, let us bow down and bend the knee : let us kneel before the LORD our Maker.

Song "We Shall Overcome"

Lord, if we are extremists : may we be extremists for love.

Psalm 78:1–3, 12–14
Hear my teaching, O my people : **incline your ears to the words of my mouth.**
I will open my mouth in a parable : **I will declare the mysteries of ancient times.**
That which we have heard and known, and what our forefathers have told us : **we will not hide from their children.**
He worked marvels in the sight of their forefathers : **in the land of Egypt, in the field of Zoan.**
He split open the sea and let them pass through : **he made the waters stand up like walls.**
He led them with a cloud by day : **and all the night through with a glow of fire.**

Lord, if we are extremists : may we be extremists for love.

Genesis 8:6–22   Galatians 4:21–31

Lord, if we are extremists : may we be extremists for love.

Martin Luther King Jr. preached, "I have a dream that one day every valley shall be exalted, every hill and mountain shall be made low, that rough places will be made straight and the glory of the Lord shall be revealed and all flesh shall see it together."

Prayers for Others

Our Father

Lord, as we wake from another night's slumber, we are reminded that your dreams are given to us and not merely conjured up by our imaginations. Help us understand both that your dreams come at a price and that their rewards are immeasurable. Amen.

May the peace of the Lord Christ go with you : wherever he may send you; may he guide you through the wilderness : protect you through the storm; may he bring you home rejoicing : at the wonders he has shown you; may he bring you home rejoicing : once again into our doors.

January 16

After twelve years of civil war and approximately seventy-five thousand deaths, El Salvador's government and rebel leaders signed a peace treaty in Mexico City on January 16, 1992. Six government negotiators, five guerilla commanders, and five rebel negotiators signed the treaty one after another.

O Lord, let my soul rise up to meet you
as the day rises to meet the sun.

Glory to the Father, and to the Son, and to the Holy Spirit, as it was in the beginning, is now, and will be forever. Amen.

Come, let us sing to the LORD : let us shout for joy to the Rock of our salvation.

Song "We Are Marching in the Light of God"

Sustain us in the struggle, Lord : and raise us to your life.

Psalm 85:1–4
You have been gracious to your land, O LORD : **you have restored the good fortune of Jacob.**
You have forgiven the iniquity of your people : **and blotted out all their sins.**
You have withdrawn all your fury : **and turned yourself from your wrathful indignation.**
Restore us then, O God our Savior : **let your anger depart from us.**

Sustain us in the struggle, Lord : and raise us to your life.

Genesis 9:18–29   Galatians 5:1–15

Sustain us in the struggle, Lord : and raise us to your life.

Morning Prayer

El Salvador's Archbishop Oscar Romero said, "I have frequently been threatened with death. I must say that, as a Christian, I do not believe in death but in the resurrection. If they kill me, I shall rise again in the Salvadoran people. Martyrdom is a great gift from God that I do not believe I have earned. But if God accepts the sacrifice of my life, then my blood will be like the seed of liberty, and a sign of the hope that will soon become a reality."

Prayers for Others

Our Father

Lord, as humans we are always moving closer to death. Each morning is a reminder that our lives are fleeting gifts. But as your children, we are also always moving toward life. May this morning remind us that we are one day closer to the life that lasts forever. Amen.

**May the peace of the Lord Christ go with you : wherever he may send you;
may he guide you through the wilderness : protect you through the storm;
may he bring you home rejoicing : at the wonders he has shown you;
may he bring you home rejoicing : once again into our doors.**

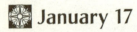

January 17

Anthony of Egypt (251 – 356)

Anthony was born in Egypt in the middle of the third century and lost his parents at a young age, inheriting a fair amount of land and wealth. Soon after, when he heard a gospel reading in church prompting him to "go sell what you possess and give to the poor," he did just that, vowing to dedicate his life thereafter to God. Anthony lived for a time in his native home, pursuing prayerful asceticism. After fifteen years, at the age of thirty-five, he withdrew to the solitude of the desert and began his monastic life of prayer, study, and work. After many years of living in the desert, Anthony remained whole and healthy, and he radiated compassion and joy. He lived to the age of 105 and is remembered as the father of the church's first monastic movement.

O Lord, let my soul rise up to meet you
as the day rises to meet the sun.

**Glory to the Father, and to the Son, and to the Holy Spirit,
as it was in the beginning, is now, and will be forever. Amen.**

Come, let us bow down and bend the knee : let us kneel before the LORD our Maker.

Song "Let All Mortal Flesh Keep Silence"

Keep our frailty before us, Lord : that we might set our hearts on you.

Psalm 89:47–52
Remember, Lord, how short life is : **how frail you have made all flesh.**
Who can live and not see death? : **who can save himself from the power of the grave?**
Where, Lord, are your loving-kindnesses of old : **which you promised David in your faithfulness?**
Remember, Lord, how your servant is mocked : **how I carry in my bosom the taunts of many peoples,**
the taunts your enemies have hurled, O Lord : **which they hurled at the heels of your anointed.**
Blessed be the Lord for evermore! : **Amen, I say, Amen.**

Keep our frailty before us, Lord : that we might set our hearts on you.

Genesis 11:1–9   Galatians 5:16–24

Keep our frailty before us, Lord : that we might set our hearts on you.

Abba Anthony wrote, "From our neighbors is life and death. If we gain our brother, we gain God, but if we cause our brother to stumble, we sin against Christ."

Prayers for Others

Our Father

Lord, we know that to live by the flesh is death, but to live by the Spirit is life. Still, you have redeemed the flesh of the world through your incarnation. Teach us how to be in the world but not of it. Amen.

May the peace of the Lord Christ go with you : wherever he may send you;
may he guide you through the wilderness : protect you through the storm;
may he bring you home rejoicing : at the wonders he has shown you;
may he bring you home rejoicing : once again into our doors.

❈ January 18

In 1893 Lorrin Thurston, the grandson of Christian missionaries, convinced US President Benjamin Harrison of the urgent need to annex Hawaii in order to protect American lives and property. When US troops arrived on Hawaiian soil, Queen Liliuokalani surrendered her throne to prevent bloodshed. One hundred years later, US President Bill Clinton apologized to Native Hawaiians, calling the overthrow of Hawaii's monarchy an illegal act.

O Lord, let my soul rise up to meet you
as the day rises to meet the sun.

Glory to the Father, and to the Son, and to the Holy Spirit,
as it was in the beginning, is now, and will be forever. Amen.

Come, let us bow down and bend the knee : let us kneel before the LORD our Maker.

Song "O Lord, Have Mercy"

Judge your earth with mercy, Lord : and teach us to love justice.

Psalm 94:1–4
O LORD God of vengeance : **O God of vengeance, show yourself.**
Rise up, O Judge of the world : **give the arrogant their just desserts.**
How long shall the wicked, O LORD : **how long shall the wicked triumph?**
They bluster in their insolence : **all evildoers are full of boasting.**

Judge your earth with mercy, Lord : and teach us to love justice.

Genesis 11:27–12:8   Galatians 5:25–6:10

Judge your earth with mercy, Lord : and teach us to love justice.

Dorothy Day, co-founder of the Catholic Worker Movement, wrote, "We want no revolution; we want the brotherhood of men. We want men to love one another. We want all men to have what is sufficient for their needs. But when we meet people who deny Christ in His poor, we feel, 'Here are the atheists.' They turned first from Christ crucified because He was a poor worker, buffeted and spat upon and beaten. And now — strange thought — the devil has so maneuvered that the people turn from Him because those who profess Him are clothed in soft raiment and sit at well-spread tables and deny the poor."

Prayers for Others

Our Father

Holy Spirit, guide us in the imprint of Christ's footsteps to pursue justice, counting our neighbors' welfare to be as important as our own. Amen.

**May the peace of the Lord Christ go with you : wherever he may send you;
may he guide you through the wilderness : protect you through the storm;
may he bring you home rejoicing : at the wonders he has shown you;
may he bring you home rejoicing : once again into our doors.**

January 19

O Lord, let my soul rise up to meet you
as the day rises to meet the sun.

**Glory to the Father, and to the Son, and to the Holy Spirit,
as it was in the beginning, is now, and will be forever. Amen.**

Come, let us sing to the LORD : let us shout for joy to the Rock of our salvation.

Song "Praise to the Lord, the Almighty"

Shout with joy to the Lord : lift up your voice, rejoice, and sing!

Psalm 98:1–4
Sing to the LORD a new song: **for he has done marvelous things.**
With his right hand and his holy arm : **has he won for himself the victory.**
The LORD has made known his victory : **his righteousness has he openly shown in the sight of the nations.**
He remembers his mercy and faithfulness to the house of Israel : **and all the ends of the earth have seen the victory of our God.**

Shout with joy to the Lord : lift up your voice, rejoice, and sing!

Genesis 12:9–13:1   Galatians 6:11–18

Shout with joy to the Lord : lift up your voice, rejoice, and sing!

Contemporary writer Madeleine L'Engle wrote, "We are all asked to do more than we can do. Every hero and heroine of the Bible does more than he would have thought it possible to do, from Gideon to Esther to Mary. Jacob, one of my favourite characters, certainly wasn't qualified. He was a liar and a cheat; and yet he was given the extraordinary vision of angels and archangels ascending and descending a ladder which reached from earth to heaven."

Prayers for Others

Our Father

Lord, this is the day that you have made. Let us rejoice and be glad in it, even as we know it will bring more than we can do. Amen.

**May the peace of the Lord Christ go with you : wherever he may send you;
may he guide you through the wilderness : protect you through the storm;
may he bring you home rejoicing : at the wonders he has shown you;
may he bring you home rejoicing : once again into our doors.**

January 20

O Lord, let my soul rise up to meet you
as the day rises to meet the sun.

**Glory to the Father, and to the Son, and to the Holy Spirit,
as it was in the beginning, is now, and will be forever. Amen.**

Come, let us sing to the LORD : let us shout for joy to the Rock of our salvation.

Song "All Creatures of Our God and King"

Bless the Lord, O my soul : how excellent is your greatness.

Psalm 104:2–6
You wrap yourself with light as with a cloak : **and spread out the heavens like a curtain.**
You lay the beams of your chambers in the waters above : **you make the clouds your chariot; you ride on the wings of the wind.**
You make the winds your messengers : **and flames of fire your servants.**
You have set the earth upon its foundations : **so that it never shall move at any time.**
You covered it with the Deep as with a mantle : **the waters stood higher than the mountains.**

Bless the Lord, O my soul : how excellent is your greatness.

Genesis 13:2–18   Ephesians 1:1–14

Bless the Lord, O my soul : how excellent is your greatness.

John Calvin, sixteenth-century theologian and reformer, wrote, "The creation is quite like a spacious and splendid house, provided and filled with the most exquisite and the most abundant furnishings. Everything in it tells us of God."

Prayers for Others

Our Father

Lord, wherever we look today, allow us to catch a glimpse of you. And whenever others look at us today, allow them to catch a glimpse of you. Amen.

**May the peace of the Lord Christ go with you : wherever he may send you;
may he guide you through the wilderness : protect you through the storm;
may he bring you home rejoicing : at the wonders he has shown you;
may he bring you home rejoicing : once again into our doors.**

✴ January 21

O Lord, let my soul rise up to meet you
as the day rises to meet the sun.

**Glory to the Father, and to the Son, and to the Holy Spirit,
as it was in the beginning, is now, and will be forever. Amen.**

Come, let us sing to the LORD : let us shout for joy to the Rock of our salvation.

Song "O Mary, Don't You Weep"

Give thanks to the Lord for he is good : his mercy endures forever.

Psalm 106:6–12
We have sinned as our forebears did : **we have done wrong and dealt wickedly.**
In Egypt they did not consider your marvelous works, nor remember the abundance of your love : **they defied the Most High at the Red Sea.**
But he saved them for his name's sake : **to make his power known.**
He rebuked the Red Sea, and it dried up : **and he led them through the deep as through a desert.**
He saved them from the hand of those who hated them : **and redeemed them from the hand of the enemy.**
The waters covered their oppressors : **not one of them was left.**
Then they believed his words : **and sang him songs of praise.**

Give thanks to the Lord for he is good : his mercy endures forever.

Genesis 14:1–24   Ephesians 1:15–23

Give thanks to the Lord for he is good : his mercy endures forever.

Irish rock star Bono has said, "Grace defies reason and logic. Love interrupts, if you like, the consequences of your actions, which in my case is very good news indeed, because I've done a lot of stupid stuff."

Prayers for Others

Our Father

Enlighten the eyes of our hearts, O Lord, so we may not only see and receive your mercy but also notice the places in our world where you call us to extend mercy. Amen.

**May the peace of the Lord Christ go with you : wherever he may send you;
may he guide you through the wilderness : protect you through the storm;
may he bring you home rejoicing : at the wonders he has shown you;
may he bring you home rejoicing : once again into our doors.**

January 22

On January 22, 1973, the US Supreme Court decided in *Roe v. Wade* that a mother has the legal right to end her pregnancy up until the point at which the fetus can live outside of her womb. We lament the death of each child lost to abortion. We pray for each parent who has chosen to terminate a pregnancy. And we commit to become a people who welcome life in a culture of death.

O Lord, let my soul rise up to meet you
as the day rises to meet the sun.

**Glory to the Father, and to the Son, and to the Holy Spirit,
as it was in the beginning, is now, and will be forever. Amen.**

Come, let us bow down and bend the knee : let us kneel before the Lord our Maker.

Song "Take My Life and Let It Be"

Today you set before us life and death : in everything we do, may we choose life.

Psalm 107:33–38
The Lord changed rivers into deserts : **and water springs into thirsty ground,**
a fruitful land into salt flats : **because of the wickedness of those who dwell there.**
He changed deserts into pools of water : **and dry land into water springs.**
He settled the hungry there : **and they founded a city to dwell in.**
They sowed fields, and planted vineyards : **and brought in a fruitful harvest.**
He blessed them, so that they increased greatly : **he did not let their herds decrease.**

Today you set before us life and death : in everything we do, may we choose life.

Genesis 15:1–11, 17–21   Ephesians 2:1–10

Today you set before us life and death : in everything we do, may we choose life.

Cyprian of Carthage, a third-century North African bishop, wrote, "The world is going mad in mutual extermination, and murder, considered as a crime when committed individually, becomes a virtue when it is committed by large numbers. It is the multiplication of the frenzy that assures impunity to the assassins."

Prayers for Others

Our Father

Lord, we all suffer varying degrees of blindness. We are blind to love, to justice, to grace, and to life. Help us not to condemn one another in our blindness, but rather to work together to help one another see more clearly by your light. Amen.

May the peace of the Lord Christ go with you : wherever he may send you;
may he guide you through the wilderness : protect you through the storm;
may he bring you home rejoicing : at the wonders he has shown you;
may he bring you home rejoicing : once again into our doors.

January 23

O Lord, let my soul rise up to meet you
as the day rises to meet the sun.

**Glory to the Father, and to the Son, and to the Holy Spirit,
as it was in the beginning, is now, and will be forever. Amen.**

Come, let us sing to the LORD : let us shout for joy to the Rock of our salvation.

Song "All Creatures of Our God and King"

May our feet skip with the mountains : as we sing and dance your praise.

Psalm 114
Hallelujah! When Israel came out of Egypt : **the house of Jacob from a people of strange speech,**
Judah became God's sanctuary : **and Israel his dominion.**
The sea beheld it and fled : **Jordan turned and went back.**
The mountains skipped like rams : **and the little hills like young sheep.**
What ailed you, O sea, that you fled? : **O Jordan, that you turned back?**
You mountains, that you skipped like rams? : **you little hills like young sheep?**
Tremble, O earth, at the presence of the Lord : **at the presence of the God of Jacob,**
who turned the hard rock into a pool of water : **and flint stone into a flowing spring.**

May our feet skip with the mountains : as we sing and dance your praise.

Genesis 16:1–14   Ephesians 2:11–22

May our feet skip with the mountains : as we sing and dance your praise.

Morning Prayer

William Law, an eighteenth-century English cleric, wrote, "All that is sweet, delightful, and amiable in this world, in the serenity of the air, the fineness of seasons, the joy of light, the melody of sounds, the beauty of colors, the fragrancy of smells, the splendor of precious stones, is nothing else but Heaven breaking through the veil of this world."

Prayers for Others

Our Father

Lord, it is fitting to rejoice in your beauty and to gaze upon your handiwork. While others may call this a waste of time, we recognize that unless we sit in adoration of you, we will forget whom we serve and for what purpose. Remind us why worship is always our first response to you. Amen.

**May the peace of the Lord Christ go with you : wherever he may send you;
may he guide you through the wilderness : protect you through the storm;
may he bring you home rejoicing : at the wonders he has shown you;
may he bring you home rejoicing : once again into our doors.**

✺ January 24

On January 24, 1848, James Marshall discovered gold in the American River, setting off the California Gold Rush. Prior to the discovery of this precious metal, one hundred and fifty thousand Native Americans lived in California. White settlers in search of gold brought with them genocide through both disease and violence. In 1851, the government of California endorsed the extermination of Native people. Offering five dollars per head in some places, they invested a total of a million dollars in the systematic murder of men, women, and children. By 1870, only an estimated thirty-one thousand California Natives had survived.

O Lord, let my soul rise up to meet you
as the day rises to meet the sun.

**Glory to the Father, and to the Son, and to the Holy Spirit,
as it was in the beginning, is now, and will be forever. Amen.**

Come, let us bow down and bend the knee : let us kneel before the Lord our Maker.

Song "I Want Jesus to Walk with Me"

Speak, Lord, for your servant is listening : give us life according to your word.

Psalm 119:25–28
My soul cleaves to the dust : **give me life according to your word.**
I have confessed my ways, and you answered me : **instruct me in your statutes.**
Make me understand the way of your commandments : **that I may meditate on your marvelous works.**
My soul melts away for sorrow : **strengthen me according to your word.**

Speak, Lord, for your servant is listening : give us life according to your word.

Genesis 16:15–17:14   Ephesians 3:1–13

Speak, Lord, for your servant is listening : give us life according to your word.

Seattle, chief of the Suquamish, said, "One thing we know, which the White Man may one day discover — our God is the same God. You may think that you own Him as you wish to own our land; but you cannot. He is the God of humanity, and his compassion is equal for the red man and the white. The earth is precious to him, and to harm the earth is to heap contempt on its Creator. Even the white man cannot be exempt from the common destiny. We may be brothers after all. We shall see."

Prayers for Others

Our Father

Thank you, Lord, that you do not claim to be God over just some people but are the creator and redeemer of all creatures. Help us spread the good news that no one can claim ownership of you, because each of us belongs to you. Amen.

May the peace of the Lord Christ go with you : wherever he may send you; may he guide you through the wilderness : protect you through the storm; may he bring you home rejoicing : at the wonders he has shown you; may he bring you home rejoicing : once again into our doors.

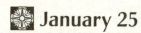 **January 25**

O Lord, let my soul rise up to meet you
as the day rises to meet the sun.

Glory to the Father, and to the Son, and to the Holy Spirit,
as it was in the beginning, is now, and will be forever. Amen.

Come, let us sing to the LORD : let us shout for joy to the Rock of our salvation.

Song   "Ubi Caritas"

Your love, O Lord, reaches to heaven : your faithfulness extends to the sky.

Psalm 119:73–76
Your hands have made me and fashioned me : **give me understanding, that I may learn your commandments.**
Those who fear you will be glad when they see me : **because I trust in your word.**
I know, O Lord, that your judgments are right : **and that in faithfulness you have afflicted me.**
Let your loving-kindness be my comfort : **as you have promised to your servant.**

Your love, O Lord, reaches to heaven : your faithfulness extends to the sky.

Genesis 17:15–27   Ephesians 3:14–21

Your love, O Lord, reaches to heaven : your faithfulness extends to the sky.

Twentieth-century Russian Georges Florovsky wrote, "Christianity entered history as a new social order, or rather a new social dimension. From the very beginning Christianity was not primarily a 'doctrine,' but exactly a 'community.' There was not only a 'Message' to be proclaimed and delivered, and 'Good News' to be declared. There was precisely a New Community, distinct and peculiar, in the process of growth and formation, to which members were called and recruited. Indeed, 'fellowship' (*koinonia*) was the basic category of Christian existence."

Prayers for Others

Our Father

Lord, when one of us hungers, make it our instinct to feed. When one of us is displaced, make it our instinct to share our home. When one of us is called illegal, make it our instinct to advocate for our sister's rights. May we find our peace in the peace of the places to which you have called us. Amen.

May the peace of the Lord Christ go with you : wherever he may send you; may he guide you through the wilderness : protect you through the storm; may he bring you home rejoicing : at the wonders he has shown you; may he bring you home rejoicing : once again into our doors.

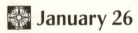 January 26

O Lord, let my soul rise up to meet you
as the day rises to meet the sun.

**Glory to the Father, and to the Son, and to the Holy Spirit,
as it was in the beginning, is now, and will be forever. Amen.**

Come, let us sing to the LORD : let us shout for joy to the Rock of our salvation.

Song "Guide My Feet"

Give us a song to guide our feet : as we're marching to freedom land.

Psalm 119:108–12
Accept, O LORD, the willing tribute of my lips : **and teach me your judgments.**
My life is always in my hand : **yet I do not forget your law.**
The wicked have set a trap for me : **but I have not strayed from your commandments.**
Your decrees are my inheritance for ever : **truly, they are the joy of my heart.**
I have applied my heart to fulfill your statutes : **for ever and to the end.**

Give us a song to guide our feet : as we're marching to freedom land.

Genesis 18:1–16   Ephesians 4:1–16

Give us a song to guide our feet : as we're marching to freedom land.

A poem from American farmer Wendell Berry:
> As soon as the generals and the politicos
> can predict the motion of your mind,
> lose it. Leave it as a sign
> to mark the false trail, the way
> you didn't go. Be like the fox
> who makes more tracks than necessary,
> some in the wrong direction.
> Practice resurrection.

Prayers for Others

Our Father

Lord, the power of song can stir our hearts to courage and break down walls of resistance. Help us compose lyrics of our lives that move enemies to compassion and make justice to rise up and dance in every corner of the world. Amen.

**May the peace of the Lord Christ go with you : wherever he may send you;
may he guide you through the wilderness : protect you through the storm;
may he bring you home rejoicing : at the wonders he has shown you;
may he bring you home rejoicing : once again into our doors.**

✦ January 27

O Lord, let my soul rise up to meet you
as the day rises to meet the sun.

Glory to the Father, and to the Son, and to the Holy Spirit,
as it was in the beginning, is now, and will be forever. Amen.

Come, let us sing to the LORD : let us shout for joy to the Rock of our salvation.

Song "Sing and Rejoice"

Restore our fortunes, Lord : like a wash in the rainy season.

Psalm 126:1–4
When the LORD restored the fortunes of Zion : **then were we like those who dream.**
Then was our mouth filled with laughter : **and our tongue with shouts of joy.**
Then they said among the nations : **"The LORD has done great things for them."**
The LORD has done great things for us : **and we are glad indeed.**

Restore our fortunes, Lord : like a wash in the rainy season.

Genesis 18:16–33   Ephesians 4:17–32

Restore our fortunes, Lord : like a wash in the rainy season.

Twelfth-century mystic Hildegard of Bingen wrote, "Rivers of living water are to be poured out over the whole world, to ensure that people, like fishes caught in a net, can be restored to wholeness."

Prayers for Others

Our Father

Lord, to laugh in the midst of trial and to rejoice in the darkest valley is another way of saying, "Our hope is in you." Fill us with laughter and joy while we work for peace and strive for justice. Amen.

**May the peace of the Lord Christ go with you : wherever he may send you;
may he guide you through the wilderness : protect you through the storm;
may he bring you home rejoicing : at the wonders he has shown you;
may he bring you home rejoicing : once again into our doors.**

✦ January 28

O Lord, let my soul rise up to meet you
as the day rises to meet the sun.

**Glory to the Father, and to the Son, and to the Holy Spirit,
as it was in the beginning, is now, and will be forever. Amen.**

Come, let us bow down and bend the knee : let us kneel before the Lord our Maker.

Song "Holy, Holy, Holy"

Worthy is the Lamb who was slain : to receive glory and honor.

Psalm 138:1–5
I will give thanks to you, O Lord, with my whole heart : **before the gods I will sing your praise.**
I will bow down toward your holy temple and praise your name : **because of your love and faithfulness;**
For you have glorified your name : **and your word above all things.**
When I called, you answered me : **you increased my strength within me.**
All the kings of the earth will praise you, O Lord : **when they have heard the words of your mouth.**

Worthy is the Lamb who was slain : to receive glory and honor.

Genesis 19:1–29   Ephesians 5:1–14

Worthy is the Lamb who was slain : to receive glory and honor.

Early Christian apologist Tertullian wrote in the second century, "It is not fitting to serve at the same time the symbol of Christ and the symbol of the devil, the power light, and the power darkness. One and the same soul cannot serve two masters. And how may we wage war without the sword that God himself has taken away from us? How can we learn the use of the sword, when Our Lord said that he who raised the sword would perish by the sword? And how can the sons of peace take part in combat?"

Prayers for Others

Our Father

Jesus, you are known as both the Lion of Judah and the Sacrificial Lamb. As we follow you, we learn both mighty power and humble submission. Teach us when to imitate you as Lion and when as Lamb. Amen.

May the peace of the Lord Christ go with you : wherever he may send you;
may he guide you through the wilderness : protect you through the storm;
may he bring you home rejoicing : at the wonders he has shown you;
may he bring you home rejoicing : once again into our doors.

❋ January 29

O Lord, let my soul rise up to meet you
as the day rises to meet the sun.

**Glory to the Father, and to the Son, and to the Holy Spirit,
as it was in the beginning, is now, and will be forever. Amen.**

Come, let us sing to the LORD : let us shout for joy to the Rock of our salvation.

Song "Great Is Thy Faithfulness"

Search me, O God, and know my heart : try me and know my restless thoughts.

Psalm 139:13–16
I will thank you because I am marvelously made : **your works are wonderful, and I know it well.**
My body was not hidden from you : **while I was being made in secret and woven in the depths of the earth.**
Your eyes beheld my limbs, yet unfinished in the womb; all of them were written in your book : **they were fashioned day by day, when as yet there was none of them.**
How deep I find your thoughts, O God! : **how great is the sum of them!**

Search me, O God, and know my heart : try me and know my restless thoughts.

Genesis 21:1–21   Ephesians 5:15–33

Search me, O God, and know my heart : try me and know my restless thoughts.

Twentieth-century Catholic writer Flannery O'Connor said, "I think there is no suffering greater than what is caused by the doubts of those who want to believe. I know what torment this is, but I can only see it, in myself anyway, as the process by which faith is deepened. What people don't realize is how much religion costs. They think faith is a big electric blanket, when of course it is the cross."

Prayers for Others

Our Father

How merciful are you, O Lord, when you receive us even with our doubts and suspicions. We pray to keep tiptoeing toward you without fear of rejection. We pray to keep up our feeble attempts at serving you even when we question the worth of our efforts. Amen.

May the peace of the Lord Christ go with you : wherever he may send you; may he guide you through the wilderness : protect you through the storm; may he bring you home rejoicing : at the wonders he has shown you; may he bring you home rejoicing : once again into our doors.

❉ January 30

While walking to evening prayer in New Delhi, India, Mohandas Gandhi was shot five times at point blank range and died almost immediately. Gandhi was the primary political and spiritual leader of India during his country's independence movement. He was one of the first in India to practice mass civil disobedience and nonviolence against the tyranny in his country, inspiring a host of twentieth-century activists.

O Lord, let my soul rise up to meet you
as the day rises to meet the sun.

Glory to the Father, and to the Son, and to the Holy Spirit,
as it was in the beginning, is now, and will be forever. Amen.

Come, let us bow down and bend the knee : let us kneel before the LORD our Maker.

Song "The Kingdom of God"

Living Christ means a living cross : without it, life is a living death.

Psalm 146:4–8
Happy are they who have the God of Jacob for their help! : **whose hope is in the LORD their God;**
who made heaven and earth, the seas, and all that is in them : **who keeps his promise for ever;**
who gives justice to those who are oppressed : **and food to those who hunger.**
The LORD sets the prisoners free; the LORD opens the eyes of the blind : **the LORD lifts up those who are bowed down;**
the LORD loves the righteous; the LORD cares for the stranger : **he sustains the orphan and widow, but frustrates the way of the wicked.**

Living Christ means a living cross : without it, life is a living death.

Morning Prayer

Genesis 22:1–18   Ephesians 6:1–9

Living Christ means a living cross : without it, life is a living death.

Gandhi said, "If I have read the Bible correctly, I know many men who have never heard the name of Jesus Christ or have even rejected the official interpretation of Christianity who will, probably, if Jesus came in our midst today in the flesh, be owned by him more than many of us."

Prayers for Others

Our Father

We know, Lord, that the world will never cease to return hatred for love and violence for peace. Still we pray for the courage and confidence to walk in love and peace for the sake of those who have never known love or peace, for the sake of our own treacherous hearts. Amen.

May the peace of the Lord Christ go with you : wherever he may send you; may he guide you through the wilderness : protect you through the storm; may he bring you home rejoicing : at the wonders he has shown you; may he bring you home rejoicing : once again into our doors.

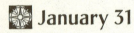# January 31

Marcella of Rome (325–410)
Marcella had an enviable life as the daughter of a prominent Roman family who married a wealthy man. But less than a year after her wedding, her husband died. She was given a chance to continue living in wealth when she was proposed to by the wealthy consul Cerealis. She chose instead to convert her mansion into one of the earliest communities of women, where she and other noblewomen used their riches to help the poor. Marcella said she preferred to "store her money in the stomachs of the needy than hide it in a purse." In 410, when the Goths invaded Rome, they broke into Marcella's home. When they demanded money, she calmly responded that she had no riches because she had given all to the poor. Though she was an elderly woman, they beat and tortured her mercilessly. Her attackers were eventually shamed by her piety and she was released, but she died within a short time.

O Lord, let my soul rise up to meet you
as the day rises to meet the sun.

Glory to the Father, and to the Son, and to the Holy Spirit,
as it was in the beginning, is now, and will be forever. Amen.

Come, let us sing to the LORD : let us shout for joy to the Rock of our salvation.

Song "Sing and Rejoice"

Fill us, Lord, with the abundance : of life that never ends.

Psalm 147:6–9
The LORD lifts up the lowly : **but casts the wicked to the ground.**
Sing to the LORD with thanksgiving : **make music to our God upon the harp.**
He covers the heavens with clouds : **and prepares rain for the earth;**
he makes grass to grow upon the mountains : **and green plants to serve mankind.**

Fill us, Lord, with the abundance : of life that never ends.

Genesis 23:1–20   Ephesians 6:10–24

Fill us, Lord, with the abundance : of life that never ends.

Marcella of Rome wrote, "By heaven's grace, captivity has found me a poor woman, not made me one. Now I shall go in want of daily bread, but I shall not feel hunger since I am full of Christ."

Prayers for Others

Our Father

Lord, some of us have found wealth in this world, while others of us are left wanting. But as we stand before you, we are all paupers save for your grace and love. Remind us that our true wealth is your gift of a sustainable way of life for all. Amen.

May the peace of the Lord Christ go with you : wherever he may send you;
may he guide you through the wilderness : protect you through the storm;
may he bring you home rejoicing : at the wonders he has shown you;
may he bring you home rejoicing : once again into our doors.

Becoming the Answer to Our Prayers: A Few Ideas

1. Try to go a whole week without spending any money. If you have to, barter or beg a little to make it through.
2. Hold a Baby Goods Exchange for parents to bring toys and clothing their kids have outgrown and trade them.
3. Join a Bible study led by someone with less formal education than yourself.
4. Attempt to repair something that is broken. Appreciate the people who repair things for you on a regular basis.
5. Defy complacency and flout despair. Believe that you can do something, right now, right here — even if you take only a baby step.

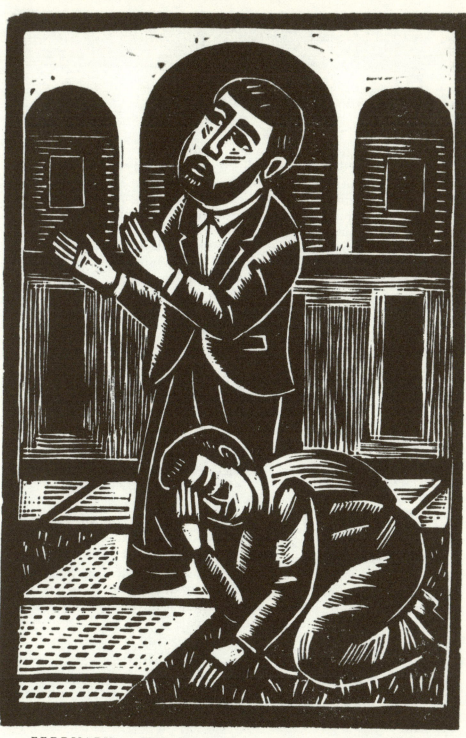

FEBRUARY — THE PUBLICAN AND THE PHARISEE

FEBRUARY

Marks of New Monasticism
Reconciliation

We lament the racial divisions within the church and pursue a just reconciliation. Martin Luther King Jr. powerfully called out one of the most heartbreaking ironies for those of us who call ourselves Christians: "The most segregated hour in the world is eleven o'clock on Sunday morning" — when we gather for worship. Of all the places we should hope and expect to see the diversity of God's family, it is not in the shopping malls and bars but in the church. But reconciliation begins on a small scale. It must begin in living rooms and at dinner tables. Reconciliation will never make its way into our worship services until it makes its way into our homes.

During Black History Month, we acknowledge the many ways racism has crippled our country, while also celebrating African-Americans who've made incredible contributions to society. Alongside the ugly stories in the bloodstained pages of church history, in which Christians justified slavery and genocide with deadly theology, there are the incredible stories of communities of faith who lived with great courage in times of oppression and conflict. In South Africa, a community of black and white South Africans bought land together and began living on it in the middle of apartheid. Their lives were at risk. They were threatened with jail time. Their kingdom-minded friendships were an offense to their society of colonialism and segregation. Reconciliation takes different shapes in different contexts and eras. There are beautiful stories of Catholics and Protestants in Northern Ireland, and Hutus

> **Suggested Reading for the Month**
> *Let Justice Roll Down* by John Perkins
> *No Future without Forgiveness* by Desmond Tutu
> *Mirror to the Church* by Emmanuel Katongole
> *Grace Matters* by Chris Rice

and Tutsis in Burundi, starting communities where they live and worship together, lamenting their history of Christians killing other Christians. These communities are a prophetic witness and a healing leaven amid a world still riddled with racism and prejudice and hatred.

When we make reconciliation our goal, we don't pretend to have it all together. Like the tax collector who beat his chest in the back of the temple, saying, "Lord, have mercy," we begin our prayer for reconciliation with lament and repentance. With us, reconciliation is impossible. But with God, all things are possible. We don't just believe it; we've seen it.

✾ February 1

Brigid of Ireland (c. 450–525)

Brigid is believed to have been the daughter of a pagan Scottish king and a Christian Pictish slave. Even as a child, she was known to have a generous spirit and a compassionate, tender heart and was drawn to help the poor, the hungry, and the cold. Eventually Brigid's father decided she must be married or taken into someone else's household, because he could no longer afford to keep her (especially in light of her excessive giving to the poor, which he feared would be the ruin of him). Brigid refused marriage and became a nun with seven other women. At Kildare, she founded a double monastery for monks and nuns, assisted by a bishop. The perpetual fire at the monastery became a symbol of its hospitality and constant, undying devotion to God and the poor.

O Lord, let my soul rise up to meet you
as the day rises to meet the sun.

**Glory to the Father, and to the Son, and to the Holy Spirit,
as it was in the beginning, is now, and will be forever. Amen.**

Come, let us bow down and bend the knee : let us kneel before the Lord our Maker.

Song "We Shall Not Be Moved"

We are happy to be your children, O Lord : make us happier still to extend the table.

Psalm 1:1–3
Happy are they who have not walked in the counsel of the wicked : **nor lingered in the way of sinners, nor sat in the seats of the scornful!**
Their delight is in the law of the Lord : **and they meditate on his law day and night.**
They are like trees planted by streams of water, bearing fruit in due season, with leaves that do not wither : **everything they do shall prosper.**

We are happy to be your children, O Lord : make us happier still to extend the table.

Genesis 24:1–27   John 13:1–20

We are happy to be your children, O Lord : make us happier still to extend the table.

Brigid of Ireland said, "I would like the angels of Heaven to be among us. I would like an abundance of peace. I would like full vessels of charity. I would like rich treasures of mercy. I would like cheerfulness to preside over all. I would like Jesus to be present."

Prayers for Others

Our Father

Lord, help us to welcome every guest as if we were welcoming you, delighting in their presence and ready to learn what good news they bring to us. Amen.

**May the peace of the Lord Christ go with you : wherever he may send you;
may he guide you through the wilderness : protect you through the storm;
may he bring you home rejoicing : at the wonders he has shown you;
may he bring you home rejoicing : once again into our doors.**

 # February 2

The Presentation of Christ in the Temple

On February 2, the church remembers Jesus' presentation at the temple in Jerusalem. Along with their newborn son, Mary and Joseph brought a sacrifice of two pigeons, the offering permitted in the law of Moses for those too poor to afford a lamb (Lev. 12:8). Despite their lack of wealth, however, these peasants from Galilee carried in their arms the salvation of the whole world. Simeon and Anna, a holy man and a devout woman of Israel, immediately recognized the incalculable value of the present they had brought. We sing "Simeon's Song" (see Saturday in the Evening Prayer section) to train our eyes to see the salvation of the world in the presents of the poor.

O Lord, let my soul rise up to meet you
as the day rises to meet the sun.

Glory to the Father, and to the Son, and to the Holy Spirit,
as it was in the beginning, is now, and will be forever. Amen.

Come, let us sing to the LORD : let us shout for joy to the Rock of our salvation.

Song "Vamos Todos al Banquete"

Our eyes have seen your salvation, Lord : which you have prepared for all to see.

Psalm 10:15–19
The helpless commit themselves to you : **for you are the helper of orphans.**
Break the power of the wicked and evil : **search out their wickedness until you find none.**

The LORD is King for ever and ever : **the ungodly shall perish from his land.**
The LORD will hear the desire of the humble : **you will strengthen their heart and your ears shall hear;**
to give justice to the orphan and oppressed : **so that mere mortals may strike terror no more.**

Our eyes have seen your salvation, Lord : which you have prepared for all to see.

Malachi 3:1–4   Luke 2:22–40

Our eyes have seen your salvation, Lord : which you have prepared for all to see.

This quote comes from the apocryphal writing known as the Acts of Peter: "Unless you make what is right left, and what is left right, what is above into what is below, and what is behind into what is in front, you will not learn to know the Kingdom."

Prayers for Others

Our Father

Things are topsy-turvy in your kingdom, God. The poor bear gifts of great worth, the dead rise, the meek inherit the earth. Teach us how to live in an upside-down world where we are called to welcome the outcast, prepare a feast for the ragged, and forgive those who offend us. Amen.

May the peace of the Lord Christ go with you : wherever he may send you;
may he guide you through the wilderness : protect you through the storm;
may he bring you home rejoicing : at the wonders he has shown you;
may he bring you home rejoicing : once again into our doors.

✸ February 3

O Lord, let my soul rise up to meet you
as the day rises to meet the sun.

Glory to the Father, and to the Son, and to the Holy Spirit,
as it was in the beginning, is now, and will be forever. Amen.

Come, let us bow down and bend the knee : let us kneel before the LORD our Maker.

Song   "Servant Song"

O God, you stretch out the universe : and wash our feet with your hands.

Psalm 18:26–28
With the faithful you show yourself faithful, O God : **with the forthright you show yourself forthright.**
With the pure you show yourself pure : **but with the crooked you are wily.**
You will save a lowly people : **but you will humble the haughty eyes.**

O God, you stretch out the universe : and wash our feet with your hands.

Genesis 24:28–38, 49–51   John 13:21–30

O God, you stretch out the universe : and wash our feet with your hands.

Fourth-century bishop Gregory of Nyssa wrote, "God has imprinted the image of the good things of His own nature on creation. But sin, in spreading out over the divine likeness, has caused this good to disappear, covering it with shameful garments. But if by life rightly led, you wash away the mud that has been put on your heart, the Godlike beauty will again shine out in you."

Prayers for Others

Our Father

Lord, we are all capable of denying you. Please help us to invite the lost back into your fold with humility, knowing all the while that we would ourselves be lost but for your grace. Amen.

May the peace of the Lord Christ go with you : wherever he may send you; may he guide you through the wilderness : protect you through the storm; may he bring you home rejoicing : at the wonders he has shown you; may he bring you home rejoicing : once again into our doors.

✻ February 4

Rosa Parks was born February 4, 1913. When she was forty-two, Parks refused to give up her seat on a city bus in Montgomery, Alabama, to a white passenger, which at the time, the law required of African-Americans. She was arrested for her act of civil disobedience and worked with others from the NAACP to start the Montgomery Bus Boycott. The resulting integration of city buses in Montgomery ignited the civil rights movement in the United States and inspired nonviolent movements for social change around the world.

O Lord, let my soul rise up to meet you
as the day rises to meet the sun.

Glory to the Father, and to the Son, and to the Holy Spirit, as it was in the beginning, is now, and will be forever. Amen.

Come, let us sing to the LORD : let us shout for joy to the Rock of our salvation.

Song "Freedom Train"

O Lord, give freedom to your people : and answer us when we call.

Psalm 20:5–8
We will shout for joy at your victory and triumph in the name of our God :
 may the LORD grant all your requests.
Now I know that the LORD gives victory to his anointed : **he will answer him
 out of his holy heaven, with the victorious strength of his right hand.**
Some put their trust in chariots and some in horses : **but we will call upon the
 name of the LORD our God.**
They collapse and fall down: **but we will arise and stand upright.**

O Lord, give freedom to your people : and answer us when we call.

Genesis 24:50–67   John 13:31–38

O Lord, give freedom to your people : and answer us when we call.

Rosa Parks commented, "People always say that I didn't give up my seat because I was tired, but that isn't true. No, the only tired I was, was tired of giving in."

Prayers for Others

Our Father

Lord, we have only to look at your life to know that reconciliation always costs something. Whether we are old or young, strong or weary, rich or poor, supply us with the conviction that reconciliation is always worth the price. Amen.

**May the peace of the Lord Christ go with you : wherever he may send you;
may he guide you through the wilderness : protect you through the storm;
may he bring you home rejoicing : at the wonders he has shown you;
may he bring you home rejoicing : once again into our doors.**

✺ February 5

On February 1, 1960, four college students — Ezell A. Blair Jr., David Richmond, Joseph McNeil, and Franklin McCain — initiated the first sit-in demonstration at a Woolworth's lunch counter in Greensboro, North Carolina. The store manager ignored the protestors, hoping they would leave. The next day, twenty-seven more students came to protest. By February 5, three hundred students had arrived, igniting a mass movement of sit-ins for desegregation throughout the South.

O Lord, let my soul rise up to meet you
as the day rises to meet the sun.

**Glory to the Father, and to the Son, and to the Holy Spirit,
as it was in the beginning, is now, and will be forever. Amen.**

Come, let us sing to the LORD : let us shout for joy to the Rock of our salvation.

Song "This Little Light of Mine"

May our sitting down and our rising up : contribute, Lord, to your kingdom's work.

Psalm 27:15–18
Show me your way, O LORD : **lead me on a level path, because of my enemies.**
Deliver me not into the hand of my adversaries : **for false witnesses have risen up against me, and also those who speak malice.**
What if I had not believed that I should see the goodness of the LORD : **in the land of the living!**
O tarry and await the LORD's pleasure; be strong, and he shall comfort your heart : **wait patiently for the LORD.**

May our sitting down and our rising up : contribute, Lord, to your kingdom's work.

Genesis 24:50–67   John 14:1–7

May our sitting down and our rising up : contribute, Lord, to your kingdom's work.

Eighteenth-century Jesuit Jean-Pierre de Caussade wrote, "The great and firm foundation of the spiritual life is the offering of ourselves to God and being subject to his will in all things. We must completely forget ourselves, so that we regard ourselves as an object which has been sold and over which we no longer have any rights. We find all our joy in fulfilling God's pleasure — his happiness, his glory and the fact that he is our great and only delight. Once we have this foundation, all we need to do is spend our lives rejoicing that God is God and being so wholly abandoned to his will that we are quite indifferent as to what we do and equally indifferent as to what use he makes of our activities."

Prayers for Others

Our Father

Lord, remind us that it is not always agitated uprisings and nonstop activity which lead to justice, but that change often comes through the quiet commitment of a small group of people. Help us raise our small body of people to set about quietly becoming the change we want to see in the world. Amen.

May the peace of the Lord Christ go with you : wherever he may send you;
may he guide you through the wilderness : protect you through the storm;
may he bring you home rejoicing : at the wonders he has shown you;
may he bring you home rejoicing : once again into our doors.

✠ February 6

O Lord, let my soul rise up to meet you
as the day rises to meet the sun.

Glory to the Father, and to the Son, and to the Holy Spirit,
as it was in the beginning, is now, and will be forever. Amen.

Come, let us bow down and bend the knee : let us kneel before the LORD our Maker.

Song "Steal Away to Jesus"

Teach us, Lord, to twist our tanks : into tractors and tilling blades.

Psalm 33:13–17
The LORD looks down from heaven : **and beholds all the people in the world.**
From where he sits enthroned he turns his gaze : **on all who dwell on the earth.**
He fashions all the hearts of them : **and understands all their works.**
There is no king that can be saved by a mighty army : **a strong man is not delivered by his great strength.**
The horse is a vain hope for deliverance : **for all its strength it cannot save.**

Teach us, Lord, to twist our tanks : into tractors and tilling blades.

Genesis 25:19–34   John 14:8–17

Teach us, Lord, to twist our tanks : into tractors and tilling blades.

Second-century Bible scholar Origen of Alexandria wrote, "We do not arm ourselves against any nation; we do not learn the art of war; because, through Jesus Christ, we have become the children of peace."

Prayers for Others

Our Father

Lord, this work of peacemaking is difficult business. But we cannot expect peace by any other way than nonviolence. Keep us even from violent thoughts and from threatening your peace with impatience. Amen.

May the peace of the Lord Christ go with you : wherever he may send you; may he guide you through the wilderness : protect you through the storm; may he bring you home rejoicing : at the wonders he has shown you; may he bring you home rejoicing : once again into our doors.

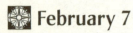 ## February 7

Dom Helder Camara of Recife (1909–1999)
Born February 7, 1909, in Fortazela, Brazil, Dom Helder Camara became a bishop of the Catholic Church and one of the twentieth century's great apostles of nonviolence. After joining a conservative political movement as a young priest, Camara experienced a conversion while ministering among the poor in the favelas of Rio de Janeiro. "When I fed the poor they called me a saint," Camara said. "When I asked why they were poor, they called me a Communist." Labeled "the red bishop," Camara worked tirelessly for democracy and human rights in Brazil, even as he watched friends and fellow priests imprisoned, tortured, and killed. When a hired assassin knocked on the elderly Camara's door, he was so moved by the sight of the bishop that he blurted out, "I can't kill you. You are one of the Lord's."

O Lord, let my soul rise up to meet you
as the day rises to meet the sun.

Glory to the Father, and to the Son, and to the Holy Spirit, as it was in the beginning, is now, and will be forever. Amen.

Come, let us sing to the LORD : let us shout for joy to the Rock of our salvation.

Song "Magnificat"

Lord, give us a good start : and the grace never to give up.

Psalm 37:5–9
Commit your way to the LORD and put your trust in him : **and he will bring it to pass.**
He will make your righteousness as clear as the light : **and your just dealing as the noonday.**
Be still before the LORD : **and wait patiently for him.**
Do not fret yourself over the one who prospers : **the one who succeeds in evil schemes.**
Refrain from anger, leave rage alone : **do not fret yourself; it leads only to evil.**

Lord, give us a good start : and the grace never to give up.

Genesis 26:1–6, 12–33   John 14:18–31

Lord, give us a good start : and the grace never to give up.

Bishop Camara wrote, "To walk alone is possible, but the good walker knows that the great trip is life and it requires companions."

Prayers for Others

Our Father

Lord, though each of us rises alone to start this new day, bind us to the faith of the saints who have gone before us, and guide us to walk with our brothers and sisters in community. Amen.

May the peace of the Lord Christ go with you : wherever he may send you; may he guide you through the wilderness : protect you through the storm; may he bring you home rejoicing : at the wonders he has shown you; may he bring you home rejoicing : once again into our doors.

✣ February 8

On February 8, 1887, the Dawes Act was approved by the United States Congress, dividing Native American reservation lands into separate properties to be owned and maintained by individuals. Tribes were to be dissolved and Native Americans were expected to assimilate into white American culture. Most of the land granted to Native Americans was desert, unable to sustain agriculture.

O Lord, let my soul rise up to meet you
as the day rises to meet the sun.

Glory to the Father, and to the Son, and to the Holy Spirit, as it was in the beginning, is now, and will be forever. Amen.

Come, let us bow down and bend the knee : let us kneel before the LORD our Maker.

Song   "Poor Wayfaring Stranger"

Forgive us, Lord, for stealing the land : Have mercy and set us free.

Psalm 39:5–8
LORD, let me know my end and the number of my days : **so that I may know how short my life is.**

You have given me a mere handful of days, and my lifetime is as nothing in your sight : **truly, even those who stand erect are but a puff of wind.**
We walk about like a shadow, and in vain we are in turmoil : **we heap up riches and cannot tell who will gather them.**
And now, what is my hope? : **O Lord, my hope is in you.**

Forgive us, Lord, for stealing the land : Have mercy and set us free.

Genesis 27:1–29   John 15:1–11

Forgive us, Lord, for stealing the land : Have mercy and set us free.

Seattle, chief of the Suquamish, said, "We know that the White Man does not understand our ways. One portion of the land is the same to him as the next, for he is a stranger who comes in the night and takes from the land whatever he needs. The earth is not his brother, but his enemy, and when he has conquered it, he moves on."

Prayers for Others

Our Father

Lord, show us that reconciling with those we imagine are different from us is not only for peace, but also to train us more deeply in the faith that honors everything created by your hand. Help us see that reconciliation leads to deeper knowledge of you. Amen.

May the peace of the Lord Christ go with you : wherever he may send you; may he guide you through the wilderness : protect you through the storm; may he bring you home rejoicing : at the wonders he has shown you; may he bring you home rejoicing : once again into our doors.

✦ February 9

O Lord, let my soul rise up to meet you
as the day rises to meet the sun.

Glory to the Father, and to the Son, and to the Holy Spirit, as it was in the beginning, is now, and will be forever. Amen.

Come, let us sing to the Lord : let us shout for joy to the Rock of our salvation.

Song   "Glory, Glory, Hallelujah"

We want to find our home in you, Lord : come and make your home with us.

Psalm 49:15–19
But God will ransom my life : **he will snatch me from the grasp of death.**
Do not be envious when some become rich : **or when the grandeur of their house increases;**
for they will carry nothing away at their death : **nor will their grandeur follow them.**
Though they thought highly of themselves while they lived : **and were praised for their success,**
they shall join the company of their forebears : **who will never see the light again.**

We want to find our home in you, Lord : come and make your home with us.

Genesis 27:30–45   John 15:12–27

We want to find our home in you, Lord : come and make your home with us.

Mississippi civil rights leader Fannie Lou Hamer said, "I am sick and tired of being sick and tired."

Prayers for Others

Our Father

Lord, when we weary of the journey, strengthen us by your Spirit to imagine new heavens and a new earth. Amen.

May the peace of the Lord Christ go with you : wherever he may send you; may he guide you through the wilderness : protect you through the storm; may he bring you home rejoicing : at the wonders he has shown you; may he bring you home rejoicing : once again into our doors.

> ### A Note on Lent
> Lent is the forty-day season of reflection and preparation for the death and resurrection of Jesus. (You'll have to check for Ash Wednesday on a calendar to see when Lent starts this year.) It is a time of repentance, of considering Christ's sufferings and rethinking how we are called to take up our own crosses. Some of us give up things like chocolate or television during this season as a sort of fasting, and others try to integrate something new into their lives, like visiting folks in prison, sewing clothes, exercising, or praying. It is a good season to rethink how we live and to let some things go, or maybe even to develop some new holy habits.
>
> Ash Wednesday marks the beginning of Lent. Traditionally, the palm branches from Palm Sunday of the previous year are burned and the ashes are placed on the foreheads of Christians as a sign of repentance.

✦ February 10

On February 10, 1990, Nelson Mandela was released after twenty-seven years in a South African prison. He had been sentenced to life imprisonment for plotting to overthrow his government as part of the African National Congress (AFM), which stood in opposition to the ruling National Party's apartheid policies. While imprisoned he became one of the most influential black leaders of South Africa. After the apartheid policy was defeated through nonviolent struggle, Mandela became South Africa's first black president.

O Lord, let my soul rise up to meet you
as the day rises to meet the sun.

**Glory to the Father, and to the Son, and to the Holy Spirit,
as it was in the beginning, is now, and will be forever. Amen.**

Come, let us sing to the LORD : let us shout for joy to the Rock of our salvation.

Song "We Are Marching in the Light of God"

Offer to God a sacrifice of thanksgiving : make good on your promises to the Most High.

Psalm 50:1–3, 6
The LORD, the God of gods, has spoken : **he has called the earth from the rising of the sun to its setting.**
Out of Zion, perfect in its beauty : **God reveals himself in glory.**
Our God will come and will not keep silence : **before him there is a consuming flame, and round about him a raging storm.**
Let the heavens declare the rightness of his cause : **for God himself is judge.**

Offer to God a sacrifice of thanksgiving : make good on your promises to the Most High.

Genesis 27:46–28:4, 10–22   John 16:1–15

Offer to God a sacrifice of thanksgiving : make good on your promises to the Most High.

Nelson Mandela said, "To be free is not merely to cast off one's chains, but to live in a way that respects and enhances the freedom of others."

Prayers for Others

Our Father

Lord, not many of us could sustain hope in the midst of such horrors as Apartheid South Africa. Thank you for the witness of people like Nelson

Mandela, who remind us that hope is a lifeline for those who hang by the threads of injustice. As long as there are people held in captivity, oppressed, and denied basic human rights, help us all to consider ourselves to be hanging by the same frail threads. Amen.

May the peace of the Lord Christ go with you : wherever he may send you; may he guide you through the wilderness : protect you through the storm; may he bring you home rejoicing : at the wonders he has shown you; may he bring you home rejoicing : once again into our doors.

February 11

O Lord, let my soul rise up to meet you
as the day rises to meet the sun.

Glory to the Father, and to the Son, and to the Holy Spirit, as it was in the beginning, is now, and will be forever. Amen.

Come, let us bow down and bend the knee : let us kneel before the LORD our Maker.

Song "Come, Ye Sinners"

My eyes are fixed on you, my strength : for you, O God, are my stronghold.

Psalm 59:11–14
My merciful God comes to meet me : **God will let me look in triumph on my enemies.**
Slay them, O God, lest my people forget : **send them reeling by your might and put them down, O Lord our shield.**
For the sins of their mouths, for the words of their lips, for the cursing and lies that they utter : **let them be caught in their pride.**
Make an end of them in your wrath : **make an end of them, and they shall be no more.**

My eyes are fixed on you, my strength : for you, O God, are my stronghold.

Genesis 29:1–20   John 16:16–33

My eyes are fixed on you, my strength : for you, O God, are my stronghold.

Bernard of Clairvaux, a twelfth-century Cistercian reformer, wrote, "The first step of pride is curiosity. How does it show itself? Here is an example. There stands a monk who up to this time had every appearance of being an excellent monk. Now you begin to notice that wherever he is, standing, walking or sitting, his eyes are wandering, his glance darts right and left, his ears are cocked. Some change has taken place in him; every movement shows it. These symptoms show that that monastic's soul has caught some disease. One who used to watch over his own conduct now is all watchfulness for others."

Prayers for Others

Our Father

Lord, we ask for singleness of mind to serve you and wisdom to seek unity without judging those closest to us. Amen.

**May the peace of the Lord Christ go with you : wherever he may send you;
may he guide you through the wilderness : protect you through the storm;
may he bring you home rejoicing : at the wonders he has shown you;
may he bring you home rejoicing : once again into our doors.**

✦ February 12

The National Association for the Advancement of Colored People (NAACP) was established on February 12, 1909, after a race riot in Springfield, Illinois. Some of the founding members included W. E. B. DuBois, Ida Wells-Barnett, and Oswald Garrison Villiard. Over the years, it has become one of the most influential justice organizations in the United States, leading movements against lynching, segregation, discrimination, and race-based violence.

O Lord, let my soul rise up to meet you
as the day rises to meet the sun.

**Glory to the Father, and to the Son, and to the Holy Spirit,
as it was in the beginning, is now, and will be forever. Amen.**

Come, let us sing to the LORD : let us shout for joy to the Rock of our salvation.

Song "When the Saints Go Marching In"

Bless our God, you peoples : make the voice of his praise to be heard.

Psalm 66:4–8
Come now and see the works of God : **how wonderful are his deeds toward all people.**
He turned the sea into dry land, so that they went through the water on foot : **and there we rejoiced in him.**
In his might he rules for ever; his eyes keep watch over the nations : **let no rebel rise up against him.**

Bless our God, you peoples : **make the voice of his praise to be heard;**
who holds our souls in life : **and will not allow our feet to slip.**

Bless our God, you peoples : make the voice of his praise to be heard.

Genesis 29:20–35   John 17:1–11

Bless our God, you peoples : make the voice of his praise to be heard.

W. E. B. DuBois, a co-founder of the NAACP, wrote, "Only by a union of intelligence and sympathy across the color-line in this critical period of the Republic shall justice and right triumph."

Prayers for Others

Our Father

Lord, help us to see that without unity and solidarity very little can be accomplished as we strive for racial harmony and economic justice. As your children, we are in this together. Amen.

May the peace of the Lord Christ go with you : wherever he may send you; may he guide you through the wilderness : protect you through the storm; may he bring you home rejoicing : at the wonders he has shown you; may he bring you home rejoicing : once again into our doors.

✺ February 13

On February 13, 2008, the prime minister of Australia, Kevin Rudd, issued a national apology to aboriginal families torn apart by Australian government agencies and church missions during the period between 1869 and 1969. Children were taken from their families and forced into institutions where they were often unable to speak their native language and were given new names and birthdates. It is estimated that between 1910 and 1971, fifty-five thousand children were taken from their families.

O Lord, let my soul rise up to meet you
as the day rises to meet the sun.

**Glory to the Father, and to the Son, and to the Holy Spirit,
as it was in the beginning, is now, and will be forever. Amen.**

Come, let us bow down and bend the knee : let us kneel before the LORD our Maker.

Song "Waters of Babylon"

Hide not your face from your servant : be swift and answer me, for I am in distress.

Psalm 69:20–23
"Draw near to me and redeem me : **because of my enemies deliver me.**
You know my reproach, my shame, and my dishonor : **my adversaries are all in your sight.**"
Reproach has broken my heart, and it cannot be healed : **I looked for sympathy, but there was none, for comforters, but I could find no one.**
They gave me gall to eat : **and when I was thirsty, they gave me vinegar to drink.**

Hide not your face from your servant : be swift and answer me, for I am in distress.

Genesis 30:1–24   John 17:12–19

Hide not your face from your servant : be swift and answer me, for I am in distress.

Zitkala-Sa, an American Indian woman who spent three years in an off-reservation boarding school, wrote this account of her experience: "Judéwin knew a few words of English, and she had overheard the paleface woman talk about cutting our long, heavy hair. Our mothers had taught us that only unskilled warriors who were captured had their hair shingled by the enemy. Among our people, short hair was worn by mourners, and shingled hair by cowards! I cried aloud, shaking my head all the while until I felt the cold blades of the scissors against my neck, and heard them gnaw off one of my thick braids. Then I lost my spirit. In my anguish I moaned for my mother, but no one came to comfort me. Not a soul reasoned quietly with me, as my own mother used to do; for now I was only one of many little animals driven by a herder."

Prayers for Others

Our Father

Lord, forgive us for not learning the cultures of your children around the world and in our communities. You speak to us in many languages and customs. Train our ears and our hearts to hear you. Amen.

**May the peace of the Lord Christ go with you : wherever he may send you;
may he guide you through the wilderness : protect you through the storm;
may he bring you home rejoicing : at the wonders he has shown you;
may he bring you home rejoicing : once again into our doors.**

February 14

Valentine of Rome (d. 269)

A Christian priest in Rome, Valentine was known for assisting Christians persecuted under Claudius II. After being caught marrying Christian couples and helping Christians escape the persecution, Valentine was arrested and imprisoned. Although Emperor Claudius originally liked Valentine, he was condemned to death when he tried to convert the emperor. Valentine was beaten with stones, clubbed, and, finally, beheaded on February 14, 269. In the year 496, February 14 was named as a day of celebration in Valentine's honor. He has since become the patron saint of engaged couples, beekeepers, happy marriages, lovers, travelers, young people, and greetings.

O Lord, let my soul rise up to meet you
as the day rises to meet the sun.

**Glory to the Father, and to the Son, and to the Holy Spirit,
as it was in the beginning, is now, and will be forever. Amen.**

Come, let us sing to the Lord : let us shout for joy to the Rock of our salvation.

Song "Ubi Caritas"

O Love that keeps the heavens turning : draw us to you in all our yearnings.

Psalm 72:16–19
May there be abundance of grain on the earth, growing thick even on the hilltops : **may its fruit flourish like Lebanon, and its grain like grass upon the earth.**
May his name remain for ever and be established as long as the sun endures : **may all the nations bless themselves in him and call him blessed.**
Blessed be the Lord God, the God of Israel : **who alone does wondrous deeds!**
And blessed be his glorious name for ever! : **And may all the earth be filled with his glory. Amen. Amen.**

O Love that keeps the heavens turning : draw us to you in all our yearnings.

Genesis 31:1–24   John 17:20–26

O Love that keeps the heavens turning : draw us to you in all our yearnings.

G. K. Chesterton said, "Let your religion be less of a theory and more of a love affair."

Prayers for Others

Our Father

Lord, help us distinguish between the love that keeps merely human affection in the center of things and the love you bore in your sacrificial life, death, and resurrection. Amen.

**May the peace of the Lord Christ go with you : wherever he may send you;
may he guide you through the wilderness : protect you through the storm;
may he bring you home rejoicing : at the wonders he has shown you;
may he bring you home rejoicing : once again into our doors.**

✣ February 15

O Lord, let my soul rise up to meet you
as the day rises to meet the sun.

Glory to the Father, and to the Son, and to the Holy Spirit,
as it was in the beginning, is now, and will be forever. Amen.

Come, let us sing to the LORD : let us shout for joy to the Rock of our salvation.

Song "Come, Thou Fount"

Shepherd us, Lord, with a faithful heart : and guide us in the way of truth.

Psalm 78:69–72
He built his sanctuary like the heights of heaven : **like the earth which he founded for ever.**
He chose David his servant : **and took him away from the sheepfolds.**
He brought him from following the ewes : **to be a shepherd over Jacob his people and over Israel his inheritance.**
So he shepherded them with a faithful and true heart : **and guided them with the skillfulness of his hands.**

Shepherd us, Lord, with a faithful heart : and guide us in the way of truth.

Genesis 31:25–50   Hebrews 7:1–28

Shepherd us, Lord, with a faithful heart : and guide us in the way of truth.

Basil of Caesarea, a fourth-century monk and bishop, wrote, "I cannot persuade myself that without love to others, and without, as far as rests with me, peaceableness towards all, I can be called a worthy servant of Jesus Christ."

Prayers for Others

Our Father

Lord, reconcile us to you anew each morning so that we might know what a fearful and wonderful thing it is to be reconciled to one another. Amen.

**May the peace of the Lord Christ go with you : wherever he may send you;
may he guide you through the wilderness : protect you through the storm;
may he bring you home rejoicing : at the wonders he has shown you;
may he bring you home rejoicing : once again into our doors.**

✤ February 16

On February 16, 2005, the Kyoto Protocol went into effect as an international attempt to reduce greenhouse gases and global warming. The protocol places more responsibility on developed countries because they are responsible for the highest levels of greenhouse gas emissions.

O Lord, let my soul rise up to meet you
as the day rises to meet the sun.

**Glory to the Father, and to the Son, and to the Holy Spirit,
as it was in the beginning, is now, and will be forever. Amen.**

Come, let us sing to the Lord : let us shout for joy to the Rock of our salvation.

Song "Sing, O Sky (Gaao Re)"

Lord God of hosts, hear my prayer : hearken, O God of Jacob.

Psalm 84:2–6
The sparrow has found her a house and the swallow a nest where she may lay her young : **by the side of your altars, O Lord of hosts, my King and my God.**
Happy are they who dwell in your house! : **they will always be praising you.**
Happy are the people whose strength is in you! : **whose hearts are set on the pilgrims' way.**
Those who go through the desolate valley will find it a place of springs : **for the early rains have covered it with pools of water.**
They will climb from height to height : **and the God of gods will reveal himself in Zion.**

Lord God of hosts, hear my prayer : hearken, O God of Jacob.

Genesis 32:3–21   Hebrews 8:1–13

Lord God of hosts, hear my prayer : hearken, O God of Jacob.

British evangelical John Stott has written, "Simplicity is the first cousin of contentment. Its motto is, 'We brought nothing into this world, and we can certainly carry nothing out.' It recognizes that we are pilgrims. It concentrates us on what we need, and measures this by what we use. It rejoices in the good things of creation, but hates waste and greed and clutter. It knows how easily the seed of the Word is smothered by the 'cares and riches of this life.' It wants to be free of distractions, in order to love and serve God and others."

Prayers for Others

Our Father

Lord, the morning is clothed with splendor from the beauty of dewdrops to the slow rising of the sun. And yet, as each day descends to night, we trust that the morning beauty will come again. Likewise, we pray to trust that you will decorate our lives with the essentials we need for today. Amen.

May the peace of the Lord Christ go with you : wherever he may send you; may he guide you through the wilderness : protect you through the storm; may he bring you home rejoicing : at the wonders he has shown you; may he bring you home rejoicing : once again into our doors.

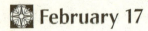
February 17

O Lord, let my soul rise up to meet you
as the day rises to meet the sun.

Glory to the Father, and to the Son, and to the Holy Spirit, as it was in the beginning, is now, and will be forever. Amen.

Come, let us sing to the LORD : let us shout for joy to the Rock of our salvation.

Song "What Wondrous Love"

Heaven and earth are full of your glory : Hosannah in the highest!

Psalm 89:1–5
Your love, O LORD, for ever will I sing : **from age to age my mouth will proclaim your faithfulness.**
For I am persuaded that your love is established for ever : **you have set your faithfulness firmly in the heavens.**
"I have made a covenant with my chosen one : **I have sworn an oath to David my servant:**
'I will establish your line for ever : **and preserve your throne for all generations.'"**

The heavens bear witness to your wonders, O LORD : **and to your faithfulness in the assembly of the holy ones.**

Heaven and earth are full of your glory : Hosannah in the highest!

Genesis 32:22–33:17   Hebrews 9:1–14

Heaven and earth are full of your glory : Hosannah in the highest!

In the second century, Tertullian wrote, "Nature is schoolmistress, the soul the pupil; and whatever one has taught or the other has learned has come from God — the Teacher of the teacher."

Prayers for Others

Our Father

Despite the fact we are all made in your image, God, we can see ourselves as brothers and sisters only by the light of your redeeming grace. Give us eyes to see that we are made from the same dirt, and help us work to reconcile ourselves to one another and to the ground beneath us. Amen.

May the peace of the Lord Christ go with you : wherever he may send you; may he guide you through the wilderness : protect you through the storm; may he bring you home rejoicing : at the wonders he has shown you; may he bring you home rejoicing : once again into our doors.

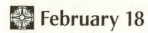

February 18

Hagar the Egyptian

When Abraham's wife, Sarah, was unable to have a child, she gave him her Egyptian slave, Hagar, as a wife. Sarah was following ancient surrogate customs, which allowed a wife to give her maid to her husband and then claim the child as her own. But after Hagar conceived a son by Abraham, Sarah turned bitter and resentful and began to treat her harshly. Hagar's response was to run away into the wilderness, but an angel of the Lord appeared to Hagar and urged her to return and submit to her mistress. The Lord directed Hagar to call the child Ishmael (meaning "God hears") and, as with Abraham, promised her descendants so numerous they could not be counted. Hagar called God *El-roi* — "the God who sees" — and was struck with awe that she had seen him.

O Lord, let my soul rise up to meet you
as the day rises to meet the sun.

**Glory to the Father, and to the Son, and to the Holy Spirit,
as it was in the beginning, is now, and will be forever. Amen.**

Come, let us bow down and bend the knee : let us kneel before the Lord our Maker.

Song "Were You There?"

Hear the cry of your children, Lord : come quickly and set us free.

Psalm 94:21–23
They conspire against the life of the just : **and condemn the innocent to death.**
But the Lord has become my stronghold : **and my God the rock of my trust.**
He will turn their wickedness back upon them and destroy them in their own malice : **the Lord our God will destroy them.**

Hear the cry of your children, Lord : come quickly and set us free.

Genesis 35:1–20   Hebrews 9:15–28

Hear the cry of your children, Lord : come quickly and set us free.

A reading from the book of Genesis: "Early the next morning Abraham took some food and a skin of water and gave them to Hagar. He set them on her shoulders and then sent her off with the boy. She went on her way and wandered in the Desert of Beersheba. When the water in the skin was gone, she put the boy under one of the bushes. Then she went off and sat down about a bowshot away, for she thought, 'I cannot watch the boy die.' And as she sat there, she began to sob. God heard the boy crying, and the angel of God called to Hagar from heaven and said to her, 'What is this matter, Hagar? Do not be afraid; God has heard the boy crying as he lies there. Lift the boy up and take him by the hand, for I will make him into a great nation.' "

Prayers for Others

Our Father

Thank you, Lord, that you never abandon us to our hopelessness. There is always room at your table for those who feel forgotten, or who have been cast out. Train us in such hospitality. Amen.

**May the peace of the Lord Christ go with you : wherever he may send you;
may he guide you through the wilderness : protect you through the storm;
may he bring you home rejoicing : at the wonders he has shown you;
may he bring you home rejoicing : once again into our doors.**

✣ February 19

On February 19, 1942, following the bombing of Pearl Harbor by Japanese warplanes the previous December, US President Franklin Roosevelt signed an executive order calling for the displacement of one hundred and twenty thousand Japanese Americans to internment camps.

O Lord, let my soul rise up to meet you
as the day rises to meet the sun.

**Glory to the Father, and to the Son, and to the Holy Spirit,
as it was in the beginning, is now, and will be forever. Amen.**

Come, let us bow down and bend the knee : let us kneel before the Lord our Maker.

Song "O Lord, Hear My Prayer"

Free us, O Lord, from fear : so we can live in peace.

Psalm 95:8–11
Harden not your hearts, as your forebears did in the wilderness : **at Meribah, and on that day at Massah, when they tempted me.**
They put me to the test : **though they had seen my works.**
Forty years long I detested that generation and said : **"This people are wayward in their hearts; they do not know my ways."**
So I swore in my wrath : **"They shall not enter into my rest."**

Free us, O Lord, from fear : so we can live in peace.

Genesis 37:1–11   Hebrews 10:1–10

Free us, O Lord, from fear : so we can live in peace.

Oscar Romero, Archbishop of El Salvador, said, "Peace is not the product of terror or fear. Peace is not the silence of cemeteries. Peace is not the silent result of violent repression. Peace is the generous, tranquil contribution of all to the good of all. Peace is dynamism. Peace is generosity. It is right and it is duty."

Prayers for Others

Our Father

Lord, keep us from fearfully persecuting the innocent among us. When we are tempted to use the cultural differences of our neighbors as excuses for injustice, convict us of our error. Keep us from turning difference into discrimination. Amen.

May the peace of the Lord Christ go with you : wherever he may send you;
may he guide you through the wilderness : protect you through the storm;
may he bring you home rejoicing : at the wonders he has shown you;
may he bring you home rejoicing : once again into our doors.

✣ February 20

Frederick Douglass (1818–1895)
Frederick Douglass was born a slave in Maryland. His mother died shortly after his birth, and he was raised by his grandparents. A resourceful youth, he learned how to read and write by giving away food in exchange for reading lessons from neighborhood kids. Before long he was able to teach other slaves to read the Bible through weekly Sunday schools. In 1838, at the age of twenty, Douglass escaped from slavery by impersonating a sailor and went on to become one of the most famous abolitionists and leaders in US history. He was a firm believer in the equality of all people, whether black, female, Native American, or recent immigrant. He was fond of saying, "I would unite with anybody to do right and with nobody to do wrong."

O Lord, let my soul rise up to meet you
as the day rises to meet the sun.

**Glory to the Father, and to the Son, and to the Holy Spirit,
as it was in the beginning, is now, and will be forever. Amen.**

Come, let us sing to the Lord : let us shout for joy to the Rock of our salvation.

Song "Woke Up This Mornin'"

Lift us by awe at the things we see : to set our minds on none but thee.

Psalm 104:25–31
O Lord, how manifold are your works! : **in wisdom you have made them all; the earth is full of your creatures.**
Yonder is the great and wide sea with its living things too many to number : **creatures both small and great.**
There move the ships, and there is that Leviathan : **which you have made for the sport of it.**
All of them look to you : **to give them their food in due season.**
You give it to them; they gather it : **you open your hand, and they are filled with good things.**
You hide your face, and they are terrified : **you take away their breath, and they die and return to their dust.**
You send forth your Spirit, and they are created : **and so you renew the face of the earth.**

Lift us by awe at the things we see : to set our minds on none but thee.

Genesis 37:12–24   Hebrews 10:11–25

Lift us by awe at the things we see : to set our minds on none but thee.

Frederick Douglass wrote in his autobiography, "Between the Christianity of this land, and the Christianity of Christ, I recognize the widest possible difference — so wide, that to receive the one as good, pure, and holy is of necessity to reject the other as bad, corrupt, and wicked. I love the pure, peaceable, and impartial Christianity of Christ; I therefore hate the corrupt, slaveholding, women-whipping, cradle-plundering, partial and hypocritical Christianity of this land. Indeed, I can see no reason, but the most deceitful one, for calling the religion of this land Christianity."

Prayers for Others

Our Father

Jesus, even in our waking, grant us dreams by which to guide our lives. Make us to dream of justice for the oppressed, reunions for those torn from loved ones, hospitality for immigrants, and the healing of all wounds. Amen.

May the peace of the Lord Christ go with you : wherever he may send you;
may he guide you through the wilderness : protect you through the storm;
may he bring you home rejoicing : at the wonders he has shown you;
may he bring you home rejoicing : once again into our doors.

February 21

On February 21, 1965, Malcolm X was assassinated while delivering a speech in Manhattan's Audubon Ballroom. Malcolm X became a well-known advocate for civil rights after joining the Nation of Islam while in prison. A brilliant, self-educated leader, Malcolm experienced multiple conversions, eventually leaving the Nation of Islam after a pilgrimage to Mecca and committing to overcome racism through an international solidarity movement. Though he was not a Christian, Malcolm X spoke prophetically about the church's complicity in Western culture's sin of racism.

O Lord, let my soul rise up to meet you
as the day rises to meet the sun.

Glory to the Father, and to the Son, and to the Holy Spirit,
as it was in the beginning, is now, and will be forever. Amen.

Come, let us sing to the Lord : let us shout for joy to the Rock of our salvation.

Song "Walk in the Light"

Give us more light about each other : that we might understand enough to love.

Psalm 105:1–3; 106:47–48
Give thanks to the LORD and call upon his name : **make known his deeds among the peoples.**
Sing to him, sing praises to him : **and speak of all his marvelous works.**
Glory in his holy name : **let the hearts of those who seek the LORD rejoice.**
Save us, O LORD our God, and gather us from among the nations : **that we may give thanks to your holy name and glory in your praise.**
Blessed be the LORD, the God of Israel, from everlasting and to everlasting : **and let all the people say, "Amen!" Hallelujah!**

Give us more light about each other : that we might understand enough to love.

Genesis 37:25–36   Hebrews 10:26–39

Give us more light about each other : that we might understand enough to love.

Thomas Aquinas, a thirteenth-century Dominican and doctor of the church, said, "Every truth without exception — and whoever may utter it — is from the Holy Spirit."

Prayers for Others

Our Father

Lord, we pray you will keep us humble enough to learn from those whom we least expect to be our teachers. Help us to listen for your truth, even in the words of our enemies. Amen.

May the peace of the Lord Christ go with you : wherever he may send you;
may he guide you through the wilderness : protect you through the storm;
may he bring you home rejoicing : at the wonders he has shown you;
may he bring you home rejoicing : once again into our doors.

❋ February 22

O Lord, let my soul rise up to meet you
as the day rises to meet the sun.

Glory to the Father, and to the Son, and to the Holy Spirit,
as it was in the beginning, is now, and will be forever. Amen.

Come, let us sing to the LORD : let us shout for joy to the Rock of our salvation.

Song "Solid Rock"

My heart is firmly fixed : O God, my heart is fixed.

Psalm 108:2–6
Wake up, my spirit; awake, lute and harp : **I myself will waken the dawn.**
I will confess you among the peoples, O LORD : **I will sing praises to you among the nations.**
For your loving-kindness is greater than the heavens : **and your faithfulness reaches to the clouds.**
Exalt yourself above the heavens, O God : **and your glory over all the earth.**
So that those who are dear to you may be delivered : **save with your right hand and answer me.**

My heart is firmly fixed : O God, my heart is fixed.

Genesis 39:1–23   Hebrews 11:1–12

My heart is firmly fixed : O God, my heart is fixed.

Catherine de Hueck Doherty, founder of the Madonna House community, wrote, "The hunger for God can only be satisfied by a love that is face to face, person to person. It is only in the eyes of another that we can find the Icon of Christ. We must make the other person aware we love him. If we do, he will know that God loves him. He will never hunger again."

Prayers for Others

Our Father

Lord God, extend our faith so that even when we fail to see the fruit of our planted seeds, we may have the assurance that every inch of soil overturned will lead to a harvest someday. Amen.

**May the peace of the Lord Christ go with you : wherever he may send you;
may he guide you through the wilderness : protect you through the storm;
may he bring you home rejoicing : at the wonders he has shown you;
may he bring you home rejoicing : once again into our doors.**

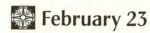

February 23

Polycarp of Smyrna (70–155)
Polycarp was arrested by Roman officials after having served as Bishop of Smyrna for many decades. When the Roman proconsul ordered him to declare that "Caesar is Lord" and to curse Christ, the elderly Polycarp

refused, saying, "Eighty-six years I have served him and he never did me any wrong. How can I blaspheme my King who saved me?" Polycarp was sentenced to death by fire, but the flames miraculously stood like a wall around him and he was not burned. The executioner then stabbed him in the heart, which issued such an abundance of blood that the fire was quenched.

O Lord, let my soul rise up to meet you
as the day rises to meet the sun.

**Glory to the Father, and to the Son, and to the Holy Spirit,
as it was in the beginning, is now, and will be forever. Amen.**

Come, let us bow down and bend the knee : let us kneel before the LORD our Maker.

Song "I Will Trust in the Lord"

You who raised Jesus from the dead : raise us also to life abundant.

Psalm 115:1–4
Not to us, O LORD, not to us, but to your name give glory : **because of your love and because of your faithfulness.**
Why should the heathen say : "Where then is their God?"
Our God is in heaven : **whatever he wills to do he does.**
Their idols are silver and gold : **the work of human hands.**

You who raised Jesus from the dead : raise us also to life abundant.

Genesis 40:1–23   Hebrews 11:13–22

You who raised Jesus from the dead : raise us also to life abundant.

Søren Kierkegaard, a nineteenth-century Danish philosopher, said, "What the age needs is not a genius but a martyr."

Prayers for Others

Our Father

Lord, in our work for justice, let us not seek after martyrdom for its own sake, but neither let us turn away from your truth because we fear suffering. Give us grace to live faithfully whatever the cost. Amen.

**May the peace of the Lord Christ go with you : wherever he may send you;
may he guide you through the wilderness : protect you through the storm;
may he bring you home rejoicing : at the wonders he has shown you;
may he bring you home rejoicing : once again into our doors.**

❋ February 24

O Lord, let my soul rise up to meet you
as the day rises to meet the sun.

**Glory to the Father, and to the Son, and to the Holy Spirit,
as it was in the beginning, is now, and will be forever. Amen.**

Come, let us bow down and bend the knee : let us kneel before the LORD our Maker.

Song "Amazing Grace"

You order your kingdom with justice, Lord : and judge the nations with loving-kindness.

Psalm 119:17–20
Deal bountifully with your servant : **that I may live and keep your word.**
Open my eyes, that I may see : **the wonders of your law.**
I am a stranger here on earth : **do not hide your commandments from me.**
My soul is consumed at all times : **with longing for your judgments.**

You order your kingdom with justice, Lord : and judge the nations with loving-kindness.

Genesis 41:1–13   Hebrews 11:23–31

You order your kingdom with justice, Lord : and judge the nations with loving-kindness.

Dag Hammarskjöld, former United Nations Secretary General, said, "In our era, the road to holiness necessarily passes through the world of action."

Prayers for Others

Our Father

Train us to be faithful, Lord, and teach us your ways so our lives may reflect you, to the glory of God the Father. Amen.

**May the peace of the Lord Christ go with you : wherever he may send you;
may he guide you through the wilderness : protect you through the storm;
may he bring you home rejoicing : at the wonders he has shown you;
may he bring you home rejoicing : once again into our doors.**

✸ February 25

On this day in 1994, a Jewish settler from New York entered the Ibrahimi Mosque in Hebron with an automatic weapon and killed twenty-nine Muslims during prayer, which has become known as the Hebron Massacre. This massacre has been a landmark in the conflict in the Middle East, which is so often fueled by religious extremists reacting to other religious extremists. It is a reminder that extremists of all faiths have distorted the best that our faiths have to offer, and it is our prayer that a new generation of extremists for love and grace will rise up.

O Lord, let my soul rise up to meet you
as the day rises to meet the sun.

**Glory to the Father, and to the Son, and to the Holy Spirit,
as it was in the beginning, is now, and will be forever. Amen.**

Come, let us sing to the LORD : let us shout for joy to the Rock of our salvation.

Song "Go, Tell It on the Mountain"

God, help us shout the good news : in our songs and in our lives.

Psalm 119:101–4
I restrain my feet from every evil way : **that I may keep your word.**
I do not shrink from your judgments : **because you yourself have taught me.**
How sweet are your words to my taste! : **they are sweeter than honey to my mouth.**
Through your commandments I gain understanding : **therefore I hate every lying way.**

God, help us shout the good news : in our songs and in our lives.

Genesis 41:14–45   Hebrews 11:32–12:2

God, help us shout the good news : in our songs and in our lives.

Mother Teresa of Calcutta said, "To show great love for God and our neighbor we need not do great things. It is how much love we put in the doing that makes our offering something beautiful for God."

Prayers for Others

Our Father

Today, Lord, help us make our lives an offering of quiet commitment to thread love through the torn garments of society. Amen.

May the peace of the Lord Christ go with you : wherever he may send you;
may he guide you through the wilderness : protect you through the storm;
may he bring you home rejoicing : at the wonders he has shown you;
may he bring you home rejoicing : once again into our doors.

> **Sacred Space: Thinking About Where We Pray**
>
> Without a doubt we can pray anywhere, but there is something to be said for having a space that is reserved for prayer. Scripture makes it clear that God doesn't dwell in buildings made by hand any more than God is in the streets or alleys. Still, most of our homes have places where we eat, play, or work. There are also places where God leaves a mark. To be sure, the church is not the building but the people. But it can be nice to have a special place to meet the God we love.
>
> One thing we see in Scripture is that folks like Jacob are commanded to mark the sacred space where God met them, to remember. As we look at spaces like a chapel or a shrine in the Holy Land, we remember not the magic of a physical space but the magic of what God did and who God is; we are reminded that this entire planet is filled with sacred spaces where God meets people.
>
> Consider creating a space where you can get on your knees in the "secret chamber" and be with God. A friend from Brazil started a tradition of tacking prayers on her wall, so she could pray simply by looking at the walls and remembering the needs of her neighborhood and all the prayers God has answered. Some of us keep things that remind us to pray for others, like dog tags of soldiers whose faith has called them to leave the military or a crack valve or a bullet from the streets in our neighborhoods. It is important to remember the things that happen on our streets, both good and bad.

February 26

O Lord, let my soul rise up to meet you
as the day rises to meet the sun.

**Glory to the Father, and to the Son, and to the Holy Spirit,
as it was in the beginning, is now, and will be forever. Amen.**

Come, let us sing to the LORD : let us shout for joy to the Rock of our salvation.

Song "When the Saints Go Marching In"

Guide us, Lord, in your good way : that all our work might speed your day.

Psalm 119:169–72
Let my cry come before you, O LORD : **give me understanding, according to your word.**
Let my supplication come before you : **deliver me, according to your promise.**

My lips shall pour forth your praise : **when you teach me your statutes.**
My tongue shall sing of your promise : **for all your commandments are righteous.**

Guide us, Lord, in your good way : that all our work might speed your day.

Genesis 41:46–57   Hebrews 12:3–11

Guide us, Lord, in your good way : that all our work might speed your day.

Francis de Sales, a sixteenth-century bishop in France, wrote, "Each of us has his own endowment from God, one to live in this way, another in that. It is an impertinence, then, to try to find out why St. Paul was not given St. Peter's grace, or St. Peter given St. Paul's. There is only one answer to such questions: the Church is a garden patterned with countless flowers, so there must be a variety of sizes, colors, scents — of perfections, after all. Each has its value, its charm, its joy; while the whole vast cluster of these variations makes for beauty in its most graceful form."

Prayers for Others

Our Father

Lord, as we continually answer the call to follow you, help us discern how to use our talents and gifts in ways that nurture your kingdom. Amen.

May the peace of the Lord Christ go with you : wherever he may send you;
may he guide you through the wilderness : protect you through the storm;
may he bring you home rejoicing : at the wonders he has shown you;
may he bring you home rejoicing : once again into our doors.

✸ February 27

In the year 280, Roman Emperor Constantine was baptized into the church, beginning Christianity's transition from a minority movement to an empire's religion. It was not long before the persecuted became the persecutors, and the cross of Christ was exchanged for the sword of Rome.

O Lord, let my soul rise up to meet you
as the day rises to meet the sun.

Glory to the Father, and to the Son, and to the Holy Spirit,
as it was in the beginning, is now, and will be forever. Amen.

Come, let us bow down and bend the knee : let us kneel before the L ORD our Maker.

Song "I Will Trust in the Lord"

You take dry bones and clothe them with bodies : create a church from those who are dead.

Psalm 127:1–4
Unless the LORD builds the house : **their labor is in vain who build it.**
Unless the LORD watches over the city : **in vain the watchman keeps his vigil.**
It is in vain that you rise so early and go to bed so late : **vain, too, to eat the bread of toil, for he gives to his beloved sleep.**
Children are a heritage from the LORD : **and the fruit of the womb is a gift.**

You take dry bones and clothe them with bodies : create a church from those who are dead.

Genesis 42:1–17   Hebrews 12:12–29

You take dry bones and clothe them with bodies : create a church from those who are dead.

Clement, an early bishop of Rome, wrote, "When the heathen hear the words of God from our lips, they marvel at them as something beautiful and great. However, when they find out that our deeds are unworthy of the words we speak, they turn from this to blasphemy. They say it is a myth and a delusion."

Prayers for Others

Our Father

Jesus, keep us from the tragedy of blaspheming your name because we have succumbed to a watered-down faith. Make our spirits restless whenever we think that the way things are is the way things have to be. Amen.

May the peace of the Lord Christ go with you : wherever he may send you; may he guide you through the wilderness : protect you through the storm; may he bring you home rejoicing : at the wonders he has shown you; may he bring you home rejoicing : once again into our doors.

✣ February 28

O Lord, let my soul rise up to meet you
as the day rises to meet the sun.

Glory to the Father, and to the Son, and to the Holy Spirit, as it was in the beginning, is now, and will be forever. Amen.

Come, let us bow down and bend the knee : let us kneel before the LORD our Maker.

Song "We Shall Not Be Moved"

Our lives, O Lord, are in your hand : hold us up that we might stand.

Psalm 138:7–9
Though the LORD be high, he cares for the lowly : **he perceives the haughty from afar.**
Though I walk in the midst of trouble, you keep me safe : **you stretch forth your hand against the fury of my enemies; your right hand shall save me.**
The LORD will make good his purpose for me : **O LORD, your love endures for ever; do not abandon the works of your hands.**

Our lives, O Lord, are in your hand : hold us up that we might stand.

Genesis 42:18–28   Hebrews 13:1–16

Our lives, O Lord, are in your hand : hold us up that we might stand.

Bonaventure, a thirteenth-century Franciscan theologian, wrote, "The outcome or the fruit of reading Holy Scripture is by no means negligible: it is the fullness of eternal happiness. These are the books which tell of eternal life, which were written, not only that we might believe, but also that we might have everlasting life. The purpose of the Scriptures, which come to us from God, is to lead us to the fullness of the truth. In order to achieve this, we must study holy Scripture carefully, and teach it and listen to it in the same way."

Prayers for Others

Our Father

Lord, convict us of the need for spiritual disciplines that call us to stillness, centeredness, and contemplation. Remind us that your word is living and present to nurture us, grow us, and sustain us through Jesus Christ our Lord. Amen.

May the peace of the Lord Christ go with you : wherever he may send you; may he guide you through the wilderness : protect you through the storm; may he bring you home rejoicing : at the wonders he has shown you; may he bring you home rejoicing : once again into our doors.

✣ February 29

O Lord, let my soul rise up to meet you
as the day rises to meet the sun.

**Glory to the Father, and to the Son, and to the Holy Spirit,
as it was in the beginning, is now, and will be forever. Amen.**

Come, let us bow down and bend the knee : let us kneel before the Lord our Maker.

Song "Steal Away to Jesus"

Whisper to us when we feel alone : sweet songs from around your throne.

Psalm 142:1–4
I cry to the Lord with my voice : **to the Lord I make loud supplication.**
I pour out my complaint before him : **and tell him all my trouble.**
When my spirit languishes within me, you know my path : **in the way wherein I walk they have hidden a trap for me.**
I look to my right hand and find no one who knows me : **I have no place to flee to, and no one cares for me.**

Whisper to us when we feel alone : sweet songs from around your throne.

Genesis 42:29–38   Hebrews 13:17–25

Whisper to us when we feel alone : sweet songs from around your throne.

Jean Vanier, founder of the L'Arche communities, has written, "Almost everyone finds their early days in a community ideal. It all seems perfect. They feel they are surrounded by saints, heroes, or at the least, most exceptional people who are everything they want to be themselves. And then comes the let-down. The greater their idealization of the community at the start, the greater the disenchantment. If people manage to get through this second period, they come to a third phase — that of realism and of true commitment. They no longer see other members of the community as saints or devils, but as people — each with a mixture of good and bad, darkness and light, each growing and each with their own hope. The community is neither heaven nor hell, but planted firmly on earth, and they are ready to walk in it, and with it. They accept the community and the other members as they are; they are confident that together they can grow towards something more beautiful."

Prayers for Others

Our Father

Lord Jesus Christ, you alone are without sin. Grant us the grace to see ourselves and one another as you see us, stained but washed in your reconciling blood. Help us maintain concord and unity among ourselves so that your people might be strengthened to go forth into the world. Amen.

May the peace of the Lord Christ go with you : wherever he may send you;
may he guide you through the wilderness : protect you through the storm;
may he bring you home rejoicing : at the wonders he has shown you;
may he bring you home rejoicing : once again into our doors.

> **Becoming the Answer to Our Prayers: A Few Ideas**
> 1. Mow your neighbor's grass.
> 2. Create a directory of spiritual mentors and help folks find them.
> 3. Practice radical hospitality, which includes the willingness to be a guest. Next time you make a vacation or business trip, stay in homes instead of hotels.
> 4. Ask the next person who asks you for change to join you for dinner.
> 5. Invest money in a micro-lending bank.

MARCH — THE ANNUNCIATION

MARCH

Marks of New Monasticism
Celebrating Singleness and Marriage

Both singleness and marriage are gifts to the church. Both can teach us about God. Both can be holy, and both can be self-centered and narcissistic. There are lots of books on marriage, and still the Christian divorce rate mirrors that of the larger society. We have much work still to do, and there aren't many good books out there on singleness or chastity, a traditional monastic vow.

Singleness is often terribly misunderstood. Catholics have often overemphasized singleness and the religious vocation of celibacy to the point that folks feel defeated if they don't end up being a nun, a priest, or a monk. (It is said that John Newton was asked if he was a monk, and he replied, "God hasn't given me the grace ... so I am only a monk on Mondays and Wednesdays.") And Protestants have nearly forgotten the gift that singleness is. Many singles groups end up being little more than opportunities to meet a spouse. Pastors pray that every kid will find the mate that God has chosen for them, forgetting the gift of singleness that Paul spoke so highly of and that Jesus celebrates when he holds up those who have "renounced marriage because of the kingdom of heaven" (Matt. 19:12). We cannot forget the saints throughout church history whose singleness has been a part of their radical faith and single-minded pursuit of God as their lover and soul mate. After all, when we think of Mother Teresa, we don't say pityingly, "If only she had met her husband!" A life of singleness helped free her up for a single-minded pursuit of God's kingdom.

> **Suggested Reading for the Month**
> *The Wounded Healer* by Henri Nouwen
> *Real Sex* by Lauren Winner
> *Families at the Crossroads* by Rodney Clapp
> *The Life of Amma Syncletica* or *The Life of St. Macrina*

March is Women's History Month. (You'll notice that most of the quotes this month come from great women in church history.) It's also when the church remembers Mary, the first of the saints, a woman who put her sexuality in the service of God's kingdom, giving birth to our Lord and thereby becoming mother to all of us. With Mary as our mother and Jesus as our brother, we are part of God's family whether we marry or remain single. Whatever the case, we know love because we've been adopted into God's family.

Our deepest longing is not for sex but for love. We can live without sex, but we cannot live without love. And there certainly are many folks who have a lot of sex but never find love, and others who may never have sex but who have found love and intimacy in the deepest core of their being. We are created to love and be loved. Marriage and biological family is a beautiful way to find love. But it is not the only place, and that is good news to the singles out there and to the many folks who do not find themselves attracted to the other gender. If our communities can create spaces where people can love and be loved as God has loved us, all the other stuff gets a little bit easier.

✦ March 1

O Lord, let my soul rise up to meet you
as the day rises to meet the sun.

**Glory to the Father, and to the Son, and to the Holy Spirit,
as it was in the beginning, is now, and will be forever. Amen.**

Come, let us bow down and bend the knee : let us kneel before the LORD our Maker.

Song "Waters of Babylon"

Take our tears, Lord : to water the seeds of prayer.

Psalm 6:6–9
I grow weary because of my groaning : **every night I drench my bed and flood my couch with tears.**
My eyes are wasted with grief : **and worn away because of all my enemies.**
Depart from me, all evildoers : **for the LORD has heard the sound of my weeping.**
The LORD has heard my supplication : **the LORD accepts my prayer.**

Take our tears, Lord : to water the seeds of prayer.

Genesis 43:1–15   Mark 1:1–13

Take our tears, Lord : to water the seeds of prayer.

Julian of Norwich wrote in the fourteenth century, "The worst has already happened and been repaired.... All shall be well, all shall be well, and all manner of things shall be well."

Prayers for Others

Our Father

Lord, we are grateful that you can use every experience to draw us closer to you. Our trials and triumphs alike can finally be sown in the garden of our faith. Amen.

**May the peace of the Lord Christ go with you : wherever he may send you;
may he guide you through the wilderness : protect you through the storm;
may he bring you home rejoicing : at the wonders he has shown you;
may he bring you home rejoicing : once again into our doors.**

March 2

O Lord, let my soul rise up to meet you
as the day rises to meet the sun.

**Glory to the Father, and to the Son, and to the Holy Spirit,
as it was in the beginning, is now, and will be forever. Amen.**

Come, let us bow down and bend the knee : let us kneel before the Lord our Maker.

Song "O Lord, Have Mercy"

Remember me in your mercy, Lord : and unite us by your cross.

Psalm 13
How long, O Lord? will you forget me for ever? : **how long will you hide your face from me?**
How long shall I have perplexity in my mind, and grief in my heart, day after day? : **how long shall my enemy triumph over me?**
Look upon me and answer me, O Lord my God : **give light to my eyes, lest I sleep in death;**
lest my enemy say, "I have prevailed over him," : **and my foes rejoice that I have fallen.**
But I put my trust in your mercy : **my heart is joyful because of your saving help.**
I will sing to the Lord, for he has dealt with me richly : **I will praise the name of the Lord Most High.**

Remember me in your mercy, Lord : and unite us by your cross.

Genesis 43:16–34   Mark 1:14–28

Remember me in your mercy, Lord : and unite us by your cross.

Twentieth-century nun and philosopher Edith Stein asked, "Do you want to be totally united to the Crucified? If you are serious about this, you will be present, by the power of His Cross, at every front, at every place of sorrow, bringing to those who suffer, healing and salvation."

Prayers for Others

Our Father

Sometimes we don't realize the intensity of the things for which we pray, Lord. Keep us courageously mindful that your way is laden with tears on the way to resurrection. Amen.

May the peace of the Lord Christ go with you : wherever he may send you;
may he guide you through the wilderness : protect you through the storm;
may he bring you home rejoicing : at the wonders he has shown you;
may he bring you home rejoicing : once again into our doors.

✹ March 3

On March 3, 1968, more than twenty thousand Mexican and Chicano students walked out of Los Angeles high schools, calling for an end to racist policies. The students were not allowed to speak Spanish in the classroom or to use the bathroom during lunchtime. Mexican-American history was often denied, and Chicano students were advised toward menial labor instead of college.

O Lord, let my soul rise up to meet you
as the day rises to meet the sun.

**Glory to the Father, and to the Son, and to the Holy Spirit,
as it was in the beginning, is now, and will be forever. Amen.**

Come, let us sing to the LORD : let us shout for joy to the Rock of our salvation.

Song   "The Kingdom of God"

Unite us in justice, Lord : that all might praise your name together.

Psalm 18:14–18
The LORD thundered out of heaven : **the Most High uttered his voice.**
He loosed his arrows and scattered them : **he hurled thunderbolts and routed them.**
The beds of the seas were uncovered, and the foundations of the world laid bare : **at your battle cry, O LORD, at the blast of the breath of your nostrils.**
He reached down from on high and grasped me : **he drew me out of great waters.**
He delivered me from my strong enemies and from those who hated me : **for they were too mighty for me.**

Unite us in justice, Lord : that all might praise your name together.

Genesis 44:1–17   Mark 1:29–45

Unite us in justice, Lord : that all might praise your name together.

Pandita Ramabai, a nineteenth-century Indian activist, said, "People must not only hear about the kingdom of God, but must see it in actual operation, on a small scale perhaps and in imperfect form, but a real demonstration nevertheless."

Prayers for Others

Our Father

Lord, where there is injustice, unite us as your children to speak out and walk out as necessary. May all of our acts of protest be steeped in love for others and for you. Amen.

May the peace of the Lord Christ go with you : wherever he may send you; may he guide you through the wilderness : protect you through the storm; may he bring you home rejoicing : at the wonders he has shown you; may he bring you home rejoicing : once again into our doors.

 March 4

O Lord, let my soul rise up to meet you
as the day rises to meet the sun.

Glory to the Father, and to the Son, and to the Holy Spirit, as it was in the beginning, is now, and will be forever. Amen.

Come, let us bow down and bend the knee : let us kneel before the LORD our Maker.

Song "Were You There?"

Be not far from me, O Lord : for you are my strength and my help.

Psalm 22:1–6
My God, my God, why have you forsaken me? : **and are so far from my cry and from the words of my distress?**
O my God, I cry in the daytime, but you do not answer : **by night as well, but I find no rest.**
Yet you are the Holy One : **enthroned upon the praises of Israel.**
Our forefathers put their trust in you : **they trusted, and you delivered them.**
They cried out to you and were delivered : **they trusted in you and were not put to shame.**
But as for me, I am a worm and no man : **scorned by all and despised by the people.**

Be not far from me, O Lord : for you are my strength and my help.

Genesis 44:18–34   Mark 2:1–12

Be not far from me, O Lord : for you are my strength and my help.

Thirteenth-century mystic Gertrude of Helfta prayed, "Inscribe with your precious blood, most merciful Lord, your wounds on my heart, that I may read in them both your sufferings and your love."

Prayers for Others

Our Father

Keep us from self-pity, Lord, and stir us to rise each morning expecting to encounter you and be caught up in your work. Amen.

May the peace of the Lord Christ go with you : wherever he may send you; may he guide you through the wilderness : protect you through the storm; may he bring you home rejoicing : at the wonders he has shown you; may he bring you home rejoicing : once again into our doors.

 ## March 5

O Lord, let my soul rise up to meet you
as the day rises to meet the sun.

Glory to the Father, and to the Son, and to the Holy Spirit, as it was in the beginning, is now, and will be forever. Amen.

Come, let us bow down and bend the knee : let us kneel before the LORD our Maker.

Song "O Lord, Hear My Prayer"

Free us, Lord, from the chains of death : that we might work for love and life.

Psalm 28:1–4
O LORD, I call to you; my Rock, do not be deaf to my cry : **lest, if you do not hear me, I become like those who go down to the Pit.**
Hear the voice of my prayer when I cry out to you : **when I lift up my hands to your holy of holies.**
Do not snatch me away with the wicked or with the evildoers : **who speak peaceably with their neighbors, while strife is in their hearts.**
Repay them according to their deeds : **and according to the wickedness of their actions.**

Free us, Lord, from the chains of death : that we might work for love and life.

Genesis 45:1–15   Mark 2:13–22

Free us, Lord, from the chains of death : that we might work for love and life.

Catherine Booth, a great nineteenth-century preacher and co-founder of the Salvation Army, said, "Cast off all bonds of prejudice and custom, and let the love of Christ, which is in you, have free course to run out in all conceivable schemes and methods of labour for the souls of men."

Prayers for Others

Our Father

As the morning casts off the darkness, Lord, help us to cast aside any feelings of ill will we might harbor against those who have hurt us. Soften our hearts to work toward their conversion and ours. Amen.

**May the peace of the Lord Christ go with you : wherever he may send you;
may he guide you through the wilderness : protect you through the storm;
may he bring you home rejoicing : at the wonders he has shown you;
may he bring you home rejoicing : once again into our doors.**

✹ March 6

O Lord, let my soul rise up to meet you
as the day rises to meet the sun.

**Glory to the Father, and to the Son, and to the Holy Spirit,
as it was in the beginning, is now, and will be forever. Amen.**

Come, let us bow down and bend the knee : let us kneel before the Lord our Maker.

Song   "Come, Ye Sinners"

Teach us, Lord, the unquenchable joy : of sins forgiven, friendship restored.

Psalm 32:6–8
I said, "I will confess my transgressions to the Lord." : **Then you forgave me the guilt of my sin.**
Therefore all the faithful will make their prayers to you in time of trouble : **when the great waters overflow, they shall not reach them.**
You are my hiding place; you preserve me from trouble : **you surround me with shouts of deliverance.**

Teach us, Lord, the unquenchable joy : of sins forgiven, friendship restored.

Genesis 45:16–28   Mark 2:23–3:6

Teach us, Lord, the unquenchable joy : of sins forgiven, friendship restored.

Twentieth-century mystic and philosopher Simone Weil said, "Today it is not nearly enough merely to be a saint; but we must have the saintliness demanded by the present moment, a new saintliness."

Prayers for Others

Our Father

Lord, guide us to act, live, and pray as the times determine. Make our faith grow to accommodate the needs of your people and the fulfillment of your kingdom. Amen.

May the peace of the Lord Christ go with you : wherever he may send you; may he guide you through the wilderness : protect you through the storm; may he bring you home rejoicing : at the wonders he has shown you; may he bring you home rejoicing : once again into our doors.

 March 7

Perpetua and Felicity (d. 203)
The relationship between Perpetua and Felicity began as that of a noblewoman and her servant girl. But when they embraced Christ, they became sisters in faith and ultimately co-martyrs. In 203 AD, Roman authorities arrested six Christians and condemned them to death by the sword for their refusal to renounce their faith. Among these six were twenty-two-year-old Perpetua, who had a young child, and her former slave, Felicity, who was eight months pregnant. Felicity gave birth while in prison, the night before their execution date, and her child was entrusted to a Christian couple. Eyewitness accounts document that just before their death, the two women, now equals in Christ, embraced one another with a holy kiss.

O Lord, let my soul rise up to meet you
as the day rises to meet the sun.

**Glory to the Father, and to the Son, and to the Holy Spirit,
as it was in the beginning, is now, and will be forever. Amen.**

Come, let us sing to the LORD : let us shout for joy to the Rock of our salvation.

Song   "Come, Thou Fount"

Giver of all good things : make us generous in our giving.

Psalm 37:19–22
The L<small>ORD</small> cares for the lives of the godly : **and their inheritance shall last for ever.**
They shall not be ashamed in bad times : **and in days of famine they shall have enough.**
As for the wicked, they shall perish : **and the enemies of the L<small>ORD</small>, like the glory of the meadows, shall vanish; they shall vanish like smoke.**
The wicked borrow and do not repay : **but the righteous are generous in giving.**

Giver of all good things : make us generous in our giving.

Genesis 46:1–7, 28–34   Mark 3:7–19a

Giver of all good things : make us generous in our giving.

The following account is found in *The Martyrdom of Perpetua*: "Perpetua followed with quick step as a true spouse of Christ, the darling of God, her brightly flashing eyes quelling the gaze of the crowd. Felicitas too, joyful because she had safely survived child-birth and was now able to participate in the contest with the wild animals, passed from one shedding of blood to another; from midwife to gladiator, about to be purified after childbirth by a second baptism."

Prayers for Others

Our Father

Lord, you have brought us in safety to this new day. Preserve us now by your mighty power that we may not fall into sin nor be overcome by adversity, but in all that we do direct us to the fulfilling of your purpose through Jesus Christ, our Lord. Amen.

May the peace of the Lord Christ go with you : wherever he may send you; may he guide you through the wilderness : protect you through the storm; may he bring you home rejoicing : at the wonders he has shown you; may he bring you home rejoicing : once again into our doors.

> **Order and Spontaneity**
>
> We must be careful in all our talk about liturgical prayer not to rule out the spontaneous moves of the Spirit. Just as liturgical traditions have much to offer us by way of roots, the charismatic and Pentecostals have much to offer us in zeal and passion. Tradition and innovation go together in God's kingdom. Jesus was Jewish. He went to synagogue "as was his tradition" and celebrated holy days such as Passover. But Jesus also healed on the Sabbath. Jesus points us to a God who is able to work within institutions and order, a God who is too big to be confined.

> God is constantly coloring outside the lines. Jesus challenges the structures that oppress and exclude, and busts through any traditions that put limitations on love. Love cannot be harnessed.
>
> Liturgy is public poetry and art. You can make beautiful art by splashing paint on a wall, and you can also make art with the careful diligence of a sculptor. Both can be lovely, and both can be ugly. Both can be marketed and robbed of their original touch, and both have the potential to inspire and move people to do something beautiful for God. So it is with worship. More important than whether something is old or new, winsome or classic is whether it is real. The Scriptures tell us to "test the spirits," and the true test of the spirit of a thing is whether it moves us closer to God and to our suffering neighbor. Does it have fruit outside of our own good feelings? Beauty must hearken to something beyond us. It should cause us to do something beautiful for God in the world.

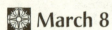

March 8

O Lord, let my soul rise up to meet you
as the day rises to meet the sun.

**Glory to the Father, and to the Son, and to the Holy Spirit,
as it was in the beginning, is now, and will be forever. Amen.**

Come, let us bow down and bend the knee : let us kneel before the LORD our Maker.

Song "Guide My Feet"

Lead us by your light, O Lord : that we might shine like the sun.

Psalm 43:1–4
Give judgment for me, O God, and defend my cause against an ungodly people : **deliver me from the deceitful and the wicked.**
For you are the God of my strength; why have you put me from you? : **and why do I go so heavily while the enemy oppresses me?**
Send out your light and your truth, that they may lead me : **and bring me to your holy hill and to your dwelling;**
that I may go to the altar of God, to the God of my joy and gladness : **and on the harp I will give thanks to you, O God my God.**

Lead us by your light, O Lord : that we might shine like the sun.

Genesis 47:1–26   Mark 3:19b–35

Lead us by your light, O Lord : that we might shine like the sun.

Maria Skobtsova, a twentieth-century nun remembered in Russia as Mother Maria, said, "I am your message, Lord. Throw me like a blazing torch into the night, that all may see and understand what it means to be a disciple."

Prayers for Others

Our Father

Lord God, when the hungry are fed, the sick healed, the lonely made family, the outcast brought in, the sinner forgiven, the tyrant transformed, and the enemy reconciled, we know your work by the fruit it produces. May our lives bear fruit worthy of your name. Amen.

May the peace of the Lord Christ go with you : wherever he may send you; may he guide you through the wilderness : protect you through the storm; may he bring you home rejoicing : at the wonders he has shown you; may he bring you home rejoicing : once again into our doors.

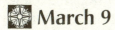 March 9

O Lord, let my soul rise up to meet you
as the day rises to meet the sun.

Glory to the Father, and to the Son, and to the Holy Spirit,
as it was in the beginning, is now, and will be forever. Amen.

Come, let us bow down and bend the knee : let us kneel before the LORD our Maker.

Song "Take My Life and Let It Be"

Forgive our greed, Lord : and free us for life together.

Psalm 49:4–8
Why should I be afraid in evil days : **when the wickedness of those at my heels surrounds me,**
the wickedness of those who put their trust in their goods : **and boast of their great riches?**
We can never ransom ourselves : **or deliver to God the price of our life;**
for the ransom of our life is so great : **that we should never have enough to pay it,**
in order to live for ever and ever : **and never see the grave.**

Forgive our greed, Lord : and free us for life together.

Genesis 47:27–48:7   Mark 4:1–20

Forgive our greed, Lord : and free us for life together.

Basil of Caesarea, a fourth-century bishop and monk, asked, "Are you not a robber, you who consider your own that which has been given you solely to distribute to others? This bread which you have set aside is the bread of the hungry; this garment you have locked away is the clothing of the naked; those shoes which you let rot are the shoes of him who is barefoot; those riches you have hoarded are the riches of the poor."

Prayers for Others

Our Father

Lord, keep us from speaking of love while hoarding the gifts you have given us. Make us full of discontent as long as there are brothers and sisters living and dying in hunger. Amen.

May the peace of the Lord Christ go with you : wherever he may send you; may he guide you through the wilderness : protect you through the storm; may he bring you home rejoicing : at the wonders he has shown you; may he bring you home rejoicing : once again into our doors.

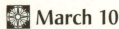# March 10

O Lord, let my soul rise up to meet you
as the day rises to meet the sun.

**Glory to the Father, and to the Son, and to the Holy Spirit,
as it was in the beginning, is now, and will be forever. Amen.**

Come, let us bow down and bend the knee : let us kneel before the LORD our Maker.

Song "I Will Trust in the Lord"

I will call upon God : and the Lord will deliver me.

Psalm 55:22–24
Cast your burden upon the LORD, and he will sustain you : **he will never let the righteous stumble.**
For you will bring the bloodthirsty and deceitful : **down to the pit of destruction, O God.**
They shall not live out half their days : **but I will put my trust in you.**

I will call upon God : and the Lord will deliver me.

Genesis 48:8–22   Mark 4:21–34

I will call upon God : and the Lord will deliver me.

Teresa of Avila, a sixteenth-century Spanish mystic, said, "Let nothing disturb you, nothing dismay you. All things are passing, God never changes. Patient endurance attains all things. God alone suffices."

Prayers for Others

Our Father

Lord, before the heat of the noonday comes, we are already feeling as though our lives are not full enough. Instill in us this morning the assurance that you are enough for us, God. Your love, your call, your work, is enough. Amen.

**May the peace of the Lord Christ go with you : wherever he may send you;
may he guide you through the wilderness : protect you through the storm;
may he bring you home rejoicing : at the wonders he has shown you;
may he bring you home rejoicing : once again into our doors.**

✣ March 11

O Lord, let my soul rise up to meet you
as the day rises to meet the sun.

**Glory to the Father, and to the Son, and to the Holy Spirit,
as it was in the beginning, is now, and will be forever. Amen.**

Come, let us bow down and bend the knee : let us kneel before the LORD our Maker.

Song "I Want Jesus to Walk with Me"

We need your help against the enemy : for human help is useless.

Psalm 60:1–4
O God, you have cast us off and broken us : **you have been angry; oh, take us back to you again.**
You have shaken the earth and split it open : **repair the cracks in it, for it totters.**
You have made your people know hardship : **you have given us wine that makes us stagger.**
You have set up a banner for those who fear you : **to be a refuge from the power of the bow.**

We need your help against the enemy : for human help is useless.

Genesis 49:1–28   Mark 4:35–41

We need your help against the enemy : for human help is useless.

Third-century martyr Agnes of Rome said, "You may stain your sword with my blood, but you will never be able to profane my body, consecrated to Christ."

Prayers for Others

Our Father

Quiet our anxious spirits, Lord, and help us enjoy the peace you give which the world cannot take away. Amen.

May the peace of the Lord Christ go with you : wherever he may send you; may he guide you through the wilderness : protect you through the storm; may he bring you home rejoicing : at the wonders he has shown you; may he bring you home rejoicing : once again into our doors.

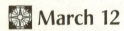 March 12

Maximilian of Thavaste (d. 295)

Maximilian, the son of a Roman soldier in present-day Algeria, was required to join the army at the age of twenty-one. Before the court of the Roman proconsul Dion, Maximilian testified, "I cannot enlist for I am a Christian. I cannot serve, I cannot do evil." Because of his refusal he was beheaded.

Also noteworthy: this is the day that Jesuit priest Rutilio Grande was murdered in El Salvador, a pivotal moment in Salvadoran history and for the witness of the church in Latin America.

O Lord, let my soul rise up to meet you
as the day rises to meet the sun.

Glory to the Father, and to the Son, and to the Holy Spirit, as it was in the beginning, is now, and will be forever. Amen.

Come, let us sing to the LORD : let us shout for joy to the Rock of our salvation.

Song "Woke Up This Mornin'"

Overwhelm us with your love : which casts out every fear.

Psalm 66:14–18
Come and listen, all you who fear God : **and I will tell you what he has done for me.**
I called out to him with my mouth : **and his praise was on my tongue.**
If I had found evil in my heart : **the Lord would not have heard me;**
but in truth God has heard me : **he has attended to the voice of my prayer.**

Blessed be God, who has not rejected my prayer : **nor withheld his love from me.**

Overwhelm us with your love : which casts out every fear.

Genesis 49:29–50:14   Mark 5:1–20

Overwhelm us with your love : which casts out every fear.

Maximilian of Thavaste said, "You can cut off my head, but I will not be a solider of this world, for I am a soldier of Christ."

Prayers for Others

Our Father

Lord, help us examine ourselves and see if we are willing to give all for you. Search our hearts and convict us where there is still fear, self-preoccupation, and lack of trust. Amen.

May the peace of the Lord Christ go with you : wherever he may send you; may he guide you through the wilderness : protect you through the storm; may he bring you home rejoicing : at the wonders he has shown you; may he bring you home rejoicing : once again into our doors.

✸ March 13

O Lord, let my soul rise up to meet you
as the day rises to meet the sun.

Glory to the Father, and to the Son, and to the Holy Spirit,
as it was in the beginning, is now, and will be forever. Amen.

Come, let us bow down and bend the knee : let us kneel before the Lord our Maker.

Song   "Swing Low, Sweet Chariot"

Answer me, Lord, for your love is kind : in your compassion, turn to me.

Psalm 69:1–5
Save me, O God : **for the waters have risen up to my neck.**
I am sinking in deep mire : **and there is no firm ground for my feet.**
I have come into deep waters : **and the torrent washes over me.**
I have grown weary with my crying; my throat is inflamed : **my eyes have failed from looking for my God.**
Those who hate me without a cause are more than the hairs of my head; my

lying foes who would destroy me are mighty : **Must I then give back what I never stole?**

Answer me, Lord, for your love is kind : in your compassion, turn to me.

Genesis 50:15–26   Mark 5:21–43

Answer me, Lord, for your love is kind : in your compassion, turn to me.

Perpetua of Carthage, a third-century martyr, said, "Stand fast in the faith, and love one another."

Prayers for Others

Our Father

Lord, you ask us not to fear but to trust. Help our unbelief and grant us faith to stand fast in our love for one another. Amen.

May the peace of the Lord Christ go with you : wherever he may send you; may he guide you through the wilderness : protect you through the storm; may he bring you home rejoicing : at the wonders he has shown you; may he bring you home rejoicing : once again into our doors.

✤ March 14

O Lord, let my soul rise up to meet you
as the day rises to meet the sun.

Glory to the Father, and to the Son, and to the Holy Spirit, as it was in the beginning, is now, and will be forever. Amen.

Come, let us bow down and bend the knee : let us kneel before the LORD our Maker.

Song   "The Kingdom of God"

Arise, O God, maintain your cause : defend the poor for your name's sake.

Psalm 74:17–20
Remember, O Lord, how the enemy scoffed : **how a foolish people despised your name.**
Do not hand over the life of your dove to wild beasts : **never forget the lives of your poor.**
Look upon your covenant : **the dark places of the earth are haunts of violence.**
Let not the oppressed turn away ashamed : **let the poor and needy praise your name.**

Arise, O God, maintain your cause : defend the poor for your name's sake.

Exodus 1:6–22   Mark 6:1–13

Arise, O God, maintain your cause : defend the poor for your name's sake.

Maria Skobtsova, a twentieth-century nun remembered in Russia as Mother Maria, said, "At the Last Judgment I shall not be asked whether I was successful in my ascetic exercises, nor how many bows and prostrations I made. Instead I shall be asked if I fed the hungry, clothed the naked, visited the sick and the prisoners."

Prayers for Others

Our Father

Lord, in our efforts to serve, help us be true to who we are in you. Make us see and understand the gifts and talents you have given us, and give us courage to use them for the building up of your kingdom. Amen.

May the peace of the Lord Christ go with you : wherever he may send you;
may he guide you through the wilderness : protect you through the storm;
may he bring you home rejoicing : at the wonders he has shown you;
may he bring you home rejoicing : once again into our doors.

✸ March 15

O Lord, let my soul rise up to meet you
as the day rises to meet the sun.

Glory to the Father, and to the Son, and to the Holy Spirit,
as it was in the beginning, is now, and will be forever. Amen.

Come, let us bow down and bend the knee : let us kneel before the Lord our Maker.

Song   "O Lord, Have Mercy"

Cleanse our hearts, Lord, by your Spirit : that we might praise your holy name.

Psalm 78:34–39
Whenever he slew them, they would seek him : **and repent, and diligently search for God.**
They would remember that God was their rock : **and the Most High God their redeemer.**
But they flattered him with their mouths : **and lied to him with their tongues.**

Morning Prayer

Their heart was not steadfast toward him : **and they were not faithful to his covenant.**
But he was so merciful that he forgave their sins and did not destroy them : **many times he held back his anger and did not permit his wrath to be roused.**
For he remembered that they were but flesh : **a breath that goes forth and does not return.**

Cleanse our hearts, Lord, by your Spirit : that we might praise your holy name.

Exodus 2:1–22   Mark 6:13–29

Cleanse our hearts, Lord, by your Spirit : that we might praise your holy name.

Katherine Drexel, the patron saint of racial justice, said, "You have no time to occupy your thoughts with that complacency or consideration of what others will think. Your business is simply, 'What will my Father in heaven think?'"

Prayers for Others

Our Father

Lord, make it second nature for us to do what is right in your sight. Make us more concerned with abiding by the tenets of your kingdom than by human law. Amen.

May the peace of the Lord Christ go with you : wherever he may send you;
may he guide you through the wilderness : protect you through the storm;
may he bring you home rejoicing : at the wonders he has shown you;
may he bring you home rejoicing : once again into our doors.

✺ March 16

Twenty-three-year-old American activist Rachel Corrie was killed on this day in 2003. While countless Palestinian people have been killed the way Rachel was, her death marks a key moment symbolizing international concern. She was crushed by a bulldozer in Gaza as she knelt in front of the home of a Palestinian friend and tried to stop the demolition of their house.

O Lord, let my soul rise up to meet you
as the day rises to meet the sun.

Glory to the Father, and to the Son, and to the Holy Spirit,
as it was in the beginning, is now, and will be forever. Amen.

Come, let us sing to the LORD : let us shout for joy to the Rock of our salvation.

Song "Praise to the Lord, the Almighty"

Lord God of hosts, hear our prayer : listen, O God of Jacob.

Psalm 84:8–12
Behold our defender, O God : **and look upon the face of your Anointed.**
For one day in your courts is better than a thousand in my own room : **and to stand at the threshold of the house of my God than to dwell in the tents of the wicked.**
For the LORD God is both sun and shield : **he will give grace and glory;**
no good thing will the LORD withhold : **from those who walk with integrity.**
O LORD of hosts : **happy are they who put their trust in you!**

Lord God of hosts, hear our prayer : listen, O God of Jacob.

Exodus 2:23–3:15   Mark 6:30–46

Lord God of hosts, hear our prayer : listen, O God of Jacob.

Nineteenth-century French mystic Therese of Lisieux wrote, "My vocation is love! In the heart of the Church, who is my Mother, I will be love. So I shall be everything and so my dreams will be fulfilled — to make Love loved."

Prayers for Others

Our Father

Lord God, please keep us balanced between the times you call us apart to be alone with you and the times when we dwell in the midst of others who claim you as Lord, that we might in every circumstance know ourselves in the beloved community of your Trinity. Amen.

**May the peace of the Lord Christ go with you : wherever he may send you;
may he guide you through the wilderness : protect you through the storm;
may he bring you home rejoicing : at the wonders he has shown you;
may he bring you home rejoicing : once again into our doors.**

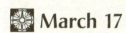 # March 17

Patrick of Ireland (389–461)
At the age of sixteen, Patrick was kidnapped from his home by Irish marauders and taken to Ireland, where he was sold as a slave to a chieftain and forced to herd livestock. After six years of slavery, Patrick escaped to his native Britain. Because he believed that his captivity and deliverance were ordained by God, Patrick devoted his life to ministry. While studying for the priesthood, he

experienced recurring dreams in which he heard voices say, "O holy youth, come back to Erin and walk once more amongst us." He convinced his superiors to let him return to Ireland in 432, not to seek revenge for injustice but to seek reconciliation and to spread his faith. Over the next thirty years, Patrick established churches and monastic communities across Ireland. When he was not engaged in the work of spreading the Christian faith, Patrick spent his time praying in his favorite places of solitude and retreat.

O Lord, let my soul rise up to meet you
as the day rises to meet the sun.

**Glory to the Father, and to the Son, and to the Holy Spirit,
as it was in the beginning, is now, and will be forever. Amen.**

Come, let us sing to the LORD : let us shout for joy to the Rock of our salvation.

Song "Be Thou My Vision"

I arise, I arise today : in the Spirit of the Trinity.

Psalm 89:34–37
I will not break my covenant : **nor change what has gone out of my lips.**
Once for all I have sworn by my holiness : **"I will not lie to David.**
His line shall endure for ever : **and his throne as the sun before me;**
it shall stand fast for evermore like the moon : **the abiding witness in the sky."**

I arise, I arise today : in the Spirit of the Trinity.

Exodus 3:16–4:12   Mark 6:47–56

I arise, I arise today : in the Spirit of the Trinity.

This prayer is attributed to Patrick:

> Christ be with me,
> Christ before me,
> Christ behind me,
> Christ in the heart of everyone who thinks of me,
> Christ in the mouth of everyone who speaks of me,
> Christ in every eye that sees me,
> Christ in every ear that hears me.

Prayers for Others

Our Father

Lord, if only we made ourselves as open and available as your saints of old, who knows what you might do through us! Speak to us in visions and dreams, make your will known to us, and be patient with us. Amen.

May the peace of the Lord Christ go with you : wherever he may send you;
may he guide you through the wilderness : protect you through the storm;
may he bring you home rejoicing : at the wonders he has shown you;
may he bring you home rejoicing : once again into our doors.

March 18

Cyril of Jerusalem (315–386)

Cyril lived in the fourth century. His gift to the church was his refusal to separate good doctrine from good living, insisting that orthodoxy (right belief) and orthopraxis (right living) must be married. He was accused of selling some gifts from the emperor and giving the money to the poor. Cyril was condemned and forced into exile. He died in 386 at the age of seventy. Of his thirty-five years as a bishop, nearly sixteen were spent in exile.

O Lord, let my soul rise up to meet you
as the day rises to meet the sun.

**Glory to the Father, and to the Son, and to the Holy Spirit,
as it was in the beginning, is now, and will be forever. Amen.**

Come, let us sing to the LORD : let us shout for joy to the Rock of our salvation.

Song   "All Creatures of Our God and King"

In the roar of a hard rain, Lord : we hear justice rolling down.

Psalm 93:4–6
The waters have lifted up, O LORD, the waters have lifted up their voice : **the waters have lifted up their pounding waves.**
Mightier than the sound of many waters, mightier than the breakers of the sea : **mightier is the LORD who dwells on high.**
Your testimonies are very sure : **and holiness adorns your house, O LORD, for ever and for evermore.**

In the roar of a hard rain, Lord : we hear justice rolling down.

Exodus 4:10–31   Mark 7:1–23

In the roar of a hard rain, Lord : we hear justice rolling down.

Cyril of Jerusalem said, "The way of godliness consists of these two parts, pious doctrines and good works. Neither are the doctrines acceptable to God without good works, nor does God accept works accomplished otherwise than as linked with pious doctrines."

Prayers for Others

Our Father

Lord, not only in the roar of a hard rain, but in the dousing, dipping, drenching of our baptism, call us to live into that new life that is your resurrection. Amen.

**May the peace of the Lord Christ go with you : wherever he may send you;
may he guide you through the wilderness : protect you through the storm;
may he bring you home rejoicing : at the wonders he has shown you;
may he bring you home rejoicing : once again into our doors.**

✸ March 19

On March 19, 2003, US and British troops began a "shock and awe" campaign to overthrow the government of Saddam Hussein, which US intelligence officials accused of possessing weapons of mass destruction (WMDs). Though no WMDs were found in Iraq, a US-sponsored occupation continued, costing thousands of soldiers' lives, tens of thousands of civilians' lives, and billions of US dollars.

O Lord, let my soul rise up to meet you
as the day rises to meet the sun.

**Glory to the Father, and to the Son, and to the Holy Spirit,
as it was in the beginning, is now, and will be forever. Amen.**

Come, let us bow down and bend the knee : let us kneel before the LORD our Maker.

Song "Waters of Babylon"

We pledge allegiance to the Lamb : and to the kingdom for which he stands.

Psalm 99:1–5
The LORD is King; let the people tremble : **he is enthroned upon the cherubim; let the earth shake.**
The LORD is great in Zion : **he is high above all peoples.**
Let them confess his name, which is great and awesome : **he is the Holy One.**
"O mighty King, lover of justice, you have established equity : **you have executed justice and righteousness in Jacob."**
Proclaim the greatness of the LORD our God and fall down before his footstool : **he is the Holy One.**

We pledge allegiance to the Lamb : and to the kingdom for which he stands.

Exodus 5:1–6:1   Mark 7:24–37

We pledge allegiance to the Lamb : and to the kingdom for which he stands.

Second-century martyr Ignatius of Antioch said, "Better to die for the sake of Jesus Christ than to be king over the utmost ends of the earth."

Prayers for Others

Our Father

Lord, keep us from making excuses for the sake of disobedience and spiritual death. Help us remember that all of humanity is invited to feast at your table, especially those we would name as enemies. Amen.

May the peace of the Lord Christ go with you : wherever he may send you; may he guide you through the wilderness : protect you through the storm; may he bring you home rejoicing : at the wonders he has shown you; may he bring you home rejoicing : once again into our doors.

✦ March 20

O Lord, let my soul rise up to meet you
as the day rises to meet the sun.

Glory to the Father, and to the Son, and to the Holy Spirit, as it was in the beginning, is now, and will be forever. Amen.

Come, let us sing to the LORD : let us shout for joy to the Rock of our salvation.

Song "Fairest Lord Jesus"

Set our hearts to sing your praise : and our bodies to do your will.

Psalm 104:1, 13–16
Bless the LORD, O my soul : **O LORD my God, how excellent is your greatness! you are clothed with majesty and splendor.**
You water the mountains from your dwelling on high : **the earth is fully satisfied by the fruit of your works.**
You make grass grow for flocks and herds : **and plants to serve mankind;**
that they may bring forth food from the earth : **and wine to gladden our hearts,**
oil to make a cheerful countenance : **and bread to strengthen the heart.**

Set our hearts to sing your praise : and our bodies to do your will.

Exodus 7:8–24   Mark 8:1–10

Set our hearts to sing your praise : and our bodies to do your will.

Maria Skobtsova, a twentieth-century nun remembered in Russia as Mother Maria, said, "The meaning of the liturgy must be translated into life."

Prayers for Others

Our Father

Lord, we begin this day praising you. May your liturgy set our souls to dancing, and may your Spirit guide our feet today. Amen.

May the peace of the Lord Christ go with you : wherever he may send you; may he guide you through the wilderness : protect you through the storm; may he bring you home rejoicing : at the wonders he has shown you; may he bring you home rejoicing : once again into our doors.

March 21

Under apartheid law, black South African men over the age of sixteen were required to carry a pass card. Anyone found without a card by the police could be arrested. On March 21, 1960, black South African men had planned to leave their pass cards at home, go to the police station, and ask to be arrested in an act of civil disobedience. When the men began their walk to the police station, officers opened fire, killing sixty-nine and injuring hundreds in what has been remembered as the Sharpeville Massacre.

O Lord, let my soul rise up to meet you
as the day rises to meet the sun.

Glory to the Father, and to the Son, and to the Holy Spirit, as it was in the beginning, is now, and will be forever. Amen.

Come, let us bow down and bend the knee : let us kneel before the Lord our Maker.

Song "We Shall Overcome"

Lord, help us to resist : the madness of our age.

Psalm 106:47–48
Save us, O Lord our God, and gather us from among the nations : **that we may give thanks to your holy name and glory in your praise.**
Blessed be the Lord, the God of Israel, from everlasting and to everlasting : **and let all the people say, "Amen!" Hallelujah!**

Lord, help us to resist : the madness of our age.

Exodus 7:25–8:19   Mark 8:11–26

Lord, help us to resist : the madness of our age.

Desert father Abba Anthony said, "A time is coming when men will go mad, and when they see someone who is not mad, they will attack him saying, 'You are mad, you are not like us.'"

Prayers for Others

Our Father

Lord, we remember those who have given their lives for the sake of justice and freedom. Help us not to take our own freedom lightly, but to use it to advocate relentlessly for the freedom of others. Amen.

May the peace of the Lord Christ go with you : wherever he may send you; may he guide you through the wilderness : protect you through the storm; may he bring you home rejoicing : at the wonders he has shown you; may he bring you home rejoicing : once again into our doors.

✤ March 22

O Lord, let my soul rise up to meet you
as the day rises to meet the sun.

**Glory to the Father, and to the Son, and to the Holy Spirit,
as it was in the beginning, is now, and will be forever. Amen.**

Come, let us sing to the Lord : let us shout for joy to the Rock of our salvation.

Song "Glory, Glory, Hallelujah"

Hold not your tongue, O God of our praise : for the air is full of empty words.

Psalm 109:29–30
I will give great thanks to the Lord with my mouth : **in the midst of the multitude will I praise him;**
because he stands at the right hand of the needy : **to save his life from those who would condemn him.**

Hold not your tongue, O God of our praise : for the air is full of empty words.

Exodus 9:13–35   Mark 8:27–9:1

Hold not your tongue, O God of our praise : for the air is full of empty words.

Benedict of Nursia, sixth-century father of communal monasticism, wrote, "How much more important it is to refrain from evil speech, remembering what such sins bring down on us in punishment. In fact so important is it to cultivate silence. After all, it is written in scripture that one who never stops talking cannot avoid falling into sin. Another text in the same book reminds us that the tongue holds the key to death and life."

Prayers for Others

Our Father

Lord, may our prayers be found in our actions today as much as they are found in these words. Amen.

**May the peace of the Lord Christ go with you : wherever he may send you;
may he guide you through the wilderness : protect you through the storm;
may he bring you home rejoicing : at the wonders he has shown you;
may he bring you home rejoicing : once again into our doors.**

March 23

O Lord, let my soul rise up to meet you
as the day rises to meet the sun.

**Glory to the Father, and to the Son, and to the Holy Spirit,
as it was in the beginning, is now, and will be forever. Amen.**

Come, let us sing to the LORD : let us shout for joy to the Rock of our salvation.

Song "Vamos Todos al Banquete"

Come now and join the feast : right here in the belly of the beast!

Psalm 115:14–18
May the LORD increase you more and more : **you and your children after you.**
May you be blessed by the LORD : **the maker of heaven and earth.**
The heaven of heavens is the LORD's : **but he entrusted the earth to its peoples.**
The dead do not praise the LORD : **nor all those who go down into silence;**
but we will bless the LORD : **from this time forth for evermore. Hallelujah!**

Come now and join the feast : right here in the belly of the beast!

Exodus 10:21–11:8   Mark 9:2–13

Come now and join the feast : right here in the belly of the beast!

John Chrysostom, a great fourth-century preacher in Constantinople, said, "When we suffer anything for Christ's sake, we should do so not only with courage, but even with joy. If we have to go hungry, let us be glad as if we were at a banquet. If we are insulted, let us be elated as though we had been showered with praises. If we lose all we possess, let us consider ourselves the gainers. If we provide for the poor, let us regard ourselves as the recipients. Do not think of the painful effort involved, but of the sweetness of the reward; and above all, remember that your struggles are for the sake of our Lord Jesus."

Prayers for Others

Our Father

Transform our memory, Lord, so that whenever we encounter suffering for your sake, we will recall all the saints who have gone before us whose courage and faith brought us this far. Amen.

**May the peace of the Lord Christ go with you : wherever he may send you;
may he guide you through the wilderness : protect you through the storm;
may he bring you home rejoicing : at the wonders he has shown you;
may he bring you home rejoicing : once again into our doors.**

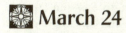

March 24

Oscar Romero (1917–1980)

Although he began as a conservative archbishop, opposed to the progressive liberation theology that was popular among those seeking to help poor farmers in El Salvador, Oscar Romero was deeply impacted when his friend, a priest, was assassinated as a result of commitment to social justice. Through weekly homilies on national radio, Romero advocated an end to the repression of the people in El Salvador, thus making himself an enemy of the government and the military. He was not successful in ending the violence: more than seventy-five thousand Salvadorans would eventually be killed, one million would leave the country, and another million would be left homeless. Because of his prophetic witness, Romero became a target of assassination. As he was saying Mass on March 24, 1980, he was shot and killed. "A bishop will die," Romero had said, foreseeing his own fate, "but the church of God — the people — will not perish."

O Lord, let my soul rise up to meet you
as the day rises to meet the sun.

**Glory to the Father, and to the Son, and to the Holy Spirit,
as it was in the beginning, is now, and will be forever. Amen.**

Come, let us sing to the LORD : let us shout for joy to the Rock of our salvation.

Song "Servant Song"

Unless a seed falls into the ground and dies : it cannot bear fruit or bless others' lives.

Psalm 119:34–37
Give me understanding, and I shall keep your law : **I shall keep it with all my heart.**
Make me go in the path of your commandments : **for that is my desire.**
Incline my heart to your decrees : **and not to unjust gain.**
Turn my eyes from watching what is worthless : **give me life in your ways.**

Unless a seed falls into the ground and dies : it cannot bear fruit or bless others' lives.

Exodus 12:1–14   Mark 9:14–29

Unless a seed falls into the ground and dies : it cannot bear fruit or bless others' lives.

Oscar Romero wrote, "It helps, now and then, to step back and take the long view. The Kingdom is not only beyond our efforts: it is beyond our vision. We accomplish in our lifetime only a tiny fraction of the magnificent enterprise that is the Lord's work. Nothing we do is complete, which is another way of saying that the Kingdom always lies beyond us. No sermon says all that should be said. No prayer fully expresses our faith. No confession brings perfection. No pastoral visit brings wholeness. No program accomplishes the Church's mission. No set of goals and objectives includes everything. That is what we are about. We plant the seeds that one day will grow. We water seeds already planted knowing they hold future promise. We lay foundations that will need further development. We provide yeast that affects far beyond our capabilities. We cannot do everything and there is a sense of liberation in realizing that. This enables us to do something, and to do it very, very well. It may be incomplete, but it is a beginning, a step along the way, an opportunity for the Lord's grace to enter and do the rest. We may never see the end results, but that is the difference between the Master Builder and the worker. We are workers, not master builders; ministers, not messiahs. We are prophets of a future that is not our own."

Prayers for Others

Our Father

Lord, we know the world will kill your prophets. Nevertheless, give us words to convict, to heal, to raise up others for justice, and to offer forgiveness for those who harm us. Amen.

May the peace of the Lord Christ go with you : wherever he may send you;
may he guide you through the wilderness : protect you through the storm;
may he bring you home rejoicing : at the wonders he has shown you;
may he bring you home rejoicing : once again into our doors.

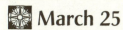 **March 25**

The Annunciation

On March 25 we remember the special role that Mary plays in the redemption of the world and celebrate the example she is to each of us as disciples of Jesus. When the angel Gabriel visited Mary, she was a teenager in occupied Palestine, as anonymous and apparently insignificant as the billions of people who live and die today in the slums of megacities. But the angel of the Lord called Mary by name and proclaimed that she would carry inside her womb God in flesh. It is a miracle we remember even as we put it into practice: however humble our circumstances, God proposes to live in and through our bodies. As a sign to remind us that anything is possible with our God, we remember that Mary conceived Jesus without the help of any man.

O Lord, let my soul rise up to meet you
as the day rises to meet the sun.

**Glory to the Father, and to the Son, and to the Holy Spirit,
as it was in the beginning, is now, and will be forever. Amen.**

Come, let us sing to the LORD : let us shout for joy to the Rock of our salvation.

Song "Magnificat"

Here am I, the servant of the Lord : let it be to me according to your will.

Psalm 119:141–44
I am small and of little account : **yet I do not forget your commandments.**
Your justice is an everlasting justice : **and your law is the truth.**
Trouble and distress have come upon me : **yet your commandments are my delight.**
The righteousness of your decrees is everlasting : **grant me understanding, that I may live.**

Here am I, the servant of the Lord : let it be to me according to your will.

Isaiah 7:10–14   Luke 1:26–38

Here am I, the servant of the Lord : let it be to me according to your will.

Twentieth-century Trappist and spiritual writer Thomas Merton said, "The Christian life — and especially the contemplative life — is a continual discovery of Christ in new and unexpected places."

Prayers for Others

Our Father

Thank you, Lord, for Mary's witness to joyful obedience, courageous faith, and the merciful truth that you dwell among those the world would forget. Amen.

May the peace of the Lord Christ go with you : wherever he may send you; may he guide you through the wilderness : protect you through the storm; may he bring you home rejoicing : at the wonders he has shown you; may he bring you home rejoicing : once again into our doors.

 ## March 26

Harriet Tubman (1820? – 1913)

Harriet Tubman was born into slavery in the 1820s. In 1849, she had a vision that compelled her to run away, traveling under the cover of night with only the North Star as her guide. Arriving safely in Pennsylvania, she felt like she was in heaven. "I had crossed the line," she wrote. "I was FREE; but there was no one to welcome me to the land of freedom." Tubman committed herself to helping others escape to freedom, guiding at least three hundred fugitive slaves to Canada over the course of fifteen years. To those who traveled under her guidance, she was known as Moses.

O Lord, let my soul rise up to meet you
as the day rises to meet the sun.

Glory to the Father, and to the Son, and to the Holy Spirit, as it was in the beginning, is now, and will be forever. Amen.

Come, let us sing to the LORD : let us shout for joy to the Rock of our salvation.

Song "Steal Away to Jesus"

Go down, Moses, way down to Egypt land : and tell old Pharaoh, "Let my people go!"

Psalm 119:153–56
Behold my affliction and deliver me : **for I do not forget your law.**
Plead my cause and redeem me : **according to your promise, give me life.**
Deliverance is far from the wicked : **for they do not study your statutes.**

Great is your compassion, O LORD : **preserve my life, according to your judgments.**

Go down, Moses, way down to Egypt land : and tell old Pharaoh, "Let my people go!"

Exodus 12:14–27   Mark 9:30–41

Go down, Moses, way down to Egypt land : and tell old Pharaoh, "Let my people go!"

In a letter to Harriet Tubman, fellow abolitionist Frederick Douglass wrote, "Most that I have done and suffered in the service of our cause has been in public, and I have received much encouragement at every step of the way. You, on the other hand, have labored in a private way ... most that you have done has been witnessed by a few trembling, scared, and foot-sore bondsmen and women, whom you have led out of the house of bondage, and whose heartfelt 'God Bless You' has been your only reward."

Prayers for Others

Our Father

Thank you, Lord, that throughout history there have been women whose steadfast faith and hope in you have brought about justice, freedom, and security for those who most needed it. We pray we can learn from women like Rahab and Esther and Harriet Tubman what it means to commit our lives to your service. Amen.

May the peace of the Lord Christ go with you : wherever he may send you; may he guide you through the wilderness : protect you through the storm; may he bring you home rejoicing : at the wonders he has shown you; may he bring you home rejoicing : once again into our doors.

✺ March 27

O Lord, let my soul rise up to meet you
as the day rises to meet the sun.

Glory to the Father, and to the Son, and to the Holy Spirit, as it was in the beginning, is now, and will be forever. Amen.

Come, let us bow down and bend the knee : let us kneel before the LORD our Maker.

Song   "It Is Well with My Soul"

My soul waits for the Lord : more than watchmen wait for the morning.

Psalm 130
Out of the depths have I called to you, O LORD; LORD, hear my voice : **let your ears consider well the voice of my supplication.**
If you, LORD, were to note what is done amiss : **O Lord, who could stand?**
For there is forgiveness with you : **therefore you shall be feared.**
I wait for the LORD; my soul waits for him : **in his word is my hope.**
My soul waits for the LORD, more than watchmen for the morning : **more than watchmen for the morning.**
O Israel, wait for the LORD : **for with the LORD there is mercy;**
with him there is plenteous redemption : **and he shall redeem Israel from all their sins.**

My soul waits for the Lord : more than watchmen wait for the morning.

Exodus 12:28–39   Mark 9:42–50

My soul waits for the Lord : more than watchmen wait for the morning.

Sadhu Sundar Singh, an early twentieth-century Indian missionary, wrote, "A silkworm was struggling out of the cocoon and an ignorant man saw it battling as if in pain, so he went and helped it to get free, but very soon after it fluttered and died. The other silkworms that struggled out without help suffered, but they came out into full life and beauty, with wings made strong for flight by their battle for fresh existence."

Prayers for Others

Our Father

Lord, mold us and form us into the kind of people you want us to be. Be patient with us when we fall short of what love demands of us. And give us patience with ourselves. Catch us in the arms of your grace. Amen.

May the peace of the Lord Christ go with you : wherever he may send you;
may he guide you through the wilderness : protect you through the storm;
may he bring you home rejoicing : at the wonders he has shown you;
may he bring you home rejoicing : once again into our doors.

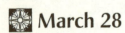 ## March 28

Amos the Prophet
Unlike other Old Testament messengers, Amos was not a professional prophet; he had no special training, nor was he related to any other prophets. He was a peasant farmer and sheep tender called by God for a special mission.

A native of the southern kingdom of Judah, Amos received a powerful commission from God to preach to the people of the northern kingdom of Israel. In the first half of the eighth century BC, during a time of great expansion and prosperity in Israel, Amos spoke out against the economic injustices between urban elites and the poor. Rich landowners were acquiring money and land, taking advantage of small farmers and peasants. Although Amos was not wealthy, he was sent to warn the wealthy and invite them back into the good way of God's justice.

O Lord, let my soul rise up to meet you
as the day rises to meet the sun.

**Glory to the Father, and to the Son, and to the Holy Spirit,
as it was in the beginning, is now, and will be forever. Amen.**

Come, let us bow down and bend the knee : let us kneel before the LORD our Maker.

Song "Jesus, Help Us Live in Peace"

Rain down justice upon us, Lord : that we might live in peace.

Psalm 133
Oh, how good and pleasant it is : **when brethren live together in unity!**
It is like fine oil upon the head : **that runs down upon the beard,**
upon the beard of Aaron : **and runs down upon the collar of his robe.**
It is like the dew of Hermon : **that falls upon the hills of Zion.**
For there the LORD has ordained the blessing : **life for evermore.**

Rain down justice upon us, Lord : that we might live in peace.

Exodus 12:40–51   Mark 10:1–16

Rain down justice upon us, Lord : that we might live in peace.

Amos spoke out, saying, "Hear this, you that trample on the needy, and bring ruin to the poor of the land. I hate, I despise your festivals, and I take no delight in your solemn assemblies. Take away from me the noise of your songs; I will not listen to the melody of your harps. But let justice roll down like waters, and righteousness like an ever-flowing stream."

Prayers for Others

Our Father

We give thanks, God, for the prophets who love us enough to tell us your hard truth. Show us where we need your words for our repentance and conversion, and teach us how to always speak your truth in love. Amen.

May the peace of the Lord Christ go with you : wherever he may send you;
may he guide you through the wilderness : protect you through the storm;
may he bring you home rejoicing : at the wonders he has shown you;
may he bring you home rejoicing : once again into our doors.

✦ March 29

O Lord, let my soul rise up to meet you
as the day rises to meet the sun.

**Glory to the Father, and to the Son, and to the Holy Spirit,
as it was in the beginning, is now, and will be forever. Amen.**

Come, let us bow down and bend the knee : let us kneel before the Lord our Maker.

Song "Nothin' but the Blood"

Receive, Lord, the offering of our lives : that every breath might be holy to you.

Psalm 141:1–3
O Lord, I call to you; come to me quickly : **hear my voice when I cry to you.**
Let my prayer be set forth in your sight as incense : **the lifting up of my hands as the evening sacrifice.**
Set a watch before my mouth, O Lord, and guard the door of my lips : **let not my heart incline to any evil thing.**

Receive, Lord, the offering of our lives : that every breath might be holy to you.

Exodus 13:3–10   Mark 10:17–31

Receive, Lord, the offering of our lives : that every breath might be holy to you.

Pierre Teilhard de Chardin, a twentieth-century Jesuit philosopher, prayed, "Since once again, Lord, I have neither bread nor wine nor altar, I will raise myself beyond these symbols, up to the pure majesty of the real itself; I, your priest, will make the whole earth my altar and on it will offer you all the labors and suffering of the world."

Prayers for Others

Our Father

Lord God, we give you thanks that no building can house you fully and no place of worship can contain your majesty. Teach us by our deeds of peace and justice and joyful celebration to erect altars in the world, so that when some other soul comes across them, they will see that you are indeed present everywhere. Amen.

May the peace of the Lord Christ go with you : wherever he may send you; may he guide you through the wilderness : protect you through the storm; may he bring you home rejoicing : at the wonders he has shown you; may he bring you home rejoicing : once again into our doors.

✺ March 30

O Lord, let my soul rise up to meet you
as the day rises to meet the sun.

Glory to the Father, and to the Son, and to the Holy Spirit,
as it was in the beginning, is now, and will be forever. Amen.

Come, let us sing to the LORD : let us shout for joy to the Rock of our salvation.

Song "Sing and Rejoice"

In you alone we put our trust : let us not be put to shame.

Psalm 146:1–3
Hallelujah! Praise the LORD, O my soul! : **I will praise the LORD as long as I live; I will sing praises to my God while I have my being.**
Put not your trust in rulers, nor in any child of earth : **for there is no help in them.**
When they breathe their last, they return to earth : **and in that day their thoughts perish.**

In you alone we put our trust : let us not be put to shame.

Exodus 13:1–2, 11–16   Mark 10:32–45

In you alone we put our trust : let us not be put to shame.

Peter Maurin, co-founder of the Catholic Worker Movement, said, "The world would be better off if people tried to become better. And people would become better if they stopped trying to become better off."

Prayers for Others

Our Father

Lord, our efforts at faithfulness are fraught with failure more often than we care to admit. Thank you that your love for us is never wasted. Keep us rooted in your word, eating at your table, and praying by your Spirit, so that we may remember when we fail that we are part of your family not because we deserve to be but because you want us. Amen.

May the peace of the Lord Christ go with you : wherever he may send you;
may he guide you through the wilderness : protect you through the storm;
may he bring you home rejoicing : at the wonders he has shown you;
may he bring you home rejoicing : once again into our doors.

March 31

O Lord, let my soul rise up to meet you
as the day rises to meet the sun.

**Glory to the Father, and to the Son, and to the Holy Spirit,
as it was in the beginning, is now, and will be forever. Amen.**

Come, let us sing to the LORD : let us shout for joy to the Rock of our salvation.

Song "All Creatures of Our God and King"

Worship the Lord, O Jerusalem : praise your God, O Zion.

Psalm 148:7–13
Praise the LORD from the earth : **you sea monsters and all deeps;**
fire and hail, snow and fog : **tempestuous wind, doing his will;**
mountains and all hills : **fruit trees and all cedars;**
wild beasts and all cattle : **creeping things and winged birds;**
kings of the earth and all peoples : **princes and all rulers of the world;**
young men and maidens : **old and young together.**
Let them praise the name of the LORD : **for his name only is exalted, his splendor is over earth and heaven.**

Worship the Lord, O Jerusalem : praise your God, O Zion.

Exodus 13:17–14:4   Mark 10:46–52

Worship the Lord, O Jerusalem : praise your God, O Zion.

Twentieth-century Jesuit theologian Henri de Lubac wrote, "The finest and boldest Christian effort, the freshest and most enduring, has always flourished from the roots of tradition."

Prayers for Others

Our Father

Lord, we mark time with hours, days, months, and years. You mark time in ways we cannot comprehend. Help us learn to mark time with worship, praise, and prayers, rooting our lives in the living tradition of your beloved community. Amen.

May the peace of the Lord Christ go with you : wherever he may send you; may he guide you through the wilderness : protect you through the storm; may he bring you home rejoicing : at the wonders he has shown you; may he bring you home rejoicing : once again into our doors.

> **Becoming the Answer to Our Prayers: A Few Ideas**
> 1. Take a break from noise. Turn off things that make noise for a day or a week, and spend the time in silence, speaking only when necessary. Also remember those in our world whose voices have been silenced.
> 2. Go to a home for the elderly and get a list of folks who don't get any visitors. Visit them each week and tell stories, read together, or play board games.
> 3. Laugh at advertisements, especially ones that teach you that you can buy happiness.
> 4. Go down a line of parked cars and add money to the meters that are expired. Leave a little note saying something nice.
> 5. Connect with a group of migrant workers or farmers who grow your food. Visit their farm. Maybe even pick some veggies with them. Ask what they get paid.

HOLY WEEK — JESUS EATS WITH FRIENDS

HOLY WEEK

A Note on Holy Week

Since we chose to organize morning prayers in this book by calendar dates, there's no way to say for sure when Easter, Ascension, and Pentecost will be this year. If you have the internet or a printed calendar, it's pretty easy to look up the date of Easter. (Or, if you want to figure it out for yourself, Easter is the first Sunday after the coming of the first full moon after the vernal equinox.) However you find the date, this is an important one to note. As Paul said in the first century, our faith means little if Jesus isn't risen from the dead. If Advent is our New Year's and Pentecost is the church's birthday, Easter is our Memorial Day, Independence Day, and Presidents' Day all in one. This is when we remember Christ's sacrifice for our sins, celebrate his victory over the powers of evil, and honor him as our true Commander in Chief. It's a big deal, so we have a special set of prayers for Holy Week.

Holy Week begins with Jesus' inaugural parade on Palm Sunday and takes us through the drama of his last week in Jerusalem. In many ways, this is the week that teaches us our rhythm for every week in God's kingdom. It's often called "passion week," because it's full of suffering. (*Passio* is Latin for "suffering.") This is one of the harder things to learn about following Jesus: his way to real life isn't easy. In the end, it'll get you killed. And most of us don't want to die. (This is why we have to practice denying ourselves through forty days of Lent, fasting from stuff that we usually enjoy so we can learn to hunger and thirst for God's kingdom.)

The good news of the cross is that dying in Christ, we're raised to new life, a life that is stronger than death. As Martin Luther King Jr. taught us, unearned suffering is redemptive. Loving your enemies, giving to whoever asks, or turning the other cheek might get you killed, but it will also get you born again. And when we're born into God's life, we know a life that will never end. That's what Easter season is about.

Resurrection is such a big deal that we don't take just one day to celebrate it. Every Sunday is resurrection day. But we also set aside fifty days for the Easter season, putting aside our normal fasts and taking extra time to celebrate what God has done in our world. Forty days after Easter, we remember Jesus' ascension, when he returned to heaven and told the disciples to wait for the Holy Spirit, so they might become his body in the world. The ascension seals the deal for the disciples. (Up to that point, many of them had headed back to their familiar world of fishing and life as usual.) For us it is a reminder that resurrection isn't just a miracle that happened two thousand years ago. It's a way of life we practice. Pentecost ends the Easter season, reminding us that we don't practice resurrection by our own strength, but have the Holy Spirit's power among us as a community called church. Jesus' story is now our story. And the next chapter begins today.

✠ Palm Sunday

O Lord, let my soul rise up to meet you
as the day rises to meet the sun.

**Glory to the Father, to the Son, and to the Holy Spirit,
as it was in the beginning, is now, and will be forever. Amen.**

Come, let us sing to the L ORD : let us shout for joy to the Rock of our salvation.

Song "Sing and Rejoice"

Lest a rock cry out in my place : I lift my whole life in praise.

Psalm 118:25–29
Hosannah, L ORD, hosannah! : **L ORD, send us now success.**
Blessed is he who comes in the name of the Lord : **we bless you from the house of the L ORD.**
God is the L ORD; he has shone upon us : **form a procession with branches up to the horns of the altar.**
"You are my God, and I will thank you : **you are my God, and I will exalt you."**
Give thanks to the L ORD, for he is good : **his mercy endures for ever.**

Lest a rock cry out in my place : I lift my whole life in praise.

Zechariah 9:9–17   Luke 19:29–40

Lest a rock cry out in my place : I lift my whole life in praise.

Eighth-century martyr Andrew of Crete wrote, "Let us say to Christ: *Blessed is he who comes in the name of the Lord,* the king of Israel. Let us wave before him like palm branches the words inscribed above him on the cross. Let us show him honor, not with olive branches, but with the splendor of merciful deeds to one another. Let us spread the thoughts and desires of our hearts under his feet like garments, so that he may draw the whole of our being into himself and place the whole of his in us."

Prayers for Others

Our Father

Jesus of Nazareth, King of the Jews, may your reign become real through the works of our hands and your love become alive in our hearts. Amen.

**May the peace of the Lord Christ go with you : wherever he may send you;
may he guide you through the wilderness : protect you through the storm;
may he bring you home rejoicing : at the wonders he has shown you;
may he bring you home rejoicing : once again into our doors.**

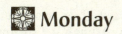 **Monday**

O Lord, let my soul rise up to meet you
as the day rises to meet the sun.

**Glory to the Father, to the Son, and to the Holy Spirit,
as it was in the beginning, is now, and will be forever. Amen.**

Come, let us sing to the Lord : let us shout for joy to the Rock of our salvation.

Song "We Are Marching in the Light of God"

With you, O Lord, is the well of life : and in your light we see light.

Psalm 36:5–10
Your love, O Lord, reaches to the heavens : **and your faithfulness to the clouds.**
Your righteousness is like the strong mountains, your justice like the great deep : **you save both man and beast, O Lord.**
How priceless is your love, O God! : **your people take refuge under the shadow of your wings.**
They feast upon the abundance of your house : **you give them drink from the river of your delights.**
For with you is the well of life : **and in your light we see light.**
Continue your loving-kindness to those who know you : **and your favor to those who are true of heart.**

With you, O Lord, is the well of life : and in your light we see light.

Isaiah 42:1–9   Mark 14:3–9

With you, O Lord, is the well of life : and in your light we see light.

Contemporary Ugandan theologian Emmanuel Katongole has written, "Mary represents the 'rebel consciousness' that is essential to Jesus' gospel. Wherever the gospel is preached, we must remember that its good news will make you crazy. Jesus will put you at odds with the economic and political systems of our world. This gospel will force you to act, interrupting the world as it is in ways that make even pious people indignant."

Prayers for Others

Our Father

While we sat in darkness, Lord Jesus Christ, you interrupted us with your life. Make us, your people, a holy interruption so that by your Spirit's power we may live as a light to the nations, even as we stumble through this world's dark night. Amen.

May the peace of the Lord Christ go with you : wherever he may send you;
may he guide you through the wilderness : protect you through the storm;
may he bring you home rejoicing : at the wonders he has shown you;
may he bring you home rejoicing : once again into our doors.

✸ Tuesday

O Lord, let my soul rise up to meet you
as the day rises to meet the sun.

**Glory to the Father, to the Son, and to the Holy Spirit,
as it was in the beginning, is now, and will be forever. Amen.**

Come, let us bow down and bend the knee : let us kneel before the LORD our Maker.

Song "Lamb of God"

Save us, Lord, but not us alone : redeem your whole creation.

Psalm 71:1–3, 9–12
In you, O LORD, have I taken refuge : **let me never be ashamed.**
In your righteousness, deliver me and set me free : **incline your ear to me and save me.**
Be my strong rock, a castle to keep me safe : **you are my crag and my stronghold.**
Do not cast me off in my old age : **forsake me not when my strength fails.**
For my enemies are talking against me : **and those who lie in wait for my life take counsel together.**
They say, "God has forsaken him; go after him and seize him : **because there is none who will save."**
O God, be not far from me : **come quickly to help me, O my God.**

Save us, Lord, but not us alone : redeem your whole creation.

Isaiah 49:1–6   Mark 11:15–19

Save us, Lord, but not us alone : redeem your whole creation.

Fourteenth-century anchorite Julian of Norwich wrote, "I often wondered why, through the great prescient wisdom of God, the beginning of sin was not prevented. For then it seemed to me that would have been well. I mourned and I sorrowed on this account, unreasonably, lacking discretion. But Jesus answered me with these words and said: Sin is necessary, but all will be well, and all will be well, and every kind of thing will be well."

Prayers for Others

Our Father

Savior of the world, save us from our sin, our sadness, and our self-deception. Give us courage to live in a world we cannot fix with hope that it has already been redeemed. Amen.

May the peace of the Lord Christ go with you : wherever he may send you;
may he guide you through the wilderness : protect you through the storm;
may he bring you home rejoicing : at the wonders he has shown you;
may he bring you home rejoicing : once again into our doors.

Wednesday

O Lord, let my soul rise up to meet you
as the day rises to meet the sun.

Glory to the Father, to the Son, and to the Holy Spirit,
as it was in the beginning, is now, and will be forever. Amen.

Come, let us bow down and bend the knee : let us kneel before the LORD our Maker.

Song "O Lord, Have Mercy"

In your great mercy, O God : answer me with your unfailing help.

Psalm 69:8–15
Surely, for your sake have I suffered reproach : and shame has covered my face.
I have become a stranger to my own kindred : an alien to my mother's children.
Zeal for your house has eaten me up : the scorn of those who scorn you has fallen upon me.
I humbled myself with fasting : but that was turned to my reproach.
I put on sackcloth also : and became a byword among them.
Those who sit at the gate murmur against me : and the drunkards make songs about me.
But as for me, this is my prayer to you : at the time you have set, O LORD:
"In your great mercy, O God : answer me with your unfailing help."

In your great mercy, O God : answer me with your unfailing help.

Isaiah 50:4–9a   Matthew 26:1–5, 14–25

In your great mercy, O God : answer me with your unfailing help.

Reflecting on her beating in the Winona County Jail, civil rights leader Fannie Lou Hamer said, "It wouldn't solve any problem for me to hate whites just because they hate me. Oh, there's so much hate, only God has kept the Negro sane."

Prayers for Others

Our Father

Merciful Lord, you revealed your glory by humbly serving the one who would betray you. Shower us with your mercy, Lord, and grow us up to be merciful. Amen.

May the peace of the Lord Christ go with you : wherever he may send you; may he guide you through the wilderness : protect you through the storm; may he bring you home rejoicing : at the wonders he has shown you; may he bring you home rejoicing : once again into our doors.

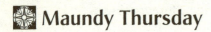 **Maundy Thursday**

O Lord, let my soul rise up to meet you
as the day rises to meet the sun.

Glory to the Father, to the Son, and to the Holy Spirit, as it was in the beginning, is now, and will be forever. Amen.

Come, let us bow down and bend the knee : let us kneel before the Lord our Maker.

Song "Guide My Feet"

Will you let me be your servant? : let me be as Christ to you?

Psalm 78:14–17
He led them with a cloud by day : **and all the night through with a glow of fire.**
He split the hard rocks in the wilderness : **and gave them drink as from the great deep.**
He brought streams out of the cliff : **and the waters gushed out like rivers.**
But they went on sinning against him : **rebelling in the desert against the Most High.**

Will you let me be your servant? : let me be as Christ to you?

Exodus 12:1–14a   John 13:1–15

Will you let me be your servant? : let me be as Christ to you?

Jean Vanier, founder of the L'Arche communities, has written, "To wash the feet of a brother or sister in Christ, to allow someone to wash our feet, is a sign that together we want to follow Jesus, to take the downward path, to find Jesus' presence in the poor and the weak. Is it not a sign that we too want to live a heart-to-heart relationship with others, to meet them as a person and a friend, and to live in communion with them? Is it not a sign that we yearn to be men and women of forgiveness, to be healed and cleansed and to heal and cleanse others and thus to live more fully in communion with Jesus?"

Prayers for Others

Our Father

Lord Jesus Christ, you knelt to wash from our feet the dirt out of which you made us. Teach us to humbly serve one another so that the world may know we are your disciples. Amen.

May the peace of the Lord Christ go with you : wherever he may send you; may he guide you through the wilderness : protect you through the storm; may he bring you home rejoicing : at the wonders he has shown you; may he bring you home rejoicing : once again into our doors.

> **Taking Liturgy to the Streets**
>
> Liturgy and worship were never meant to be confined to the cathedrals and sanctuaries. Liturgy at its best can be performed like a circus or theater, making the gospel visible as a witness to the world around us. Consider some services that happened in Philadelphia around Good Friday, just before Easter.
>
> Hundreds of Christians gathered on Good Friday to remember Jesus, and also to remember Jesus disguised as the "least of these," those who continue to be tortured, spit on, slapped, insulted, misunderstood, those who ache, bleed, cry, love, forgive, and ask God, "Have you forsaken me?" The morning started with a slow meditative reading of the passion narrative from the gospel. We sat still, praying that we would have the courage to follow the way of the cross in a world of the sword. Then, as many Christians do throughout the world, we spent Good Friday remembering the "stations of the cross," the various stages of Christ's execution.
>
> But we didn't keep things inside the walls of cathedrals; we took to the streets. At one gathering, hundreds of us assembled outside of a gun store notorious for selling weapons that are later traced to violent crimes. On the makeshift stage outside the gun shop, alongside a Pentecostal dance team and a host of collared clergy from all sorts of denominations, there was a giant gun next to a cross and a coffin. After some songs, testimonies, and preaching, we read aloud the same Scripture we had read in the morning, only this time what stood out was how the heartbroken women went to the tomb with all the perfumes and spices and found no body there. We heard from women who had lost their children from gunshots on the streets of Philadelphia, who wept and prayed that tomorrow "the casket and

tomb would be empty." One of them lost her eighteen-year-old Harvard-bound son to a stray bullet outside a movie theater. We could almost taste the salt in the tears of those childless mothers as they wept, like Mary. (This gun shop was closed down and had its license revoked. Prayer also works!)

A few miles away, another group of folks gathered on that same Good Friday outside the headquarters of Lockheed Martin, the world's largest arms contractor. We walked the stations of the cross, one by one, remembering Jesus. And we heard stories of suffering, stories of God's little ones groaning in the midst of killing, displacement, and torture. We heard statistics about weapons manufacturers like the one on whose property we were standing. And again we read the passion narrative. This time as we listened to the words, it seemed that we could almost hear the wailing of women in Iraq and Afghanistan and Palestine, women like Mary.

As we approached the final station of the cross, about twenty of us crossed onto the property at Lockheed Martin. We bowed on our knees and began to pray the Lord's Prayer, but were interrupted by police officers, who placed us under arrest. As we stepped into the police van, there was a solemn sense of peace. It was the right place to be. It was a magnificent thing to hear folks honk as they went by. One of the police officers who had arrested even us thanked us for our witness and decried the evils of violence and war.

This is what we mean by taking liturgy to the streets. There are hosts of creative liturgical witnesses that happen throughout the year, and all over the world. Consider joining with others and taking liturgy to the streets in your city or town this year.

✸ Good Friday

O Lord, let my soul rise up to meet you
as the day rises to meet the sun.

**Glory to the Father, to the Son, and to the Holy Spirit,
as it was in the beginning, is now, and will be forever. Amen.**

Come, let us bow down and bend the knee : let us kneel before the LORD our Maker.

Song "Were You There?"

He who hung the earth upon the waters : today he is hung upon the cross.

Psalm 22:1–2, 9–11
My God, my God, why have you forsaken me? : **and are so far from my cry and from the words of my distress?**
O my God, I cry in the daytime, but you do not answer : **by night as well, but I find no rest.**

Yet you are he who took me out of the womb : **and kept me safe upon my mother's breast.**
I have been entrusted to you ever since I was born : **you were my God when I was still in my mother's womb.**
Be not far from me, for trouble is near : **and there is none to help.**

He who hung the earth upon the waters : today he is hung upon the cross.

Genesis 22:1–18   John 19:1–37

He who hung the earth upon the waters : today he is hung upon the cross.

John Chrysostom, a fourth-century bishop and preacher in Constantinople, asked, "Do you see how the devil is defeated by the very weapons of his prior victory? The devil had vanquished Adam by means of a tree. Christ vanquished the devil by means of the tree of the Cross. The tree sent Adam to hell. The tree of the Cross brought him back from there. The tree revealed Adam in his weakness, laying prostrate, naked and low. The tree of the Cross manifested to all the world the victorious Christ, naked and nailed on high. Adam's death sentence passed on to all who came after him. Christ's death gave life to all his children."

Prayers for Others

Our Father

While we were still your enemies, Lord Jesus Christ, you suffered and died for us, winning the victory over death for our sakes. Give us grace to lift you up as we follow the way of your cross so that all people may be drawn unto you. Amen.

**May the peace of the Lord Christ go with you : wherever he may send you;
may he guide you through the wilderness : protect you through the storm;
may he bring you home rejoicing : at the wonders he has shown you;
may he bring you home rejoicing : once again into our doors.**

✤ Holy Saturday

O Lord, let my soul rise up to meet you
as the day rises to meet the sun.

**Glory to the Father, to the Son, and to the Holy Spirit,
as it was in the beginning, is now, and will be forever. Amen.**

Come, let us bow down and bend the knee : let us kneel before the LORD our Maker.

Silence

Listen, Lord, to the cries of your poor : break hell's hold, fling wide heaven's door.

Psalm 31:1–5
In you, O Lord, have I taken refuge; let me never be put to shame : **deliver me in your righteousness.**
Incline your ear to me : **make haste to deliver me.**
Be my strong rock, a castle to keep me safe, for you are my crag and my stronghold : **for the sake of your name, lead me and guide me.**
Take me out of the net that they have secretly set for me : **for you are my tower of strength.**
Into your hands I commend my spirit : **for you have redeemed me, O Lord, O God of truth.**

Listen, Lord, to the cries of your poor : break hell's hold, fling wide heaven's door.

Job 14:1–14   John 19:38–42

Listen, Lord, to the cries of your poor : break hell's hold, fling wide heaven's door.

These words are from an ancient homily for Holy Saturday: "Something strange is happening — there is a great silence on earth today, a great silence and stillness. The whole earth keeps silence because the King is asleep. The earth trembled and is still because God has fallen asleep in the flesh and he has raised up all who have slept ever since the world began. God has died in the flesh and hell trembles with fear. He has gone to search for our first parents, as for lost sheep. Greatly desiring to visit those who live in darkness and in the shadow of death, he has gone to free from sorrow the captives Adam and Eve, he who is both God and the son of Eve. The Lord approached them bearing the cross, the weapon that had won him the victory. At the sight of him, Adam, the first man he had created, struck his breast in terror and cried out to everyone: 'My Lord be with you all.' Christ answered him: 'And with your spirit.' He took him by the hand and raised him up, saying: 'Awake, O sleeper, and rise from the dead, and Christ will give you light.' "

Prayers for Others

Our Father

As you hovered over the darkness that covered the earth at the beginning of time, may your Spirit move among us in the silence of this day, preparing us for new life. Amen.

May the peace of the Lord Christ go with you : wherever he may send you;
may he guide you through the wilderness : protect you through the storm;
may he bring you home rejoicing : at the wonders he has shown you;
may he bring you home rejoicing : once again into our doors.

✺ Easter Sunday

O Lord, let my soul rise up to meet you
as the day rises to meet the sun.

**Glory to the Father, to the Son, and to the Holy Spirit,
as it was in the beginning, is now, and will be forever. Amen.**

Come, let us sing to the LORD : let us shout for joy to the Rock of our salvation.

Song "Vamos Todos al Banquete"

Just when I thought I was lost : my dungeon shook and the chains fell off.

Psalm 114
Hallelujah! When Israel came out of Egypt : **the house of Jacob from a people of strange speech,**
Judah became God's sanctuary : **and Israel his dominion.**
The sea beheld it and fled : **Jordan turned and went back.**
The mountains skipped like rams : **and the little hills like young sheep.**
What ailed you, O sea, that you fled? : **O Jordan, that you turned back?**
you mountains, that you skipped like rams? : **you little hills like young sheep?**
Tremble, O earth, at the presence of the Lord : **at the presence of the God of Jacob,**
who turned the hard rock into a pool of water : **and flint-stone into a flowing spring.**

Just when I thought I was lost : my dungeon shook and the chains fell off.

Exodus 14:10–15:1   Matthew 28:1–10

Just when I thought I was lost : my dungeon shook and the chains fell off.

Clarence Jordan, co-founder of Koinonia Farm, wrote, "The resurrection of Jesus was simply God's unwillingness to take our 'no' for an answer. He raised Jesus, not as an invitation to us to come to heaven when we die, but as a declaration that he himself has now established permanent, eternal residence here on earth. He is standing beside us, strengthening us in this life. The good news of the resurrection of Jesus is not that we shall die and go home to be with him, but that he has risen and comes home with us, bringing all his hungry, naked, thirsty, sick prisoner brothers with him."

Prayers for Others

Our Father

Lord, you have risen! We praise you. We worship you. We give you thanks. Alleluia.

**May the peace of the Lord Christ go with you : wherever he may send you;
may he guide you through the wilderness : protect you through the storm;
may he bring you home rejoicing : at the wonders he has shown you;
may he bring you home rejoicing : once again into our doors.**

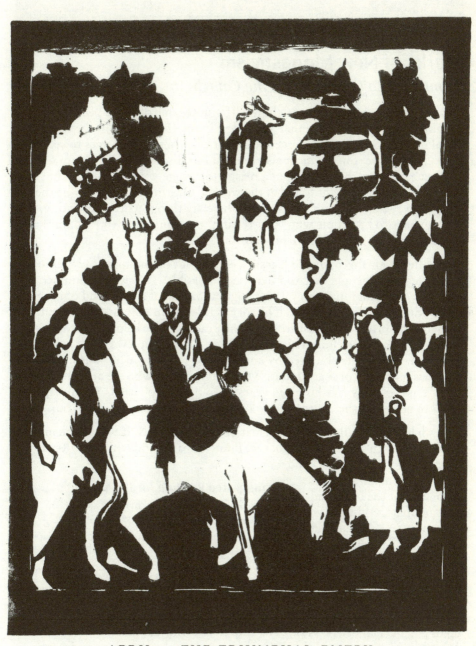

APRIL — THE TRIUMPHAL ENTRY

APRIL

Marks of New Monasticism
Submission to Christ's Body, the Church

Discontentment is a gift to the church. If you are one of those people who has the ability to see the things that are wrong in the church and in the world, you should thank God for that perception. Not everyone has the eyes to see, or to notice, or to care. But we must also see that our discontentment is not a reason to disengage from the church but a reason to engage with it. As Gandhi said, "Be the change you want to see in the world." Our invitation is to "be the change" we want to see in the church. There are things worth protesting, but we also have to be people who "pro-testify," proclaiming the kingdom that we're for, not just the evils we're against.

Jesus offered an alternative to Caesar's empire not by mounting a rebellion but by teaching people that another way is possible. That way is summed up well in Jesus' triumphal entry, the inaugural parade of a new kind of king for a new kind of kingdom. Church history is filled with holy dissenters, rabble-rousers, and prophets — disturbers of the peace who've helped to show us a better way. As some church historians have pointed out, every few hundred years the church gets cluttered by and infected with the materialism and militarism of the world around it. We begin to forget who we are. One bishop said, "And so every five hundred years or so the church needs a rummage sale," to get rid of the clutter and to remember the true treasures of our faith.

Church history is filled with reformations and renewals. It was in the middle of Italy's wealth and crusades that St. Francis heard God whisper, "Repair my church which is in ruins," and he began to repair the ruins. At one point the pope had a vision that the church was beginning to crumble, but the corner was being held up by Francis and the little youth movement in Assisi. The call to repair the church is a call we continue to hear from God, and a movement we are invited to participate in.

> **Suggested Reading for the Month**
> *The Great Emergence* by Phyllis Tickle
> *Beyond Smells and Bells* by Mark Galli
> *For the Life of the World* by Alexander Schmemann

We shouldn't be too surprised that the church is a mess. After all, it's made up of people. Augustine said, "The church is a whore, but she's our mother." The early Christians said that if we do not accept the church as our mother, we cannot call God our Father. We are not to leave her, but we are to work for her healing, as we would with a dysfunctional parent. Our work is not "para-church" but "pro-church." The church needs our discontent, and we need the rest of the body of Christ. One pastor said it like this: "The church is sort of like Noah's ark. It's a stinky mess inside, but if you get out, you'll drown."

April 1

O Lord, let my soul rise up to meet you
as the day rises to meet the sun.

Glory to the Father, and to the Son, and to the Holy Spirit,
as it was in the beginning, is now, and will be forever. Amen.

Come, let us sing to the LORD : let us shout for joy to the Rock of our salvation.

Song "We Are Marching in the Light of God"

Our delight is in the law of love : may we walk in Christ's light day and night.

Psalm 1:1–3, 6
Happy are they who have not walked in the counsel of the wicked : **nor lingered in the way of sinners, nor sat in the seats of the scornful!**
Their delight is in the law of the LORD : **and they meditate on his law day and night.**
They are like trees planted by streams of water, bearing fruit in due season, with leaves that do not wither : **everything they do shall prosper.**
For the LORD knows the way of the righteous : **but the way of the wicked is doomed.**

Our delight is in the law of love : may we walk in Christ's light day and night.

Exodus 14:5–22   1 John 1:1–10

Our delight is in the law of love : may we walk in Christ's light day and night.

American humorist Garrison Keillor has said, "Some people think it is difficult to be a Christian and to laugh, but I think it's the other way around. God writes a lot of comedy, it's just that he has so many bad actors."

Prayers for Others

Our Father

You who led Israel through the waters, plant us by streams of living water. Root us in your love and grow us up to bear the fruit of your Spirit: love, joy, peace, patience, kindness, goodness, faithfulness, gentleness, and self-control. Amen.

May the peace of the Lord Christ go with you : wherever he may send you;
may he guide you through the wilderness : protect you through the storm;
may he bring you home rejoicing : at the wonders he has shown you;
may he bring you home rejoicing : once again into our doors.

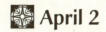 **April 2**

O Lord, let my soul rise up to meet you
as the day rises to meet the sun.

**Glory to the Father, and to the Son, and to the Holy Spirit,
as it was in the beginning, is now, and will be forever. Amen.**

Come, let us sing to the Lord: let us shout for joy to the Rock of our salvation.

Song "Be Thou My Vision"

Awake, O sleeper, rise from the dead : and Christ will shine on you.

Psalm 9:1–3, 9–10
I will give thanks to you, O Lord, with my whole heart : **I will tell of all your marvelous works.**
I will be glad and rejoice in you : **I will sing to your name, O Most High.**
When my enemies are driven back : **they will stumble and perish at your presence.**
The Lord will be a refuge for the oppressed : **a refuge in time of trouble.**
Those who know your name will put their trust in you : **for you never forsake those who seek you, O Lord.**

Awake, O sleeper, rise from the dead : and Christ will shine on you.

Exodus 14:21–31   1 John 2:1–11

Awake, O sleeper, rise from the dead : and Christ will shine on you.

Fourth-century bishop Athanasius of Alexandria wrote, "That mystery the Jews traduce, the Greeks deride, but we adore. For it is a fact that the more unbelievers pour scorn on him, so much the more does he makes his Godhead evident. Thus by what seems his utter poverty and weakness on the cross he overturns the pomp and parade of idols, and quietly and hiddenly wins over the mockers and unbelievers to recognize him as God."

Prayers for Others

Our Father

God of power and might, you raised Jesus from the dead after you had raised Israel out of Egypt. As we arise in the light of this new day, raise us to live by your power the life that only you can give.

**May the peace of the Lord Christ go with you : wherever he may send you;
may he guide you through the wilderness : protect you through the storm;
may he bring you home rejoicing : at the wonders he has shown you;
may he bring you home rejoicing : once again into our doors.**

Eucharist and Communion

Eucharist is from the Greek *eucharistein*, meaning "thanksgiving."

Communion is from the Latin, meaning "union with."

One of the church's peculiar practices is communion, also called the Lord's Supper or the Eucharist. The early Christians were accused of being cannibals because they talked of eating flesh and drinking blood together. It was a way of remembering, as Christ had asked them to remember him in this way.

"Re-member-ing" has to do with becoming something new, the body of Christ, in which we lose ourselves in something bigger than ourselves; we are re-membered into a new body.

Sadly, and ironically, the sharing of the Eucharist or communion table is both the most unifying and the most divisive practice in the Christian church. After all, sacrament is a "mystery," so we don't want to try to systematically analyze the practice of Holy Communion. What we want to do is invite you into the deepest part of this mystery. We are what we eat.

When we take the wine and bread and eat it, we are digesting Christ—or an even better way of understanding might be that we are made into a new creation as we are digested into the body of Christ. Performing the Eucharist with a community makes us into the body of Christ. As often as Christians take the common elements of bread and wine, they re-member themselves into Jesus. In the Eucharist, we don't just remember Jesus in general; we remember his suffering. The bread is a *broken* body, and the wine is poured like *shed* blood. Both grain and grapes have to be crushed and broken to become something new together. If you are what you eat, the Eucharist is indeed the act of uniting yourself with the one who lovingly suffered at the hands of his enemies. If you ritually cross yourself (like Catholics do), you are stamping upon yourself the sign of the cross; you are identifying with Jesus' suffering love. Those who ingest and become one with the suffering body of Christ all together become the body of Christ.

We pray as we take the elements that the blood of Jesus would run through our veins and that we would be digested into the body of Christ. The early church used to say, "God became man that we might become God." Certainly none of us is God alone, but all of us are God's body together. God has chosen to have no hands but ours, no feet but ours. Maybe this is the greatest sacrament or mystery of our faith—that these broken pieces become one body.

April 3

O Lord, let my soul rise up to meet you
as the day rises to meet the sun.

**Glory to the Father, and to the Son, and to the Holy Spirit,
as it was in the beginning, is now, and will be forever. Amen.**

Come, let us sing to the Lord : let us shout for joy to the Rock of our salvation.

Song "O Mary, Don't You Weep"

The Lord is my strength and my song : you have become my salvation.

Psalm 16:5–9
O Lord, you are my portion and my cup : **it is you who uphold my lot.**
My boundaries enclose a pleasant land : **indeed, I have a goodly heritage.**
I will bless the Lord who gives me counsel : **my heart teaches me, night after night.**
I have set the Lord always before me : **because he is at my right hand I shall not fall.**
My heart, therefore, is glad, and my spirit rejoices : **my body also shall rest in hope.**

The Lord is my strength and my song : you have become my salvation.

Exodus 15:1–21   1 John 2:12–17

The Lord is my strength and my song : you have become my salvation.

A reading from Paul's letter to the Colossians: "The Son is the image of the invisible God, the firstborn over all creation. For in him all things were created: things in heaven and on earth, visible and invisible, whether thrones or powers or rulers or authorities; all things have been created through him and for him. He is before all things, and in him all things hold together. And he is the head of the body, the church; he is the beginning and the firstborn from among the dead, so that in everything he might have the supremacy. For God was pleased to have all his fullness dwell in him, and through him to reconcile to himself all things, whether things on earth or things in heaven, by making peace through his blood, shed on the cross."

Prayers for Others

Our Father

We thank you, Lord Jesus, that you have risen from the dead and won victory over the powers to save us from our sin. We praise you for our salvation, and ask for grace to praise you with our whole lives. Amen.

**May the peace of the Lord Christ go with you : wherever he may send you;
may he guide you through the wilderness : protect you through the storm;
may he bring you home rejoicing : at the wonders he has shown you;
may he bring you home rejoicing : once again into our doors.**

✳ April 4

Martin Luther King Jr. (1929–1968)

Martin Luther King Jr. was a black American preacher who became a civil rights leader, teaching nonviolent resistance to evil, and opposing racism and segregation. Working out of his home in the church, King organized a diverse coalition of people to combat the evils of racism, poverty, and militarism. In many ways he was a flawed hero, but he was a committed man who died for his faith and for the freedom of his people. It was while he was advocating for sanitation workers that he was killed in Memphis, Tennessee, on April 4, 1968.

O Lord, let my soul rise up to meet you
as the day rises to meet the sun.

**Glory to the Father, and to the Son, and to the Holy Spirit,
as it was in the beginning, is now, and will be forever. Amen.**

Come, let us bow down and bend the knee : let us kneel before the Lord our Maker.

Song "I Will Trust in the Lord"

In our lives this day, O Lord : may we love you among the least.

Psalm 20:1–4, 6–7
May the Lord answer you in the day of trouble : **the name of the God of Jacob defend you;**
send you help from his holy place : **and strengthen you out of Zion;**
remember all your offerings : **and accept your burnt sacrifice;**
grant you your heart's desire : **and prosper all your plans.**
Now I know that the Lord gives victory to his anointed : **he will answer him out of his holy heaven, with the victorious strength of his right hand.**
Some put their trust in chariots and some in horses : **but we will call upon the name of the Lord our God.**

In our lives this day, O Lord : may we love you among the least.

Exodus 15:22–16:10   1 John 2:18–29

In our lives this day, O Lord : may we love you among the least.

Martin Luther King Jr. reflected in a sermon, "Every now and then I think about my own death, and I think about my own funeral. Every now and then I ask myself, 'What is it that I want said?' I'd like somebody to mention that day, that Martin Luther King Jr. tried to give his life serving others. I'd like for somebody to say that day, that Martin Luther King Jr. tried to love somebody. I want you to say that day, that I tried to be right on the war question. I want you to be able to say that day, that I did try to feed the hungry. And I want you to be able to say that day, that I did try, in my life, to clothe those who were naked. I want you to say, on that day, that I did try, in my life, to visit those who were in prison. I want you to say that I tried to love and serve humanity."

Prayers for Others

Our Father

We give thanks today for our brother Martin and for the ways you spoke through him to expose the poverty of our wealth, the insecurity of our war-making, and the contradictions of our racism. Give us grace to love you among the least today, O Lord, and to live the good news Martin preached in his life and in his death. Amen.

**May the peace of the Lord Christ go with you : wherever he may send you;
may he guide you through the wilderness : protect you through the storm;
may he bring you home rejoicing : at the wonders he has shown you;
may he bring you home rejoicing : once again into our doors.**

April 5

O Lord, let my soul rise up to meet you
as the day rises to meet the sun.

**Glory to the Father, and to the Son, and to the Holy Spirit,
as it was in the beginning, is now, and will be forever. Amen.**

Come, let us sing to the LORD : let us shout for joy to the Rock of our salvation.

Song "Praise to the Lord, the Almighty"

Who is the King of glory? : The Lord of hosts is King!

Psalm 24:1–6
The earth is the LORD's and all that is in it : **the world and all who dwell therein.**
For it is he who founded it upon the seas : **and made it firm upon the rivers of the deep.**
"Who can ascend the hill of the LORD? : **and who can stand in his holy place?"**
"Those who have clean hands and a pure heart : **who have not pledged themselves to falsehood, nor sworn by what is a fraud.**
They shall receive a blessing from the LORD : **and a just reward from the God of their salvation."**

Such is the generation of those who seek him : **of those who seek your face, O God of Jacob.**

Who is the King of glory? : The Lord of hosts is King!

Exodus 16:10–21   1 John 3:1–10

Who is the King of glory? : The Lord of hosts is King!

Oscar Romero, a martyr of the church's struggle in El Salvador, wrote, "I do not tire of telling everyone, especially young people who long for their people's liberation, that I admire their social and political sensitivity, but it saddens me when they waste it by going on ways that are false. Let us, too, all take notice that the great leader of our liberation is the Lord's Anointed One, who comes to announce good news to the poor, to give freedom to the captives, to give news of the missing, to give joy to so many homes in mourning, so that society may be renewed as in the sabbatical years of Israel."

Prayers for Others

Our Father

Jesus, you are the King of Glory and the King of Creation. Teach us to recognize the ways of your kingdom that we might participate as faithful and devout residents in the space between a broken world and the coming kingdom of God. Amen.

May the peace of the Lord Christ go with you : wherever he may send you; may he guide you through the wilderness : protect you through the storm; may he bring you home rejoicing : at the wonders he has shown you; may he bring you home rejoicing : once again into our doors.

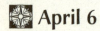

April 6

O Lord, let my soul rise up to meet you
as the day rises to meet the sun.

Glory to the Father, and to the Son, and to the Holy Spirit,
as it was in the beginning, is now, and will be forever. Amen.

Come, let us sing to the LORD : let us shout for joy to the Rock of our salvation.

Song "Ubi Caritas"

When we love and learn to share : when we love, Christ is there.

Psalm 30:1–3, 12–13
I will exalt you, O LORD, because you have lifted me up : **and have not let my enemies triumph over me.**
O LORD my God, I cried out to you : **and you restored me to health.**
You brought me up, O LORD, from the dead : **you restored my life as I was going down to the grave.**
You have turned my wailing into dancing : **you have put off my sack-cloth and clothed me with joy.**
Therefore my heart sings to you without ceasing : **O LORD my God, I will give you thanks for ever.**

When we love and learn to share : when we love, Christ is there.

Exodus 16:22–36   1 John 3:11–18

When we love and learn to share : when we love, Christ is there.

Elizabeth of the Trinity, a nineteenth-century Carmelite nun, said, "Let us ask God to make us true in our love, to make us sacrificial beings, for it seems to me that sacrifice is only love put into action."

Prayers for Others

Our Father

God of love, forgive us when we make a mockery of love by only speaking of love. Burden us with your embodied love so that our first response may be to love with our hands and feet. May our love take on the flesh you so humbly bore. Amen.

May the peace of the Lord Christ go with you : wherever he may send you; may he guide you through the wilderness : protect you through the storm; may he bring you home rejoicing : at the wonders he has shown you; may he bring you home rejoicing : once again into our doors.

✹ April 7

On April 7, 1994, a civil war broke out in Rwanda as Hutu extremists began brutally killing Tutsis and moderate Hutus. Over the next one hundred days, nearly a million people were killed in the worst occurrence of genocide since the Holocaust. An estimated 75 percent of the Tutsis living in Rwanda were murdered.

O Lord, let my soul rise up to meet you
as the day rises to meet the sun.

Glory to the Father, and to the Son, and to the Holy Spirit,
as it was in the beginning, is now, and will be forever. Amen.

Come, let us bow down and bend the knee : let us kneel before the LORD our Maker.

Song "We Shall Overcome"

Give us water from the Rock, O Lord : and sustain us in the struggle for justice.

Psalm 35:1, 24–28
Fight those who fight me, O LORD : **attack those who are attacking me.**
Give me justice, O LORD my God, according to your righteousness : **do not let them triumph over me.**
Do not let them say in their hearts, "Aha! just what we want!" : **Do not let them say, "We have swallowed him up."**
Let all who rejoice at my ruin be ashamed and disgraced : **let those who boast against me be clothed with dismay and shame.**
Let those who favor my cause sing out with joy and be glad : **let them say always, "Great is the LORD, who desires the prosperity of his servant."**
And my tongue shall be talking of your righteousness : **and of your praise all the day long.**

Give us water from the Rock, O Lord : and sustain us in the struggle for justice.

Exodus 17:1–16   1 John 3:19–4:6

Give us water from the Rock, O Lord : and sustain us in the struggle for justice.

When Cardinal Roger Etchegary visited Rwanda on behalf of the pope in 1994, he asked the assembled church leaders, "Are you saying that the blood of tribalism is deeper than the waters of baptism?" One leader answered, "Yes, it is."

Prayers for Others

Our Father

LORD God, King of the Universe, we lift up our hands to you and ask you to help us bear the burden of injustice. Grant us a discerning spirit to follow your path to justice. Equip us with your patience and your grace so that as we walk with those who suffer, we might strengthen and uphold one another. Amen.

May the peace of the Lord Christ go with you : wherever he may send you;
may he guide you through the wilderness : protect you through the storm;
may he bring you home rejoicing : at the wonders he has shown you;
may he bring you home rejoicing : once again into our doors.

✸ April 8

O Lord, let my soul rise up to meet you
as the day rises to meet the sun.

**Glory to the Father, and to the Son, and to the Holy Spirit,
as it was in the beginning, is now, and will be forever. Amen.**

Come, let us bow down and bend the knee : let us kneel before the LORD our Maker.

Song "I Will Trust in the Lord"

I do not think that I shall fear you : when I see you face to face.

Psalm 38:1–2, 14–15, 21–22
O LORD, do not rebuke me in your anger : **do not punish me in your wrath.**
For your arrows have already pierced me : **and your hand presses hard upon me.**
I have become like one who does not hear : **and from whose mouth comes no defense.**
For in you, O LORD, have I fixed my hope : **you will answer me, O Lord my God.**
O LORD, do not forsake me : **be not far from me, O my God.**
Make haste to help me : **O Lord of my salvation.**

I do not think that I shall fear you : when I see you face to face.

Exodus 18:1–12   1 John 4:7–21

I do not think that I shall fear you : when I see you face to face.

Jack Bernard, a co-founder of the Church of the Sojourners in San Francisco, wrote, "The key element in beginning to learn to embody the love of God is not heroic faith and determination. It has to do with whether or not we can take hold of the love of God as a power that includes us within it. The difference is between seeing life from the inside of God versus seeing it from within my own sensibilities and capacities. From inside the love of God, suffering becomes not only bearable, but a privilege of participating with Christ in his love for the world. This cannot be rationally explained or justified, but it is the fruit of a life trustingly lived in and for God who is all love."

Prayers for Others

Our Father

Holy Spirit, you dwell within us and you teach us perfect love, which drives out all fear. Give us a spirit of courage, and make us bold enough to love one another without fear. Enable us to see that perfect love calls us to persevere in suffering and to trust beyond what is visible. Amen.

**May the peace of the Lord Christ go with you : wherever he may send you;
may he guide you through the wilderness : protect you through the storm;
may he bring you home rejoicing : at the wonders he has shown you;
may he bring you home rejoicing : once again into our doors.**

April 9

Dietrich Bonhoeffer (1906–1945)
Dietrich Bonhoeffer studied theology in Germany and the United States and pastored a church in London before returning to Germany as a leader of the Confessing Church, which tried to resist Adolf Hitler. Though Bonhoeffer returned to Germany a pacifist, he became a resistance worker and was part of a failed plot to assassinate Hitler. But it was his evasion of the call-up for military service that led to his arrest. Perhaps he died because of his political convictions and not as a Christian martyr, but he would have said that there is no distinction between the two.

O Lord, let my soul rise up to meet you
as the day rises to meet the sun.

**Glory to the Father, and to the Son, and to the Holy Spirit,
as it was in the beginning, is now, and will be forever. Amen.**

Come, let us bow down and bend the knee : let us kneel before the LORD our Maker.

Song "Swing Low, Sweet Chariot"

Freedom, how long have we sought you : dying, we now may behold you.

Psalm 44:1–2, 9–10, 22, 25–26
We have heard with our ears, O God, our forefathers have told us : **the deeds you did in their days, in the days of old.**
How with your hand you drove the peoples out and planted our forefathers in the land : **how you destroyed nations and made your people flourish.**
Nevertheless, you have rejected and humbled us : **and do not go forth with our armies.**

You have made us fall back before our adversary : **and our enemies have plundered us.**
Indeed, for your sake we are killed all the day long : **we are accounted as sheep for the slaughter.**
We sink down into the dust : **our body cleaves to the ground.**
Rise up, and help us : **and save us, for the sake of your steadfast love.**

Freedom, how long have we sought you : dying, we now may behold you.

Exodus 18:13–27   1 John 5:1–12

Freedom, how long have we sought you : dying, we now may behold you.

Dietrich Bonhoeffer wrote, "Jesus Christ lived in the midst of his enemies. At the end, all of his disciples deserted him. On the cross he was utterly alone, surrounded by evildoers and mockers. For this cause he had come, to bring peace to the enemies of God. So the Christian, too, belongs not in the seclusion of a cloistered life, but in the thick of foes."

Prayers for Others

Our Father

Lord, reveal to us all that makes itself an enemy to the life you want for us. Help us hunger so deeply for the freedom of all your people that we risk walking among enemies who pervert justice. Reveal to us when we ourselves act as enemies to your kingdom of justice and peace. Amen.

May the peace of the Lord Christ go with you : wherever he may send you; may he guide you through the wilderness : protect you through the storm; may he bring you home rejoicing : at the wonders he has shown you; may he bring you home rejoicing : once again into our doors.

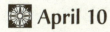

April 10

William Booth (1829–1912)

William Booth was a Methodist preacher in Britain who co-founded the Salvation Army. He was born in Nottingham and ended up living and working with his wife, Catherine, among the poor and ostracized. Out of their work on the streets was born the Salvation Army, with its uniforms and discipline. The movement became structured as a quasi-military organization with no physical weaponry, but with an army of people passionate about salvation and healing the broken wounds of our world.

O Lord, let my soul rise up to meet you
as the day rises to meet the sun.

**Glory to the Father, and to the Son, and to the Holy Spirit,
as it was in the beginning, is now, and will be forever. Amen.**

Come, let us sing to the LORD : **let us shout for joy to the Rock of our salvation.**

Song "Fairest Lord Jesus"

You who shine in all that's fair : season our works with your love.

Psalm 50:1–3, 6
The LORD, the God of gods, has spoken : **he has called the earth from the rising of the sun to its setting.**
Out of Zion, perfect in its beauty : **God reveals himself in glory.**
Our God will come and will not keep silence : **before him there is a consuming flame, and round about him a raging storm.**
Let the heavens declare the rightness of his cause : **for God himself is judge.**

You who shine in all that's fair : season our works with your love.

Exodus 19:1–16   1 John 5:13–21

You who shine in all that's fair : season our works with your love.

William Booth said, "Consider that the chief dangers which confront the coming century will be religion without the Holy Ghost, Christianity without Christ, forgiveness without repentance, salvation without regeneration, politics without God, and heaven without hell."

Prayers for Others

Our Father

Lord, help us become so familiar with your word and with your presence that thoughts of you consume our waking moments and holy fear of you brings us to worship. Then even our smallest actions will speak of you. Amen.

**May the peace of the Lord Christ go with you : wherever he may send you;
may he guide you through the wilderness : protect you through the storm;
may he bring you home rejoicing : at the wonders he has shown you;
may he bring you home rejoicing : once again into our doors.**

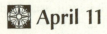 # April 11

O Lord, let my soul rise up to meet you
as the day rises to meet the sun.

Glory to the Father, and to the Son, and to the Holy Spirit,
as it was in the beginning, is now, and will be forever. Amen.

Come, let us bow down and bend the knee : let us kneel before the LORD our Maker.

Song "Swing Low, Sweet Chariot"

In God the Lord whose word I praise : in God I trust and will not be afraid.

Psalm 56:1–2, 11–12
Have mercy on me, O God, for my enemies are hounding me : **all day long they assault and oppress me.**
They hound me all the day long : **truly there are many who fight against me, O Most High.**
I am bound by the vow I made to you, O God : **I will present to you thank-offerings;**
For you have rescued my soul from death and my feet from stumbling : **that I may walk before God in the light of the living.**

In God the Lord whose word I praise : in God I trust and will not be afraid.

Exodus 19:16–25   2 John 1–13

In God the Lord whose word I praise : in God I trust and will not be afraid.

A reading from a fourteenth-century anonymous work, *The Cloud of Unknowing*: "For I tell you this: one loving, blind desire for God alone is more valuable in itself, more pleasing to God and to the saints, more beneficial to your own growth, and more helpful to your friends, both living and dead, than anything else you could do."

Prayers for Others

Our Father

Transform our desires to mirror yours, Lord. Bind us to you and to one another in vows of peace, in obedience to your word, and in the love of the Holy Spirit, which binds you to the Father, one God both now and forever. Amen.

**May the peace of the Lord Christ go with you : wherever he may send you;
may he guide you through the wilderness : protect you through the storm;
may he bring you home rejoicing : at the wonders he has shown you;
may he bring you home rejoicing : once again into our doors.**

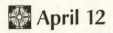 **April 12**

O Lord, let my soul rise up to meet you
as the day rises to meet the sun.

**Glory to the Father, and to the Son, and to the Holy Spirit,
as it was in the beginning, is now, and will be forever. Amen.**

Come, let us bow down and bend the knee : let us kneel before the LORD our Maker.

Song "I Will Trust in the Lord"

I will trust in the Lord and shout with my life : that power belongs to God.

Psalm 62:1–3, 13–14
For God alone my soul in silence waits : **from him comes my salvation.**
He alone is my rock and my salvation : **my stronghold, so that I shall not be greatly shaken.**
How long will you assail me to crush me, all of you together : **as if you were a leaning fence, a toppling wall?**
God has spoken once, twice have I heard it : **that power belongs to God.**
Steadfast love is yours, O Lord : **for you repay everyone according to his deeds.**

I will trust in the Lord and shout with my life : that power belongs to God.

Exodus 20:1–21   3 John 1–13

I will trust in the Lord and shout with my life : that power belongs to God.

Dorothy Day, co-founder of the Catholic Worker Movement, wrote, "What we do is very little. But it is like the little boy with a few loaves and fishes. Christ took that little and increased it. He will do the rest. What we do is so little that we may seem to be constantly failing. But so did he fail. He met with apparent failure on the Cross. But unless the seeds fall into the earth and die, there is no harvest."

Prayers for Others

Our Father

Give us patience and humility with our feeble efforts at faithfulness. Bless the minute things we do in your name so that our small acts of faith may find witness among many and thereby glorify you.

**May the peace of the Lord Christ go with you : wherever he may send you;
may he guide you through the wilderness : protect you through the storm;
may he bring you home rejoicing : at the wonders he has shown you;
may he bring you home rejoicing : once again into our doors.**

April 13

O Lord, let my soul rise up to meet you
as the day rises to meet the sun.

**Glory to the Father, and to the Son, and to the Holy Spirit,
as it was in the beginning, is now, and will be forever. Amen.**

Come, let us sing to the LORD : let us shout for joy to the Rock of our salvation.

Song "When the Saints Go Marching In"

Some say this world of trouble is the only one we need : but I'm waiting for that morning when the new world is revealed.

Psalm 68:4–6, 24–26, 36
Sing to God, sing praises to his name; exalt him who rides upon the heavens : **YAHWEH is his name, rejoice before him!**
Father of orphans, defender of widows : **God in his holy habitation!**
God gives the solitary a home and brings forth prisoners into freedom : **but the rebels shall live in dry places.**
They see your procession, O God : **your procession into the sanctuary, my God and my King.**
The singers go before, musicians follow after : **in the midst of maidens playing upon the hand-drums.**
Bless God in the congregation : **bless the LORD, you that are of the fountain of Israel.**
How wonderful is God in his holy places! : **the God of Israel giving strength and power to his people! Blessed be God!**

Some say this world of trouble is the only one we need : but I'm waiting for that morning when the new world is revealed.

Exodus 24:1–18   1 Thessalonians 1:1–10

Some say this world of trouble is the only one we need : but I'm waiting for that morning when the new world is revealed.

Julian of Norwich, a fourteenth-century anchorite, wrote about a vision she had in the midst of suffering: "What, do you wish to know your Lord's meaning in this thing? Know it well, love was his meaning. Who reveals it to you? Love. What did he reveal to you? Love. Why does he reveal it to you? For love. Remain in this, and you will know more of the same."

Prayers for Others

Our Father

God of heaven and earth, help us to live in this world faithfully guided by your love, which manifests itself in our love toward one another. Prepare us for that great gettin' up morning when your new world is fully revealed. Amen.

May the peace of the Lord Christ go with you : wherever he may send you; may he guide you through the wilderness : protect you through the storm; may he bring you home rejoicing : at the wonders he has shown you; may he bring you home rejoicing : once again into our doors.

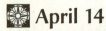
April 14

Kateri Tekakwitha (1656 – 1680)
Kateri Tekakwitha was born in 1656 in present-day New York. Her mother was Algonquin, a Christian Native, and her father was a non-Christian Mohawk Turtle chief. When Tekakwitha was four years old, a smallpox epidemic killed her parents and her brother, and left her with seriously impaired eyesight and a disfigured face. Inspired by Jesuit missionaries at an early age, Tekakwitha was baptized and assumed the name Kateri, probably in honor of Catherine of Siena. The following year, French conquerors reached her community of Ossernenon and destroyed much of it, burning it to the ground and massacring many of the Natives. Kateri escaped on the St. Lawrence River to a village of Christian Natives, where she dedicated her life to chastity, prayer, and care for the sick. She was the first Native American saint in the Catholic Church and is often called the Lily of the Mohawks, and the Apostle of the Indians.

O Lord, let my soul rise up to meet you
as the day rises to meet the sun.

Glory to the Father, and to the Son, and to the Holy Spirit, as it was in the beginning, is now, and will be forever. Amen.

Come, let us bow down and bend the knee : let us kneel before the Lord our Maker.

Song "Be Thou My Vision"

May the guarding of God shelter us : against the winds and the wiles of the devil.

Psalm 71:1–3, 15–17
In you, O Lord, have I taken refuge : **let me never be ashamed.**
In your righteousness, deliver me and set me free : **incline your ear to me and save me.**

Be my strong rock, a castle to keep me safe : **you are my crag and my stronghold.**
My mouth shall recount your mighty acts and saving deeds all day long : **though I cannot know the number of them.**
I will begin with the mighty works of the Lord God : **I will recall your righteousness, yours alone.**
O God, you have taught me since I was young : **and to this day I tell of your wonderful works.**

May the guarding of God shelter us : against the winds and the wiles of the devil.

Exodus 25:1–22   1 Thessalonians 2:1–12

May the guarding of God shelter us : against the winds and the wiles of the devil.

Martin Niemoller, a Lutheran pastor in Nazi Germany, wrote, "First they came for the Jews and I did not speak out because I was not a Jew. Then they came for the Communists and I did not speak out because I was not a Communist. Then they came for the trade unionists and I did not speak out because I was not a trade unionist. Then they came for me and there was no one left to speak out for me."

Prayers for Others

Our Father

Go before us, God, that we may follow in your steps. Go behind us, God, to steer us when we stray. Go beside us, God, as our strength and our joy for the journey. Amen.

**May the peace of the Lord Christ go with you : wherever he may send you;
may he guide you through the wilderness : protect you through the storm;
may he bring you home rejoicing : at the wonders he has shown you;
may he bring you home rejoicing : once again into our doors.**

✸ April 15

O Lord, let my soul rise up to meet you
as the day rises to meet the sun.

Glory to the Father, and to the Son, and to the Holy Spirit,
as it was in the beginning, is now, and will be forever. Amen.

Come, let us sing to the Lord : let us shout for joy to the Rock of our salvation.

Song "Vamos Todos al Banquete"

You have stamped your image on us, Lord : to mark us as your own.

Psalm 75:1–2, 7–10
We give you thanks, O God, we give you thanks : **calling upon your name and declaring all your wonderful deeds.**
"I will appoint a time," says God : **I will judge with equity."**
It is God who judges : **he puts down one and lifts up another.**
For in the LORD's hand there is a cup, full of spiced and foaming wine, which he pours out : **and all the wicked of the earth shall drink and drain the dregs.**
But I will rejoice for ever : **I will sing praises to the God of Jacob.**
He shall break off all the horns of the wicked : **but the horns of the righteous shall be exalted.**

You have stamped your image on us, Lord : to mark us as your own.

Exodus 28:1–4, 30–38   1 Thessalonians 2:13–20

You have stamped your image on us, Lord : to mark us as your own.

A reading from the gospel according to Mark: "They came to him and said, 'Teacher, we know that you are a man of integrity.... Is it right to pay the imperial tax to Caesar or not?' ... But Jesus knew their hypocrisy. 'Why are you trying to trap me?' he asked. 'Bring me a denarius and let me look at it.' They brought the coin, and he asked them, 'Whose image is this? And whose inscription?' 'Caesar's,' they replied. Then Jesus said to them, 'Give back to Caesar what is Caesar's and to God what is God's.'"

Prayers for Others

Our Father

Lord, we long to be your people in this world where other powers claim our allegiance. You have stamped your image on us. Guide us by your light that we might see clearly who we are and what it means to give ourselves to you. Amen.

May the peace of the Lord Christ go with you : wherever he may send you; may he guide you through the wilderness : protect you through the storm; may he bring you home rejoicing : at the wonders he has shown you; may he bring you home rejoicing : once again into our doors.

April 16

O Lord, let my soul rise up to meet you
as the day rises to meet the sun.

**Glory to the Father, and to the Son, and to the Holy Spirit,
as it was in the beginning, is now, and will be forever. Amen.**

Come, let us bow down and bend the knee : let us kneel before the Lord our Maker.

Song "Servant Song"

Save us and make us small, O God : small enough to walk your little way.

Psalm 79:1, 9–13
O God, the heathen have come into your inheritance : **they have profaned your holy temple; they have made Jerusalem a heap of rubble.**
Help us, O God our Savior, for the glory of your name : **deliver us and forgive us our sins, for your name's sake.**
Why should the heathen say, "Where is their God?" : **Let it be known among the heathen and in our sight that you avenge the shedding of your servants' blood.**
Let the sorrowful sighing of the prisoners come before you : **and by your great might spare those who are condemned to die.**
May the revilings with which they reviled you, O Lord : **return seven-fold into their bosoms.**
For we are your people and the sheep of your pasture : **we will give you thanks for ever and show forth your praise from age to age.**

Save us and make us small, O God : small enough to walk your little way.

Exodus 32:1–20   1 Thessalonians 3:1–13

Save us and make us small, O God : small enough to walk your little way.

Therese of Lisieux, a nineteenth-century Carmelite who sought to follow Christ's "little way," wrote, "The only way to make rapid progress along the path of divine love is to remain very little and put all our trust in Almighty God."

Prayers for Others

Our Father

Lord, teach us to dwell in the corners and crevices, to find an abundance of your love in those pockets of our lives where the poverty of our abilities crowds out our pride and ego. Amen.

May the peace of the Lord Christ go with you : wherever he may send you;
may he guide you through the wilderness : protect you through the storm;
may he bring you home rejoicing : at the wonders he has shown you;
may he bring you home rejoicing : once again into our doors.

✸ April 17

On April 17, 1961, the CIA launched its Bay of Pigs invasion of Cuba, an unsuccessful attempt to overthrow Fidel Castro's Communist government. When US President John F. Kennedy recognized this action of his own intelligence agency as an attempt to escalate the Cold War, he refused to send in US troops, saying that he would like to "splinter the CIA in a thousand pieces and scatter it to the wind."

O Lord, let my soul rise up to meet you
as the day rises to meet the sun.

**Glory to the Father, and to the Son, and to the Holy Spirit,
as it was in the beginning, is now, and will be forever. Amen.**

Come, let us bow down and bend the knee : let us kneel before the LORD our Maker.

Song "Guide My Feet"

We stoop to lift up our souls, O God : rain down heaven in our hearts and in your world.

Psalm 86:3–5, 11–13
Be merciful to me, O LORD, for you are my God : **I call upon you all the day long.**
Gladden the soul of your servant : **for to you, O LORD, I lift up my soul.**
For you, O LORD, are good and forgiving : **and great is your love toward all who call upon you.**
Teach me your way, O LORD, and I will walk in your truth : **knit my heart to you that I may fear your name.**
I will thank you, O LORD my God, with all my heart : **and glorify your name for evermore.**
For great is your love toward me : **you have delivered me from the nethermost pit.**

We stoop to lift up our souls, O God : rain down heaven in our hearts and in your world.

Exodus 32:21–34   1 Thessalonians 4:1–12

We stoop to lift up our souls, O God : rain down heaven in our hearts and in your world.

John Chrysostom, a fourth-century bishop of Constantinople, wrote, "Prayer is the light of the spirit, and the spirit, raised up to heaven by prayer, clings to God with the utmost tenderness. Like a child crying tearfully for its mother, it craves the milk that God provides. Prayer also stands before God as an honored ambassador. It gives joy to the spirit, peace to the heart. I speak of prayer, not words. It is the longing for God, love too deep for words, a gift not given by humans, but by God's grace."

Prayers for Others

Our Father

Lord, we cup our hands to gather the pieces of heaven you shower upon us. Help us to open our hands with generous spirits and scatter your divine love in the darkest places. Amen.

May the peace of the Lord Christ go with you : wherever he may send you; may he guide you through the wilderness : protect you through the storm; may he bring you home rejoicing : at the wonders he has shown you; may he bring you home rejoicing : once again into our doors.

April 18

O Lord, let my soul rise up to meet you
as the day rises to meet the sun.

Glory to the Father, and to the Son, and to the Holy Spirit, as it was in the beginning, is now, and will be forever. Amen.

Come, let us bow down and bend the knee : let us kneel before the Lord our Maker.

Song "Were You There?"

Even in the darkness, we will trust : that our lives are still in your hands.

Psalm 90:1–4, 12
Lord, you have been our refuge : **from one generation to another.**
Before the mountains were brought forth, or the land and the earth were born : **from age to age you are God.**
You turn us back to the dust and say : **"Go back, O child of earth."**
For a thousand years in your sight are like yesterday when it is past : **and like a watch in the night.**
So teach us to number our days : **that we may apply our hearts to wisdom.**

Even in the darkness, we will trust : that our lives are still in your hands.

Exodus 33:1–23   1 Thessalonians 4:13–18

Even in the darkness, we will trust : that our lives are still in your hands.

Sixteenth-century Spanish mystic John of the Cross wrote:
> Oh, night that guided me
> oh, night more lovely than the dawn,
> oh, night that joined Beloved with lover
> Lover transformed in the Beloved!

Prayers for Others

Our Father

Guide us, Lord, through the dark places of our day that we might trust you when shadows overcome the light. Remind us that darkness is as light to you. Amen.

May the peace of the Lord Christ go with you : wherever he may send you;
may he guide you through the wilderness : protect you through the storm;
may he bring you home rejoicing : at the wonders he has shown you;
may he bring you home rejoicing : once again into our doors.

April 19

O Lord, let my soul rise up to meet you
as the day rises to meet the sun.

Glory to the Father, and to the Son, and to the Holy Spirit,
as it was in the beginning, is now, and will be forever. Amen.

Come, let us sing to the Lord : let us shout for joy to the Rock of our salvation.

Song   "Sing and Rejoice"

Alabare! Alabare! Alabare a mi Senor : Praise to the Lord! Praise to the Lord! Sing praises now, forevermore.

Psalm 96:1–4, 11–13
Sing to the Lord a new song : **sing to the Lord, all the whole earth.**
Sing to the Lord and bless his name : **proclaim the good news of his salvation from day to day.**
Declare his glory among the nations : **and his wonders among all peoples.**

For great is the Lord and greatly to be praised : **he is more to be feared than all gods.**
Let the heavens rejoice, and let the earth be glad; let the sea thunder and all that is in it : **let the field be joyful and all that is therein.**
Then shall all the trees of the wood shout for joy before the Lord when he comes : **when he comes to judge the earth.**
He will judge the world with righteousness : **and the peoples with his truth.**

Alabare! Alabare! Alabare a mi Senor : Praise to the Lord! Praise to the Lord! Sing praises now, forevermore.

Exodus 34:1–9   1 Thessalonians 5:1–11

Alabare! Alabare! Alabare a mi Senor : Praise to the Lord! Praise to the Lord! Sing praises now, forevermore.

An aboriginal activist sister said, "If you have come to help me, you are wasting your time. But if you have come because your liberation is bound up with mine, then let us walk together."

Prayers for Others

Our Father

Lord of the captive and Lord of the free, fill our voices with songs that proclaim hope, joy, and justice for all creation. Guide us this day to walk alongside the oppressed as fellow sojourners. Amen.

May the peace of the Lord Christ go with you : wherever he may send you; may he guide you through the wilderness : protect you through the storm; may he bring you home rejoicing : at the wonders he has shown you; may he bring you home rejoicing : once again into our doors.

Liturgy Is Magical, but Not Magic

As we pray to and worship the God of the universe, there is something that remains at some level incomprehensible. It gives us a taste of something dazzling and transcendent. Historians say the phrase *hocus pocus* originated from liturgical worship services, in which the priest held up the bread and proclaimed, *Hoc est corpus Christi*. There were lots of folks on the fringes of the church who looked through the doors and windows, marveling at the mystery and magic of the moment. Many of them were unfamiliar with liturgy and had little education, so all they picked up was *hocus pocus*, and it seemed quite magical.

Although the liturgy is not magic or illusion or sorcery, it captures our imagination—this idea that God came to earth and died and now lives in us. It is a mystery. So while there is nothing of a magical formula in the liturgy, there is plenty that points us toward a world beyond this one. Perhaps one of the sure signs that we

> have worshiped God is that we walk away saying, "I didn't understand everything that happened there. It must be bigger than my comprehension." Too much of our worship has boxed God in as if we were going to see a play on Broadway. But in worship we become a part of the play. Though we can't understand it all, we can come onstage and participate in the divine drama.

April 20

O Lord, let my soul rise up to meet you
as the day rises to meet the sun.

**Glory to the Father, and to the Son, and to the Holy Spirit,
as it was in the beginning, is now, and will be forever. Amen.**

Come, let us bow down and bend the knee : let us kneel before the Lord our Maker.

Song "Come, Ye Sinners"

Lord, you have the words of life : you have the words of eternal life.

Psalm 102:1–4
Lord, hear my prayer, and let my cry come before you : **hide not your face from me in the day of my trouble.**
Incline your ear to me : **when I call, make haste to answer me,**
for my days drift away like smoke : **and my bones are hot as burning coals.**
My heart is smitten like grass and withered : **so that I forget to eat my bread.**

Lord, you have the words of life : you have the words of eternal life.

Exodus 34:10–17   1 Thessalonians 5:12–28

Lord, you have the words of life : you have the words of eternal life.

A theologian and poet of the seventeenth and eighteenth centuries, François Fenelon wrote, "We must have faith during the period of our grief. We think that our afflictions will be greater than we can bear, but we do not know the strength of our own hearts, nor the power of God. He knows all. He knows every folding of the heart and also the extent of the sorrow that he inflicts. What we think will overwhelm us entirely only subdues and conquers our pride. Our renewed spirit rises from its subjugation with a celestial strength and consolation."

Prayers for Others

Our Father

Lord, some of us are never far from tears, and some of us have forced ourselves not to cry. Direct our tears that they might flow with yours and cease when you smile upon us. Amen.

May the peace of the Lord Christ go with you : wherever he may send you; may he guide you through the wilderness : protect you through the storm; may he bring you home rejoicing : at the wonders he has shown you; may he bring you home rejoicing : once again into our doors.

April 21

O Lord, let my soul rise up to meet you
as the day rises to meet the sun.

Glory to the Father, and to the Son, and to the Holy Spirit, as it was in the beginning, is now, and will be forever. Amen.

Come, let us sing to the Lord : let us shout for joy to the Rock of our salvation.

Song "Great Is Thy Faithfulness"

If I stand, let me stand on your promise : when I fall, let me fall on your grace.

Psalm 105:1–2, 8–11
Give thanks to the Lord and call upon his name : **make known his deeds among the peoples.**
Sing to him, sing praises to him : **and speak of all his marvelous works.**
He has always been mindful of his covenant : **the promise he made for a thousand generations:**
the covenant he made with Abraham : **the oath that he swore to Isaac,**
which he established as a statute for Jacob : **an everlasting covenant for Israel,**
saying, "To you will I give the land of Canaan : **to be your allotted inheritance."**

If I stand, let me stand on your promise : when I fall, let me fall on your grace.

Exodus 34:18–35   2 Thessalonians 1:1–12

If I stand, let me stand on your promise : when I fall, let me fall on your grace.

Peter Maurin, co-founder of the Catholic Worker Movement, liked to say, "They say that I am crazy because I refuse to be crazy the way everyone else is crazy."

Prayers for Others

Our Father

Lord, help us to be foolish enough today to stand for you, foolish enough to trust you, foolish enough to call upon you, and foolish enough to wait on you. Amen.

**May the peace of the Lord Christ go with you : wherever he may send you;
may he guide you through the wilderness : protect you through the storm;
may he bring you home rejoicing : at the wonders he has shown you;
may he bring you home rejoicing : once again into our doors.**

April 22

In the spring of 1970, Gaylord Nelson announced that a demonstration about the environment would happen on April 22. Approximately twenty million people showed up to celebrate the first Earth Day. Since then, environmental concerns such as oil spills, global warming, extinction of wildlife, and pollution have been pushed to the forefront of political agendas and popular concern.

O Lord, let my soul rise up to meet you
as the day rises to meet the sun.

**Glory to the Father, and to the Son, and to the Holy Spirit,
as it was in the beginning, is now, and will be forever. Amen.**

Come, let us sing to the LORD : let us shout for joy to the Rock of our salvation.

Song "All Creatures of Our God and King"

The LORD has lifted up the lowly : and has filled us with good things.

Psalm 107:1–3, 8–9
Give thanks to the LORD, for he is good : **and his mercy endures for ever.**
Let all those whom the LORD has redeemed proclaim : **that he redeemed them from the hand of the foe.**
He gathered them out of the lands : **from the east and from the west, from the north and from the south.**
Let them give thanks to the LORD for his mercy : **and the wonders he does for his children.**
For he satisfies the thirsty : **and fills the hungry with good things.**

The LORD has lifted up the lowly : and has filled us with good things.

Exodus 40:18–38   2 Thessalonians 2:1–12

The LORD has lifted up the lowly : and has filled us with good things.

A sixth-century rabbi wrote, "God, from the very beginning of creation, was occupied before all else with planting, as it is written, 'And first of all, the Eternal God planted a Garden in Eden.' Therefore, occupy yourselves first and foremost with planting."

Prayers for Others

Our Father

Lord, give us humility to remember that we are made from dirt so that we might till the dirt and love it as we love ourselves. Amen.

May the peace of the Lord Christ go with you : wherever he may send you; may he guide you through the wilderness : protect you through the storm; may he bring you home rejoicing : at the wonders he has shown you; may he bring you home rejoicing : once again into our doors.

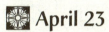 **April 23**

Cesar Chavez (1927–1993)

Cesar Chavez was a Latino farmworker in the United States who organized the United Farmworkers Union (UFW). Inspired by a priest who taught him God's desire for social justice, Chavez gave himself to voluntary poverty and a nonviolent struggle on behalf of America's poorest and most exploited workers. "When you sacrifice, you force others to sacrifice," he said. "It's an extremely powerful weapon."

O Lord, let my soul rise up to meet you
as the day rises to meet the sun.

Glory to the Father, and to the Son, and to the Holy Spirit, as it was in the beginning, is now, and will be forever. Amen.

Come, let us sing to the LORD : let us shout for joy to the Rock of our salvation.

Song "Vamos Todos al Banquete"

O Mighty God, our Prince of Peace : you order your kingdom with justice.

Psalm 110:1–5
The LORD said to my Lord, "Sit at my right hand : **until I make your enemies your footstool."**
The LORD will send the scepter of your power out of Zion : **saying, "Rule over your enemies round about you.**
Princely state has been yours from the day of your birth : **in the beauty of holiness have I begotten you, like dew from the womb of the morning."**

The LORD has sworn and he will not recant : **"You are a priest for ever after the order of Melchizedek."**
The Lord who is at your right hand will smite kings in the day of his wrath : **he will rule over the nations.**

O Mighty God, our Prince of Peace : you order your kingdom with justice.

Leviticus 16:1–19   2 Thessalonians 2:13–17

O Mighty God, our Prince of Peace : you order your kingdom with justice.

A prayer by Cesar Chavez: "Show me the suffering of the most miserable, so I will know my people's plight. Free me to pray for others, for you are present in every person. Help me take responsibility for my own life, so that I can be free at last. Grant me courage to serve others, for in service there is true life. Give me honesty and patience, so that the Spirit will be alive among us. Let the Spirit flourish and grow, so that we will never tire of the struggle. Let us remember those who have died for justice, for they have given us life. Help us love even those who hate us, so we can change the world. Amen."

Prayers for Others

Our Father

Loving God, teach us to order the desires of our hearts according to the call to do justice, love kindness, and walk humbly with you. Amen.

May the peace of the Lord Christ go with you : wherever he may send you;
may he guide you through the wilderness : protect you through the storm;
may he bring you home rejoicing : at the wonders he has shown you;
may he bring you home rejoicing : once again into our doors.

✣ April 24

O Lord, let my soul rise up to meet you
as the day rises to meet the sun.

Glory to the Father, and to the Son, and to the Holy Spirit,
as it was in the beginning, is now, and will be forever. Amen.

Come, let us bow down and bend the knee : let us kneel before the LORD our Maker.

Song "Swing Low, Sweet Chariot"

May the Lord direct our hearts : into God's love and Christ's perseverance.

Psalm 116:1–4
I love the LORD, because he has heard the voice of my supplication : **because he has inclined his ear to me whenever I called upon him.**
The chords of death entangled me; the grip of the grave took hold of me : **I came to grief and sorrow.**
Then I called upon the name of the LORD : **"O LORD, I pray you, save my life."**
Gracious is the LORD and righteous : **our God is full of compassion.**

May the Lord direct our hearts : into God's love and Christ's perseverance.

Leviticus 16:20–34   2 Thessalonians 3:1–18

May the Lord direct our hearts : into God's love and Christ's perseverance.

Francis of Assisi, a twelfth-century mendicant preacher, said, "Above all the graces and gifts of the Holy Spirit, which Christ grants to His friends, is that of self-conquest and of willingly bearing sufferings, injuries and reproaches and discomforts for the love of Christ. If we shall bear all these things patiently and with cheerfulness, thinking on the suffering of Christ the blessed, which we ought to bear patiently for His love, O Brother Leo, write that here and in this is perfect joy."

Prayers for Others

Our Father

Christ of the cross and of the empty tomb, strengthen us to bear the burdens of the day, to seek you amid the hurts and questions, and to trust you for mercy enough for this day. Amen.

May the peace of the Lord Christ go with you : wherever he may send you; may he guide you through the wilderness : protect you through the storm; may he bring you home rejoicing : at the wonders he has shown you; may he bring you home rejoicing : once again into our doors.

✣ April 25

O Lord, let my soul rise up to meet you
as the day rises to meet the sun.

Glory to the Father, and to the Son, and to the Holy Spirit,
as it was in the beginning, is now, and will be forever. Amen.

Come, let us bow down and bend the knee : **let us kneel before the LORD our Maker.**

Song "I Want Jesus to Walk with Me"

Show us your way, O Lord : and we will walk it to the end.

Psalm 119:33–38
Teach me, O Lord, the way of your statutes : **and I shall keep it to the end.**
Give me understanding, and I shall keep your law : **I shall keep it with all my heart.**
Make me go in the path of your commandments : **for that is my desire.**
Incline my heart to your decrees : **and not to unjust gain.**
Turn my eyes from watching what is worthless : **give me life in your ways.**
Fulfill your promise to your servant : **which you make to those who fear you.**

Show us your way, O Lord : and we will walk it to the end.

Leviticus 19:1–18   1 Peter 1:1–12

Show us your way, O Lord : and we will walk it to the end.

Sixth-century hermit Dorotheos of Gaza wrote, "Scripture says, *Love your neighbor as yourself.* And yet, you ask, 'How can I love my neighbor as myself when I have things hidden in my heart which I cannot see, or even know?' Do not consider virtues excessively difficult or unattainable, but make at least a little effort and have confidence in God. If our brother or sister needs something, give it freely. By this we go up the ladder of righteousness one rung at a time, until finally, with God's help, we reach the top. For through this repeated coming to your neighbor's rescue, you do what is advantageous for both your neighbor and yourself."

Prayers for Others

Our Father

Lord, help us to see that our well-being is inextricably bound to the well-being of our neighbor. Our sorrows are shared. Our longings are shared. Our fears are shared. Enable us also to share compassion, patience, and courage today. Amen.

May the peace of the Lord Christ go with you : wherever he may send you; may he guide you through the wilderness : protect you through the storm; may he bring you home rejoicing : at the wonders he has shown you; may he bring you home rejoicing : once again into our doors.

April 26

On April 26, 1986, a nuclear power accident in Chernobyl, Ukraine, dispersed large amounts of radioactive debris into the air. The plume drifted over parts of the Soviet Union and Europe, extending as far as Ireland. The most contaminated areas were in Ukraine, Belarus, and Russia, forcing the evacuation and resettlement of 336,000 people. There were fifty-six direct deaths; it is estimated that eight hundred thousand others suffered radiation exposure.

O Lord, let my soul rise up to meet you
as the day rises to meet the sun.

**Glory to the Father, and to the Son, and to the Holy Spirit,
as it was in the beginning, is now, and will be forever. Amen.**

Come, let us bow down and bend the knee : let us kneel before the LORD our Maker.

Song "Guide My Feet"

Guide my feet and hold my hand : set my heart on heaven's way.

Psalm 119:105–8, 111–12
Your word is a lantern to my feet : **and a light upon my path.**
I have sworn and am determined : **to keep your righteous judgments.**
I am deeply troubled : **preserve my life, O LORD, according to your word.**
Accept, O LORD, the willing tribute of my lips : **and teach me your judgments.**
Your decrees are my inheritance for ever : **truly, they are the joy of my heart.**
I have applied my heart to fulfill your statutes : **for ever and to the end.**

Guide my feet and hold my hand : set my heart on heaven's way.

Leviticus 19:26–37   1 Peter 1:13–25

Guide my feet and hold my hand : set my heart on heaven's way.

Dorothy Day, co-founder of the Catholic Worker Movement, wrote, "We believe that spiritual action is the hardest of all — to praise and worship God, to thank Him, to petition Him for our brothers, to repent of our sins and those of others. This is action, just as the taking of cities is action, as revolution is action, as the Corporal Works of Mercy are action. And just to lie in the sun and let God work on you is to be sitting in the light of the Sun of Justice, and the growth will be there, and joy will grow and spread from us to others. That is why I like to use so often that saying of St. Catherine of Siena: 'All the Way to heaven is Heaven, because He said I am the Way.'"

Prayers for Others

Our Father

Open our eyes to see your glory in the smallest things, that we would live with the faith and the boldness required to believe that all the way to heaven truly is heaven. Amen.

May the peace of the Lord Christ go with you : wherever he may send you;
may he guide you through the wilderness : protect you through the storm;
may he bring you home rejoicing : at the wonders he has shown you;
may he bring you home rejoicing : once again into our doors.

April 27

On April 27, 1977, mothers of abducted children in Buenos Aires, Argentina, held their first rally for the "disappeared." The mothers organized after losing numerous children during Argentina's Dirty War between 1976 and 1983. Many of the children were tortured and killed during this time. The military claims that nine thousand such children are unaccounted for, while the mothers say it is closer to thirty thousand.

O Lord, let my soul rise up to meet you
as the day rises to meet the sun.

**Glory to the Father, and to the Son, and to the Holy Spirit,
as it was in the beginning, is now, and will be forever. Amen.**

Come, let us bow down and bend the knee : let us kneel before the Lord our Maker.

Song "O Mary, Don't You Weep"

God, grant me courage : that I may plant seeds of peace.

Psalm 120:1–3, 6–7
When I was in trouble, I called to the Lord : **I called to the Lord, and he answered me.**
Deliver me, O Lord, from lying lips : **and from the deceitful tongue.**
What shall be done to you, and what more besides : **O you deceitful tongue?**
Too long have I had to live : **among the enemies of peace.**
I am on the side of peace : **but when I speak of it, they are for war.**

God, grant me courage : that I may plant seeds of peace.

Leviticus 23:1–22   1 Peter 2:1–10

God, grant me courage : that I may plant seeds of peace.

Contemporary Christian activist Jim Wallis has said, "People who believe in war leave all behind, prepared to die: what price are we prepared to pay to be a people who believe in peace? Those who keep faith to the end will know their weakness the best. God, grant me the courage; help me, that I may plant seeds of peace."

Prayers for Others

Our Father

We profess to be people of peace, Lord, but keep us from the temptation to proclaim peace when there is no peace. Show us today where peace is most needed in our community and in our world. Show us which of us must plant the seeds of peace, which of us must water them, and which of us must yet become gardeners of your peace. Amen.

May the peace of the Lord Christ go with you : wherever he may send you; may he guide you through the wilderness : protect you through the storm; may he bring you home rejoicing : at the wonders he has shown you; may he bring you home rejoicing : once again into our doors.

✣ April 28

O Lord, let my soul rise up to meet you
as the day rises to meet the sun.

Glory to the Father, and to the Son, and to the Holy Spirit,
as it was in the beginning, is now, and will be forever. Amen.

Come, let us bow down and bend the knee : let us kneel before the Lord our Maker.

Song "Let All Mortal Flesh Keep Silence"

I greet the Christ in you, my sister : I greet the Christ in you, my brother.

Psalm 133
Oh, how good and pleasant it is : **when brethren live together in unity!**
It is like fine oil upon the head : **that runs down upon the beard,**
upon the beard of Aaron : **and runs down upon the collar of his robe.**
It is like the dew of Hermon : **that falls upon the hills of Zion.**
For there the Lord has ordained the blessing : **life for evermore.**

I greet the Christ in you, my sister : I greet the Christ in you, my brother.

Leviticus 23:23–44   1 Peter 2:11–25

I greet the Christ in you, my sister : I greet the Christ in you, my brother.

Albert Luthuli, who struggled nonviolently against apartheid in South Africa, said, "It is inevitable that in working for freedom some individuals and some families must take the lead and suffer: the road to freedom is via the cross."

Prayers for Others

Our Father

Lord, we pray we never find ourselves without hope, without a glimpse of the empty tomb each time we happen upon a cross. Help us begin our daily journey expecting both crosses and empty tombs and rejoicing when we encounter either because we know you are with us. Amen.

May the peace of the Lord Christ go with you : wherever he may send you; may he guide you through the wilderness : protect you through the storm; may he bring you home rejoicing : at the wonders he has shown you; may he bring you home rejoicing : once again into our doors.

April 29

O Lord, let my soul rise up to meet you
as the day rises to meet the sun.

Glory to the Father, and to the Son, and to the Holy Spirit,
as it was in the beginning, is now, and will be forever. Amen.

Come, let us bow down and bend the knee : let us kneel before the Lord our Maker.

Song "Be Thou My Vision"

There is a crack, a crack in everything : that's how the light gets in.

Psalm 139:1, 6–9
Lord, you have searched me out and known me : **you know my sitting down and my rising up; you discern my thoughts from afar.**
Where can I go then from your Spirit? : **where can I flee from your presence?**
If I climb up to heaven, you are there : **if I make the grave my bed, you are there also.**
If I take the wings of the morning : **and dwell in the uttermost parts of the sea,**
even there your hand will lead me : **and your right hand hold me fast.**

256   *Morning Prayer*

There is a crack, a crack in everything : that's how the light gets in.

Leviticus 25:1–17   1 Peter 3:13–4:6

There is a crack, a crack in everything : that's how the light gets in.

Francis de Sales, a sixteenth-century bishop, said, "We often say that we are nothing, that we are misery itself and the refuse of the world, but we would be very sorry if anyone took us at our word or told others that we are really such as we say."

Prayers for Others

Our Father

Lord, we thank you for our brokenness because it makes us depend on you. Yet you are continually remaking us into a new creation. Keep us from false humilities and help us to reflect back to one another what it means to be created in your image. Amen.

**May the peace of the Lord Christ go with you : wherever he may send you;
may he guide you through the wilderness : protect you through the storm;
may he bring you home rejoicing : at the wonders he has shown you;
may he bring you home rejoicing : once again into our doors.**

✺ April 30

North and South Vietnam were reunited on April 30, 1975, bringing an end to the Vietnam War.

O Lord, let my soul rise up to meet you
as the day rises to meet the sun.

**Glory to the Father, and to the Son, and to the Holy Spirit,
as it was in the beginning, is now, and will be forever. Amen.**

Come, let us sing to the LORD : let us shout for joy to the Rock of our salvation.

Song   "We Are Marching in the Light of God"

Establish the work of our hands, O God : establish the work of our hands.

Psalm 144:1–2, 13–16
Blessed be the LORD my rock! : **who trains my hand to fight and my fingers to battle;**
my help and my fortress, my stronghold and my deliverer : **my shield in whom I trust, who subdues the peoples under me.**

Morning Prayer

May our sons be like plants well nurtured from their youth : **and our daughters like sculptured corners of a palace.**
May our barns be filled to overflowing with all manner of crops : **may the flocks in our pastures increase by thousands and tens of thousands; may our cattle be fat and sleek.**
May there be no breaching of the walls, no going into exile : **no wailing in the public squares.**
Happy are the people of whom this is so! : **happy are the people whose God is the Lord!**

Establish the work of our hands, O God : establish the work of our hands.

Leviticus 25:35–55   1 Peter 4:7–19

Establish the work of our hands, O God : establish the work of our hands.

Twentieth-century novelist Georges Bernarnos said, "Every particle of Christ's divine charity is today more precious for your security — for your security, I say — than all the atom bombs in all the stockpiles."

Prayers for Others

Our Father

If our days do not begin and end in you, O Lord, they come to nothing. Bless our efforts at faithfulness; work through us despite our supposed strengths. Establish the work of our hands, O God, and be merciful. Amen.

May the peace of the Lord Christ go with you : wherever he may send you; may he guide you through the wilderness : protect you through the storm; may he bring you home rejoicing : at the wonders he has shown you; may he bring you home rejoicing : once again into our doors.

Becoming the Answer to Our Prayers: A Few Ideas

1. Track to its source one item of food you eat regularly. Then each time you eat that food, remember the folks who made it possible for you to eat it.
2. Become a pen pal with someone who is in prison.
3. Try recycling water from the washer or sink by using it to flush your toilet. Remember the 1.2 billion folks who don't have clean water.
4. Leave a tip for someone cleaning the streets or the public restroom.
5. Write one CEO each month this year. Affirm or critique the ethics of their companies. (You may need to do a little research first.)

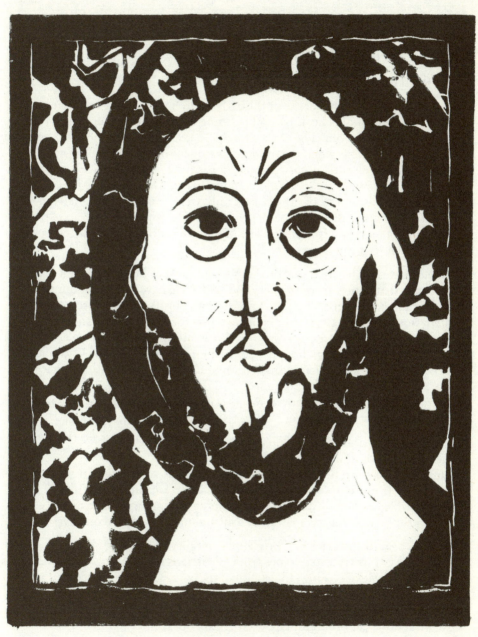

MAY — CHRIST

Marks of New Monasticism
Hospitality

Hospitality is one of the marks of the early church. Jesus was always going to people's homes, and his healings and teaching often happened around a dinner table or in a living room. The early church ate and met in each other's homes. It has been noted that when the disciples were sent out with nothing at all (no money, no extra clothes, no provisions), it was not because Jesus wanted them to suffer in poverty or to be left alone in the street; it was because they were to rely on the hospitality of others. Not only were the early Christians to practice hospitality; they were to depend on it. There was no "us" and "them." *My* became a cussword for Christians. My house is no longer mine but is God's, which means it is open to all.

One of the early Christians pointed out the miracle of hospitality and the abundance that comes from sharing, and said, "We have no house, but we have homes everywhere we go." Our Mennonite brothers and sisters have known this for a long time; they created a directory of Christian homes that are open to folks who are in crisis or who are traveling and need a place to stay (before there was couchhopper.com!). Dorothy Day and the Catholic Worker Movement also shared this vision of hospitality and insisted that if every Christian home made room for the stranger, we would end poverty and homelessness.

Suggested Reading for the Month
Making Room by Christine Pohl
Selected Writings of Dorothy Day

Our Savior came into the world dependent on hospitality, from the moment he was born in a borrowed manger until he was buried in a donated tomb. What is more, Jesus longs to meet us face to face in the disguise of the stranger, the guest at our door. Christ looks at us longingly, as in our icon for this month, eager for us to answer the call and invite him into our lives.

There are beautiful stories of Christian hospitality happening all over the world. One of our favorites comes from Christians living along the border of the US and Mexico. They, like many of us, became deeply concerned about the struggles of undocumented brothers and sisters and the plight of many recent immigrants to the US. They insisted that laws don't dictate how we are to treat immigrants, but Scripture does, and the Bible speaks unquestionably about a God of hospitality and grace, who is a refuge to the widow and orphan and alien. As God's people, we are to be like that. So these Christians on the border opened up their homes as sanctuary houses, and helped undocumented friends get legal help. But they did not stop there. They decided they also wanted their lives to be a witness to the world, so they organized worship services along the border, in which hundreds of Christians on the Mexican side of the wall joined hundreds of Christians on the US side of the wall. There they worshiped Jesus together. And then they served each other communion by throwing it over the wall.

May 1

On May 1, 1886, one hundred and eighty thousand US workers went on strike for an eight-hour workday. Rallies continued until May 3, when a bomb was thrown into a crowd and shots were fired, killing eight policemen and an unknown number of civilians. Ever since this incident, remembered as the Haymarket Massacre, May 1 has been remembered as International Workers Day.

O Lord, let my soul rise up to meet you
as the day rises to meet the sun.

**Glory to the Father, and to the Son, and to the Holy Spirit,
as it was in the beginning, is now, and will be forever. Amen.**

Come, let us bow down and bend the knee : let us kneel before the Lord our Maker.

Song "Steal Away to Jesus"

Gather us to you, O Lord : and whisper justice in our ears.

Psalm 2:1–2, 11–13
Why are the nations in an uproar? : **Why do the peoples mutter empty threats?**
Why do the kings of the earth rise up in revolt, and the princes plot together : **against the Lord and against his Anointed?**
Submit to the Lord with fear : **and with trembling bow before him;**
lest he be angry and you perish : **for his wrath is quickly kindled.**
Happy are they all : **who take refuge in him!**

Gather us to you, O Lord : and whisper justice in our ears.

Leviticus 26:1–20   Luke 3:1–14

Gather us to You, O Lord : and whisper justice in our ears.

American labor organizer and activist Cesar Chavez said, "When we are really honest with ourselves, we must admit that our lives are all that really belong to us. So it is how we use our lives that determines what kind of men we are. It is my deepest belief that only by giving our lives do we find life. I am convinced that the truest act of courage, the strongest act of manliness is to sacrifice ourselves for others in totally nonviolent struggle for justice. To be a man is to suffer for others. God help us to be men!"

Prayers for Others

Our Father

God, help us to imitate you as we feed those who hunger for bread, for justice, for companionship, for forgiveness, for alternate ways of living in this world. Give us your words, equip our hands, and guide our feet. Sustain us, Lord, with your healing love. Amen.

May the peace of the Lord Christ go with you : wherever he may send you; may he guide you through the wilderness : protect you through the storm; may he bring you home rejoicing : at the wonders he has shown you; may he bring you home rejoicing : once again into our doors.

✣ May 2

O Lord, let my soul rise up to meet you
as the day rises to meet the sun.

Glory to the Father, and to the Son, and to the Holy Spirit, as it was in the beginning, is now, and will be forever. Amen.

Come, let us bow down and bend the knee : let us kneel before the Lord our Maker.

Song "O Lord, Hear My Prayer"

Rise up and lift your hand, O God : forget not your afflicted.

Psalm 10:1–3, 10–11
Why do you stand so far off, O Lord : **and hide yourself in time of trouble?**
The wicked arrogantly persecute the poor : **but they are trapped in the schemes they have devised.**
The wicked boast of their heart's desire : **the covetous curse and revile the Lord.**
The innocent are broken and humbled before them : **the helpless fall before their power.**
They say in their heart, "God has forgotten : **he hides his face; he will never notice."**

Rise up and lift your hand, O God : forget not your afflicted.

Leviticus 26:27–42   Luke 3:15–22

Rise up and lift your hand, O God : forget not your afflicted.

Russian novelist Leo Tolstoy said, "Men of our time believe that all the insanity and cruelty of our lives, the enormous wealth of few, the envious poverty of the majority, the wars and every form of violence, are perceived by nobody, and that nothing prevents us from continuing to live thus."

Prayers for Others

Our Father

God, we know you see us in our suffering and in our sin. It is we who are forgetful. Be patient with us and receive even our forgetful prayers and pleas. Remind us again and again of your presence, and help us to be that memory for others. Amen.

May the peace of the Lord Christ go with you : wherever he may send you;
may he guide you through the wilderness : protect you through the storm;
may he bring you home rejoicing : at the wonders he has shown you;
may he bring you home rejoicing : once again into our doors.

 May 3

Septima Poinsette Clark (1898 – 1987)

Septima Poinsette Clark was born in Charleston, South Carolina, to a father who was an ex-slave and a mother who had been raised in the Caribbean. While her parents had very little formal education, they emphasized the need for Septima to go to school. Though Septima was eligible to teach after completing the eighth grade, her parents and teachers encouraged her to finish high school. After graduating she took a post as a teacher on Johns Island, off the coast of Charleston. There she began to notice the extreme disparity between the education of African-Americans and that of their white counterparts. This experience stayed with her and fueled her quest for educational reform. An avid social activist during the civil rights era, Septima traveled throughout the South to educate African-Americans about their voting rights. She worked closely with Myles Horton of the Highlander Folk School. Together they trained many civil rights activists, including Rosa Parks, in nonviolent resistance and local leadership. Although Septima was thrown in jail, threatened, fired from jobs, and falsely accused of wrongdoing, she never turned from her task of working against an unjust educational system. Septima Poinsette Clark has become known as the Grandmother of the Civil Rights Movement.

O Lord, let my soul rise up to meet you
as the day rises to meet the sun.

**Glory to the Father, and to the Son, and to the Holy Spirit,
as it was in the beginning, is now, and will be forever. Amen.**

Come, let us sing to the LORD : let us shout for joy to the Rock of our salvation.

Song "Solid Rock"

Root us, Lord, in your life : the life that lasts forever.

Psalm 15

LORD, who may dwell in your tabernacle? **: who may abide upon your holy hill?**

Whoever leads a blameless life and does what is right **: who speaks the truth from his heart.**

There is no guile upon his tongue; he does no evil to his friend **: he does not heap contempt upon his neighbor.**

In his sight the wicked is rejected **: but he honors those who fear the LORD.**

He has sworn to do no wrong **: and does not take back his word.**

He does not give his money in hope of gain **: nor does he take a bribe against the innocent.**

Whoever does these things **: shall never be overthrown.**

Root us, Lord, in your life : the life that lasts forever.

Numbers 3:1–13   Luke 4:1–13

Root us, Lord, in your life : the life that lasts forever.

Septima Poinsette Clark liked to say, "I have a great belief in the fact that whenever there is chaos, it creates wonderful thinking. I consider chaos a gift."

Prayers for Others

Our Father

Like a tree planted by living water is the person who commits to your ways, O Lord. Nourish us with your disciplining love; prune our branches for growth. Teach us also to recognize good fruit and to recoil from the bitterness of the bad. Amen.

May the peace of the Lord Christ go with you : wherever he may send you; may he guide you through the wilderness : protect you through the storm; may he bring you home rejoicing : at the wonders he has shown you; may he bring you home rejoicing : once again into our doors.

 ## May 4

O Lord, let my soul rise up to meet you
as the day rises to meet the sun.

**Glory to the Father, and to the Son, and to the Holy Spirit,
as it was in the beginning, is now, and will be forever. Amen.**

Morning Prayer

Come, let us sing to the LORD : let us shout for joy to the Rock of our salvation.

Song "Come, Thou Fount"

May the words we say and the prayers we pray : echo heaven's praise.

Psalm 19:1–4
The heavens declare the glory of God : **and the firmament shows his handiwork.**
One day tells its tale to another : **and one night imparts knowledge to another.**
Although they have no words or language : **and their voices are not heard,**
their sound has gone out into all lands : **and their message to the ends of the world.**

May the words we say and the prayers we pray : echo heaven's praise.

Numbers 6:22–27   Luke 4:14–30

May the words we say and the prayers we pray : echo heaven's praise.

Mechthild of Magdeburg, a thirteenth-century mystic, prayed, "I cannot dance, Lord, unless you lead me. If you want me to leap with abandon, you must intone the song. Then I shall leap into love, from love into knowledge, from knowledge into enjoyment, and from enjoyment beyond all human sensations. There I want to remain, yet want also to circle higher still."

Prayers for Others

Our Father

We will proclaim your bounty and your blessing, O Lord. We will sing to one another the song you have put in our hearts. Our feet will bring good news to the ends of the earth. Help us, Lord, to live out our promises. Amen.

May the peace of the Lord Christ go with you : wherever he may send you;
may he guide you through the wilderness : protect you through the storm;
may he bring you home rejoicing : at the wonders he has shown you;
may he bring you home rejoicing : once again into our doors.

Smells and Bells

We worship a God who came as a material Savior. So when we pray, we can use all of our senses. We see symbols of our faith. We hear words and songs. We smell the incense of our prayers rising to God. We touch and taste Christ in the sacramental life. Just as a whiff of apple pie can conjure up nostalgic memories of home, so our incense can help us pray. But, as Amos declares, if all we have is incense, without justice for the poor and fruit from our prayers, we should snuff out the incense and shut up with our songs, because they are nauseating to God. If our material tools help us worship the eternal God and bear fruit for the kingdom, then we keep them. If our material tools lead to narcissism or to an obsession with having the right incense or the correct color of candle, then we need to let go of them.

Disagreements in church history have led many Christians to feel like the physical world and the spiritual world are at odds, but it's important to see them as complements, not opposites. After all, God breathed into the dirt to make humanity. (The very name *human* comes from the word *humus*, meaning "dirt.") The incarnation of Jesus is all about God taking on flesh and being born as a baby who cries, eats, and poops. Jesus uses physical stuff like dirt and spit to heal people, and God is always communicating—through rocks and fire (even through a donkey).

Physical stuff can help us pray. In the celebration of communion, or the Eucharist, we eat bread and drink wine (or juice) in remembrance of Jesus. The physical elements help us literally "re-member" Jesus as we are knit together into his body. We are what we eat. *Sacrament* comes from the Latin translation of the Greek word for *mystery*. A lot of the most sacred and beautiful rituals of Christianity are mysterious. There is more going on than what we see, but what we see can help us know God at work in the world.

Take water, for example. When we see water, we think of the waters of creation, the waters that swallowed up the Egyptian armies, the flood in Noah's day, the baptism of Jesus. It may seem odd that Jesus identified himself with things of the earth such as "living water" and "the bread of life." But just as much as Jesus used the stuff of earth to show us something about himself, he also showed us that there is something of God in the creation around us. Even mud and spit can be used as healing balms. God is everywhere.

Think of the power of candlelight vigils or how the Scriptures speak about our prayers going up to God like incense. Certain parts of the church regularly use oil and water, not as magic potions but as material signs of the Spirit's touch. Pentecostals often anoint the sick with oil as a sign of healing.

"Is any one of you sick? Call the elders of the church to pray over you and anoint you with oil" (James 5:14).

Catholics often dip an olive branch in water and fling the water out on the people as a reminder of their baptism. We want to give you an invitation to use material things in prayer. You may want to burn incense as you say prayers for others. Or maybe you could do a foot-washing ceremony during confession, or light a candle as we suggest during evening prayer, remembering the light that shines in the darkness and is not overwhelmed.

Maybe you want to get even more creative. One pastor created an Easter service by putting snow on the altar, on Saturday, when the world was cold and the sun stopped shining. He made icicles out of red liquid and placed them in a crown above the snow so that as they melted, they dripped red onto the snow. Members of the congregation were invited to come and chisel their sins on ice tablets on the altar. Then, as Easter approached, the ice melted and the world came to life again.

May 5

O Lord, let my soul rise up to meet you
as the day rises to meet the sun.

**Glory to the Father, and to the Son, and to the Holy Spirit,
as it was in the beginning, is now, and will be forever. Amen.**

Come, let us sing to the LORD : let us shout for joy to the Rock of our salvation.

Song "I Will Trust in the Lord"

Rise up, O LORD : and may your enemies be scattered.

Psalm 25:1–5
To you, O LORD, I lift up my soul; my God, I put my trust in you : **let me not be humiliated, nor let my enemies triumph over me.**
Let none who look to you be put to shame : **let the treacherous be disappointed in their schemes.**
Show me your ways, O LORD : **and teach me your paths.**
Lead me in your truth and teach me : **for you are the God of my salvation; in you have I trusted all the day long.**
Remember, O LORD, your compassion and love : **for they are from everlasting.**

Rise up, O LORD : and may your enemies be scattered.

Numbers 10:29–36   Luke 4:31–37

Rise up, O LORD : and may your enemies be scattered.

French sociologist Jacques Ellul wrote, "One thing, however, is sure: unless Christians fulfill their prophetic role, unless they become the advocates and defenders of the truly poor, witness to their misery, then, infallibly, violence will suddenly break out. In one way or other 'their blood cries to heaven,' and violence will seem the only way out. It will be too late to try to calm them and create harmony."

Prayers for Others

Our Father

God, you call us to walk alongside the poor, all the while reminding us of our own poverty in spirit. Grant us courage to cry out against injustice. Grant us burdened hearts that ache to see the enemies of hunger, violence, and economic injustice scattered.

May the peace of the Lord Christ go with you : wherever he may send you;
may he guide you through the wilderness : protect you through the storm;
may he bring you home rejoicing : at the wonders he has shown you;
may he bring you home rejoicing : once again into our doors.

May 6

O Lord, let my soul rise up to meet you
as the day rises to meet the sun.

**Glory to the Father, and to the Son, and to the Holy Spirit,
as it was in the beginning, is now, and will be forever. Amen.**

Come, let us sing to the LORD : let us shout for joy to the Rock of our salvation.

Song "Praise to the Lord, the Almighty"

In the light of the morning : we will sing for joy.

Psalm 30:4–7
Sing to the LORD, you servants of his : **give thanks for the remembrance of his holiness.**
For his wrath endures but the twinkling of an eye : **his favor for a lifetime.**
Weeping may spend the night : **but joy comes in the morning.**
While I felt secure, I said, "I shall never be disturbed : **You, LORD, with your favor, made me as strong as the mountains."**

In the light of the morning : we will sing for joy.

Numbers 11:1–23   Luke 4:38–44

In the light of the morning : we will sing for joy.

Rabbi Abraham Joshua Heschel prayed, "I did not ask for success; I asked for wonder. And You gave it to me."

Prayers for Others

Our Father

You hear our prayers whether they are full of thanksgiving or full of complaints. Your mercy is unending. Even in your discipline you restrain yourself in ways we cannot know. May our mumbled words of gratitude and our fleeting praises find crevices where they can grow within your presence, Lord of light and morning. Amen.

May the peace of the Lord Christ go with you : wherever he may send you;
may he guide you through the wilderness : protect you through the storm;
may he bring you home rejoicing : at the wonders he has shown you;
may he bring you home rejoicing : once again into our doors.

✦ May 7

O Lord, let my soul rise up to meet you
as the day rises to meet the sun.

**Glory to the Father, and to the Son, and to the Holy Spirit,
as it was in the beginning, is now, and will be forever. Amen.**

Come, let us bow down and bend the knee : let us kneel before the LORD our Maker.

Song "Come, Ye Sinners"

Lord Jesus Christ, Son of God : have mercy on me, a sinner.

Psalm 36:1–4
There is a voice of rebellion deep in the heart of the wicked : **there is no fear of God before his eyes.**
He flatters himself in his own eyes : **that his hateful sin will not be found out.**
The words of his mouth are wicked and deceitful : **he has left off acting wisely and doing good.**
He thinks up wickedness upon his bed and has set himself in no good way : **he does not abhor that which is evil.**

Lord Jesus Christ, Son of God : have mercy on me, a sinner.

Numbers 11:24–33   Luke 5:1–11

Lord Jesus Christ, Son of God : have mercy on me, a sinner.

American Quaker and spiritual writer Richard Foster has said, "We have real difficulty here because everyone thinks of changing the world, but where, oh where, are those who think of changing themselves? People may genuinely want to be good, but seldom are they prepared to do what it takes to produce the inward life of goodness that can form the soul. Personal formation into the likeness of Christ is arduous and lifelong."

Prayers for Others

Our Father

Gracious God, by your Son, Jesus Christ, you call us forth from sin and into the baptism of new life. Help us work out our salvation with the fear and trembling necessary for any genuine disciple. Forgive us when we imagine that you are done with your re-creative work in us. Amen.

May the peace of the Lord Christ go with you : wherever he may send you;
may he guide you through the wilderness : protect you through the storm;
may he bring you home rejoicing : at the wonders he has shown you;
may he bring you home rejoicing : once again into our doors.

✹ May 8

O Lord, let my soul rise up to meet you
as the day rises to meet the sun.

**Glory to the Father, and to the Son, and to the Holy Spirit,
as it was in the beginning, is now, and will be forever. Amen.**

Come, let us bow down and bend the knee : let us kneel before the LORD our Maker.

Song "I Want Jesus to Walk with Me"

Walk with us, Lord : the journey is long.

Psalm 39:5 – 8
LORD, let me know my end and the number of my days : **so that I may know how short my life is.**
You have given me a mere handful of days, and my lifetime is as nothing in your sight : **truly, even those who stand erect are but a puff of wind.**
We walk about like a shadow, and in vain we are in turmoil : **we heap up riches and cannot tell who will gather them.**
And now, what is my hope? : **O Lord, my hope is in you.**

Walk with us, Lord : the journey is long.

Numbers 12:1 – 6   Luke 5:12 – 26

Walk with us, Lord : the journey is long.

Seventeenth-century French mystic Madame Guyon said, "Praying scripture is not judged by how much you read but by the way in which you read. If you read quickly, it will benefit you little. You will be like a bee that merely skims the surface of a flower. Instead, in this new way of reading with prayer, you must become as the bee that penetrates into the depths of the flower. You plunge deeply within to remove its deepest nectar."

Prayers for Others

Our Father

Lord, we pray for humility of mind to discern you in our visions and our dreams. We pray for wisdom to know what to do with your revelations. We pray for innocence to trust that you are walking with us. Amen.

**May the peace of the Lord Christ go with you : wherever he may send you;
may he guide you through the wilderness : protect you through the storm;
may he bring you home rejoicing : at the wonders he has shown you;
may he bring you home rejoicing : once again into our doors.**

 May 9

Columba of Iona (521 – 597)
An Irish prince who chose the monastic life, Columba left Ireland in 563 and settled in Iona in Scotland. He was a large man with a big, resonant singing voice. He was also an excellent scribe and illuminator of manuscripts. A much-loved abbot, he had a missionary zeal and great prophetic insight. His faithfulness to the Celtic tradition fueled the spread of vital Christianity through Britain and beyond as he planted monastic communities to be hubs of prayer and mission, modeling a radical life of discipleship.

O Lord, let my soul rise up to meet you
as the day rises to meet the sun.

Glory to the Father, and to the Son, and to the Holy Spirit,
as it was in the beginning, is now, and will be forever. Amen.

Come, let us sing to the LORD : let us shout for joy to the Rock of our salvation.

Song "Go, Tell It on the Mountain"

How happy upon the hills : are the feet of those who bring good news.

Psalm 45:1 – 4
My heart is stirring with a noble song; let me recite what I have fashioned for the king : **my tongue shall be the pen of a skilled writer.**
You are the fairest of men : **grace flows from your lips, because God has blessed you for ever.**
Strap your sword upon your thigh, O mighty warrior : **in your pride and in your majesty.**
Ride out and conquer in the cause of truth : **and for the sake of justice.**

How happy upon the hills : are the feet of those who bring good news.

Numbers 13:1–3, 21–30   Luke 5:27–39

How happy upon the hills : are the feet of those who bring good news.

Columba of Iona said, "Joy is the echo of God's life in us."

Prayers for Others

Our Father

Surprise us with your joy, O Lord, and let it resound in all we do. Amen.

May the peace of the Lord Christ go with you : wherever he may send you; may he guide you through the wilderness : protect you through the storm; may he bring you home rejoicing : at the wonders he has shown you; may he bring you home rejoicing : once again into our doors.

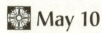 May 10

Isidore the Farmer (1070–1130)

In March 1622, Rome surprised many people by recognizing Isidore as a saint. He founded no order, nor did he write a single book. He was a simple farmworker who spent his life tilling the land, mostly for the same wealthy landowner. With his wife, Maria, he bore a son who died in childhood. Isidore knew the hardship, toil, and sorrow that are very familiar to many. He went to worship daily and prayed continuously in the fields, displaying the simple and profound faith shared by campesinos around the globe. It was said that angels could be seen assisting Isidore in the fields as he plowed. Though he had very little wealth, he became known for generosity and hospitality, especially to the stranger or the lonely. He died on May 15, 1130.

O Lord, let my soul rise up to meet you
as the day rises to meet the sun.

**Glory to the Father, and to the Son, and to the Holy Spirit,
as it was in the beginning, is now, and will be forever. Amen.**

Come, let us bow down and bend the knee : let us kneel before the Lord our Maker.

Song   "We Are Marching in the Light of God"

Shine the light of your justice, God : in our hearts and on our world.

Morning Prayer

Psalm 51:11–13
Create in me a clean heart, O God : **and renew a right spirit within me.**
Cast me not away from your presence : **and take not your holy Spirit from me.**
Give me the joy of your saving help again : **and sustain me with your bountiful Spirit.**

Shine the light of your justice, God : in our hearts and on our world.

Numbers 13:31–14:25   Luke 6:1–11

Shine the light of your justice, God : in our hearts and on our world.

This instruction is found in the ancient *Codex Bezae*: "Seek to grow from smallness, and from the higher place move down to the lowest."

Prayers for Others

Our Father

Jesus, we believe in your kingdom coming. Even amid pain and despair, we believe that with each brave prophet — with each unknown disciple who stretches her arm as a bridge between a broken world and a holy kingdom — you are laying another brick for the New Jerusalem. Amen.

**May the peace of the Lord Christ go with you : wherever he may send you;
may he guide you through the wilderness : protect you through the storm;
may he bring you home rejoicing : at the wonders he has shown you;
may he bring you home rejoicing : once again into our doors.**

✣ May 11

O Lord, let my soul rise up to meet you
as the day rises to meet the sun.

**Glory to the Father, and to the Son, and to the Holy Spirit,
as it was in the beginning, is now, and will be forever. Amen.**

Come, let us sing to the LORD : let us shout for joy to the Rock of our salvation.

Song   "Woke Up This Mornin' "

Exalt yourself above the heavens, God : and your glory over all the earth.

Psalm 57:6–10
Exalt yourself above the heavens, O God : **and your glory over all the earth.**
My heart is firmly fixed, O God, my heart is fixed : **I will sing and make melody.**
Wake up, my spirit; awake, lute and harp : **I myself will waken the dawn.**

I will confess you among the peoples, O LORD : **I will sing praise to you among the nations.**
For your loving-kindness is greater than the heavens : **and your faithfulness reaches to the clouds.**

Exalt yourself above the heavens, God : and your glory over all the earth.

Numbers 14:26–45   Luke 6:12–26

Exalt yourself above the heavens, God : and your glory over all the earth.

Francis de Sales, a sixteenth-century bishop in France, wrote, "Love the poor and love poverty, for it is by such love that we become truly poor. As the Scripture says, we become like the things we love. If you love the poor you will share their poverty and be poor like them. If you love the poor be often with them. Be glad to see them in your own home and to visit with them in theirs. Be glad to talk to them and be pleased to have them near you in church, on the street, and elsewhere. Be poor in conversing with them and speak to them as their companions do, but be rich in assisting them by sharing some of your more abundant goods with them."

Prayers for Others

Our Father

Lord, turn our praises into hands that clothe the naked, arms that comfort the afflicted, tables that host the stranger, and shoulders that support the weary so that your name may be praised by those who live and die with their backs against the wall. Amen.

**May the peace of the Lord Christ go with you : wherever he may send you;
may he guide you through the wilderness : protect you through the storm;
may he bring you home rejoicing : at the wonders he has shown you;
may he bring you home rejoicing : once again into our doors.**

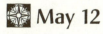 # May 12

O Lord, let my soul rise up to meet you
as the day rises to meet the sun.

Glory to the Father, and to the Son, and to the Holy Spirit,
as it was in the beginning, is now, and will be forever. Amen.

Come, let us sing to the LORD : let us shout for joy to the Rock of our salvation.

Song   "Nothin' but the Blood"

Make us friends of the thirsty, Lord : and teach us to thirst for you.

Psalm 63:1–4
O God, you are my God; eagerly I seek you : **my soul thirsts for you, my flesh faints for you, as in a barren and dry land where there is no water.**
Therefore I have gazed upon you in your holy place : **that I might behold your power and your glory.**
For your loving-kindness is better than life itself : **my lips shall give you praise.**
So will I bless you as long as I live : **and lift up my hands in your name.**

Make us friends of the thirsty, Lord : and teach us to thirst for you.

Numbers 16:1–19   Luke 6:27–38

Make us friends of the thirsty, Lord : and teach us to thirst for you.

These words were spoken to Catherine of Siena, a fourteenth-century mystic: "Beloved daughter, everything I give to you comes from the love and care I have for them. I desire to show my mercy to the whole world and my protective love to those want it. My care is constant. I did all this so that they will know me and rejoice to see me forever."

Prayers for Others

Our Father

Lord, your patience exceeds our comfort. We pray to step beyond the boundaries of what we call kindness. Expand our notion of mercy and enable us to turn toward our enemies even when they do not turn toward us. Amen.

May the peace of the Lord Christ go with you : wherever he may send you; may he guide you through the wilderness : protect you through the storm; may he bring you home rejoicing : at the wonders he has shown you; may he bring you home rejoicing : once again into our doors.

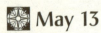 May 13

Julian of Norwich (1342–1416)
Born during a tumultuous period of England's history, Julian witnessed tremendous suffering in her lifetime. At age thirty, when she was seriously ill, Julian received the first of sixteen visions that centered on the crucified Christ. She interpreted her visions to mean that God loves us unconditionally, and she likened Christ to a mother who suffers when a child is hurt. Julian became an anchorite, voluntarily restricting herself to a tiny cell in the church

building at Norwich. She lived the rest of her days in almost total isolation so that she could pray for the community and offer spiritual counsel. Her *Showings* has been praised as being among the most important spiritual writing in the English language.

O Lord, let my soul rise up to meet you
as the day rises to meet the sun.

**Glory to the Father, and to the Son, and to the Holy Spirit,
as it was in the beginning, is now, and will be forever. Amen.**

Come, let us sing to the LORD : let us shout for joy to the Rock of our salvation.

Song "Ubi Caritas"

Let the peoples praise you, O God : let all the peoples praise you.

Psalm 67:1–4
May God be merciful to us and bless us : **show us the light of his countenance and come to us.**
Let your ways be known upon earth : **your saving health among all nations.**
Let the peoples praise you, O God : **let all the peoples praise you.**
Let the nations be glad and sing for joy : **for you judge the peoples with equity and guide all the nations upon earth.**

Let the peoples praise you, O God : let all the peoples praise you.

Numbers 16:20–35   Luke 6:39–49

Let the peoples praise you, O God : let all the peoples praise you.

Julian of Norwich prayed, "God, of your goodness, give me yourself, for you are enough for me. I may ask nothing less that is fully to your worship, and if I do ask anything less, ever shall I be in want. Only in you I have all."

Prayers for Others

Our Father

God, you are present in our joys and in our sorrows. Help us expect to live lives that mirror the suffering and joy of Christ our Savior. No disciple is above her master. Amen.

**May the peace of the Lord Christ go with you : wherever he may send you;
may he guide you through the wilderness : protect you through the storm;
may he bring you home rejoicing : at the wonders he has shown you;
may he bring you home rejoicing : once again into our doors.**

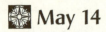 **May 14**

Brother Juniper (d. 1258)

A companion of Francis of Assisi, Brother Juniper is remembered as a "fool for Christ," and there are all sorts of wild stories about his antics. He was notorious for constantly giving his possessions away and living with a winsomeness that sometimes got him into trouble. At one point, he was ordered by a superior not to give away his outer garment to the beggars anymore. But it wasn't long before he met someone in need who asked him for some clothing. He said, "My superior has told me under obedience not to give my clothing to anyone. But if you pull it off my back, I certainly will not prevent you." Francis is said to have joked about how he wished for a forest of Junipers.

O Lord, let my soul rise up to meet you
as the day rises to meet the sun.

**Glory to the Father, and to the Son, and to the Holy Spirit,
as it was in the beginning, is now, and will be forever. Amen.**

Come, let us bow down and bend the knee : let us kneel before the LORD our Maker.

Song "Servant Song"

Blessed are you who are poor : for yours is the kingdom of God.

Psalm 72:1–2, 12–14
Give the king your justice, O God : **and your righteousness to the king's son;**
that he may rule your people righteously : **and the poor with justice.**
For he shall deliver the poor who cries out in distress : **and the oppressed who has no helper.**
He shall have pity on the lowly and poor : **he shall preserve the lives of the needy.**
He shall redeem their lives from oppression and violence : **and dear shall their blood be in his sight.**

Blessed are you who are poor : for yours is the kingdom of God.

Numbers 16:36–50   Luke 7:1–17

Blessed are you who are poor : for yours is the kingdom of God.

John Chrysostom, a fourth-century preacher and bishop of Constantinople, wrote, "Tell me then, how is it that you are rich? From whom did you receive it, and from whom did he transmit it to you? From his father and his grandfather. But can you, ascending through many generations, show the acquisition just? It cannot be. The root and origin of it must have been injustice. Why? Because God in the beginning did not make one person rich and another poor. He left the earth free to all alike. Why then if it is common, have you so many acres of land, while your neighbor has not a portion of it?"

Prayers for Others

Our Father

Lord, you did not withhold even your life for our benefit. If nothing is too much to offer you, remind us that nothing is too much to sacrifice for our brothers and sisters in need. Amen.

**May the peace of the Lord Christ go with you : wherever he may send you;
may he guide you through the wilderness : protect you through the storm;
may he bring you home rejoicing : at the wonders he has shown you;
may he bring you home rejoicing : once again into our doors.**

✱ May 15

On May 15 each year, many people gather for International Conscientious Objector's Day, holding vigils, protests, seminars, and campaigns to draw attention to conscientious objection. A conscientious objector is someone who refuses to serve in the armed forces or to bear arms in a military conflict. This refusal is based on moral or religious beliefs. It is also noteworthy that May 15 is celebrated as Israel's independence day and lamented by Palestinians as "Al Nakba," meaning "the day of catastrophe." We remember on this day the conflict in the Middle East. And we also celebrate conscientious objectors known as the Israeli Refuseniks.

O Lord, let my soul rise up to meet you
as the day rises to meet the sun.

**Glory to the Father, and to the Son, and to the Holy Spirit,
as it was in the beginning, is now, and will be forever. Amen.**

Come, let us sing to the LORD : let us shout for joy to the Rock of our salvation.

Song "Lamb of God"

The Lamb has conquered : let us follow him!

Psalm 76:1–4
In Judah is God known : **his name is great in Israel.**
At Salem is his tabernacle : **and his dwelling is in Zion.**
There he broke the flashing arrows : **the shield, the sword, and the weapons of battle.**

How glorious you are! : **more splendid than the everlasting mountains!**

The Lamb has conquered : let us follow him!

Numbers 17:1–11   Luke 7:18–35

The Lamb has conquered : let us follow him!

Fourth-century martyr Maximilian said, "I cannot enlist, for I am a Christian. I cannot serve, I cannot do evil. You can cut off my head, but I will not be a soldier of this world, for I am a soldier of Christ."

Prayers for Others

Our Father

Lord, grant us courage to stand firm by the tenets of your kingdom — to seek peace and pursue it, to hunger and thirst for righteousness, to uphold the cause of the voiceless, to worship no other God before you. Amen.

May the peace of the Lord Christ go with you : wherever he may send you; may he guide you through the wilderness : protect you through the storm; may he bring you home rejoicing : at the wonders he has shown you; may he bring you home rejoicing : once again into our doors.

May 16

On May 16, 1792, Denmark decided that it was immoral to participate in the trading of human beings and became the first European country to ban the transportation of slaves from their country.

It is also worth noting that this day marks the martyrdom of Dirk Willems. Willems is one of the most celebrated martyrs in the Anabaptist tradition (which includes Mennonites, Brethren, and Amish). He was born in the Netherlands and lived during a tumultuous time in Christendom. He is most famous for escaping from prison and turning around to rescue one of his pursuers, who had fallen through the thin ice of a frozen pond while chasing him. He was burned at the stake on May 16, 1569.

O Lord, let my soul rise up to meet you
as the day rises to meet the sun.

Glory to the Father, and to the Son, and to the Holy Spirit, as it was in the beginning, is now, and will be forever. Amen.

Come, let us bow down and bend the knee : let us kneel before the Lord our Maker.

Song "O Mary, Don't You Weep"

Restore us, O God of hosts : show the light of your countenance, and we shall be saved.

Psalm 80:4–7
O Lord God of hosts : **how long will you be angered despite the prayers of your people?**
You have fed them with the bread of tears : **you have given them bowls of tears to drink.**
You have made us the derision of our neighbors : **and our enemies laugh us to scorn.**
Restore us, O God of hosts : **show the light of your countenance, and we shall be saved.**

Restore us, O God of hosts : show the light of your countenance, and we shall be saved.

Numbers 20:1–13   Luke 7:36–50

Restore us, O God of hosts : show the light of your countenance, and we shall be saved.

Clare of Assisi, a friend of St. Francis in the twelfth century, said, "Place your mind before the mirror of eternity! Place your soul in the brilliance of glory! Place your heart in the figure of the divine substance! And transform your whole being into the image of the Godhead itself through contemplation!"

Prayers for Others

Our Father

Merciful God, nothing can separate us from you. When the distance between you and us seems unbearable, help us to move closer to you, knowing that by your mercy you are never beyond our reach. Amen.

**May the peace of the Lord Christ go with you : wherever he may send you;
may he guide you through the wilderness : protect you through the storm;
may he bring you home rejoicing : at the wonders he has shown you;
may he bring you home rejoicing : once again into our doors.**

✹ May 17

On May 17, 1968, the Catonsville Nine, which included two Catholic priests, went into the Selective Service offices in Catonsville, Maryland, and burned several hundred draft records in a direct action against the Vietnam War. They were arrested, tried, and found guilty of destroying government property. After the nine were sentenced, one of the priests, Dan Berrigan, asked the judge if the Lord's Prayer could be recited. All in the courtroom, including the judge and prosecuting attorneys, rose and joined in the prayer.

O Lord, let my soul rise up to meet you
as the day rises to meet the sun.

**Glory to the Father, and to the Son, and to the Holy Spirit,
as it was in the beginning, is now, and will be forever. Amen.**

Come, let us bow down and bend the knee : let us kneel before the Lord our Maker.

Song "Freedom Train"

We who believe in freedom : cannot rest until it comes.

Psalm 86:6–10
Give ear, O Lord, to my prayer : **and attend to the voice of my supplications.**
In the time of my trouble I will call upon you : **for you will answer me.**
Among the gods there is none like you, O Lord : **nor anything like your works.**
All nations you have made will come and worship you, O Lord : **and glorify your name.**
For you are great; you do wondrous things : **and you alone are God.**

We who believe in freedom : cannot rest until it comes.

Numbers 20:14–29   Luke 8:1–15

We who believe in freedom : cannot rest until it comes.

Dan Berrigan has said, "If you're going to follow Jesus, well, he got killed. That's just part of the job description: making trouble for peace."

Prayers for Others

Our Father

Today we pray for courage to dig ourselves deeper into the good soil, so that your word may take root in us and bring forth fruit that nourishes those who hunger for freedom. Amen.

May the peace of the Lord Christ go with you : wherever he may send you; may he guide you through the wilderness : protect you through the storm; may he bring you home rejoicing : at the wonders he has shown you; may he bring you home rejoicing : once again into our doors.

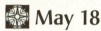 May 18

Origen of Alexandria (c. 185 – c. 254)

The oldest of seven children, Origen was born in Alexandria, and witnessed at a very young age the public death of his father, who was martyred during the persecutions in 202. While still in his teens, Origen became a teacher, philosopher, and student of Scripture — and a prolific writer, all the while practicing a strict discipline of prayer, fasting, celibacy, and poverty. Though his self-denial was extreme to the point of abuse and some of his teachings were ultimately considered heresy, Origen is still considered one of the greatest early interpreters of Scripture and Christian doctrine. By helping Christians find meaning in the riches of Scripture, he taught a love for truth, sanctity, and God above all else.

O Lord, let my soul rise up to meet you
as the day rises to meet the sun.

Glory to the Father, and to the Son, and to the Holy Spirit, as it was in the beginning, is now, and will be forever. Amen.

Come, let us sing to the LORD : let us shout for joy to the Rock of our salvation.

Song "Magnificat"

Steep us in your story, Lord : that we may live its truth today.

Psalm 92:1–4
It is a good thing to give thanks to the LORD : **and to sing praises to your name, O Most High;**
to tell of your loving-kindness early in the morning : **and of your faithfulness in the night season;**
on the psaltery, and on the lyre : **and to the melody of the harp.**
For you have made me glad by your acts, O LORD : **and I shout for joy because of the works of your hands.**

Steep us in your story, Lord : that we may live its truth today.

Numbers 21:4–9, 21–35   Luke 8:16–25

Steep us in your story, Lord : that we may live its truth today.

Origen of Alexandria wrote, "I do not call the Law an 'Old Testament' if I understand it in the Spirit. The Law becomes an 'Old Testament' only for those who wish to understand it carnally, but for those who understand it and apply it in the Spirit and in the Gospel sense, the Law is ever new and the two Testaments are a new Testament for us, not because of their date in time but because of the newness of the meaning. For those who do not respect the covenant of love, even the Gospels are 'old.' "

Prayers for Others

Our Father

Help us, Lord, to see in your Scripture the good news that never grows old. Amen.

**May the peace of the Lord Christ go with you : wherever he may send you;
may he guide you through the wilderness : protect you through the storm;
may he bring you home rejoicing : at the wonders he has shown you;
may he bring you home rejoicing : once again into our doors.**

✺ May 19

O Lord, let my soul rise up to meet you
as the day rises to meet the sun.

**Glory to the Father, and to the Son, and to the Holy Spirit,
as it was in the beginning, is now, and will be forever. Amen.**

Come, let us sing to the Lord : let us shout for joy to the Rock of our salvation.

Song   "Vamos Todos al Banquete"

God is good all the time : all the time, God is good.

Psalm 95:1–5
Come, let us sing to the Lord : **let us shout for joy to the Rock of our salvation.**
Let us come before his presence with thanksgiving : **and raise a loud shout to him with psalms.**
For the Lord is a great God : **and a great King above all gods.**
In his hand are the caverns of the earth : **and the heights of the hills are his also.**
The sea is his, for he made it : **and his hands have molded the dry land.**

God is good all the time : all the time, God is good.

Numbers 22:1–21   Luke 8:26–39

God is good all the time : all the time, God is good.

Paulo Freire wrote in his *Pedagogy of the Oppressed*, "To speak a true word is to transform the world."

Prayers for Others

Our Father

More often than not, Lord, we are afraid of truth. It threatens the identities we have created for ourselves and the ways we are comfortable perceiving others. Give us ears to hear your truth as blessing and mouths to celebrate your truth as gift. Amen.

May the peace of the Lord Christ go with you : wherever he may send you; may he guide you through the wilderness : protect you through the storm; may he bring you home rejoicing : at the wonders he has shown you; may he bring you home rejoicing : once again into our doors.

❁ May 20

In 1976, Indonesia annexed East Timor after the sudden withdrawal of the Portuguese. It is estimated that two hundred thousand Timorese died under the brutal and violent Indonesian rule. After years of violence between separatist guerillas and pro-Indonesian paramilitary forces, East Timor gained its independence on May 20, 2002. Today East Timor is one of the world's poorest countries.

O Lord, let my soul rise up to meet you
as the day rises to meet the sun.

**Glory to the Father, and to the Son, and to the Holy Spirit,
as it was in the beginning, is now, and will be forever. Amen.**

Come, let us sing to the LORD : let us shout for joy to the Rock of our salvation.

Song   "What Wondrous Love"

Find us in your love, O Lord : and lead us in your path.

Psalm 103:1–5
Bless the LORD, O my soul : **and all that is within me, bless his holy name.**
Bless the LORD, O my soul : **and forget not all his benefits.**

He forgives all your sins : **and heals all your infirmities;**
he redeems your life from the grave : **and crowns you with mercy and loving-kindness;**
he satisfies you with good things : **and your youth is renewed like an eagle's.**

Find us in your love, O Lord : and lead us in your path.

Numbers 22:21–38   Luke 8:40–56

Find us in your love, O Lord : and lead us in your path.

Twentieth-century Presbyterian theologian and writer Frederick Buechner has written, "Who knows how the awareness of God's love first hits people? Every person has his own tale to tell, including the person who would not believe in God if you paid him. Some moment happens in your life that makes you say Yes right up to the roots of your hair, that makes it worth having been born just to have happen. Laughing with somebody till the tears run down your cheeks. Waking up to the first snow. Being in bed with somebody you love. Whether you thank God for such a moment or thank your lucky stars, it is a moment that is trying to open up your whole life. If you try to turn your back on such a moment and hurry along to Business as Usual, it may lose you the whole ball game. If you throw your arms around such a moment and hug it like crazy, it may save your soul. How about the person you know who as far as you can possibly tell has never had such a moment? Maybe for that person the moment that has to happen is you."

Prayers for Others

Our Father

Give us grace to be present to those moments, Lord, when your love is real enough to taste. Amen.

**May the peace of the Lord Christ go with you : wherever he may send you;
may he guide you through the wilderness : protect you through the storm;
may he bring you home rejoicing : at the wonders he has shown you;
may he bring you home rejoicing : once again into our doors.**

✸ May 21

O Lord, let my soul rise up to meet you
as the day rises to meet the sun.

**Glory to the Father, and to the Son, and to the Holy Spirit,
as it was in the beginning, is now, and will be forever. Amen.**

Come, let us sing to the Lord : let us shout for joy to the Rock of our salvation.

Song "Glory, Glory, Hallelujah"

Give thanks to the Lord and call upon his name : make known his deeds among the peoples.

Psalm 105:24, 42–45
The Lord made his people exceedingly fruitful : **he made them stronger than their enemies;**
for God remembered his holy word : **and Abraham his servant.**
So he led forth his people with gladness : **his chosen with shouts of joy.**
He gave his people the lands of the nations : **and they took the fruit of others' toil,**
that they might keep his statutes : **and observe his laws. Hallelujah!**

Give thanks to the Lord and call upon his name : make known his deeds among the peoples.

Numbers 22:41–23:12   Luke 9:1–17

Give thanks to the Lord and call upon his name : make known his deeds among the peoples.

Evelyn Underhill wrote, "Adoration, as it more deeply possesses us, inevitably leads on to self-offering. Charity is the live wire along which the power of God, indwelling our finite spirits, can and does act on other souls and other things, rescuing, healing, giving support and light. Such secret intercessory prayer ought to penetrate and accompany all our active work. It is the supreme expression of the spiritual life on earth. It moves from God to others through us, because we have ceased to be self-centered units, but are woven into the great fabric of praying souls, the 'mystical body' through which the work of Christ on earth goes on being done."

Prayers for Others

Our Father

Lord, give us true words to pray for one another. Burden our hearts with shared sorrows, and delight our spirits with mutual joy. Let genuine love provoke in us words of blessing and inform our intercessions. Amen.

May the peace of the Lord Christ go with you : wherever he may send you; may he guide you through the wilderness : protect you through the storm; may he bring you home rejoicing : at the wonders he has shown you; may he bring you home rejoicing : once again into our doors.

May 22

In 1838, four thousand Cherokee died in the forced removal that the Cherokee called *Nunna dual Isunyi* — "the Trail Where They Cried." The removal of the Cherokee people resulted from the Indian Removal Act of 1830, which was violently implemented by Andrew Jackson. In 1831 the Choctaw were the first to be uprooted, followed by the Seminole in 1832, the Creek in 1834, the Chickasaw in 1837, and finally the Cherokee in 1838. By 1837, forty-six thousand Native Americans had been removed from their homes.

O Lord, let my soul rise up to meet you
as the day rises to meet the sun.

**Glory to the Father, and to the Son, and to the Holy Spirit,
as it was in the beginning, is now, and will be forever. Amen.**

Come, let us bow down and bend the knee : let us kneel before the LORD our Maker.

Song "Were You There?"

O Lord, have mercy : have mercy on us.

Psalm 109:20–25
But you, O Lord my GOD, oh, deal with me according to your name : **for your tender mercy's sake, deliver me.**
For I am poor and needy : **and my heart is wounded within me.**
I have faded away like a shadow when it lengthens : **I am shaken off like a locust.**
My knees are weak through fasting : **and my flesh is wasted and gaunt.**
I have become a reproach to them : **they see and shake their heads.**
Help me, O LORD my God : **save me for your mercy's sake.**

O Lord, have mercy : have mercy on us.

Numbers 23:11–26   Luke 9:18–27

O Lord, have mercy : have mercy on us.

Native theologian Randy Woodley has asked, "When will the American church awake from her slumber? If they want Native Americans to heal, if they want them to finally meet Jesus, then let them begin by speaking truth as Jesus did and say the only words Indians want to hear: 'We stole your land.' Our First Nations people have heard the Gospel over and over again, but rarely have they seen anyone truly live it."

Prayers for Others

Our Father

Teach us, Lord, to deny ourselves for the sake of your kingdom. Help us distinguish self-righteous suffering from the suffering that comes from bearing our crosses as we follow you. Amen.

**May the peace of the Lord Christ go with you : wherever he may send you;
may he guide you through the wilderness : protect you through the storm;
may he bring you home rejoicing : at the wonders he has shown you;
may he bring you home rejoicing : once again into our doors.**

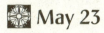 ## May 23

O Lord, let my soul rise up to meet you
as the day rises to meet the sun.

**Glory to the Father, and to the Son, and to the Holy Spirit,
as it was in the beginning, is now, and will be forever. Amen.**

Come, let us sing to the LORD : let us shout for joy to the Rock of our salvation.

Song "Holy, Holy, Holy"

With the saints around your throne : we praise you for your glory.

Psalm 111:1–2, 9–10
Hallelujah! I will give thanks to the LORD with my whole heart : **in the assembly of the upright, in the congregation.**
Great are the deeds of the LORD! : **they are studied by all who delight in them.**
He sent redemption to his people; he commanded his covenant for ever : **holy and awesome is his name.**
The fear of the LORD is the beginning of wisdom : **those who act accordingly have a good understanding; his praise endures for ever.**

With the saints around your throne : we praise you for your glory.

Numbers 24:1–13   Luke 9:28–36

With the saints around your throne : we praise you for your glory.

Now we hear the "Dance Hymn" from a manuscript titled Acts of John: "Grace leads the dance, I will make music. You shall all dance in a ring. I will lament, you shall all beat your breasts. I will flee, and I will stay. I will adorn, and I will be adorned. I will be united, and I will unite. I have no house, and I have houses. I have no home, and I have homes. I have no temple, and I have temples. I am a lamp to you who perceive me. I am a door to you who knock at me. I am a way to you, a traveler. Join yourself now to my dancing."

Prayers for Others

Our Father

Protect us, Lord, from being so offended by your revelations that we curse your prophets. Guard us from being so foolishly blinded by your majesty that we lose any sense of how to speak as your witness. Rather, help our lips praise you for your glory. Amen.

May the peace of the Lord Christ go with you : wherever he may send you;
may he guide you through the wilderness : protect you through the storm;
may he bring you home rejoicing : at the wonders he has shown you;
may he bring you home rejoicing : once again into our doors.

✣ May 24

O Lord, let my soul rise up to meet you
as the day rises to meet the sun.

Glory to the Father, and to the Son, and to the Holy Spirit,
as it was in the beginning, is now, and will be forever. Amen.

Come, let us sing to the LORD : let us shout for joy to the Rock of our salvation.

Song "Sing, O Sky (Gaao Re)"

Alabare! Alabare! : Alabare a mi Senor!

Psalm 117
Praise the LORD, all you nations : **laud him, all you peoples.**
For his loving-kindness toward us is great : **and the faithfulness of the LORD endures for ever. Hallelujah!**

Alabare! Alabare! : Alabare a mi Senor!

Numbers 24:12–25   Luke 9:37–50

Alabare! Alabare! : Alabare a mi Senor!

Ambrose, a fourth-century bishop of Milan, said, "Yes, a psalm is a blessing on the lips of the people, a hymn in praise of God, the assembly's homage, a general acclamation, a word that speaks for all, the voice of the church, a confession of faith in song. It is the voice of complete assent, the joy of freedom, a cry of happiness, the echo of gladness. It soothes the temper, distracts from care, lightens the burden of sorrow. Day begins to the music of a psalm. Day closes to the echo of a psalm."

Prayers for Others

Our Father

Let the moments and the hours of this day reverberate with sounds of our singing, with the words of the psalm, and with the praises we offer to you, O Lord. Amen.

**May the peace of the Lord Christ go with you : wherever he may send you;
may he guide you through the wilderness : protect you through the storm;
may he bring you home rejoicing : at the wonders he has shown you;
may he bring you home rejoicing : once again into our doors.**

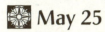 ## May 25

O Lord, let my soul rise up to meet you
as the day rises to meet the sun.

**Glory to the Father, and to the Son, and to the Holy Spirit,
as it was in the beginning, is now, and will be forever. Amen.**

Come, let us sing to the LORD : let us shout for joy to the Rock of our salvation.

Song "Guide My Feet"

Guide us, Lord, to walk : in courage, wisdom, and love.

Psalm 119:44–48
I shall continue to keep your law : **I shall keep it for ever and ever.**
I will walk at liberty : **because I study your commandments.**
I will tell of your decrees before kings : **and will not be ashamed.**
I delight in your commandments : **which I have always loved.**
I will lift up my hands to your commandments : **and I will meditate on your statutes.**

Guide us, Lord, to walk : in courage, wisdom, and love.

Numbers 27:12–23   Luke 9:51–62

Guide us, Lord, to walk : in courage, wisdom, and love.

Ammon Hennacy, a Catholic Worker, said, "Love without courage and wisdom is sentimentality, as with the ordinary church member. Courage without love and wisdom is foolhardiness, as with the ordinary soldier. Wisdom without love and courage is cowardice, as with the ordinary intellectual."

Prayers for Others

Our Father

Lord, you give life to our understanding of love, courage, and wisdom. Today there are so many paths we might follow. Help us discern the direction to set our own faces so that we might meet you at the cross in our willingness to deny ourselves for your kingdom, and at the empty tomb in our living the resurrection life. Amen.

**May the peace of the Lord Christ go with you : wherever he may send you;
may he guide you through the wilderness : protect you through the storm;
may he bring you home rejoicing : at the wonders he has shown you;
may he bring you home rejoicing : once again into our doors.**

> **Prayer Beads**
>
> Many different religions use beads as a tool for prayer, and Catholics have a rosary. Consider creating a chain of beads that you can use as a physical tool as you pray throughout the day. Prayer beads aren't magic, but they can help cure some minor cases of ADD (attention deficit disorder). For instance, create a chain of different-sized beads (or different-colored or different-textured beads) for various prayers. You might have a large bead for the Lord's Prayer. You might have seven rough beads for praying against the seven deadly sins—pride, envy, lust, anger, gluttony, greed, and sloth—and you might have nine little ones for the fruit of the Spirit listed in Galatians, so that you can rest on each one and pray that it would take root and grow like a seed inside of you—love, joy, peace, patience, kindness, goodness, gentleness, faithfulness, and self-control.

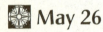 May 26

O Lord, let my soul rise up to meet you
as the day rises to meet the sun.

**Glory to the Father, and to the Son, and to the Holy Spirit,
as it was in the beginning, is now, and will be forever. Amen.**

Come, let us bow down and bend the knee : let us kneel before the Lord our Maker.

Song "Take My Life and Let It Be"

Like a hen gathers her brood, O Lord : shelter us under your wing.

Psalm 119:114–17
You are my refuge and shield : **my hope is in your word.**
Away from me, you wicked! : **I will keep the commandments of my God.**
Sustain me according to your promise, that I may live : **and let me not be disappointed in my hope.**

Hold me up, and I shall be safe : **and my delight shall be ever in your statutes.**

Like a hen gathers her brood, O Lord : shelter us under your wing.

Numbers 32:1–6, 16–27   Luke 10:1–17

Like a hen gathers her brood, O Lord : shelter us under your wing.

Indian priest Anthony de Mello told this story:

"A rich industrialist from the North was horrified to find a Southern fisherman lying leisurely beside his boat. 'Why aren't you fishing?' asked the industrialist.

" 'Because I have caught enough fish for the day,' said the fisherman.

" 'Why don't you catch some more?'

" 'What would I do with them?'

" 'You could earn more money,' was the reply. 'With that, you could fix a motor to your boat, go into deeper waters and catch more fish. Then you would make enough money to buy nylon nets. These would bring you more fish and more money. Soon you would have enough money to own two boats … maybe even a fleet of boats. Then you would be a rich man like me.'

" 'What would I do then?'

" 'Then you could really enjoy life.'

" 'What do you think I am doing right now?' said the fisherman."

Prayers for Others

Our Father

Lord, may your Holy Spirit dwell within us and among us that we might remember to hope in your word, to heed your instruction, and to delight in your statutes. Grant us humility to obey everything you have commanded us. Amen.

May the peace of the Lord Christ go with you : wherever he may send you; may he guide you through the wilderness : protect you through the storm; may he bring you home rejoicing : at the wonders he has shown you; may he bring you home rejoicing : once again into our doors.

May 27

Rahab

Rahab's story is found in the book of Joshua. Rahab was a prostitute who hid Hebrew spies in her home while they were on a reconnaissance mission in Jericho. Fearing the God of Israel more than her own king, Rahab agreed to help the spies if they would protect her and her family when God delivered her city to them. Though she is an unlikely saint, Rahab is remembered by the authors of Matthew, Hebrews, and James as a faithful witness and an ancestor of Jesus. Her story is a reminder that sinners make the best saints in God's story.

O Lord, let my soul rise up to meet you
as the day rises to meet the sun.

**Glory to the Father, and to the Son, and to the Holy Spirit,
as it was in the beginning, is now, and will be forever. Amen.**

Come, let us sing to the LORD: let us shout for joy to the Rock of our salvation.

Song "It Is Well with My Soul"

The LORD is God in heaven above : as he is on earth below.

Psalm 121:1–3, 7–8
I lift up my eyes to the hills : **from where is my help to come?**
My help comes from the LORD : **the maker of heaven and earth.**
He will not let your foot be moved : **and he who watches over you will not fall asleep.**
The LORD shall preserve you from all evil : **it is he who shall keep you safe.**
The LORD shall watch over your going out and your coming in : **from this time forth for evermore.**

The LORD is God in heaven above : as he is on earth below.

Joshua 2:1–21   Luke 10:17–24

The LORD is God in heaven above : as he is on earth below.

In his *Rule* for monastic community, Benedict of Nursia wrote, "Any guest who happens to arrive at the monastery should be received just as we would receive Christ himself, because he promised that on the last day he will say: I was a stranger and you welcomed me. Proper respect should be shown to everyone while a special welcome is reserved for those who are of the household of our Christian faith and for pilgrims. As soon as the arrival of a guest is announced, the superior and members of the community should hurry to offer a welcome with warm-hearted courtesy. First of all, they should pray together so as to seal their encounter in the peace of Christ. Prayer should come first and then the kiss of peace, so to evade any delusions which the devil may contrive."

Prayers for Others

Our Father

Lord, you receive all of us sinners, asking only that we turn from death toward life. Today we choose life wherever we find a stranger and welcome her. Amen.

May the peace of the Lord Christ go with you : wherever he may send you; may he guide you through the wilderness : protect you through the storm; may he bring you home rejoicing : at the wonders he has shown you; may he bring you home rejoicing : once again into our doors.

 **May 28**

O Lord, let my soul rise up to meet you
as the day rises to meet the sun.

Glory to the Father, and to the Son, and to the Holy Spirit, as it was in the beginning, is now, and will be forever. Amen.

Come, let us sing to the LORD: let us shout for joy to the Rock of our salvation.

Song "All Creatures of Our God and King"

Praise to you who dwell among us : keeping promise by your presence.

Psalm 132:8–13
Arise, O LORD, into your resting place : **you and the ark of your strength.**
Let your priests be clothed with righteousness : **let your faithful people sing with joy.**
For your servant David's sake : **do not turn away the face of your Anointed.**
The LORD has sworn an oath to David : **in truth, he will not break it:**
"A son, the fruit of your body : **will I set upon your throne.**
If your children keep my covenant and my testimonies that I shall teach them : **their children will sit upon your throne for evermore."**

Praise to you who dwell among us : keeping promise by your presence.

Numbers 35:1–3, 9–15, 30–34   Luke 10:25–37

Praise to you who dwell among us : keeping promise by your presence.

Irenaeus of Lyon, a second-century bishop, wrote, "The church has been planted as a paradise in this world."

Prayers for Others

Our Father

Lord, enable us today to see our neighbor in those whom the world rejects — the guilt-ridden, the foreigner, the unprotected, and the refugee. Open our eyes and make us present to these neighbors both in our various expressions of community and in the wider world. Amen.

May the peace of the Lord Christ go with you : wherever he may send you; may he guide you through the wilderness : protect you through the storm; may he bring you home rejoicing : at the wonders he has shown you; may he bring you home rejoicing : once again into our doors.

May 29

On May 29, 1968, the Poor People's Campaign arrived in Washington, D.C. The campaign was established to broaden the civil rights movement to include disadvantaged people of all races. The main demonstration was held at the Mall in Washington, D.C., where people camped out in tents called Resurrection City. Seven thousand demonstrators made this tent city their home to bring attention to issues of poverty and injustice.

O Lord, let my soul rise up to meet you
as the day rises to meet the sun.

Glory to the Father, and to the Son, and to the Holy Spirit, as it was in the beginning, is now, and will be forever. Amen.

Come, let us bow down and bend the knee : let us kneel before the Lord our Maker.

Song "We Shall Not Be Moved"

Lord, help us stand for justice : and find you among the poor.

Psalm 140:4–6
Keep me, O Lord, from the hands of the wicked : **protect me from the violent, who are determined to trip me up.**
The proud have hidden a snare for me and stretched out a net of cords : **they have set traps for me along the path.**
I have said to the Lord, "You are my God : **listen, O Lord, to my supplication."**

Lord, help us stand for justice : and find you among the poor.

Deuteronomy 1:1–18   Luke 10:38–42

Lord, help us stand for justice : and find you among the poor.

Mississippi civil rights activist Fannie Lou Hamer said, "Christianity is being concerned about your fellow man, not building a million-dollar church while people are starving right around the corner. Christ was a revolutionary person, out there where it was happening. That's what God is all about, and that's where I get my strength."

Prayers for Others

Our Father

Help us, Lord, to do the one thing that is necessary: to tend to the poor, to walk alongside the poor, to find you among the poor, to declare ourselves poor as long as anyone suffers need. May we begin this journey with just one person today. Amen.

**May the peace of the Lord Christ go with you : wherever he may send you;
may he guide you through the wilderness : protect you through the storm;
may he bring you home rejoicing : at the wonders he has shown you;
may he bring you home rejoicing : once again into our doors.**

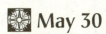 ## May 30

O Lord, let my soul rise up to meet you
as the day rises to meet the sun.

Glory to the Father, and to the Son, and to the Holy Spirit,
as it was in the beginning, is now, and will be forever. Amen.

Come, let us bow down and bend the knee : let us kneel before the Lord our Maker.

Song   "Let All Mortal Flesh Keep Silence"

Lord, we must decrease : so that you might increase.

Psalm 144:3–8
O Lord, what are we that you should care for us? : **mere mortals that you should think of us?**
We are like a puff of wind : **our days are like a passing shadow.**
Bow your heavens, O Lord, and come down : **touch the mountains, and they shall smoke.**

Morning Prayer   297

Hurl the lightning and scatter them : **shoot out your arrows and rout them.**
Stretch out your hand from on high : **rescue me and deliver me from the great waters, from the hand of foreign peoples,**
whose mouths speak deceitfully : **and whose right hand is raised in falsehood.**

Lord, we must decrease : so that you might increase.

Deuteronomy 3:18–28   Luke 11:1–13

Lord, we must decrease : so that you might increase.

Augustine of Hippo, a fifth-century bishop and theologian, wrote, "The way to Christ is first through humility, second through humility, third through humility. If humility does not precede and accompany and follow every good work we do, if it is not before us to focus on, if it is not beside us to lean upon, if it is not behind us to fence us in, pride will wrench from our hand any good deed we do at the very moment we do it."

Prayers for Others

Our Father

Lord, we expect good things from you because you are good and you promise to give to those who ask. Teach us to know not only how to ask but also for what we should ask. May all our asking, seeking, and knocking be to further your kingdom in some way, no matter how small or mundane. Amen.

**May the peace of the Lord Christ go with you : wherever he may send you;
may he guide you through the wilderness : protect you through the storm;
may he bring you home rejoicing : at the wonders he has shown you;
may he bring you home rejoicing : once again into our doors.**

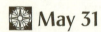 May 31

Feast of the Visitation

On May 31, the church celebrates Mary's visit with her cousin Elizabeth, after she had learned from the angel Gabriel that she was carrying the creator of the universe in her womb. Elizabeth was herself pregnant with John the Baptist at the time, and the gospel account tells us that he leapt for joy inside his mother when she embraced Mary. The joy of these two hosts — Mary and Elizabeth — is a reminder to us of the delight that comes when we practice hospitality, inviting God to come right into our lives.

O Lord, let my soul rise up to meet you
as the day rises to meet the sun.

Glory to the Father, and to the Son, and to the Holy Spirit,
as it was in the beginning, is now, and will be forever. Amen.

Come, let us sing to the Lord : let us shout for joy to the Rock of our salvation.

Song "This Little Light of Mine"

Sing and rejoice, O daughters of Zion : the Lord is coming and has now come.

Psalm 149:1–4
Hallelujah! Sing to the Lord a new song : **sing his praise in the congregation of the faithful.**
Let Israel rejoice in his Maker : **let the children of Zion be joyful in their King.**
Let them praise his name in the dance : **let them sing praise to him with timbrel and harp.**
For the Lord takes pleasure in his people : **and adorns the poor with victory.**

Sing and rejoice, O daughters of Zion : the Lord is coming and has now come.

Zephaniah 3:14–18a   Luke 1:39–49

Sing and rejoice, O daughters of Zion : the Lord is coming and has now come.

Jeanne de Chantal, seventeenth-century founder of the Order of the Visitation, said, "No matter what happens, be gentle with yourself."

Prayers for Others

Our Father

Lord, you have done great things for us, many of which we have hardly noticed. You are Lord over the past, sovereign in the present, and victorious in the future. Even in our trials, we celebrate you. Amen.

**May the peace of the Lord Christ go with you : wherever he may send you;
may he guide you through the wilderness : protect you through the storm;
may he bring you home rejoicing : at the wonders he has shown you;
may he bring you home rejoicing : once again into our doors.**

Becoming the Answer to Our Prayers: A Few Ideas

1. Wash your clothes by hand and dry them on a line. Remember the 1.6 billion people who do not have electricity.
2. Learn to sew. Try making your own clothes for a year.
3. Eat only one bowl of rice a day for a week. (Be sure also to take a multivitamin.) And remember the twenty-five thousand people who die of malnutrition and starvation each day.
4. Keep the Sabbath holy. Rest one day a week this year—don't answer the phone or the door, and don't use the internet. Do something that brings you life that day.
5. Go to a city council meeting. Pray. Speak as the Spirit leads.

JUNE — THE HOLY TRINITY

JUNE

Marks of New Monasticism
Care for Creation

Fifty days after Pentecost Sunday, the church celebrates the Holy Trinity, worshiping the one God who lives and reigns forever as Father, Son, and Holy Spirit. The Holy Trinity icon is a reminder that Abraham and Sarah had the chance to welcome God in three visitors who showed up at their door. Theology is never far removed from the people and places outside our door.

Much of our theology has been so concentrated on heaven that it invalidates any concern for the earth. Some images in Scripture have even been misconstrued to perpetuate a disregard for the creation, such as the image that in the last days the world will be consumed by fire. But nearly every other time the "consumed by fire" image is evoked in Scripture, it is a fire that purifies rather than burns up, a fire that frees up life rather than destroys it. No doubt, the way we live is shaped by how we imagine the end of the world — whether we think God's final plan is for everything to go up in flames or for everything to be brought back to life.

Creation care is not just about theology. It is about having the creativity to embody our theology imaginatively — flushing toilets with dirty sink water, riding a bike to work as an act of prophetic dissent, or helping an institution become carbon neutral. At its core, creation care is about loving our global neighbor, because the poor suffer the most from the degradation of the earth and the struggle for clean water. For many kids in the concrete jungle of the ghettoes and slums, there can be such a disconnection from creation that they feel disconnected from the Creator.

> **Suggested Reading for the Month**
> *For the Beauty of the Earth* by Steven Bouma-Prediger
> *Serve God, Save the Planet* by Matthew Sleeth
> *Go Green, Save Green* by Nancy Sleeth
> *Eaarth* by Bill McKibben

A community of folks moved into Camden, New Jersey, because the neighborhood has suffered so deeply from environmental degradation that it was rated one of the worst places to live in America. More than half the kids have chronic asthma. But part of what we do as we plant urban gardens is reconnect to the beauty of the earth. Kids get to see grass pierce concrete. Their eyes light up as they pull a carrot out of the ground, and digging for potatoes can feel like digging up lost treasure. At the heart of it all is a God who so loved the world and who called everything in it good. Our story began in a garden, but it ends in a city — a beautiful restored city the Scriptures describe as the New Jerusalem, coming on earth as it is in heaven. Christianity is not just about going up when we die; it's about bringing God's kingdom down, all the way to the dirt in our gardens.

✸ June 1

O Lord, let my soul rise up to meet you
as the day rises to meet the sun.

**Glory to the Father, and to the Son, and to the Holy Spirit,
as it was in the beginning, is now, and will be forever. Amen.**

Come, let us bow down and bend the knee : let us kneel before the LORD our Maker.

Song "Swing Low, Sweet Chariot"

Lord, we wait on you : guide us in the time of trouble.

Psalm 3:1–5
LORD, how many adversaries I have! : **how many there are who rise up against me!**
How many there are who say of me : **"There is no help for him in his God."**
But you, O LORD, are a shield about me : **you are my glory, the one who lifts up my head.**
I call aloud upon the LORD : **and he answers me from his holy hill;**
I lie down and go to sleep : **I wake again, because the LORD sustains me.**

Lord, we wait on you : guide us in the time of trouble.

Deuteronomy 4:1–9   Acts 1:1–14

Lord, we wait on you : guide us in the time of trouble.

Desert father Abba Anthony said, "Pay attention to what I tell you: whoever you may be, always have God before your eyes; whatever you do, do it according to the testimony of the holy Scriptures; in whatever place you live, do not easily leave it. Keep these three precepts and you will be saved."

Prayers for Others

Our Father

Grow us slowly, persistently, and deeply, Lord, to be people who watch without distraction, listen without interruption, and stay put without inclination to flee. Amen.

**May the peace of the Lord Christ go with you : wherever he may send you;
may he guide you through the wilderness : protect you through the storm;
may he bring you home rejoicing : at the wonders he has shown you;
may he bring you home rejoicing : once again into our doors.**

✶ June 2

On June 2, 1872, Julia Ward Howe began the celebration of Mother's Day as a holiday to honor mothers by working for an end to all war.

O Lord, let my soul rise up to meet you
as the day rises to meet the sun.

**Glory to the Father, and to the Son, and to the Holy Spirit,
as it was in the beginning, is now, and will be forever. Amen.**

Come, let us bow down and bend the knee : let us kneel before the LORD our Maker.

Song "Jesus, Help Us Live in Peace"

Make us students of your way, Lord : that we might study war no more.

Psalm 11:1–6
In the LORD have I taken refuge : **how then can you say to me, "Fly away like a bird to the hilltop;**
for see how the wicked bend the bow and fit their arrows to the string : **to shoot from ambush at the true of heart.**
When the foundations are being destroyed : **what can the righteous do?"**
The LORD is in his holy temple : **the LORD's throne is in heaven.**
His eyes behold the inhabited world : **his piercing eye weighs our worth.**
The LORD weighs the righteous as well as the wicked : **but those who delight in violence he abhors.**

Make us students of your way, Lord : that we might study war no more.

Deuteronomy 4:9–14   Acts 1:15–26

Make us students of your way, Lord : that we might study war no more.

Julia Ward Howe made this proclamation on the first Mother's Day: "Arise, then, women of this day! Arise, all women who have hearts, whether our baptism be of water or of tears! Say firmly: 'We will not have great questions decided by irrelevant agencies. Our husbands will not come to us, reeking with carnage, for caresses and applause. Our sons shall not be taken from us to unlearn all that we have been able to teach them of charity, mercy and patience.' From the bosom of the devastated Earth a voice goes up with our own. It says: 'Disarm! Disarm! The sword of murder is not the balance of justice.' Blood does not wipe out dishonor, nor violence indicate possession. As men have often forsaken the plough and the anvil at the summons of war, let women now leave all that may be left of home for a great and earnest day of counsel."

Prayers for Others

Our Father

Lord, help us assemble ourselves before you today through our acts of peace and reconciliation with neighbors near and far. Help us to teach the children in our communities what it means to be children of a God who loves us like a mother. Amen.

May the peace of the Lord Christ go with you : wherever he may send you; may he guide you through the wilderness : protect you through the storm; may he bring you home rejoicing : at the wonders he has shown you; may he bring you home rejoicing : once again into our doors.

 ## June 3

O Lord, let my soul rise up to meet you
as the day rises to meet the sun.

Glory to the Father, and to the Son, and to the Holy Spirit,
as it was in the beginning, is now, and will be forever. Amen.

Come, let us bow down and bend the knee : let us kneel before the Lord our Maker.

Song "I Will Trust in the Lord"

Pour out your Spirit, Lord : that we might dream your dream.

Psalm 17:1–3, 8–9
Hear my plea of innocence, O Lord; give heed to my cry : **listen to my prayer, which does not come from lying lips.**
Let my vindication come forth from your presence : **let your eyes be fixed on justice.**
Weigh my heart, summon me by night : **melt me down; you will find no impurity in me.**
Keep me as the apple of your eye : **hide me under the shadow of your wings,** from the wicked who assault me : **from my deadly enemies who surround me.**

Pour out your Spirit, Lord : that we might dream your dream.

Deuteronomy 4:15–24   Acts 2:1–21

Pour out your Spirit, Lord : that we might dream your dream.

William Booth, co-founder of the Salvation Army, said, "While women weep, as they do now, I'll fight; while children go hungry, as they do now, I'll fight;

while men go to prison, in and out, in and out, as they do now, I'll fight; while there is a drunkard left, while there is a poor lost girl upon the streets, while there remains one dark soul without the light of God, I'll fight — I'll fight to the very end!"

Prayers for Others

Our Father

Lord, grant us courage to fight the good fight by treating everybody right. Amen.

May the peace of the Lord Christ go with you : wherever he may send you; may he guide you through the wilderness : protect you through the storm; may he bring you home rejoicing : at the wonders he has shown you; may he bring you home rejoicing : once again into our doors.

 # June 4

In 1989, crowds of university students filled Tiananmen Square in Beijing to protest their government's oppressive regime. Though they were allowed to gather for weeks, on the night of June 3, the Chinese Army massacred hundreds of peaceful protestors.

O Lord, let my soul rise up to meet you
as the day rises to meet the sun.

Glory to the Father, and to the Son, and to the Holy Spirit,
as it was in the beginning, is now, and will be forever. Amen.

Come, let us sing to the LORD : let us shout for joy to the Rock of our salvation.

Song "Freedom Train"

You who were exalted on a cross : compel us with passion for justice and mercy.

Psalm 21:8–14
Your hand will lay hold upon all your enemies : **your right hand will seize all those who hate you.**
You will make them like a fiery furnace : **at the time of your appearing, O LORD;**
you will swallow them up in your wrath : **and fire shall consume them.**
You will destroy their offspring from the land : **and their descendants from among the peoples of the earth.**
Though they intend evil against you and devise wicked schemes : **yet they shall not prevail.**

For you will put them to flight : **and aim your arrows at them.**
Be exalted, O LORD, in your might : **we will sing and praise your power.**

You who were exalted on a cross : compel us with passion for justice and mercy.

Deuteronomy 4:25–31   Acts 2:22–36

You who were exalted on a cross : compel us with passion for justice and mercy.

Nineteenth-century Danish philosopher Søren Kierkegaard wrote, "The first form of rulers in the world were the tyrants, the last will be the martyrs. Between a tyrant and a martyr there is of course an enormous difference, although they both have one thing in common: the power to compel. The tyrant, himself ambitious to dominate, compels people through his power; the martyr, himself unconditionally obedient to God, compels others through his suffering. The tyrant dies and his rule is over; the martyr dies and his rule begins."

Prayers for Others

Our Father

God, give us discomfort at easy answers, half-truths, and superficial relationships, so that instead we may live deep within our hearts. Grant us anger at injustice, oppression, and exploitation of people, so that we may wish for justice, freedom, and peace. Bless us with enough foolishness to believe that we can make a difference in this world, so that we can do what others claim cannot be done. Amen.

**May the peace of the Lord Christ go with you : wherever he may send you;
may he guide you through the wilderness : protect you through the storm;
may he bring you home rejoicing : at the wonders he has shown you;
may he bring you home rejoicing : once again into our doors.**

June 5

In 1967, the Six-Day War erupted and lasted from June 5 to June 11. Israel fought neighboring nations Egypt, UAR, Jordan, and Syria in this historic war that has framed the ongoing conflict in the Middle East. At the war's end, Israel had seized the Gaza Strip and the Sinai Peninsula from Egypt, the West Bank and East Jerusalem from Jordan, and the Golan Heights from Syria. The status of these territories and the resulting refugee crisis continue to be central concerns in the ongoing Israeli-Palestinian conflict, raising issues of fairness, entitlement, theology, and international law.

O Lord, let my soul rise up to meet you
as the day rises to meet the sun.

**Glory to the Father, and to the Son, and to the Holy Spirit,
as it was in the beginning, is now, and will be forever. Amen.**

Come, let us sing to the LORD : let us shout for joy to the Rock of our salvation.

Song "Praise to the Lord, the Almighty"

Surely God is in this place : we stand on holy ground.

Psalm 26:8–12
LORD, I love the house in which you dwell : **and the place where your glory abides.**
Do not sweep me away with sinners : **nor my life with those who thirst for blood,**
whose hands are full of evil plots : **and their right hand full of bribes.**
As for me, I will live with integrity : **redeem me, O LORD, and have pity on me.**
My foot stands on level ground : **in the full assembly I will bless the LORD.**

Surely God is in this place : we stand on holy ground.

Deuteronomy 5:1–22   Acts 2:37–47

Surely God is in this place : we stand on holy ground.

Twentieth-century spiritual writer Henri Nouwen prayed, "Dear Lord, I will remain restless, tense and dissatisfied until I can be totally at peace in your house. There is no certainty that my life will be any easier in the years ahead, or that my heart will be any calmer. But there is the certainty that you are waiting for me and will welcome me home when I have persevered in my long journey to your house."

Prayers for Others

Our Father

Lord, meet us wherever goods are held in common for love and justice, wherever bread is broken for worship and praise, and wherever life witnesses to repentance and reconciliation. Amen.

**May the peace of the Lord Christ go with you : wherever he may send you;
may he guide you through the wilderness : protect you through the storm;
may he bring you home rejoicing : at the wonders he has shown you;
may he bring you home rejoicing : once again into our doors.**

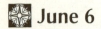 **June 6**

O Lord, let my soul rise up to meet you
as the day rises to meet the sun.

**Glory to the Father, and to the Son, and to the Holy Spirit,
as it was in the beginning, is now, and will be forever. Amen.**

Come, let us sing to the Lord : let us shout for joy to the Rock of our salvation.

Song "Nothin' but the Blood"

Lord Jesus Christ, Son of God : have mercy on me, a sinner.

Psalm 32:1–7
Happy are they whose transgressions are forgiven : **and whose sin is put away!**
Happy are they to whom the Lord imputes no guilt : **and in whose spirit there is no guile!**
While I held my tongue, my bones withered away : **because of my groaning all day long.**
For your hand was heavy upon me day and night : **my moisture was dried up as in the heat of summer.**
Then I acknowledged my sin to you : **and did not conceal my guilt.**
I said, "I will confess my transgressions to the Lord." : **Then you forgave me the guilt of my sin.**
Therefore all the faithful will make their prayers to you in time of trouble : **when the great waters overflow, they shall not reach them.**

Lord Jesus Christ, Son of God : have mercy on me, a sinner.

Deuteronomy 5:22–33   Acts 4:32–5:11

Lord Jesus Christ, Son of God : have mercy on me, a sinner.

Holocaust survivor Corrie ten Boom wrote, "Forgiveness is the key that unlocks the door of resentment and the handcuffs of hate. It is a power that breaks the chains of bitterness and the shackles of selfishness."

Prayers for Others

Our Father

Lord, you invite us to follow you on the way that leads to life, and yet so often we stray toward death. Thank you that we are still alive because of your patience and mercy. Teach us to mirror your forgiveness in our relationships with one another. Amen.

May the peace of the Lord Christ go with you : wherever he may send you;
may he guide you through the wilderness : protect you through the storm;
may he bring you home rejoicing : at the wonders he has shown you;
may he bring you home rejoicing : once again into our doors.

 June 7

Seattle (1786? – 1866)
Seattle was born in a Suquamish village along the Puget Sound. As a child he witnessed the arrival of the first white folks in the Northwest. In his early twenties, he was named chief of his tribe and inherited the responsibility of dealing with the white settlers. He rejected the option of violent resistance and insisted on peaceful discourse. In 1830 he and many other Natives converted to Christianity. Seattle became a leader committed to integrating his faith within his Native culture and traditions. He eventually became very disheartened with the way he saw the white settlers treating the creation. He died on June 7, 1866, on the Port Madison Reservation near the city which today bears his name.

O Lord, let my soul rise up to meet you
as the day rises to meet the sun.

Glory to the Father, and to the Son, and to the Holy Spirit,
as it was in the beginning, is now, and will be forever. Amen.

Come, let us sing to the LORD : let us shout for joy to the Rock of our salvation.

Song "Sing, O Sky (Gaao Re)"

We are part of the earth : and it is part of us.

Psalm 36:5 – 10
Your love, O LORD, reaches to the heavens : **and your faithfulness to the clouds.**
Your righteousness is like the strong mountains, your justice like the great deep : **you save both man and beast, O LORD.**
How priceless is your love, O God! : **your people take refuge under the shadow of your wings.**
They feast upon the abundance of your house : **you give them drink from the river of your delights.**
For with you is the well of life : **and in your light we see light.**
Continue your loving-kindness to those who know you : **and your favor to those who are true of heart.**

We are part of the earth : and it is part of us.

Deuteronomy 11:1–12   Acts 5:12–26

We are part of the earth : and it is part of us.

Seattle said, "Humankind did not weave the web of life. We are but one strand within it. Whatever we do to the web we do to ourselves."

Prayers for Others

Our Father

Lord, you care for all of creation and watch over the earth and its inhabitants day and night. Help us learn to love all things created by your hand. Teach us that we are part of a larger tapestry woven together for the good of all. Amen.

**May the peace of the Lord Christ go with you : wherever he may send you;
may he guide you through the wilderness : protect you through the storm;
may he bring you home rejoicing : at the wonders he has shown you;
may he bring you home rejoicing : once again into our doors.**

June 8

O Lord, let my soul rise up to meet you
as the day rises to meet the sun.

**Glory to the Father, and to the Son, and to the Holy Spirit,
as it was in the beginning, is now, and will be forever. Amen.**

Come, let us bow down and bend the knee : let us kneel before the Lord our Maker.

Song   "Poor Wayfaring Stranger"

Give ear to our cry, O Lord : listen to your children praying.

Psalm 39:11–15
Take your affliction from me : **I am worn down by the blows of your hand.**
With rebukes for sin you punish us; like a moth you eat away all that is dear to us : **truly, everyone is but a puff of wind.**
Hear my prayer, O Lord, and give ear to my cry : **hold not your peace at my tears.**
For I am but a sojourner with you : **a wayfarer, as all my forebears were.**
Turn your gaze from me, that I may be glad again : **before I go my way and am no more.**

Give ear to our cry, O Lord : listen to your children praying.

Deuteronomy 11:13–19   Acts 5:27–42

Give ear to our cry, O Lord : listen to your children praying.

In his *Rule* for monastic community, Benedict of Nursia wrote, "The first step of humility is to cherish at all times the sense of awe with which we should turn to God."

Prayers for Others

Our Father

Lord, send us forth into the day to rejoice in all things, to trust you in all circumstances, and to proclaim your coming kingdom to all people. Amen.

May the peace of the Lord Christ go with you : wherever he may send you; may he guide you through the wilderness : protect you through the storm; may he bring you home rejoicing : at the wonders he has shown you; may he bring you home rejoicing : once again into our doors.

> **Prayer Bowl**
>
> Some families and communities find it helpful to have a prayer bowl on the coffee table or in the room where they gather to pray each day. Whenever someone asks for prayer, they write the request on a little slip of paper and put it in the bowl. Then when it's time for morning or evening prayer, each person can take a few slips of paper from the bowl and read out the requests during the time for prayers for others. This is also a good way to remember people we don't see every day, like children in war zones, victims of human trafficking, or our political leaders.

June 9

O Lord, let my soul rise up to meet you
as the day rises to meet the sun.

Glory to the Father, and to the Son, and to the Holy Spirit, as it was in the beginning, is now, and will be forever. Amen.

Come, let us sing to the LORD : let us shout for joy to the Rock of our salvation.

Song "Solid Rock"

The Lord of hosts is with us : the God of Jacob is our stronghold.

Psalm 46:1–4
God is our refuge and strength : **a very present help in trouble.**
Therefore we will not fear, though the earth be moved : **and though the mountains be toppled into the depths of the sea;**

though its waters rage and foam : **and though the mountains tremble at its tumult.**
The L ORD of hosts is with us : **the God of Jacob is our stronghold.**

The Lord of hosts is with us : the God of Jacob is our stronghold.

Deuteronomy 12:1 – 12   Acts 6:1 – 15

The Lord of hosts is with us : the God of Jacob is our stronghold.

John Wesley, who founded the Methodist movement, wrote, "One of the principle rules of religion is to lose no occasion of serving God. And since he is invisible to our eyes, we are to serve him in our neighbor; which he receives as if done to himself in person, standing visibly before us."

Prayers for Others

Our Father

Lord, we want to serve you in the love we show our neighbors. Teach us to embrace each person made in your image as if we were greeting you. Amen.

May the peace of the Lord Christ go with you : wherever he may send you;
may he guide you through the wilderness : protect you through the storm;
may he bring you home rejoicing : at the wonders he has shown you;
may he bring you home rejoicing : once again into our doors.

June 10

O Lord, let my soul rise up to meet you
as the day rises to meet the sun.

Glory to the Father, and to the Son, and to the Holy Spirit,
as it was in the beginning, is now, and will be forever. Amen.

Come, let us bow down and bend the knee : let us kneel before the L ORD our Maker.

Song   "O Mary, Don't You Weep"

Root out wickedness from our hearts : and scatter our evil thoughts.

Psalm 52:1 – 5
You tyrant, why do you boast of wickedness : **against the godly all day long?**
You plot ruin; your tongue is like a sharpened razor : **O worker of deception.**
You love evil more than good : **and lying more than speaking the truth.**
You love all words that hurt : **O you deceitful tongue.**

Oh, that God would demolish you utterly : **topple you, and snatch you from your dwelling, and root you out of the land of the living!**

Root out wickedness from our hearts : and scatter our evil thoughts.

Deuteronomy 13:1–11   Acts 6:15–7:16

Root out wickedness from our hearts : and scatter our evil thoughts.

Desert father Joseph of Panephysis said, "If you want to find rest here below, and hereafter, in all circumstances say, Who am I? and do not judge anyone."

Prayers for Others

Our Father

Lord Jesus Christ, set our sights on your kingdom this day that we may keep from false idols and tempting voices. You alone are God, who keeps us and directs our steps for your glory. Amen.

May the peace of the Lord Christ go with you : wherever he may send you; may he guide you through the wilderness : protect you through the storm; may he bring you home rejoicing : at the wonders he has shown you; may he bring you home rejoicing : once again into our doors.

✺ June 11

O Lord, let my soul rise up to meet you
as the day rises to meet the sun.

**Glory to the Father, and to the Son, and to the Holy Spirit,
as it was in the beginning, is now, and will be forever. Amen.**

Come, let us bow down and bend the knee : let us kneel before the Lord our Maker.

Song   "Waters of Babylon"

Yea, though you slay me : yet will I praise you.

Psalm 58:3–8
The wicked are perverse from the womb : **liars go astray from their birth.**
They are as venomous as a serpent : **they are like the deaf adder which stops its ears,**
which does not heed the voice of the charmer : **no matter how skillful his charming.**
O God, break their teeth in their mouths : **pull the fangs of the young lions, O Lord.**

Morning Prayer   315

Let them vanish like water that runs off : **let them wither like trodden grass. Let them be like the snail that melts away : like a stillborn child that never sees the sun.**

Yea, though you slay me : yet will I praise you.

Deuteronomy 16:18–20; 17:14–20   Acts 7:17–29

Yea, though you slay me : yet will I praise you.

A victim of the Holocaust, Anne Frank wrote, "I see the world gradually being turned into a wilderness. I hear the ever-approaching thunder, which will destroy us too. I can feel the sufferings of millions and yet, if I look up into the heavens, I think that it will all come right. In the meantime, I must uphold my ideals, for perhaps the time will come when I shall be able to carry them out."

Prayers for Others

Our Father

God, you alone are the judge of humankind, yet you call us to work toward justice. Help us make the judgments necessary for faithful living without becoming judgmental, that we may celebrate the mystery by which your justice is your mercy, through Jesus Christ our Lord. Amen.

May the peace of the Lord Christ go with you : wherever he may send you; may he guide you through the wilderness : protect you through the storm; may he bring you home rejoicing : at the wonders he has shown you; may he bring you home rejoicing : once again into our doors.

✤ June 12

O Lord, let my soul rise up to meet you
as the day rises to meet the sun.

Glory to the Father, and to the Son, and to the Holy Spirit,
as it was in the beginning, is now, and will be forever. Amen.

Come, let us bow down and bend the knee : let us kneel before the LORD our Maker.

Song   "We Shall Not Be Moved"

Satan is defeated! : Deliver us from fear.

Psalm 64:1–4, 8–10
Hear my voice, O God, when I complain : **protect my life from fear of the enemy.**
Hide me from the conspiracy of the wicked : **from the mob of evildoers.**
They sharpen their tongue like a sword : **and aim their bitter words like arrows,**
that they may shoot down the blameless from ambush : **they shoot without warning and are not afraid.**
He will make them trip over their tongues : **and all who see them will shake their heads.**
Everyone will stand in awe and declare God's deeds : **they will recognize his works.**
The righteous will rejoice in the Lord and put their trust in him : **and all who are true of heart will glory.**

Satan is defeated! Deliver us from fear.

Deuteronomy 26:1–11   Acts 7:30–43

Satan is defeated! Deliver us from fear.

Contemporary theologian Scott Bader-Saye has written, "Following Jesus will mean surrendering the power that masquerades as security in order to love the neighbor and welcome the stranger. It will mean avoiding the safe path in order to pursue the good. But in a culture of fear, we find such risks all the more difficult since our natural inclinations lead us to close in on ourselves when we face danger. How can we maintain the posture of the open hand toward a world that scares us?"

Prayers for Others

Our Father

You alone secure us in our place, O Lord. In our going out and coming in, deliver us from fear, that we may, by your Spirit's power, let down our defenses in love. Amen.

May the peace of the Lord Christ go with you : wherever he may send you;
may he guide you through the wilderness : protect you through the storm;
may he bring you home rejoicing : at the wonders he has shown you;
may he bring you home rejoicing : once again into our doors.

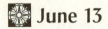 **June 13**

O Lord, let my soul rise up to meet you
as the day rises to meet the sun.

**Glory to the Father, and to the Son, and to the Holy Spirit,
as it was in the beginning, is now, and will be forever. Amen.**

Come, let us bow down and bend the knee : let us kneel before the Lord our Maker.

Song "I Will Trust in the Lord"

Father, I stretch my hand to you : no other help I know.

Psalm 70:1–6
Be pleased, O God, to deliver me : **O Lord, make haste to help me.**
Let those who seek my life be ashamed and altogether dismayed : **let those who take pleasure in my misfortune draw back and be disgraced.**
Let those who say to me "Aha!" and gloat over me turn back : **because they are ashamed.**
Let all who seek you rejoice and be glad in you : **let those who love your salvation say for ever, "Great is the Lord!"**
But as for me, I am poor and needy : **come to me speedily, O God.**
You are my helper and my deliverer : **O Lord, do not tarry.**

Father, I stretch my hand to you : no other help I know.

Deuteronomy 29:2–15   Acts 7:44–8:1a

Father, I stretch my hand to you : no other help I know.

Mennonite theologian John Howard Yoder wrote, "The work of God is the calling of a people, whether in the Old Covenant or the New. The church is then not simply the bearer of the message of reconciliation, in the way a newspaper or a telephone company can bear any message with which it is entrusted. Nor is the church simply the result of a message, as an alumni association is the product of a school or the crowds in a theater are the product of the reputation of the film. That men and women are called together to a new social wholeness is itself the work of God, which gives meaning to history."

Prayers for Others

Our Father

Lord, you call us out of captivity into the freedom of your beloved community. As we pass through the wilderness spaces of our lives, grant us ears to hear you, eyes to see you, and hearts that ache for you, that we might not turn away from the brothers and sisters who help us remember who we are. Amen.

May the peace of the Lord Christ go with you : wherever he may send you;
may he guide you through the wilderness : protect you through the storm;
may he bring you home rejoicing : at the wonders he has shown you;
may he bring you home rejoicing : once again into our doors.

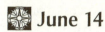 **June 14**

Gilbert Keith Chesterton (1874 – 1936)

A towering presence, G. K. Chesterton was an excitable and opinionated man who was also blessed with a sense of humor that has much to offer a world polarized by politics. He passionately critiqued liberals and conservatives, and maintained a lively and genuine friendship with George Bernard Shaw, with whom he disagreed on nearly everything. Chesterton set out to rethink the faith, but laughingly compared his quest to a voyager who set out to find a lost land only to rediscover England. At forty-eight, he formally converted to Catholicism. Amid very serious discourse, he insisted that despair comes not from being weary of suffering but from being weary of joy. He died on this day, and his epitaph describes him as one who helped restore the world to sanity by exaggerating whatever the world neglects.

O Lord, let my soul rise up to meet you
as the day rises to meet the sun.

Glory to the Father, and to the Son, and to the Holy Spirit,
as it was in the beginning, is now, and will be forever. Amen.

Come, let us bow down and bend the knee : let us kneel before the LORD our Maker.

Song "Guide My Feet"

May our minds stay fixed on you : the perfecter of our faith.

Psalm 73:1 – 6
Truly, God is good to Israel : **to those who are pure in heart.**
But as for me, my feet had nearly slipped : **I had almost tripped and fallen;**
because I envied the proud : **and saw the prosperity of the wicked:**
for they suffer no pain : **and their bodies are sleek and sound;**

in the misfortunes of others they have no share : **they are not afflicted as others are;**
therefore they wear their pride like a necklace : **and wrap their violence about them like a cloak.**

May our minds stay fixed on you : the perfecter of our faith.

Deuteronomy 29:16–29   Acts 8:1–13

May our minds stay fixed on you : the perfecter of our faith.

G. K. Chesterton said, "The whole modern world has divided itself into Conservatives and Progressives. The business of Progressives is to go on making mistakes. The business of the Conservatives is to prevent the mistakes from being corrected."

Prayers for Others

Our Father

Lord, free us from our self-deception and attune our hearts to your Spirit, that we might remember how you humbled yourself, and learn to serve one another, whatever our disagreements. Amen.

May the peace of the Lord Christ go with you : wherever he may send you; may he guide you through the wilderness : protect you through the storm; may he bring you home rejoicing : at the wonders he has shown you; may he bring you home rejoicing : once again into our doors.

✺ June 15

In 1955, twenty-nine people were arrested in New York City for refusing to participate in a civil defense drill requiring all citizens to take shelter from a simulated nuclear attack. "We refused to take part in the war maneuvers, if you can call them that," wrote Dorothy Day, who was among the pacifist resisters. Civil defense drills were discontinued six years later when the annual protest in City Hall Park drew a crowd of thousands.

O Lord, let my soul rise up to meet you
as the day rises to meet the sun.

Glory to the Father, and to the Son, and to the Holy Spirit,
as it was in the beginning, is now, and will be forever. Amen.

Come, let us sing to the L ORD : let us shout for joy to the Rock of our salvation.

Song   "What Wondrous Love"

O Lord, you have been our dwelling place : through every generation.

Psalm 78:1–4
Hear my teaching, O my people : **incline your ears to the words of my mouth.**
I will open my mouth in a parable : **I will declare the mysteries of ancient times.**
That which we have heard and known, and what our forefathers have told us : **we will not hide from their children.**
We will recount to generations to come the praiseworthy deeds and the power of the Lord : **and the wonderful works he has done.**

O Lord, you have been our dwelling place : through every generation.

Deuteronomy 30:1–10   Acts 8:14–25

O Lord, you have been our dwelling place : through every generation.

Ignatius of Antioch said, "Take heed, then, to come together often to give thanks to God, and show his praise. For when you come frequently together in the same place, the powers of Satan are destroyed, and his fiery darts of sin fall back, worthless. For your unity and harmonious faith prove his destruction, and the torment of his assistants. Nothing is better than Christ's peace, by which all war, both of heavenly and earthly spirits, is brought to an end."

Prayers for Others

Our Father

God, set our hearts on you alone, that we might not be distracted by the schemes of the devil but race on with all of our being to receive the gift of life that never ends, through Jesus Christ our Lord. Amen.

**May the peace of the Lord Christ go with you : wherever he may send you;
may he guide you through the wilderness : protect you through the storm;
may he bring you home rejoicing : at the wonders he has shown you;
may he bring you home rejoicing : once again into our doors.**

✦ June 16

In 1976, seven hundred students were killed in Soweto, South Africa, as they struggled against the forces of apartheid.

O Lord, let my soul rise up to meet you
as the day rises to meet the sun.

Morning Prayer 321

**Glory to the Father, and to the Son, and to the Holy Spirit,
as it was in the beginning, is now, and will be forever. Amen.**

Come, let us sing to the LORD : let us shout for joy to the Rock of our salvation.

Song "We Are Marching in the Light of God"

Shine your light on our darkness, Lord : and teach us the duty of delight.

Psalm 81:1–5
Sing with joy to God our strength : **and raise a loud shout to the God of Jacob.**
Raise a song and sound the timbrel : **the merry harp, and the lyre.**
Blow the ram's horn at the new moon : **and at the full moon, the day of our feast.**
For this is a statute for Israel : **a law of the God of Jacob.**
He laid it as a solemn charge upon Joseph : **when he came out of the land of Egypt.**

Shine your light on our darkness, Lord : and teach us the duty of delight.

Deuteronomy 30:11–20   Acts 8:26–40

Shine your light on our darkness, Lord : and teach us the duty of delight.

American preacher Howard Thurman wrote, "Too often the price exacted by society for security and respectability is that the Christian movement in its formal expression must be on the side of the strong against the weak. This is a matter of tremendous significance, for it reveals to what extent a religion that was born of a people acquainted with persecution and suffering has become the cornerstone of a civilization and of nations whose very position in modern life too often has been secured by a ruthless use of power applied to defenseless peoples."

Prayers for Others

Our Father

Lord, help us stand up both to the demons that hide behind ungodly laws, and the false religion that props up injustice. Make us into a people who shine out your love so that the world might know another way is possible. Amen.

**May the peace of the Lord Christ go with you : wherever he may send you;
may he guide you through the wilderness : protect you through the storm;
may he bring you home rejoicing : at the wonders he has shown you;
may he bring you home rejoicing : once again into our doors.**

June 17

John Wesley (1703–1791)

Though his studies led him to become an Anglican cleric, John Wesley did not at first have a vibrant spiritual life. While en route to the colony of Georgia as a missionary, his ship lost its mast in a violent storm. Witnessing the Moravian passengers sing and pray peacefully through the storm, Wesley realized that he lacked "the one thing necessary." After his heart was "strangely warmed" in a moving conversion experience, Wesley became a popular preacher among the working class of England and led the movement now called Methodism. The core of his message was that Christianity is based on the experience of God's grace, which bears fruit through a life of love. Wesley said, "When I have money, I get rid of it quickly, lest it find a way into my heart." He died at the age of eighty-eight, lifting his arms and saying, "The best of all, God is with us."

O Lord, let my soul rise up to meet you
as the day rises to meet the sun.

**Glory to the Father, and to the Son, and to the Holy Spirit,
as it was in the beginning, is now, and will be forever. Amen.**

Come, let us bow down and bend the knee : let us kneel before the LORD our Maker.

Song "Come, Thou Fount"

Best of all, God : you are with us.

Psalm 88:15–19
LORD, why have you rejected me? : **why have you hidden your face from me?**
Ever since my youth, I have been wretched and at the point of death : **I have borne your terrors with a troubled mind.**
Your blazing anger has swept over me : **your terrors have destroyed me;**
they surround me all day long like a flood : **they encompass me on every side.**
My friend and my neighbor you have put away from me : **and darkness is my only companion.**

Best of all, God : you are with us.

Deuteronomy 31:30–32:14   Acts 9:1–9

Best of all, God : you are with us.

Prayers for Others

Our Father

This prayer of John Wesley is used by many Christians at the beginning of each year: "I am no longer my own, but thine. Put me to what thou wilt, rank me with whom thou wilt. Put me to doing, put me to suffering. Let me be employed for thee or laid aside for thee, exalted for thee or brought low for thee. Let me be full, let me be empty. Let me have all things, let me have nothing. I freely and heartily yield all things to thy pleasure and disposal. And now, O glorious and blessed God, Father, Son, and Holy Spirit, thou art mine, and I am thine. So be it. And the covenant which I have made on earth, let it be ratified in heaven. Amen."

May the peace of the Lord Christ go with you : wherever he may send you; may he guide you through the wilderness : protect you through the storm; may he bring you home rejoicing : at the wonders he has shown you; may he bring you home rejoicing : once again into our doors.

✺ June 18

O Lord, let my soul rise up to meet you
as the day rises to meet the sun.

Glory to the Father, and to the Son, and to the Holy Spirit,
as it was in the beginning, is now, and will be forever. Amen.

Come, let us sing to the Lord : let us shout for joy to the Rock of our salvation.

Song "Steal Away to Jesus"

Hide us under the shadow of your wing : and deliver us from fear.

Psalm 91:1–4
He who dwells in the shelter of the Most High : **abides under the shadow of the Almighty.**
He shall say to the Lord, "You are my refuge and my stronghold : **my God in whom I put my trust."**
He shall deliver you from the snare of the hunter : **and from the deadly pestilence.**
He shall cover you with his pinions, and you shall find refuge under his wings : **his faithfulness shall be a shield and buckler.**

Hide us under the shadow of your wing : and deliver us from fear.

Ruth 1:1–18   Acts 9:10–19a

Hide us under the shadow of your wing : and deliver us from fear.

This story is recorded in the Acts of Eusebius: "When the proconsul was present in Pergamum, Carpus and Papylus, joyful martyrs of Christ, were brought to him. The proconsul sat down and asked, 'What is your name?' The one who was questioned answered, 'My first and chosen name is Christian. But if you are asking for my name in the world, then I call myself Carpus. It is impossible for me to offer sacrifices to these delusive phantoms, these demons, for they who sacrifice to them become like them. The living do not sacrifice to the dead."

Prayers for Others

Our Father

Lord, embolden us to go wherever you call us, to greet whoever you send us, and to do whatever you ask of us, that we might know no fear except that reverence which leads to wisdom. Amen.

May the peace of the Lord Christ go with you : wherever he may send you; may he guide you through the wilderness : protect you through the storm; may he bring you home rejoicing : at the wonders he has shown you; may he bring you home rejoicing : once again into our doors.

❖ June 19

In 1865, slaves in Texas were the last to learn of their emancipation following the defeat of the Confederate States of America. In African-American communities throughout the United States, this good news of liberation to the captives is still celebrated as Juneteenth.

O Lord, let my soul rise up to meet you
as the day rises to meet the sun.

Glory to the Father, and to the Son, and to the Holy Spirit, as it was in the beginning, is now, and will be forever. Amen.

Come, let us sing to the LORD : let us shout for joy to the Rock of our salvation.

Song "Go, Tell It on the Mountain"

How beautiful are the feet : of those who bring good news.

Psalm 97:1–3, 10–12
The LORD is King; let the earth rejoice : **let the multitude of the isles be glad.**
Clouds and darkness are round about him : **righteousness and justice are the foundations of his throne.**
A fire goes before him : **and burns up his enemies on every side.**

The LORD loves those who hate evil : **he preserves the lives of his saints and delivers them from the hand of the wicked.**
Light has sprung up for the righteous : **and joyful gladness for those who are truehearted.**
Rejoice in the LORD, you righteous : **and give thanks to his holy name.**

How beautiful are the feet : of those who bring good news.

Ruth 1:19–2:13   Acts 9:19b–31

How beautiful are the feet : of those who bring good news.

When an angry heckler once declared, "Old woman, I don't care any more for your talk than I do for the bite of a flea," abolitionist Sojourner Truth replied, "The Lord willing, I'll keep you scratching."

Prayers for Others

Our Father

Lord, wherever there is mercy, justice, freedom, and kindness, we know your good news is echoing in human history. Give us ears to recognize the sound of glad feet coming and grant us grace to join you wherever you are moving. Amen.

May the peace of the Lord Christ go with you : wherever he may send you; may he guide you through the wilderness : protect you through the storm; may he bring you home rejoicing : at the wonders he has shown you; may he bring you home rejoicing : once again into our doors.

 # June 20

Osanna of Mantua (1449–1505)
Born to wealthy parents in Mantua, Italy, Osanna Andreasi, at age five, heard the voice of God saying, "Life and death consist in loving God." She was then given a vision of heaven and the Trinity. Tradition has it that Osanna learned to read and write by divine revelation and began studying theology after this vision. Against her parents' wishes, she longed to join the Third Order of Dominicans, but she would have to wait thirty-seven years to complete her vows. Upon the untimely death of her parents, Osanna committed her life to serving Christ and caring for her family of siblings. She was privy to ongoing holy visions and was reputed to have received the stigmata — the wounds of Christ. She spent her life aiding the poor and sick and speaking out boldly against aristocrats who lived lavish lives while others suffered.

O Lord, let my soul rise up to meet you
as the day rises to meet the sun.

**Glory to the Father, and to the Son, and to the Holy Spirit,
as it was in the beginning, is now, and will be forever. Amen.**

Come, let us sing to the Lord : let us shout for joy to the Rock of our salvation.

Song "Holy, Holy, Holy"

Life and death consist : in loving you, O God.

Psalm 104:32–37
May the glory of the Lord endure for ever : **may the Lord rejoice in all his works.**
He looks at the earth and it trembles : **he touches the mountains and they smoke.**
I will sing to the Lord as long as I live : **I will praise my God while I have my being.**
May these words of mine please him : **I will rejoice in the Lord.**
Let sinners be consumed out of the earth : **and the wicked be no more.**
Bless the Lord, O my soul : **Hallelujah!**

Life and death consist : in loving you, O God.

Ruth 2:14–23   Acts 9:32–43

Life and death consist : in loving you, O God.

John Chrysostom, a fourth-century preacher and bishop of Constantinople, said, "Our spirit should be quick to reach out toward God, not only when it is engaged in meditation; at other times also, when it is carrying out its duties, caring for the needy, performing works of charity, or giving generously in the service of others. Our spirit should long for God and call him to mind, so that these works may be seasoned with the salt of God's love, and so make a palatable offering to the Lord of the universe."

Prayers for Others

Our Father

Lord, we know that you will come again in glory to raise the living and the dead. Resurrect us now from the death of comfort, complacency, sloth, and shallowness that we might witness to your love in life and death. Amen.

**May the peace of the Lord Christ go with you : wherever he may send you;
may he guide you through the wilderness : protect you through the storm;
may he bring you home rejoicing : at the wonders he has shown you;
may he bring you home rejoicing : once again into our doors.**

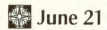 **June 21**

In 1964, civil rights activists James Chaney, Andrew Goodman, and Michael Schwerner were murdered as they participated in the Freedom Summer campaign to register black voters in Mississippi.

O Lord, let my soul rise up to meet you
as the day rises to meet the sun.

**Glory to the Father, and to the Son, and to the Holy Spirit,
as it was in the beginning, is now, and will be forever. Amen.**

Come, let us bow down and bend the knee : let us kneel before the LORD our Maker.

Song "Were You There?"

Have mercy, Lord, have mercy : the violent are raging against us.

Psalm 106:8–12
The Most High saved them for his name's sake : **to make his power known.**
He rebuked the Red Sea, and it dried up : **and he led them through the deep as through a desert.**
He saved them from the hand of those who hated them : **and redeemed them from the hand of the enemy.**
The waters covered their oppressors : **not one of them was left.**
Then they believed his words : **and sang him songs of praise.**

Have mercy, Lord, have mercy : the violent are raging against us.

Ruth 3:1–18   Acts 10:1–16

Have mercy, Lord, have mercy : the violent are raging against us.

Cyprian of Carthage taught in the early church, saying, "My friends, anyone who worships should remember the way in which the tax collector prayed in the temple alongside the Pharisee. He did not raise his eyes immodestly to heaven or lift up his hands arrogantly. Instead he struck his breast, and confessing the sins hidden within his heart, he implored the assistance of God's mercy. While the Pharisee was pleased with himself, the tax collector deserved to be cleansed much more because of the manner in which he prayed. For he did not place his hope of salvation in the certainty of his own innocence — indeed no one is innocent. Rather he prayed humbly, confessing his sins. And the Lord who forgives the lowly heard his prayer."

Prayers for Others

Our Father

Lord, you have brought us safely out of Egypt and prepared a table before us in the presence of our enemies. Have mercy on us today that we might not be overwhelmed by evil attacks or distracted by bad thoughts, but humbly trust in your power to save. Amen.

**May the peace of the Lord Christ go with you : wherever he may send you;
may he guide you through the wilderness : protect you through the storm;
may he bring you home rejoicing : at the wonders he has shown you;
may he bring you home rejoicing : once again into our doors.**

June 22

O Lord, let my soul rise up to meet you
as the day rises to meet the sun.

**Glory to the Father, and to the Son, and to the Holy Spirit,
as it was in the beginning, is now, and will be forever. Amen.**

Come, let us sing to the LORD : let us shout for joy to the Rock of our salvation.

Song "All Creatures of Our God and King"

Exalt yourself above the heavens : and your glory over all the earth.

Psalm 108:1–4
My heart is firmly fixed, O God, my heart is fixed : **I will sing and make melody.**
Wake up, my spirit; awake, lute and harp : **I myself will waken the dawn.**
I will confess you among the peoples, O LORD : **I will sing praises to you among the nations.**
For your loving-kindness is greater than the heavens : **and your faithfulness reaches to the clouds.**

Exalt yourself above the heavens : and your glory over all the earth.

Ruth 4:1–17   Acts 10:17–33

Exalt yourself above the heavens : and your glory over all the earth.

Catherine of Genoa said, "All goodness is a participation in God and his love for his creatures."

Prayers for Others

Our Father

Your love, O Lord, reaches to the heavens; your faithfulness stretches to the sky. Lift us by the power of your Holy Spirit to participate in your goodness and bear witness to your loving-kindness in every move we make today. Amen.

May the peace of the Lord Christ go with you : wherever he may send you;
may he guide you through the wilderness : protect you through the storm;
may he bring you home rejoicing : at the wonders he has shown you;
may he bring you home rejoicing : once again into our doors.

 # June 23

O Lord, let my soul rise up to meet you
as the day rises to meet the sun.

Glory to the Father, and to the Son, and to the Holy Spirit,
as it was in the beginning, is now, and will be forever. Amen.

Come, let us sing to the LORD : let us shout for joy to the Rock of our salvation.

Song "Vamos Todos al Banquete"

Glory to God in the highest : and on the earth, peace.

Psalm 112:1–3, 9–10
Hallelujah! Happy are they who fear the Lord : **and have great delight in his commandments!**
Their descendants will be mighty in the land : **the generation of the upright will be blessed.**
Wealth and riches will be in their house : **and their righteousness will last for ever.**
They have given freely to the poor : **and their righteousness stands fast for ever; they will hold up their head with honor.**
The wicked will see it and be angry; they will gnash their teeth and pine away : **the desires of the wicked will perish.**

Glory to God in the highest : and on the earth, peace.

Ezekiel 33:1–11   Acts 10:34–48

Glory to God in the highest : and on the earth, peace.

Sixteenth-century mystic Teresa of Avila said, "Prayer, in my view, is nothing but friendly intercourse and frequent solitary converse with him who we know loves us."

Prayers for Others

Our Father

Lord, you spoke all things into being and call us each to speak your truth in our corner of the world. Save us from ourselves and grant us holy confidence to speak aloud as we have been spoken to. Amen.

May the peace of the Lord Christ go with you : wherever he may send you;
may he guide you through the wilderness : protect you through the storm;
may he bring you home rejoicing : at the wonders he has shown you;
may he bring you home rejoicing : once again into our doors.

✸ June 24

O Lord, let my soul rise up to meet you
as the day rises to meet the sun.

**Glory to the Father, and to the Son, and to the Holy Spirit,
as it was in the beginning, is now, and will be forever. Amen.**

Come, let us sing to the Lord : let us shout for joy to the Rock of our salvation.

Song "Magnificat"

I will enter your gates with thanksgiving : I will dance in your courts with praise.

Psalm 118:19–24
Open for me the gates of righteousness : **I will enter them; I will offer thanks to the Lord.**
"This is the gate of the Lord : **he who is righteous may enter."**
I will give thanks to you, for you answered me : **and have become my salvation.**
The same stone which the builders rejected : **has become the chief cornerstone.**
This is the Lord's doing : **and it is marvelous in our eyes.**
On this day the Lord has acted : **we will rejoice and be glad in it.**

I will enter your gates with thanksgiving : I will dance in your courts with praise.

Ezekiel 33:21–33   Acts 11:1–18

I will enter your gates with thanksgiving : I will dance in your courts with praise.

Mary Oliver's poem "Praying" reads:

> It doesn't have to be
> the blue iris, it could be
> weeds in a vacant lot, or a few
> small stones; just
> pay attention, then patch
>
> a few words together and don't try
> to make them elaborate, this isn't
> a contest but the doorway
>
> into thanks, and a silence in which
> another voice may speak.

Prayers for Others

Our Father

Lord, you have appointed some to be prophets; give us ears to hear and mouths to speak. You have appointed some to sing of your goodness in the streets; make us bold to celebrate you. You have called some to be still, listen, and act; give us steadiness of mind and singularity of purpose. Amen.

May the peace of the Lord Christ go with you : wherever he may send you; may he guide you through the wilderness : protect you through the storm; may he bring you home rejoicing : at the wonders he has shown you; may he bring you home rejoicing : once again into our doors.

✣ June 25

In 1945, following the end of the Second World War, fifty countries signed the original charter of the United Nations in San Francisco.

O Lord, let my soul rise up to meet you
as the day rises to meet the sun.

Glory to the Father, and to the Son, and to the Holy Spirit,
as it was in the beginning, is now, and will be forever. Amen.

Come, let us sing to the LORD : let us shout for joy to the Rock of our salvation.

Song "What Is This Place?"

Speak, Lord : for your servants are listening.

Psalm 119:41–44, 48
Let your loving-kindness come to me, O Lord : **and your salvation, according to your promise.**
Then shall I have a word for those who taunt me : **because I trust in your words.**
Do not take the word of truth out of my mouth : **for my hope is in your judgments.**
I shall continue to keep your law : **I shall keep it for ever and ever.**
I will lift up my hands to your commandments : **and I will meditate on your statutes.**

Speak, Lord : for your servants are listening.

Ezekiel 34:1–16   Acts 11:19–30

Speak, Lord : for your servants are listening.

Archbishop Oscar Romero of El Salvador asked, "A church that doesn't provoke any crises, a gospel that doesn't unsettle, a word of God that doesn't get under anyone's skin, a word of God that doesn't touch the real sin of the society in which it is being proclaimed — what gospel is that?"

Prayers for Others

Our Father

Listen to your children praying, Lord. Send us love, send us power, and send us grace, that we might hear what you are saying and do it. Amen.

May the peace of the Lord Christ go with you : wherever he may send you;
may he guide you through the wilderness : protect you through the storm;
may he bring you home rejoicing : at the wonders he has shown you;
may he bring you home rejoicing : once again into our doors.

❋ June 26

O Lord, let my soul rise up to meet you
as the day rises to meet the sun.

Glory to the Father, and to the Son, and to the Holy Spirit,
as it was in the beginning, is now, and will be forever. Amen.

Come, let us bow down and bend the knee : let us kneel before the Lord our Maker.

Song   "Take My Life and Let It Be"

Speed the day of your salvation : come, Lord Jesus, come.

Psalm 119:131–36
I open my mouth and pant : **I long for your commandments.**
Turn to me in mercy : **as you always do to those who love your name.**
Steady my footsteps in your word : **let no iniquity have dominion over me.**
Rescue me from those who oppress me : **and I will keep your commandments.**
Let your countenance shine upon your servant : **and teach me your statutes.**
My eyes shed streams of tears : **because people do not keep your law.**

Speed the day of your salvation : come, Lord Jesus, come.

Ezekiel 34:17–24   Acts 12:1–17

Speed the day of your salvation : come, Lord Jesus, come.

Sixteenth-century reformer Lazarus Spengler prayed, "For my feet your holy word is a lantern, a light that shows me the way forward; as this morning star rises upon us we understand the great gifts that God's Spirit has certainly promised to us, and in these we have our hope."

Prayers for Others

Our Father

Lord, we have nothing to fear in your presence. Your purposes always come to pass. Help us to live with such certainty in your power that we expect miracles in our daily lives. Amen.

**May the peace of the Lord Christ go with you : wherever he may send you;
may he guide you through the wilderness : protect you through the storm;
may he bring you home rejoicing : at the wonders he has shown you;
may he bring you home rejoicing : once again into our doors.**

❋ June 27

O Lord, let my soul rise up to meet you
as the day rises to meet the sun.

**Glory to the Father, and to the Son, and to the Holy Spirit,
as it was in the beginning, is now, and will be forever. Amen.**

Come, let us sing to the LORD : let us shout for joy to the Rock of our salvation.

Song   "Be Thou My Vision"

Surely God is in this place : and I did not know it.

Psalm 122:1–5
I was glad when they said to me : **"Let us go to the house of the LORD."**
Now our feet are standing : **within your gates, O Jerusalem.**
Jerusalem is built as a city : **that is at unity with itself;**
to which the tribes go up, the tribes of the LORD : **the assembly of Israel, to praise the name of the LORD.**
For there are the thrones of judgment : **the thrones of the house of David.**

Surely God is in this place : and I did not know it.

Ezekiel 37:1–14   Acts 12:18–25

Surely God is in this place : and I did not know it.

Pierre Teilhard de Chardin said, "Above all, trust in the slow work of God. We are quite naturally impatient in everything to reach the end without delay. We would like to skip the intermediate stages. We are impatient of being on the way to something unknown, something new. And yet, it is the law of all progress that it is made by passing through some stages of instability — and that it may take a very long time. Above all, trust in the slow work of God, our loving vine-dresser."

Prayers for Others

Our Father

You show up, Jesus, in the most unlikely places. Give us patience to wait and watch when we cannot sense your presence so that we may be ready to greet you where we are. Amen.

May the peace of the Lord Christ go with you : wherever he may send you;
may he guide you through the wilderness : protect you through the storm;
may he bring you home rejoicing : at the wonders he has shown you;
may he bring you home rejoicing : once again into our doors.

 **June 28**

Irenaeus of Lyon (130–200)
The first systematic theologian of the church, Irenaeus lived in a time when Christianity was young and fragile. He was appointed bishop of Lyon and combated the dualistic notion that matter and spirit are entirely separate, with matter being wholly corrupt. Irenaeus insisted that there is nothing inherently corrupt in creation but that humans lost their "likeness to God" through the

distortion of sin. That likeness was restored, Irenaeus proclaimed, through Christ, the "second Adam" who corrected the story of the first Adam. In a time when so much of Christianity has been reduced to disembodied doctrine and otherworldly sentiment, Irenaeus' voice rings out like a prophet's.

O Lord, let my soul rise up to meet you
as the day rises to meet the sun.

**Glory to the Father, and to the Son, and to the Holy Spirit,
as it was in the beginning, is now, and will be forever. Amen.**

Come, let us sing to the LORD : let us shout for joy to the Rock of our salvation.

Song "Glory, Glory, Hallelujah"

Make us fully alive, O God : that our lives might shine like the sun.

Psalm 134
Behold now, bless the LORD, all you servants of the LORD : **you that stand by night in the house of the LORD.**
Lift up your hands in the holy place and bless the LORD : **the LORD who made heaven and earth bless you out of Zion.**

Make us fully alive, O God : that our lives might shine like the sun.

Ezekiel 37:15–28   Acts 13:1–12

Make us fully alive, O God : that our lives might shine like the sun.

Irenaeus of Lyon wrote, "For the glory of God is the human person fully alive; and life consists in beholding God. For if the vision of God which is made by means of the creation, gives life to all the living in the earth, much more does the revelation of the Father, which comes through the Word, give life to those who see God."

Prayers for Others

Our Father

Taking on our flesh, you have made flesh holy, Lord. Help us die to our selfish ways and our faithless habits that we might know the fullness of your new creation in our communities as it is in your resurrected body. Amen.

**May the peace of the Lord Christ go with you : wherever he may send you;
may he guide you through the wilderness : protect you through the storm;
may he bring you home rejoicing : at the wonders he has shown you;
may he bring you home rejoicing : once again into our doors.**

June 29

Peter and Paul

One of the ways we see the wisdom of the early church is in their placing Peter and Paul's saint days together so that they have a shared celebration, thereby making sure that there was no room for divisions over their leadership, even with their disagreements. (It may be that the church forgot this wisdom in the Reformation, with Rome claiming Peter's authority and Paul becoming the hero of Protestants.) The early church was quite clear that the first pastor and the first theologian of the faith had to be held in equal respect and in equal balance of authority. One without the other leaves us incomplete and unbalanced.

O Lord, let my soul rise up to meet you
as the day rises to meet the sun.

**Glory to the Father, and to the Son, and to the Holy Spirit,
as it was in the beginning, is now, and will be forever. Amen.**

Come, let us bow down and bend the knee : let us kneel before the Lord our Maker.

Song "O Lord, Hear My Prayer"

Our eyes are turned to you, O Lord : our eyes are turned to you.

Psalm 141:1, 3–6
O Lord, I call to you; come to me quickly : **hear my voice when I cry to you.**
Set a watch before my mouth, O Lord, and guard the door of my lips : **let not my heart incline to any evil thing.**
Let me not be occupied in wickedness with evildoers : **nor eat of their choice foods.**
Let the righteous smite me in friendly rebuke; let not the oil of the unrighteous anoint my head : **for my prayer is continually against their wicked deeds.**
Let their rulers be overthrown in stony places : **that they may know my words are true.**

Our eyes are turned to you, O Lord : our eyes are turned to you.

Ezekiel 39:21–29   Acts 13:13–25

Our eyes are turned to you, O Lord : our eyes are turned to you.

Archbishop Desmond Tutu, a leader in South Africa's struggle against apartheid, wrote, "The first law of our being is that we are set in a delicate network of interdependence with our fellow human beings and with the rest of God's creation."

Prayers for Others

Our Father

Lord, you promise never to leave us or forsake us. Since we are always in your presence, help us always to keep our eyes fixed upon you that we might follow your lead in the never-ending dance of your life as Father, Son, and Holy Spirit. Amen.

**May the peace of the Lord Christ go with you : wherever he may send you;
may he guide you through the wilderness : protect you through the storm;
may he bring you home rejoicing : at the wonders he has shown you;
may he bring you home rejoicing : once again into our doors.**

 June 30

O Lord, let my soul rise up to meet you
as the day rises to meet the sun.

Glory to the Father, and to the Son, and to the Holy Spirit,
as it was in the beginning, is now, and will be forever. Amen.

Come, let us sing to the LORD : let us shout for joy to the Rock of our salvation.

Song "Amazing Grace"

Here I am, Lord : here again because I need you.

Psalm 145:1–4
I will exalt you, O God my King : **and bless your name for ever and ever.**
Every day will I bless you : **and praise your name for ever and ever.**
Great is the LORD and greatly to be praised : **there is no end to his greatness.**
One generation shall praise your works to another : **and shall declare your power.**

Here I am, Lord : here again because I need you.

Ezekiel 47:1–12   Acts 13:26–43

Here I am, Lord : here again because I need you.

Jeanne Jugan has written, "Go and find Jesus when your patience and strength give out and you feel alone and helpless. He is waiting for you. Say to him, 'Jesus, you know exactly what is going on. You are all I have, and you know all. Come to my help.' And then go and don't worry about how you are going to manage. That you have told God about it is enough. He has a good memory."

Prayers for Others

Our Father

Thank you, Lord, that you remember the lilies when we cannot remember our own best interests. Open our eyes to wonder in awe at your greatness, that we might learn to see how all things are possible with you, Maker of heaven and earth. Amen.

May the peace of the Lord Christ go with you : wherever he may send you; may he guide you through the wilderness : protect you through the storm; may he bring you home rejoicing : at the wonders he has shown you; may he bring you home rejoicing : once again into our doors.

Becoming the Answer to Our Prayers: A Few Ideas

1. Hang out with folks who will inherit the earth. (For details, see the Sermon on the Mount.)
2. Set up a retreat center with pastoral care and spiritual guidance—free of charge—for persons who have little money.
3. Look through your clothes. Learn about one of the countries where they are manufactured. Do some research to discover the working conditions of the people who made them, and commit to doing one thing to improve the lives of people who live in that country.
4. Look for everything you have two of, and give one away.
5. Dig up a bucket of soil and look through it to see the elements and organisms that make our daily meals possible.

JULY — JOACHIM AND ANNA

JULY

Marks of New Monasticism
Geographical Proximity

There is something to be said for a "theology of place" — choosing to orient our lives around community for the sake of the gospel. So much of our culture is built around moving away from people rather than closer to them. In many of the wealthiest countries in the world, we have lost the sense of a village. And we have some of the highest rates of home ownership and some of the highest rates of depression. We are some of the wealthiest *and* loneliest societies the world has ever seen. We live in a mobile culture in which people are used to moving every few years, and in which many folks will uproot without question to move for a higher-paying job.

Commitment to a people and a place is one of the countercultural values at the heart of the gospel. It means recapturing the notion of the parish, a word which shares a root with *parochial*, meaning "localized and particular." Many folks these days are learning from village cultures, where people often have fewer resources but more life and joy. Even our geography has to be rethought, because our neighborhoods and homes are often built around values different from the gospel and community. What we often lament as a "breakdown of the family" is really a breakdown of local community, which has stripped away the support structures that help all of us survive. Joachim and Anna, whom tradition names as Jesus' maternal grandparents and who nurtured the mother of the Lord, remind us how important the basic institutions of family and community are.

Movements of co-housing and new urbanism are helping to cultivate spaces for shared life. People in one cul-de-sac began to rethink suburban sprawl and started sharing stuff. They decided each home didn't need a washer and dryer and a lawn mower. So one family agreed to have the laundry machines, and another had all the lawn equipment, and so on. Before long, they were homeschooling their kids together and providing hospitality to the homeless with all of the energy and resources that were freed up by sharing. When people make choices like these, life starts to look like a village, and a village is a beautiful thing.

> **Suggested Reading for the Month**
> *Sex, Economy, Freedom and Community* by Wendell Berry
> *A Theology as Big as the City* by Ray Bakke
> *The Wisdom of Stability* by Jonathan Wilson-Hartgrove

July 1

O Lord, let my soul rise up to meet you
as the day rises to meet the sun.

**Glory to the Father, and to the Son, and to the Holy Spirit,
as it was in the beginning, is now, and will be forever. Amen.**

Come, let us bow down and bend the knee : let us kneel before the LORD our Maker.

Song "O Lord, Hear My Prayer"

We have come this far by faith : leaning on the Lord.

Psalm 4:1–3
Answer me when I call, O God, defender of my cause : **you set me free when I am hard-pressed; have mercy on me and hear my prayer.**
"You mortals, how long will you dishonor my glory? : **How long will you worship dumb idols and run after false gods?"**
Know that the LORD does wonders for the faithful : **when I call upon the LORD, he will hear me.**

We have come this far by faith : leaning on the Lord.

Judges 2:1–5, 11–23   Acts 13:44–52

We have come this far by faith : leaning on the Lord.

Irish missionary Columbanus wrote, "Seek then the highest wisdom, not by arguments in words but by the perfection of your life; not by speech but by the faith that comes from simplicity of heart."

Prayers for Others

Our Father

Thank you, Lord, for your mercy and forgiveness. Help us to hear your word and to follow you today. Numb our ears to the persistent call of idols like vanity, consumerism, power, and pride. Enable us to lead lives tempered by the awareness of others' needs and propelled by your love. Amen.

**May the peace of the Lord Christ go with you : wherever he may send you;
may he guide you through the wilderness : protect you through the storm;
may he bring you home rejoicing : at the wonders he has shown you;
may he bring you home rejoicing : once again into our doors.**

July 2

O Lord, let my soul rise up to meet you
as the day rises to meet the sun.

**Glory to the Father, and to the Son, and to the Holy Spirit,
as it was in the beginning, is now, and will be forever. Amen.**

Come, let us bow down and bend the knee : let us kneel before the LORD our Maker.

Song "Steal Away to Jesus"

In the time of trouble : hide us in the shadow of your wing.

Psalm 12:1–2, 5–6
Help me, LORD, for there is no godly one left : **the faithful have vanished from among us.**
Everyone speaks falsely with his neighbor : **with a smooth tongue they speak from a double heart.**
"Because the needy are oppressed, and the poor cry out in misery : **I will rise up," says the LORD, "and give them the help they long for."**
The words of the LORD are pure words : **like silver refined from ore and purified seven times in the fire.**

In the time of trouble : hide us in the shadow of your wing.

Judges 3:12–30   Acts 14:1–18

In the time of trouble : hide us in the shadow of your wing.

English mystic Julian of Norwich said, "The mother's service is nearest, readiest, and surest. It is nearest because it is more natural; readiest because it is most loving; and surest because it is truest. No one ever might or could perform this office fully, except only Jesus. We know that all our mothers bear us for pain and for death. Oh, what is that? But our true Mother Jesus, he alone bears us for joy and for endless life. So he carries us with him in love and travail."

Prayers for Others

Our Father

Lord God, time and again you provide for us with your near, ready, and sure love. Give us eyes to recognize that all goodness and joy are from your hand, that we may praise you with our lives, forever and ever. Amen.

May the peace of the Lord Christ go with you : wherever he may send you;
may he guide you through the wilderness : protect you through the storm;
may he bring you home rejoicing : at the wonders he has shown you;
may he bring you home rejoicing : once again into our doors.

✣ July 3

O Lord, let my soul rise up to meet you
as the day rises to meet the sun.

**Glory to the Father, and to the Son, and to the Holy Spirit,
as it was in the beginning, is now, and will be forever. Amen.**

Come, let us sing to the LORD : let us shout for joy to the Rock of our salvation.

Song "O Mary, Don't You Weep"

Jesus, Savior of the world : come to us in your mercy.

Psalm 18:1–3, 18–20
I love you, O LORD my strength : **O LORD my stronghold, my crag, and my haven.**
My God, my rock in whom I put my trust : **my shield, the horn of my salvation, and my refuge; you are worthy of praise.**
I will call upon the LORD : **and so shall I be saved from my enemies.**
He delivered me from my strong enemies and from those who hated me : **for they were too mighty for me.**
They confronted me in the day of my disaster : **but the LORD was my support.**
He brought me out into an open place : **he rescued me because he delighted in me.**

Jesus, Savior of the world : come to us in your mercy.

Judges 4:4–23   Acts 14:19–28

Jesus, Savior of the world : come to us in your mercy.

Twentieth-century Presbyterian theologian and writer Frederick Buechner has written, "The grace of God means something like: Here is your life. You might never have been, but you are because the party wouldn't have been complete without you. Here is the world. Beautiful and terrible things will happen. Don't be afraid. I am with you. Nothing can ever separate us. It's for you I created the universe. I love you. There's only one catch. Like any other gift, the gift of grace can be yours only if you'll reach out and take it. Maybe being able to reach out and take it is a gift too."

Prayers for Others

Our Father

Lord, we pray for strength and trust in times of trouble. Equip us to be your hands and feet in the world. May we bring good news to all we meet this day, with our words and with our lives. We ask this through Christ our Lord. Amen.

May the peace of the Lord Christ go with you : wherever he may send you; may he guide you through the wilderness : protect you through the storm; may he bring you home rejoicing : at the wonders he has shown you; may he bring you home rejoicing : once again into our doors.

 July 4

Martin of Tours (d. 397)

Martin of Tours saw Christ in the face of the poor and in the commitment to nonviolence. He was born in what is now Hungary and as a young man was involuntarily enlisted in the Roman Army. Martin's conversion to Christianity occurred after he met a beggar seeking alms. Without money to offer the man, Martin tore his own coat in half and gave one part to the beggar. The following night, Martin dreamed of Christ wearing half of his coat. Once Martin was baptized he resolved to leave the army because Christ called him to nonviolence. His superiors mistakenly saw his request as one of cowardice until Martin offered to face the front lines without weapons as a sign of Christian pacifism. Denied this offer, Martin spent time in prison. Afterward he joined the monastery at Solesmes and eventually served for ten years as bishop of Tours.

O Lord, let my soul rise up to meet you
as the day rises to meet the sun.

Glory to the Father, and to the Son, and to the Holy Spirit, as it was in the beginning, is now, and will be forever. Amen.

Come, let us sing to the LORD : let us shout for joy to the Rock of our salvation.

Song "Be Thou My Vision"

I'm a soldier in the army of the Lord : I'm a soldier in the Lord's army.

Psalm 22:22–25
Praise the LORD, you that fear him : **stand in awe of him, O offspring of Israel; all you of Jacob's line, give glory.**
For he does not despise nor abhor the poor in their poverty; neither does he hide his face from them : **but when they cry to him he hears them.**

My praise is of him in the great assembly : **I will perform my vows in the presence of those who worship him.**
The poor shall eat and be satisfied, and those who seek the LORD shall praise him : **"May your heart live for ever!"**

I'm a soldier in the army of the Lord : I'm a soldier in the Lord's army.

Judges 5:1–18   Acts 15:1–21

I'm a soldier in the army of the Lord : I'm a soldier in the Lord's army.

Martin of Tours said, "I am a soldier of Christ; it is not lawful for me to fight."

Prayers for Others

Our Father

Almighty God, you are King of all creation. You created order out of chaos, and you call us to strive for the peace that is not like the peace empires bring. Teach us to drop the weapons we carry in our hands, in our hearts, and on our tongues. Enable us to be soldiers of yours who destroy the weapons of our oppressors with your grace. Amen.

May the peace of the Lord Christ go with you : wherever he may send you; may he guide you through the wilderness : protect you through the storm; may he bring you home rejoicing : at the wonders he has shown you; may he bring you home rejoicing : once again into our doors.

> Wanting to celebrate the reign of God rather than Independence Day, the Church of the Sojourners in San Francisco, California, has declared July 4 the Celebration of Yahweh's Kingship. Debbie Gish explains, "By choosing this day to celebrate Yahweh's kingship, we are symbolically and concretely declaring our ultimate allegiance. It may appear to be a statement *against* the United States, but in fact it is a statement *for* the kingdom of God."

✦ July 5

O Lord, let my soul rise up to meet you
as the day rises to meet the sun.

**Glory to the Father, and to the Son, and to the Holy Spirit,
as it was in the beginning, is now, and will be forever. Amen.**

Come, let us sing to the LORD : let us shout for joy to the Rock of our salvation.

Song "Magnificat"

Show me your way, O Lord : lead me on a level path.

Psalm 27:1–4
The LORD is my light and my salvation; whom then shall I fear? : **the LORD is the strength of my life; of whom then shall I be afraid?**
When evildoers came upon me to eat up my flesh : **it was they, my foes and my adversaries, who stumbled and fell.**
Though an army should encamp against me : **yet my heart shall not be afraid;**
and though war should rise up against me : **yet will I put my trust in him.**

Show me your way, O Lord : lead me on a level path.

Judges 5:19–31   Acts 15:22–35

Show me your way, O Lord : lead me on a level path.

Hear this proverb often quoted by John Perkins, pioneer of Christian community development:

> Go to the people.
> Live among them.
> Learn from them.
> Love them.
> Start with what they know.
> Build on what they have.
> But of the best leaders,
> when their task is accomplished,
> when their work is done ...
> the people will remark:
> "We have done it ourselves."

Prayers for Others

Our Father

Lord God, grant us grace to be faithful witnesses to those we encounter today. May we share your love in a way that sparks others to catch your fire. Amen.

May the peace of the Lord Christ go with you : wherever he may send you; may he guide you through the wilderness : protect you through the storm; may he bring you home rejoicing : at the wonders he has shown you; may he bring you home rejoicing : once again into our doors.

July 6

Jan Hus (1372 – 1415)

Jan Hus was born in Bohemia (now part of the Czech Republic). He helped launch a vigorous reform of the church in a particularly difficult time in our history known as the Great Schism. Amid highly politicized divisions of God's people, Hus pursued a mystical and evangelical approach, insisting that Christ alone is head of the church. To partisans on both sides, his views seemed idealistic at best, and at worst a dreamy anarchism or heresy. Hus maintained a creative loyalty to the church while challenging its pathologies. He was burned at the stake during the Council of Constance in 1415, and his death helped give birth to the Moravian Church. As he died, he said this: "It is better to die well than to live wickedly…. Truth conquers all things."

O Lord, let my soul rise up to meet you
as the day rises to meet the sun.

**Glory to the Father, and to the Son, and to the Holy Spirit,
as it was in the beginning, is now, and will be forever. Amen.**

Come, let us sing to the LORD : let us shout for joy to the Rock of our salvation.

Song "I Want Jesus to Walk with Me"

Let your loving-kindness, O LORD, be upon us : as we put our trust in you.

Psalm 33:12 – 15
Happy is the nation whose God is the LORD! : **happy the people he has chosen to be his own!**
The LORD looks down from heaven : **and beholds all the people in the world.**
From where he sits enthroned he turns his gaze : **on all who dwell on the earth.**
He fashions all the hearts of them : **and understands all their works.**

Let your loving-kindness, O LORD, be upon us : as we put our trust in you.

Judges 6:1 – 24   Acts 15:36 – 16:5

Let your loving-kindness, O LORD, be upon us : as we put our trust in you.

Mother Teresa once said, "Our vocation is to belong to Jesus so completely that nothing can separate us from the love of Christ. What you and I must do is nothing less than putting our love for Christ into practice. The important thing is not how much we accomplish, but how much love we put into our deeds every day. That is the measure of our love for God."

Prayers for Others

Our Father

Lord, we are bound to you by grace, grafted into your kingdom by love. Since the beginning of time you have found ways to be present with us, your children. Teach us to embody your loving presence in all that we do this day. Amen.

May the peace of the Lord Christ go with you : wherever he may send you;
may he guide you through the wilderness : protect you through the storm;
may he bring you home rejoicing : at the wonders he has shown you;
may he bring you home rejoicing : once again into our doors.

July 7

O Lord, let my soul rise up to meet you
as the day rises to meet the sun.

**Glory to the Father, and to the Son, and to the Holy Spirit,
as it was in the beginning, is now, and will be forever. Amen.**

Come, let us bow down and bend the knee : let us kneel before the LORD our Maker.

Song "I Will Trust in the Lord"

Quiet our troubled souls, O Lord : with peace that passes understanding.

Psalm 37:7–10
Be still before the LORD : **and wait patiently for him.**
Do not fret yourself over the one who prospers : **the one who succeeds in evil schemes.**
Refrain from anger, leave rage alone : **do not fret yourself; it leads only to evil.**
For evildoers shall be cut off : **but those who wait upon the LORD shall possess the land.**

Quiet our troubled souls, O Lord : with peace that passes understanding.

Judges 6:25–40   Acts 16:16–40

Quiet our troubled souls, O Lord : with peace that passes understanding.

Martin Luther King Jr. said this: "Injustice anywhere is a threat to justice everywhere. We are caught in an inescapable network of mutuality, tied in a single garment of destiny. Whatever affects one directly affects all indirectly."

Prayers for Others

Our Father

Lord God, some of us still ask for signs to know where you call us to go and who you desire us to become. Be merciful and reveal yourself to us in manageable ways, just enough to see us through today. Amen.

May the peace of the Lord Christ go with you : wherever he may send you; may he guide you through the wilderness : protect you through the storm; may he bring you home rejoicing : at the wonders he has shown you; may he bring you home rejoicing : once again into our doors.

 July 8

O Lord, let my soul rise up to meet you
as the day rises to meet the sun.

Glory to the Father, and to the Son, and to the Holy Spirit, as it was in the beginning, is now, and will be forever. Amen.

Come, let us sing to the LORD : let us shout for joy to the Rock of our salvation.

Song "Praise to the Lord, the Almighty"

Raise us up, O Lord : and let our light break forth like the dawn.

Psalm 41:1–3
Happy are they who consider the poor and needy! : **the LORD will deliver them in the time of trouble.**
The LORD preserves them and keeps them alive, so that they may be happy in the land : **he does not hand them over to the will of their enemies.**
The LORD sustains them on their sickbed : **and ministers to them in their illness.**

Raise us up, O Lord : and let our light break forth like the dawn.

Judges 7:1–18   Acts 17:1–15

Raise us up, O Lord : and let our light break forth like the dawn.

Hear these words of church father Augustine of Hippo: "In affliction, then, we do not know what it is right to pray for. Because affliction is difficult, troublesome and against the grain for us, weak as we are, we do what every human would do. We pray that it may be taken away from us. However, if he does not take it away, we must not imagine that he has forgotten us. In this way, power shines forth more perfectly in weakness."

Prayers for Others

Our Father

Lord, throughout history you have used the seemingly weak to nurture justice, to fight poverty, and to walk bravely toward human thrones of power proclaiming another way. Help us find comfort and hope in our afflictions, knowing that you are able to use all things for good. Amen.

May the peace of the Lord Christ go with you : wherever he may send you; may he guide you through the wilderness : protect you through the storm; may he bring you home rejoicing : at the wonders he has shown you; may he bring you home rejoicing : once again into our doors.

 July 9

On July 9, 2004, the International Court of Justice ruled that the wall being built by the Israeli government in the contested Palestinian territories is illegal and should be taken down. This historic Holy Land continues to be some of the most troubled and segregated land in the world and has been called the site of "the most sophisticated apartheid system in the world."

O Lord, let my soul rise up to meet you
as the day rises to meet the sun.

Glory to the Father, and to the Son, and to the Holy Spirit, as it was in the beginning, is now, and will be forever. Amen.

Come, let us sing to the LORD : let us shout for joy to the Rock of our salvation.

Song   "All Creatures of Our God and King"

We shout to God with a cry of joy : Let us shout with our whole lives!

Psalm 47:6–10
Sing praises to God, sing praises : **sing praises to our King, sing praises.**
For God is King of all the earth : **sing praises with all your skill.**
God reigns over the nations : **God sits upon his holy throne.**
The nobles of the peoples have gathered together : **with the people of the God of Abraham.**
The rulers of the earth belong to God : **and he is highly exalted.**

We shout to God with a cry of joy : Let us shout with our whole lives!

Judges 7:19–8:12   Acts 17:16–34

We shout to God with a cry of joy : Let us shout with our whole lives!

Second-century Christian thinker Athenagoras wrote, "Our life does not consist in making up beautiful phrases but in performing beautiful deeds."

Prayers for Others

Our Father

Lord God, we rejoice in your resurrection and in your promise to return. Help us live today as people who await the fulfillment of your kingdom. Bend our knees to the hard work of prayer, worship, repentance, and intercession. Amen.

May the peace of the Lord Christ go with you : wherever he may send you; may he guide you through the wilderness : protect you through the storm; may he bring you home rejoicing : at the wonders he has shown you; may he bring you home rejoicing : once again into our doors.

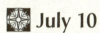
July 10

Toyohiko Kagawa (1888–1960)

Toyohiko Kagawa was a Japanese pacifist, Christian reformer, evangelist, and labor activist. He wrote, spoke, and worked at length on ways to employ Christian principles in the ordering of society. His vocation to help the poor led him to live among them, and he established schools, hospitals, and churches. He was also an innovator and a critical thinker, in everything from economics and theology to cutting-edge gardening techniques. One of his great lines is, "I read in a book that a man called Christ went about doing good. It is very disconcerting to me that I am so easily satisfied with just going about."

O Lord, let my soul rise up to meet you
as the day rises to meet the sun.

Glory to the Father, and to the Son, and to the Holy Spirit, as it was in the beginning, is now, and will be forever. Amen.

Come, let us bow down and bend the knee : let us kneel before the Lord our Maker.

Song "We Shall Overcome"

Deliver us from ourselves, O God : and bring us home to life with you.

Psalm 53:1–3, 6
The fool has said in his heart, "There is no God." : **All are corrupt and commit abominable acts; there is none who does any good.**

Morning Prayer

God looks down from heaven upon us all : **to see if there is any who is wise, if there is one who seeks after God.**
Every one has proved faithless; all alike have turned bad : **there is none who does good; no, not one.**
Oh, that Israel's deliverance would come out of Zion! : **when God restores the fortunes of his people Jacob will rejoice and Israel be glad.**

Deliver us from ourselves, O God : and bring us home to life with you.

Judges 8:22–35   Acts 18:1–11

Deliver us from ourselves, O God : and bring us home to life with you.

John Wesley, an eighteenth-century British evangelist and church reformer, said, "I believe the merciful God regards the lives and tempers of men more than their ideas. I believe he respects the goodness of the heart, rather than the clearness of the head."

Prayers for Others

Our Father

Lord God, thank you that we are unable to save ourselves and that each time we try, we fail. Have mercy on us. Be the strength in our weakness. Clear our heads of the foolishness of believing we can be our own gods. Steer our hearts to utter dependence on you. Amen.

May the peace of the Lord Christ go with you : wherever he may send you; may he guide you through the wilderness : protect you through the storm; may he bring you home rejoicing : at the wonders he has shown you; may he bring you home rejoicing : once again into our doors.

 ## July 11

Benedict of Nursia (c. 480 – c. 547)

Benedict was born in the town of Nursia, near Rome. At age twenty, he left home and lived for three years as a hermit in a desolate cave. There he practiced severe asceticism, maturing in both mind and character. Though he had little contact with the outside world, Benedict gained a reputation for his holy life and discipline. Eventually he was asked to lead a monastery in a remote area near Monte Cassino. Drawing on older rules and the wisdom of experience, Benedict outlined in his rule a simple way of life for monks, centered on praying the daily office, studying Scripture, engaging in common labor for the good of the community, and performing works of charity. His vision of the holy life became the standard for Western monasticism and a model for how to live simply — in health, wholeness, and community.

O Lord, let my soul rise up to meet you
as the day rises to meet the sun.

**Glory to the Father, and to the Son, and to the Holy Spirit,
as it was in the beginning, is now, and will be forever. Amen.**

Come, let us bow down and the bend the knee : let us kneel before the LORD our Maker.

Song "We Shall Not Be Moved"

Meet me, God, in the time of trial : and deliver me by your power.

Psalm 59:10–12, 15
My eyes are fixed on you, O my Strength : **for you, O God, are my stronghold.**
My merciful God comes to meet me : **God will let me look in triumph on my enemies.**
Slay them, O God, lest my people forget : **send them reeling by your might and put them down, O Lord our shield.**
Let everyone know that God rules in Jacob : **and to the ends of the earth.**

Meet me, God, in the time of trial : and deliver me by your power.

Judges 9:1–16, 19–21   Acts 18:12–28

Meet me, God, in the time of trial : and deliver me by your power.

Benedict of Nursia said, "However late, then, it may seem, let us rouse ourselves from lethargy. That is what scripture urges on us when it says: the time has come for us to rouse ourselves from sleep. Let us open our eyes to the light that can change us into the likeness of God. Let our ears be alert to the stirring call of his voice crying to us every day: today, if you should hear his voice, do not harden your hearts."

Prayers for Others

Our Father

God, make us bold enough to question tyranny, impassioned enough to submit ourselves to good teachers, and discerning enough to know when it is our turn to lead. Amen.

**May the peace of the Lord Christ go with you : wherever he may send you;
may he guide you through the wilderness : protect you through the storm;
may he bring you home rejoicing : at the wonders he has shown you;
may he bring you home rejoicing : once again into our doors.**

✦ July 12

O Lord, let my soul rise up to meet you
as the day rises to meet the sun.

**Glory to the Father, and to the Son, and to the Holy Spirit,
as it was in the beginning, is now, and will be forever. Amen.**

Come, let us sing to the LORD : let us shout for joy to the Rock of our salvation.

Song "Sing, O Sky (Gaao Re)"

Our sins are stronger than we are : but you will blot them out.

Psalm 65:4–7
Happy are they whom you choose and draw to your courts to dwell there! :
   they will be satisfied by the beauty of your house, by the holiness of your temple.
Awesome things will you show us in your righteousness, O God of our
   salvation : **O Hope of all the ends of the earth and of the seas that are far away.**
You make fast the mountains by your power : **they are girded about with might.**
You still the roaring of the seas : **the roaring of their waves, and the clamor of the peoples.**

Our sins are stronger than we are : but you will blot them out.

Judges 9:22–25, 50–57   Acts 19:1–20

Our sins are stronger than we are : but you will blot them out.

Desert father John Cassian said, "It is a bigger miracle to eject a passion from your own body than it is to eject an evil spirit from another's body. It is a bigger miracle to be patient and refrain from anger than it is to control the demons which fly through the air."

Prayers for Others

Our Father

Lord God, you gave us your Holy Spirit to teach us and to remind us of your words. We claim your Spirit's power today to convict us of our sin, to call us to repentance, and to remind us that your mercy enables us to choose you again and again. Amen.

May the peace of the Lord Christ go with you : wherever he may send you;
may he guide you through the wilderness : protect you through the storm;
may he bring you home rejoicing : at the wonders he has shown you;
may he bring you home rejoicing : once again into our doors.

July 13

O Lord, let my soul rise up to meet you
as the day rises to meet the sun.

**Glory to the Father, and to the Son, and to the Holy Spirit,
as it was in the beginning, is now, and will be forever. Amen.**

Come, let us bow down and bend the knee : let us kneel before the LORD our Maker.

Song   "Nothin' but the Blood"

Against the torrent of oblivion : we plead the blood of Jesus.

Psalm 69:1–3, 18
Save me, O God : **for the waters have risen up to my neck.**
I am sinking in deep mire : **and there is no firm ground for my feet.**
I have come into deep waters : **and the torrent washes over me.**
"Answer me, O LORD, for your love is kind : **in your great compassion, turn to me."**

Against the torrent of oblivion : we plead the blood of Jesus.

Judges 11:1–11, 29–40   Acts 19:21–41

Against the torrent of oblivion : we plead the blood of Jesus.

This prayer is from the second-century Christian writings known as the Acts of John: "To thee I call who art God alone: the one who is exceedingly great, the Unutterable One, the Incomprehensible One; to whom all powers of government are subject; before whom every authority bows, and before whom all that is high falls down and remains silent; at whose voice the demons take fright; and beholding whom all creation surrenders in silent adoration."

Prayers for Others

Our Father

God of all grace, in foolishness and humility we often dare to speak on your behalf, claiming to know your ways and making promises we struggle to keep. Help us learn to be still, trusting that you indeed are God. Amen.

May the peace of the Lord Christ go with you : wherever he may send you;
may he guide you through the wilderness : protect you through the storm;
may he bring you home rejoicing : at the wonders he has shown you;
may he bring you home rejoicing : once again into our doors.

✤ July 14

O Lord, let my soul rise up to meet you
as the day rises to meet the sun.

**Glory to the Father, and to the Son, and to the Holy Spirit,
as it was in the beginning, is now, and will be forever. Amen.**

Come, let us bow down and bend the knee : let us kneel before the LORD our Maker.

Song "Swing Low, Sweet Chariot"

Rise up, O God! Maintain your cause : Deliver us from the endless ruins.

Psalm 74:1–3, 9
O God, why have you utterly cast us off? : **why is your wrath so hot against the sheep of your pasture?**
Remember your congregation that you purchased long ago : **the tribe you redeemed to be your inheritance, and Mount Zion where you dwell.**
Turn your steps toward the endless ruins : **the enemy has laid waste everything in your sanctuary.**
How long, O God, will the adversary scoff? : **will the enemy blaspheme your name for ever?**

Rise up, O God! Maintain your cause : Deliver us from the endless ruins.

Judges 12:1–7   Acts 20:1–16

Rise up, O God! Maintain your cause : Deliver us from the endless ruins.

Listen to these words from the Shepherd of Hermas, whose second-century writings were cherished by the early Christians: "You know that you who are God's servants are living in a foreign country, for your own city-state is far away from this City-state. Knowing, then, which one is to be your own City-state, why do you acquire fields, costly furnishings, buildings, and frail dwellings here? Instead of fields, buy for yourselves people in distress in accordance with your means. It is far, far better to buy this kind of field, property, or building, which is quite different and which you can find again in your own City when you come home. This 'extravagance' is beautiful and holy; it brings no grief and no fear; it brings nothing but joy."

Prayers for Others

Our Father

Lord, apart from you our fragile lives would crumble into ruins. Sustain us by your mighty power, and help us rebuild our lives among those who have no home to call their own — the poor of heart and pocket, the homeless, the hungry, the unattended sick, and the imprisoned. Amen.

May the peace of the Lord Christ go with you : wherever he may send you; may he guide you through the wilderness : protect you through the storm; may he bring you home rejoicing : at the wonders he has shown you; may he bring you home rejoicing : once again into our doors.

 July 15

O Lord, let my soul rise up to meet you
as the day rises to meet the sun.

Glory to the Father, and to the Son, and to the Holy Spirit, as it was in the beginning, is now, and will be forever. Amen.

Come, let us sing to the LORD : let us shout for joy to the Rock of our salvation.

Song   "Solid Rock"

Lead us, Good Shepherd, through the waters : be the rock on which we stand.

Psalm 77:14–16, 19–20
You are the God who works wonders : **and have declared your power among the peoples.**
By your strength you have redeemed your people : **the children of Jacob and Joseph.**
The waters saw you, O God; the waters saw you and trembled : **the very depths were shaken.**
Your way was in the sea, and your paths in the great waters : **yet your footsteps were not seen.**
You led your people like a flock : **by the hand of Moses and Aaron.**

Lead us, Good Shepherd, through the waters : be the rock on which we stand.

Judges 13:1–24   Acts 20:17–38

Lead us, Good Shepherd, through the waters : be the rock on which we stand.

Benedict of Nursia said this: "The Lord himself in the gospel teaches us the same when he says: I shall liken anyone who hears my words and carries them out in deed to one who is wise enough to build on a rock; then the floods came and the winds blew and struck that house, but it did not fall because it was built on a rock. It is in the light of that teaching that the Lord waits for us every day to see if we will respond by our deeds, as we should, to his holy guidance. For that very reason also, so that we may mend our evil ways, the days of our mortal lives are allowed us as a sort of truce for improvement. So St Paul says: Do you not know that God is patient with us so as to lead us to repentance? The Lord himself says in his gentle care for us: I do not want the death of a sinner; let all sinners rather turn away from sin and live."

Prayers for Others

Our Father

God of the Ages, through your ancient prophets and disciples, your saints of old, and your Spirit, you have told us what is good — to do justice, to love kindness, and to walk humbly with you. Help us to stand on you, our Rock of salvation, for all other ground is sinking sand. Amen.

**May the peace of the Lord Christ go with you : wherever he may send you;
may he guide you through the wilderness : protect you through the storm;
may he bring you home rejoicing : at the wonders he has shown you;
may he bring you home rejoicing : once again into our doors.**

July 16

O Lord, let my soul rise up to meet you
as the day rises to meet the sun.

**Glory to the Father, and to the Son, and to the Holy Spirit,
as it was in the beginning, is now, and will be forever. Amen.**

Come, let us bow down and bend the knee : let us kneel before the Lord our Maker.

Song "O Lord, Have Mercy"

Arise, O God, and rule the earth : hear the cries from forgotten slums.

Psalm 82:1–4
God takes his stand in the council of heaven : **he gives judgment in the midst of the gods:**
"How long will you judge unjustly : **and show favor to the wicked?**
Save the weak and the orphan : **defend the humble and needy;**
rescue the weak and the poor : **deliver them from the power of the wicked."**

Arise, O God, and rule the earth : hear the cries from forgotten slums.

Judges 14:1–19   Acts 21:1–14

Arise, O God, and rule the earth : hear the cries from forgotten slums.

South African pastor and bishop Peter Storey said, "American preachers have a task more difficult, perhaps, than those faced by us under South Africa's apartheid, or Christians under Communism. We had obvious evils to engage; you have to unwrap your culture from years of red, white and blue myth. You have to expose, and confront, the great disconnection between the kindness, compassion and caring of most American people, and the ruthless way American power is experienced, directly and indirectly, by the poor of the earth. You have to help good people see how they have let their institutions do their sinning for them. This is not easy among people who really believe that their country does nothing but good, but it is necessary, not only for their future, but for us all."

Prayers for Others

Our Father

Lord, grant us the ability to think with your mind, to hear with your ears, to see with your eyes, to speak with your mouth, to walk with your feet, to love with your heart. We ask this through Christ our Lord. Amen.

May the peace of the Lord Christ go with you : wherever he may send you; may he guide you through the wilderness : protect you through the storm; may he bring you home rejoicing : at the wonders he has shown you; may he bring you home rejoicing : once again into our doors.

> **Whole Body Prayer**
>
> Worship is a physical act. Just as some folks see lifting their hands to God as a sign of worship, we also see lifting our hands out to a neighbor as an act of worship. When we "pass the peace" and give each other a hug or handshake, it is part of worship. In fact, if there is anyone we feel we cannot shake hands with, Scripture says that this stands in the way of worship, and we should get up from the altar and reconcile with our neighbor first. Homeless friends, who sometimes smell a little, have told us the only hugs they get during the week are in Mass on Sunday. It is a sad thing to hear, but thanks be to God that they get hugs on Sunday. And hopefully we have a church that is living a life of worship outside of Sunday, passing the peace on the streets and giving hugs away during the week, especially to those who smell a little.
>
> Prayer doesn't need to be boring. Consider mixing things up, perhaps kneeling during confessional sins or lifting your hands as you give thanks for something. One way many Christians gesture during prayer is by making the "sign of the

> cross," using their right hand to touch the forehead, then the middle of the breast, then the left shoulder, and finally the right shoulder. As they do this, they say, "In the name of the Father, and of the Son, and of the Holy Spirit. Amen." It is a way that we can remember that we are to take up our own crosses. And it is a way we can remember that, as Paul said, "I no longer live, but Christ lives in me" (Gal. 2:20). As we cross ourselves, we pray that Christ will be in our minds and in our hearts, and will live in us.

July 17

O Lord, let my soul rise up to meet you
as the day rises to meet the sun.

**Glory to the Father, and to the Son, and to the Holy Spirit,
as it was in the beginning, is now, and will be forever. Amen.**

Come, let us sing to the LORD : let us shout for joy to the Rock of our salvation.

Song "Oh the Deep, Deep Love of Jesus"

Root us in your love, O Lord : and set us free from fear.

Psalm 89:1–2, 18
Your love, O LORD, for ever will I sing : **from age to age my mouth will proclaim your faithfulness.**
For I am persuaded that your love is established for ever : **you have set your faithfulness firmly in the heavens.**
Truly, the LORD is our ruler : **the Holy One of Israel is our King.**

Root us in your love, O Lord : and set us free from fear.

Judges 14:20–15:20   Acts 21:15–36

Root us in your love, O Lord : and set us free from fear.

Hear these words from Martin Luther King Jr.: "It is not enough to say 'We must not wage war.' It is necessary to love peace and sacrifice for it."

Prayers for Others

Our Father

Lord God, protect us from the pointing finger and malicious talk. Give us the courage to win over our enemies by our love and to wear them down with grace. Amen.

May the peace of the Lord Christ go with you : wherever he may send you;
may he guide you through the wilderness : protect you through the storm;
may he bring you home rejoicing : at the wonders he has shown you;
may he bring you home rejoicing : once again into our doors.

❈ July 18

O Lord, let my soul rise up to meet you
as the day rises to meet the sun.

**Glory to the Father, and to the Son, and to the Holy Spirit,
as it was in the beginning, is now, and will be forever. Amen.**

Come, let us bow down and bend the knee : let us kneel before the LORD our Maker.

Song "Let All Mortal Flesh Keep Silence"

We fall down at your feet to find our way : lift us up to sing your praise.

Psalm 93:1–3
The LORD is King; he has put on splendid apparel : **the LORD has put on his apparel and girded himself with strength.**
He has made the whole world so sure : **that it cannot be moved;**
ever since the world began, your throne has been established : **you are from everlasting.**

We fall down at your feet to find our way : lift us up to sing your praise.

Judges 16:1–14   Acts 21:37–22:16

We fall down at your feet to find our way : lift us up to sing your praise.

A word from Benedict of Nursia: "The first step of humility is to cherish at all times the sense of awe with which we should turn to God."

Prayers for Others

Our Father

Lord, our strength and purpose come from you. Direct our steps today, and turn us from the perishable things at which we grasp. Cast your light upon us so that our lives may bear witness to the light of Christ. Amen.

**May the peace of the Lord Christ go with you : wherever he may send you;
may he guide you through the wilderness : protect you through the storm;
may he bring you home rejoicing : at the wonders he has shown you;
may he bring you home rejoicing : once again into our doors.**

✹ July 19

On July 19, 1848, the first Women's Rights Convention was held in Seneca Falls, New York, sparking a women's movement that challenged both the church and the world with the good news that in Jesus Christ, there is neither male nor female.

O Lord, let my soul rise up to meet you
as the day rises to meet the sun.

**Glory to the Father, and to the Son, and to the Holy Spirit,
as it was in the beginning, is now, and will be forever. Amen.**

Come, let us sing to the LORD : let us shout for joy to the Rock of our salvation.

Song "The Kingdom of God"

Sing and rejoice, O daughters of Zion : sing a new song of freedom.

Psalm 98:6–10
Sing to the LORD with the harp : **with the harp and the voice of song.**
With trumpets and the sound of the horn : **shout with joy before the King, the LORD.**
Let the sea make a noise and all that is in it : **the lands and those who dwell therein.**
Let the rivers clap their hands : **and let the hills ring out with joy before the LORD, when he comes to judge the earth.**
In righteousness shall he judge the world : **and the peoples with equity.**

Sing and rejoice, O daughters of Zion : sing a new song of freedom.

Judges 16:15–31   Acts 22:17–29

Sing and rejoice, O daughters of Zion : sing a new song of freedom.

African-American abolitionist and women's rights advocate Sojourner Truth said, "I have plowed and planted and gathered into barns, and no man could head me — and ain't I a woman? I have born'd five childrun and seen 'em mos' all sold off into slavery, and when I cried out with mother's grief, none but Jesus heard — and ain't I a woman?… Den dat little man is back dar, he say women can't have as much rights as man, 'cause Christ warn't a woman. Whar did your Christ come from? From God and a woman! Man had nothing to do with him!"

Prayers for Others

Our Father

Creator God, you made us in your image. Male and female, you created us. We give thanks that you use us, women and men, to bear your image to the world. Open our eyes to see you where we have failed to see you before. Amen.

May the peace of the Lord Christ go with you : wherever he may send you; may he guide you through the wilderness : protect you through the storm; may he bring you home rejoicing : at the wonders he has shown you; may he bring you home rejoicing : once again into our doors.

✸ July 20

O Lord, let my soul rise up to meet you
as the day rises to meet the sun.

Glory to the Father, and to the Son, and to the Holy Spirit, as it was in the beginning, is now, and will be forever. Amen.

Come, let us sing to the LORD : let us shout for joy to the Rock of our salvation.

Song   "All Creatures of Our God and King"

In all we say, please give us grace : to voice creation's praise.

Psalm 104:1, 10–12
Bless the LORD, O my soul : **O LORD my God, how excellent is your greatness! you are clothed with majesty and splendor.**
You send the springs into the valleys : **they flow between the mountains.**
All the beasts of the field drink their fill from them : **and the wild asses quench their thirst.**
Beside them the birds of the air make their nests : **and sing among the branches.**

In all we say, please give us grace : to voice creation's praise.

Judges 17:1–13   Acts 22:30–23:11

In all we say, please give us grace : to voice creation's praise.

Contemporary Anglican bishop, poet, and theologian Rowan Williams has said, "Our present ecological crisis, the biggest single practical threat to our human existence in the middle to long term, has, religious people would say, a great deal to do with our failure to think of the world as existing in relation to the mystery of God, not just as a huge warehouse of stuff to be used for our convenience."

Prayers for Others

Our Father

We praise you, O Lord, for the waters, the mountains and hills, the deserts and valleys, the wilderness spaces, and for all living creatures. Forgive us when we have not been good caretakers of the earth. Make us into people who practice resurrection by bringing dead things back to life and by making ugly things beautiful again. Amen.

May the peace of the Lord Christ go with you : wherever he may send you; may he guide you through the wilderness : protect you through the storm; may he bring you home rejoicing : at the wonders he has shown you; may he bring you home rejoicing : once again into our doors.

July 21

O Lord, let my soul rise up to meet you
as the day rises to meet the sun.

Glory to the Father, and to the Son, and to the Holy Spirit, as it was in the beginning, is now, and will be forever. Amen.

Come, let us sing to the LORD : let us shout for joy to the Rock of our salvation.

Song "Great Is Thy Faithfulness"

We have come this far by faith : leaning on the Lord who saves.

Psalm 106:47–48
Save us, O LORD our God, and gather us from among the nations : **that we may give thanks to your holy name and glory in your praise.**
Blessed be the LORD, the God of Israel, from everlasting and to everlasting : **and let all the people say, "Amen!" Hallelujah!**

We have come this far by faith : leaning on the Lord who saves.

Judges 18:1–15   Acts 23:12–24

We have come this far by faith : leaning on the Lord who saves.

Jean Vanier, founder of the L'Arche communities, said, "My experience has shown that when we welcome people from this world of anguish, brokenness and depression, and when they gradually discover that they are wanted and loved as they are and that they have a place, then we witness a real transformation — I would even say 'resurrection.' Their tense, angry, fearful, depressed body gradually becomes relaxed, peaceful and trusting. This shows through the expression on the face and through all their flesh. As they discover a sense of belonging, that they are part of a 'family,' then the will to live begins to emerge. I do not believe it is of any value to push people into doing things unless this desire to live and to grow has begun to emerge."

Prayers for Others

Our Father

Lord, save us from trouble, but help us to be people who get in the way of injustice and trouble the waters of oppression. Thank you for whispering to us that we are beloved. Help us now to whisper your love to those who long to hear that there is a loving God. Amen.

May the peace of the Lord Christ go with you : wherever he may send you; may he guide you through the wilderness : protect you through the storm; may he bring you home rejoicing : at the wonders he has shown you; may he bring you home rejoicing : once again into our doors.

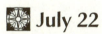 July 22

Mary Magdalene

Mary of Magdala was the most prominent of the women from Galilee who accompanied Jesus in his ministry. So devoted to Jesus was Mary that, after his death, she returned to the tomb to clean his body. Finding Jesus alive in the garden, she was sent to proclaim the news of his resurrection to the disciples, thus becoming "the apostle to the Apostles." Although she may not have been acknowledged for her discipleship, Mary stands for all those who see and proclaim Jesus as the risen Christ, bringing to others his gifts of peace, forgiveness, and justice.

O Lord, let my soul rise up to meet you
as the day rises to meet the sun.

**Glory to the Father, and to the Son, and to the Holy Spirit,
as it was in the beginning, is now, and will be forever. Amen.**

Come, let us bow down and the bend the knee : let us kneel before the LORD our Maker.

Song "Take My Life and Let It Be"

Speak, Lord, for we are listening : call us, like you called Mary, by name.

Psalm 109:1–3
Hold not your tongue, O God of my praise : **for the mouth of the wicked, the mouth of the deceitful, is opened against me.**
They speak to me with a lying tongue : **they encompass me with hateful words and fight against me without a cause.**
Despite my love, they accuse me : **but as for me, I pray for them.**

Speak, Lord, for we are listening : call us, like you called Mary, by name.

Judges 18:16–31   Acts 23:23–35

Speak, Lord, for we are listening : call us, like you called Mary, by name.

A reading from the gospel according to John: "Then the disciples went back to where they were staying. Now Mary stood outside the tomb crying. As she wept, she bent over to look into the tomb and saw two angels in white, seated where Jesus' body had been, one at the head and the other at the foot. They asked her, 'Woman, why are you crying?' 'They have taken my Lord away,' she said, 'and I don't know where they have put him.' At this, she turned around and saw Jesus standing there.... Jesus said, 'Do not hold on to me, for I have not yet ascended to the Father. Go instead to my brothers and tell them, "I am ascending to my Father and your Father, to my God and your God."' Mary Magdalene went to the disciples with the news: 'I have seen the Lord!'"

Prayers for Others

Our Father

Lord God, you reveal yourself to us in so many subversive and unassuming ways. Give us the eyes to see the miracles and resurrection that happen every day. Unclog our ears to hear you, and show us how to get rid of the clutter of our lives that we might make room for you. Amen.

**May the peace of the Lord Christ go with you : wherever he may send you;
may he guide you through the wilderness : protect you through the storm;
may he bring you home rejoicing : at the wonders he has shown you;
may he bring you home rejoicing : once again into our doors.**

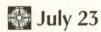
July 23

O Lord, let my soul rise up to meet you
as the day rises to meet the sun.

**Glory to the Father, and to the Son, and to the Holy Spirit,
as it was in the beginning, is now, and will be forever. Amen.**

Come, let us sing to the LORD : let us shout for joy to the Rock of our salvation.

Song "Vamos Todos al Banquete"

Praise be to God, who gives beauty for ashes : hope in the morning, strength for today.

Psalm 113:1–3, 8
Hallelujah! Give praise, you servants of the LORD : **praise the name of the LORD.**
Let the name of the LORD be blessed : **from this time forth for evermore.**
From the rising of the sun to its going down : **let the name of the LORD be praised.**
He makes the woman of a childless house : **to be a joyful mother of children.**

Praise be to God, who gives beauty for ashes : hope in the morning, strength for today.

1 Samuel 1:1–20   Acts 24:1–23

Praise be to God, who gives beauty for ashes : hope in the morning, strength for today.

These words were written in the early Christian writing known as the *Letter to Diognetus,* whose author is unknown: "Christians live in their own countries, but only as guests and aliens. They take part in everything as citizens and endure everything as aliens.... They are as poor as beggars, and yet they make many rich. They lack everything, and yet they have everything in abundance. They are dishonored, and yet have their glory in this very dishonor.... They are abused, yet they bless.... In a word: what the soul is in the body, the Christians are in the world."

Prayers for Others

Our Father

Dear God, form us into a peculiar people who live differently because we have been transformed by you. May the courage of the early Christians teach us to laugh at fear, to starve greed, and to live with the winsome freedom of the lilies and the sparrows. Amen.

May the peace of the Lord Christ go with you : wherever he may send you; may he guide you through the wilderness : protect you through the storm; may he bring you home rejoicing : at the wonders he has shown you; may he bring you home rejoicing : once again into our doors.

July 24

O Lord, let my soul rise up to meet you
as the day rises to meet the sun.

**Glory to the Father, and to the Son, and to the Holy Spirit,
as it was in the beginning, is now, and will be forever. Amen.**

Come, let us bow down and bend the knee : let us kneel before the LORD our Maker.

Song "Guide My Feet"

Guide my feet, Lord, guide me : make straight the way to your house.

Psalm 119:1–5
Happy are they whose way is blameless : **who walk in the law of the LORD!**
Happy are they who observe his decrees : **and seek him with all their hearts!**
who never do any wrong : **but always walk in his ways.**
You laid down your commandments : **that we should fully keep them.**
Oh, that my ways were made so direct : **that I might keep your statutes!**

Guide my feet, Lord, guide me : make straight the way to your house.

1 Samuel 1:21–2:11   Acts 24:24–25:12

Guide my feet, Lord, guide me : make straight the way to your house.

Listen to these words from Quaker author and educator Parker Palmer: "The power of a fully lived life or a truly learned mind is not a power to be sought or contrived. It comes only as we let go of what we possess and find ourselves possessed by a truth greater than our own."

Prayers for Others

Our Father

Lord God, our hands are open to you. Our ears are listening to you. Our eyes are watching you. Our hearts are trying to beat with yours. Live in us and love others through us today. Amen.

**May the peace of the Lord Christ go with you : wherever he may send you;
may he guide you through the wilderness : protect you through the storm;
may he bring you home rejoicing : at the wonders he has shown you;
may he bring you home rejoicing : once again into our doors.**

✦ July 25

In 1898, United States troops invaded Puerto Rico, recolonizing its people after their struggle for independence under Spanish rule. US citizenship was given to Puerto Ricans, but in the 1930s, a nationalist movement gained popularity and US assimilation was opposed. A struggle still exists in Puerto Rico between gaining independence and remaining a colony of the United States.

O Lord, let my soul rise up to meet you
as the day rises to meet the sun.

**Glory to the Father, and to the Son, and to the Holy Spirit,
as it was in the beginning, is now, and will be forever. Amen.**

Come, let us sing to the LORD : let us shout for joy to the Rock of our salvation.

Song "The Kingdom of God"

Give justice to your people, God : and set the captives free.

Psalm 119:53–56
I am filled with a burning rage : **because of the wicked who forsake your law.**
Your statutes have been like songs to me : **wherever I have lived as a stranger.**
I remember your name in the night, O LORD : **and dwell upon your law.**
This is how it has been with me : **because I have kept your commandments.**

Give justice to your people, God : and set the captives free.

1 Samuel 2:12–26   Acts 25:13–27

Give justice to your people, God : and set the captives free.

Jesuit leader and Latino theologian Pedro Arrupe said, "Today our prime educational objective must be to form men-for-others; men who will live not for themselves but for God and his Christ — for the God-man who lived and died for all the world; men who cannot even conceive of love of God which does not include love for the least of their neighbors; men completely convinced that love of God which does not issue in justice for men is a farce."

Prayers for Others

Our Father

Almighty God, thank you for the cloud of witnesses who have gone before us. Surround us with living saints who remind us of the sort of people we are trying to become. When we fall short of who we want to be, catch us in the arms of your grace. We ask this through Christ our Lord. Amen.

May the peace of the Lord Christ go with you : wherever he may send you;
may he guide you through the wilderness : protect you through the storm;
may he bring you home rejoicing : at the wonders he has shown you;
may he bring you home rejoicing : once again into our doors.

❋ July 26

On July 26, 1990, US President George Bush signed the world's first civil rights law for people with disabilities. Since its signing in 1990, the Americans with Disabilities Act has served as legal protection for equal opportunity in all aspects of life, independent living, and economic self-sufficiency for people with disabilities.

O Lord, let my soul rise up to meet you
as the day rises to meet the sun.

**Glory to the Father, and to the Son, and to the Holy Spirit,
as it was in the beginning, is now, and will be forever. Amen.**

Come, let us bow down and bend the knee : let us kneel before the Lord our Maker.

Song "Freedom Train"

Make us one with your poor, O Lord : that we might see the salvation of our God.

Psalm 119:121–25
I have done what is just and right : **do not deliver me to my oppressors.**
Be surety for your servant's good : **let not the proud oppress me.**
My eyes have failed from watching for your salvation : **and for your righteous promise.**
Deal with your servant according to your loving-kindness : **and teach me your statutes.**
I am your servant; grant me understanding : **that I may know your decrees.**

Make us one with your poor, O Lord : that we might see the salvation of our God.

1 Samuel 2:27–36   Acts 26:1–23

Make us one with your poor, O Lord : that we might see the salvation of our God.

Hear these words of L'Arche founder Jean Vanier: "People may come to our communities because they want to serve the poor; they will only stay once they have discovered that they themselves are the poor."

372 *Morning Prayer*

Prayers for Others

Our Father

Lord, thank you for using the foolish to confound the wise and the weak ones to shame the strong. Help us live with the shrewdness of serpents and the innocence of doves. Keep our feet from fatigue, our spirits from despair, and our hands from failing to rise in praise to you. Amen.

May the peace of the Lord Christ go with you : wherever he may send you; may he guide you through the wilderness : protect you through the storm; may he bring you home rejoicing : at the wonders he has shown you; may he bring you home rejoicing : once again into our doors.

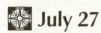 July 27

O Lord, let my soul rise up to meet you
as the day rises to meet the sun.

Glory to the Father, and to the Son, and to the Holy Spirit, as it was in the beginning, is now, and will be forever. Amen.

Come, let us bow down and bend the knee : let us kneel before the Lord our Maker.

Song "Lamb of God"

We look to you alone, O Lord : we look to you for help.

Psalm 123
To you I lift up my eyes : **to you enthroned in the heavens.**
As the eyes of servants look to the hand of their masters : **and the eyes of a maid to the hand of her mistress,**
so our eyes look to the Lord our God : **until he shows us his mercy.**
Have mercy upon us, O Lord, have mercy : **for we have had more than enough of contempt,**
too much of the scorn of the indolent rich : **and of the derision of the proud.**

We look to you alone, O Lord : we look to you for help.

1 Samuel 3:1–12   Acts 26:24–27:8

We look to you alone, O Lord : we look to you for help.

Egyptian monk Macarius said this in the fourth century: "There is no need at all to make long discourses; it is enough to stretch out one's hands and say, 'Lord, as you will, and as you know, have mercy.' And if the conflict grows fiercer say, 'Lord, help!' He knows very well what we need and he shows us his mercy."

Prayers for Others

Our Father

Holy One, so often we claim to see but prefer our blindness. Send us teachers and saints whose lives speak loudly of faith and perseverance to guide us when we unknowingly stray from wisdom's course. Help us to find the Way, the Truth, and the Life in this world of shortcuts, deception, and death. Amen.

May the peace of the Lord Christ go with you : wherever he may send you; may he guide you through the wilderness : protect you through the storm; may he bring you home rejoicing : at the wonders he has shown you; may he bring you home rejoicing : once again into our doors.

 July 28

O Lord, let my soul rise up to meet you
as the day rises to meet the sun.

**Glory to the Father, and to the Son, and to the Holy Spirit,
as it was in the beginning, is now, and will be forever. Amen.**

Come, let us sing to the LORD : let us shout for joy to the Rock of our salvation.

Song "Woke Up This Mornin'"

Give me neither poverty nor riches, Lord : but bread for today, hope for tomorrow.

Psalm 135:1–2, 15–18
Hallelujah! Praise the name of the LORD : **give praise, you servants of the LORD,**
you who stand in the house of the LORD : **in the courts of the house of our God.**
The idols of the heathen are silver and gold : **the work of human hands.**
They have mouths, but they cannot speak : **eyes have they, but they cannot see.**
They have ears, but they cannot hear : **neither is there any breath in their mouth.**
Those who make them are like them : **and so are all who put their trust in them.**

Give me neither poverty nor riches, Lord : but bread for today, hope for tomorrow.

1 Samuel 9:1–14   Acts 27:9–26

Give me neither poverty nor riches, Lord : but bread for today, hope for tomorrow.

In the second century, church father Justin Martyr described the Christian community like this: "We who formerly treasured money and possessions more than anything else now hand over everything we have to a treasury for all and share it with everyone who needs it. We who formerly hated and murdered one another … now live together and share the same table. Now we pray for our enemies and try to win those who hate us."

Prayers for Others

Our Father

Lord, it takes humility to acknowledge that our ways are not your ways. Surround us with your subtle and hidden prophets, that we might have help to overcome self-deception and face the truth that sets us free. Amen.

**May the peace of the Lord Christ go with you : wherever he may send you;
may he guide you through the wilderness : protect you through the storm;
may he bring you home rejoicing : at the wonders he has shown you;
may he bring you home rejoicing : once again into our doors.**

✸ July 29

O Lord, let my soul rise up to meet you
as the day rises to meet the sun.

**Glory to the Father, and to the Son, and to the Holy Spirit,
as it was in the beginning, is now, and will be forever. Amen.**

Come, let us bow down and bend the knee : let us kneel before the Lord our Maker.

Song "Were You There?"

When our spirits fail, you know our paths : guide us, O Lord, as we stumble.

Psalm 142:1–2, 5–7
I cry to the Lord with my voice : **to the Lord I make loud supplication.**
I pour out my complaint before him : **and tell him all my trouble.**
I cry out to you, O Lord : **I say, "You are my refuge, my portion in the land of the living."**
Listen to my cry for help, for I have been brought very low : **save me from those who pursue me, for they are too strong for me.**

Bring me out of prison, that I may give thanks to your name : **when you have dealt bountifully with me, the righteous will gather around me.**

When our spirits fail, you know our paths : guide us, O Lord, as we stumble.

1 Samuel 9:15–10:1   Acts 27:27–44

When our spirits fail, you know our paths : guide us, O Lord, as we stumble.

Listen to these words of Martin Luther King Jr.: "Truth crushed to earth will rise again. How long? Not long! Because no lie can live forever. How long? Not long! Truth forever on the scaffold, wrong forever on the throne. Yet that scaffold sways the future and behind the dim unknown standeth God within the shadow, keeping watch over his own. How long? Not long! Because the arc of the mortal universe is long but it bends toward justice."

Prayers for Others

Our Father

Lord, raise us up as servants who are willing to bear one another's burdens. Surround us with others who will help make the burdens lighter. And help us rest in the assurance that you will not put more on our shoulders than we are able to carry. We ask this through Christ Jesus, our Lord, who both told us to take up our cross and had help carrying his own. Amen.

May the peace of the Lord Christ go with you : wherever he may send you; may he guide you through the wilderness : protect you through the storm; may he bring you home rejoicing : at the wonders he has shown you; may he bring you home rejoicing : once again into our doors.

July 30

William Wilberforce (1759–1833)

William Wilberforce, an evangelical Christian in eighteenth-century England, dedicated his life to abolishing slavery. In 1780, Wilberforce was elected to Parliament. After an experience of spiritual rebirth, Wilberforce began to see his life's purpose: to use his political life in the service of God. He believed that there was no evil greater than the institution of slavery. "Let the consequences be what they would," he wrote. "I from this time determined that I would never rest until I had effected its abolition." In 1798, he began his campaign: speaking, circulating flyers and petitions, and introducing bills in Parliament. In 1806, Wilberforce managed to get a bill in Parliament passed that prohibited slavery in all British colonies. By the time Wilberforce died in 1833, Parliament had finally passed a bill that would free all slaves throughout the British Empire.

O Lord, let my soul rise up to meet you
as the day rises to meet the sun.

**Glory to the Father, and to the Son, and to the Holy Spirit,
as it was in the beginning, is now, and will be forever. Amen.**

Come, let us sing to the LORD : let us shout for joy to the Rock of our salvation.

Song "Amazing Grace"

Give us holy boldness, Lord : to struggle for justice until we die.

Psalm 144:9–12
O God, I will sing to you a new song : **I will play to you on a ten-stringed lyre.**
You give victory to kings : **and have rescued David your servant.**
Rescue me from the hurtful sword : **and deliver me from the hand of foreign peoples,**
whose mouths speak deceitfully : **and whose right hand is raised in falsehood.**

Give us holy boldness, Lord : to struggle for justice until we die.

1 Samuel 10:1–16   Acts 28:1–16

Give us holy boldness, Lord : to struggle for justice until we die.

A few words from William Wilberforce: "Never, never will we desist till we have wiped away this scandal that is slavery from the load of guilt under which we at present labor, and until we have extinguished every trace of this bloody traffic which our posterity will scarcely believe had been suffered to exist so long, a disgrace and dishonor to our country."

Prayers for Others

Our Father

Stir our hearts that we might have the holy boldness to struggle for justice until we die. Give us visions larger than those we create for ourselves. And root us in humility, Lord, that we might climb toward your heights through service. Amen.

**May the peace of the Lord Christ go with you : wherever he may send you;
may he guide you through the wilderness : protect you through the storm;
may he bring you home rejoicing : at the wonders he has shown you;
may he bring you home rejoicing : once again into our doors.**

July 31

Ignatius of Loyola (1491 – 1556)

Ignatius was born to a noble Spanish family. As a young man, he joined the military, but a war injury ended his military career. While recuperating, Ignatius became bored and asked for novels about knights and battles. But all that could be found in the castle where he stayed were books on the life of Christ and the saints of the church. Legend has it that Ignatius read these stories in a competitive manner, imagining how he could beat the various saints at practicing the spiritual disciplines. He soon found that his thoughts on the saints left him with more peaceful and satisfied feelings than his daydreams about the noble life he had known before his injury. After his illness, Ignatius began practicing his competitive notions of rivaling the saints, and wrote about his experiences of Christian disciplines. His scribblings became the spiritual classic *The Spiritual Exercises of Saint Ignatius*, used by Christians for centuries in the practice of discernment. He eventually founded the Society of Jesus, an order still known widely for a commitment to foreign missions and religious education.

O Lord, let my soul rise up to meet you
as the day rises to meet the sun.

**Glory to the Father, and to the Son, and to the Holy Spirit,
as it was in the beginning, is now, and will be forever. Amen.**

Come, let us sing to the LORD : let us shout for joy to the Rock of our salvation.

Song "Ubi Caritas"

Teach us to give : and not to count the cost.

Psalm 145:5 – 9
I will ponder the glorious splendor of your majesty : **and all your marvelous works.**
They shall speak of the might of your wondrous acts : **and I will tell of your greatness.**
They shall publish the remembrance of your great goodness : **they shall sing of your righteous deeds.**
The LORD is gracious and full of compassion : **slow to anger and of great kindness.**
The LORD is loving to everyone : **and his compassion is over all his works.**

Teach us to give : and not to count the cost.

1 Samuel 10:17 – 27   Acts 28:17 – 31

Teach us to give : and not to count the cost.

These are the words of Ignatius of Loyola, founder of the Jesuits: "Consider that the blessed life we so long for consists in an intimate and true love of God, our Creator and Lord, which binds and obliges us all to a sincere love."

Prayers for Others

Our Father

Jesus, it is enough to tell others of your works of mercy, of your resurrection, of your imminent return. It is enough to praise you in the sanctuary, to kneel before you, to wait in silence for you. Lord, it is enough to be named as one of your children, to be bound in eternal love and freedom to give up our lives for you. Amen.

May the peace of the Lord Christ go with you : wherever he may send you; may he guide you through the wilderness : protect you through the storm; may he bring you home rejoicing : at the wonders he has shown you; may he bring you home rejoicing : once again into our doors.

Becoming the Answer to Our Prayers: A Few Ideas

1. Begin a scholarship fund so that for every one of your own children you send to college, you can create a scholarship for an at-risk youth. Get to know their families and learn from each other.
2. Visit a worship service in which you will be a minority. Invite someone to a meal after the service.
3. Confess something you have done wrong to someone you have wronged or or offended and ask forgiveness.
4. Serve in a homeless shelter. For extra credit, go back to that shelter and eat or sleep there and allow yourself to be served.
5. Go through a local thrift store and drop dollar bills in the pockets of clothing in the store.

AUGUST — THE TRANSFIGURATION

AUGUST

Marks of New Monasticism
Peacemaking

Peace is not just about the absence of conflict; it's also about the presence of justice. Martin Luther King Jr. even distinguished between "the devil's peace" and God's true peace. A counterfeit peace exists when people are pacified or distracted or so beat up and tired of fighting that all seems calm. But true peace does not exist until there is justice, restoration, forgiveness. Peacemaking doesn't mean passivity. It is the act of interrupting injustice without mirroring injustice, the act of disarming evil without destroying the evildoer, the act of finding a third way that is neither fight nor flight but the careful, arduous pursuit of reconciliation and justice. It is about a revolution of love that is big enough to set both the oppressed and the oppressors free.

Peace is about being able to recognize in the face of the oppressed our own faces, and in the hands of the oppressors our own hands. Peace, like most beautiful things, begins small. Matthew 18 gives us a clear process for approaching someone who has hurt or offended us; first we are to talk directly with them, not at them or around them. Most communities that have been around a while (like a few decades or centuries) identify "straight talk," or creating an environment where people do not avoid conflict but speak honestly to one another, as one of the core values of healthy community. Straight talk is countercultural in a world that prefers politeness to honesty. In his Rule, Benedict of Nursia speaks passionately about the deadly poison of "murmuring," the negativity and dissension that can infect community and rot the fabric of love.

Peacemaking begins with what we can change — ourselves. But it doesn't end there. We are to be peacemakers in a world riddled with violence. That means interrupting violence with imagination, on our streets and in our world. This peace that is "not like any way the empire brings peace" is rooted in the nonviolence of the cross, where we see a Savior who loves his enemies so much he died for them. Peace is often not our instinct,

> **Suggested Reading for the Month**
> *The Politics of Jesus* by John Howard Yoder
> *Resident Aliens* by Stanley Hauerwas and William Willimon
> *The Powers That Be* by Walter Wink
> *The Violence of Love* by Oscar Romero
> "Riverside Speech" by Martin Luther King Jr. (audio; good for August 6, the anniversary of the bombing of Hiroshima)

which is why it must be cultivated and grown in us. Even Jesus' key disciple, Peter, picks up his sword when the soldiers approach Jesus. Jesus' response is brilliant: he scolds Peter, and then he heals the wounded persecutor, only to be dragged away and hung on a Roman cross. If ever there were a case for "just war" or justified violence to protect the innocent, Peter had it. Yet Jesus rebukes his logic of the sword.

The early Christians said, "When Jesus disarmed Peter, he disarmed every Christian." For hundreds of years, Christians were never seen carrying swords, and they followed the way of the Prince of Peace even unto death, loving their enemies and blessing those who cursed them. It doesn't look like a good strategy for running an empire, but it is the narrow way that leads to life. Undoubtedly, it doesn't always seem to "work." As we look at history, and even as we read the Scriptures, there seems to be evidence that violence has worked at times and failed at times, just as nonviolence has worked at times and failed at times. In the end, the question is, Which looks most like Jesus? For we are called not just to be successful but to be faithful to the way of the cross, even unto death. The way of the cross did not seem to work on Friday, but the promise is that Sunday is coming. In the end, Love wins.

This can be hard to remember as we go about our lives. But the transfiguration reminds us how the disciples' eyes were opened to the reality of Jesus' power even before the resurrection. If we have eyes to see, the lightning that flashes east to west in the nonviolent coming of God can illuminate the world wherever we are. "If you are willing," one of the desert fathers said, "you can become all flame."

✦ August 1

O Lord, let my soul rise up to meet you
as the day rises to meet the sun.

**Glory to the Father, and to the Son, and to the Holy Spirit,
as it was in the beginning, is now, and will be forever. Amen.**

Come, let us bow down and bend the knee : let us kneel before the LORD our Maker.

Song "Come, Thou Fount"

Listen, Lord, in your mercy : not to our words but to our hearts.

Psalm 5:1–4
Give ear to my words, O LORD : **consider my meditation.**
Hearken to my cry for help, my King and my God : **for I make my prayer to you.**
In the morning, LORD, you hear my voice : **early in the morning I make my appeal and watch for you.**
For you are not a God who takes pleasure in wickedness : **and evil cannot dwell with you.**

Listen, Lord, in your mercy : not to our words but to our hearts.

1 Samuel 11:1–15   Matthew 25:1–13

Listen, Lord, in your mercy : not to our words but to our hearts.

Irish monk Columbanus wrote, "Blessed is the time of waiting, when we stay awake for the Lord, the Creator of the universe, who fills all things and transcends all things. How I wish he would awaken me, his humble servant, from the sleep of slothfulness, even though I am of little worth. How I wish he would enkindle me with that fire of divine love. The flames of his love burn beyond the stars; the longing for his overwhelming delights and the divine fire ever burns within me!"

Prayers for Others

Our Father

Lord, you are coming in glory to bring the fullness of peace, healing, and justice. Teach us to wait when you would have us wait. And teach us to act when you would have us act. Fill us up with so much expectation for your coming kingdom that we cannot help but enact it now. Amen.

May the peace of the Lord Christ go with you : wherever he may send you;
may he guide you through the wilderness : protect you through the storm;
may he bring you home rejoicing : at the wonders he has shown you;
may he bring you home rejoicing : once again into our doors.

August 2

Basil the Blessed (1464 – 1552)

Basil was born to a peasant family near Moscow in the late 1400s. He left home at age sixteen to devote himself to a life of asceticism. He did not have a permanent home but instead walked around barefoot and in rags, exhibiting extraordinary humility in the face of punishment, ridicule, and derision. Like an Old Testament prophet, Basil challenged those in power about their treatment of the poor, marginalized, and afflicted. He foretold misfortunes and preached the gospel to all who would listen, including the Tsar, Ivan the Terrible, who respected and feared Basil's gift of prophecy. Once, when Basil offered the Tsar a piece of raw meat during the lenten season, the Tsar rejected it. Basil then boldly and truthfully asked him, "Then why do you drink the blood of men?" noting the Tsar's violent behavior toward innocent people.

O Lord, let my soul rise up to meet you
as the day rises to meet the sun.

**Glory to the Father, and to the Son, and to the Holy Spirit,
as it was in the beginning, is now, and will be forever. Amen.**

Come, let us bow down and bend the knee : let us kneel before the LORD our Maker.

Song "Poor Wayfaring Stranger"

If we are fools in this world, Lord : may we be fools for Christ.

Psalm 13:3 – 6
Look upon me and answer me, O LORD my God : **give light to my eyes, lest I sleep in death;**
lest my enemy say, "I have prevailed over him," : **and my foes rejoice that I have fallen.**
But I put my trust in your mercy : **my heart is joyful because of your saving help.**
I will sing to the LORD, for he has dealt with me richly : **I will praise the name of the Lord Most High.**

If we are fools in this world, Lord : may we be fools for Christ.

1 Samuel 12:1 – 6, 16 – 25   Matthew 25:14 – 30

If we are fools in this world, Lord : **may we be fools for Christ.**

British preacher and radical John Wesley wrote in a letter to his sister, "Money never stays with me. It would burn me if it did. I throw it out of my hands as soon as possible, lest it should find its way into my heart." Wesley committed his life to living in poverty, insisting that if he were to die with more than a few pounds to his name, he would be a liar and a thief.

Prayers for Others

Our Father

God our provider, all good gifts come from you. Make us so thankful for your gifts that we cannot help but share them with others. Own us as your fools as we abandon the stuff of this world for the treasures of your kingdom. Amen.

**May the peace of the Lord Christ go with you : wherever he may send you;
may he guide you through the wilderness : protect you through the storm;
may he bring you home rejoicing : at the wonders he has shown you;
may he bring you home rejoicing : once again into our doors.**

✦ August 3

O Lord, let my soul rise up to meet you
as the day rises to meet the sun.

**Glory to the Father, and to the Son, and to the Holy Spirit,
as it was in the beginning, is now, and will be forever. Amen.**

Come, let us sing to the LORD : let us shout for joy to the Rock of our salvation.

Song "Servant Song"

Help us to serve in our weakness, Lord : and to see your power come down.

Psalm 18:6–11
I called upon the LORD in my distress : **and cried out to my God for help.**
He heard my voice from his heavenly dwelling : **my cry of anguish came to his ears.**
The earth reeled and rocked : **the roots of the mountains shook; they reeled because of his anger.**
Smoke rose from his nostrils and a consuming fire out of his mouth : **hot burning coals blazed forth from him.**
He parted the heavens and came down : **with a storm cloud under his feet.**
He mounted on cherubim and flew : **he swooped on the wings of the wind.**

Help us to serve in our weakness, Lord : and to see your power come down.

1 Samuel 13:5–18   Matthew 25:31–46

Help us to serve in our weakness, Lord : and to see your power come down.

In his book *From Brokenness to Community*, Jean Vanier writes, "Those with whom Jesus identifies himself are regarded by society as misfits. And yet Jesus is that person who is hungry; Jesus is that woman who is confused and naked. Wouldn't it be extraordinary if we all discovered that? The face of the world would be changed. We would then no longer want to compete in going up the ladder to meet God in the light, in the sun and in beauty, to be honored because of our theological knowledge. Or if we did want knowledge, it would be because we believe that our knowledge and theology are important only so long as they are used to serve and honor the poor."

Prayers for Others

Our Father

O God of the poor and meek, form us into people who do not conform to the patterns of this world but rather conform to the norms of your upside-down kingdom. Give us eyes to see you in those who suffer. Move us to the margins of this world, and help us to find you there, in your most distressing disguises. Amen.

**May the peace of the Lord Christ go with you : wherever he may send you;
may he guide you through the wilderness : protect you through the storm;
may he bring you home rejoicing : at the wonders he has shown you;
may he bring you home rejoicing : once again into our doors.**

✼ August 4

O Lord, let my soul rise up to meet you
as the day rises to meet the sun.

Glory to the Father, and to the Son, and to the Holy Spirit,
as it was in the beginning, is now, and will be forever. Amen.

Come, let us sing to the Lord : let us shout for joy to the Rock of our salvation.

Song   "What Is This Place?"

Bring us home to you, O God : here in this place, and wherever we may go.

Psalm 23
The LORD is my shepherd : **I shall not be in want.**
He makes me lie down in green pastures : **and leads me beside still waters.**
He revives my soul : **and guides me along right pathways for his name's sake.**
Though I walk through the valley of the shadow of death, I shall fear no evil : **for you are with me; your rod and your staff, they comfort me.**
You spread a table before me in the presence of those who trouble me : **you have anointed my head with oil, and my cup is running over.**
Surely your goodness and mercy shall follow me all the days of my life : **and I will dwell in the house of the LORD for ever.**

Bring us home to you, O God : here in this place, and wherever we may go.

1 Samuel 13:19 – 14:15   Matthew 26:1 – 16

Bring us home to you, O God : here in this place, and wherever we may go.

Mother Teresa of Calcutta said, "God has identified himself with the hungry, the sick, the naked, the homeless; hunger, not only for bread, but for love, for care, to be somebody to someone; nakedness, not of clothing only, but nakedness of that compassion that very few people give to the unknown; homelessness, not only for a shelter made of stone, but that homelessness that comes from having no one to call your own."

Prayers for Others

Our Father

God, we know that you never fail us. Even in our suffering and loneliness, help us to hear the whisper of your love. Be our refuge and shelter, and remind us over and over that we are your beloved children. Amen.

May the peace of the Lord Christ go with you : wherever he may send you; may he guide you through the wilderness : protect you through the storm; may he bring you home rejoicing : at the wonders he has shown you; may he bring you home rejoicing : once again into our doors.

✳ August 5

In 1963, the United States, the USSR, and Great Britain signed a treaty banning nuclear testing in the atmosphere. President John F. Kennedy quoted Soviet leader Nikita Krushchev, saying they both hoped to avoid a nuclear war in which "the survivors would envy the dead."

O Lord, let my soul rise up to meet you
as the day rises to meet the sun.

**Glory to the Father, and to the Son, and to the Holy Spirit,
as it was in the beginning, is now, and will be forever. Amen.**

Come, let us sing to the LORD : let us shout for joy to the Rock of our salvation.

Song "Jesus, Help Us Live in Peace"

Show us your beauty, Lord : in the face of an enemy, creation restored!

Psalm 27:5–9
One thing have I asked of the LORD; one thing I seek : **that I may dwell in the house of the LORD all the days of my life;**
to behold the fair beauty of the LORD : **and to seek him in his temple.**
For in the day of trouble he shall keep me safe in his shelter : **he shall hide me in the secrecy of his dwelling and set me high upon a rock.**
Even now he lifts up my head : **above my enemies round about me.**
Therefore I will offer in his dwelling an oblation with sounds of great gladness : **I will sing and make music to the LORD.**

Show us your beauty, Lord : in the face of an enemy, creation restored!

1 Samuel 14:16–45   Matthew 26:17–25

Show us your beauty, Lord : in the face of an enemy, creation restored!

Twentieth-century priest and spiritual writer Henri Nouwen said, "That is our vocation: to convert the enemy into a guest and to create the free and fearless space where brotherhood and sisterhood can be formed and fully experienced."

Prayers for Others

Our Father

Dear Lord, remind us that no one is above reproach, and no one is beyond redemption. Help us to look into the eyes of people we find hard to like, and see your image. Assure us this day that your mercy triumphs over judgment. Amen.

**May the peace of the Lord Christ go with you : wherever he may send you;
may he guide you through the wilderness : protect you through the storm;
may he bring you home rejoicing : at the wonders he has shown you;
may he bring you home rejoicing : once again into our doors.**

August 6

The Transfiguration

In 1945, the United States dropped an atomic bomb on Hiroshima, Japan, marking the first use of a nuclear weapon against people. As we remember the transfiguration of Christ in the mysterious light of glory, we also remember all those who were tragically and senselessly transfigured by the first nuclear blast. May their memory help us to see a way toward peace in our time.

O Lord, let my soul rise up to meet you
as the day rises to meet the sun.

**Glory to the Father, and to the Son, and to the Holy Spirit,
as it was in the beginning, is now, and will be forever. Amen.**

Come, let us sing to the Lord : let us shout for joy to the Rock of our salvation.

Song "We Are Marching in the Light of God"

Overwhelm us with your beauty, Lord : and make us to shine like stars.

Psalm 99:5–9
Proclaim the greatness of the Lord our God and fall down before his footstool : **he is the Holy One.**
Moses and Aaron among his priests, and Samuel among those who call upon his name : **they called upon the Lord, and he answered them.**
He spoke to them out of the pillar of cloud : **they kept his testimonies and the decree that he gave them.**
"O Lord our God, you answered them indeed : **you were a God who forgave them, yet punished them for their evil deeds.**"
Proclaim the greatness of the Lord our God and worship him upon his holy hill : **for the Lord our God is the Holy One.**

Overwhelm us with your beauty, Lord : and make us to shine like stars.

Exodus 34:29–35   Luke 9:28–36

Overwhelm us with your beauty, Lord : and make us to shine like stars.

Hear this story of the desert fathers: "Abba Lot went to see Abba Joseph and said to him, 'Abba, as far as I can I say my little office, I fast a little, I pray and meditate, I live in peace and as far as I can, I purify my thoughts. What else can I do?' Then the old man stood up and stretched his hands towards heaven. His fingers became like ten lamps of fire and he said to him, 'If you will, you can become all flame.'"

Prayers for Others

Our Father

Creator of the Universe, thank you for your dazzling imagination. Set a fire inside us that burns with your love. Help us to shine as you shine, so that people might not see us but see you shining through us. Amen.

May the peace of the Lord Christ go with you : wherever he may send you; may he guide you through the wilderness : protect you through the storm; may he bring you home rejoicing : at the wonders he has shown you; may he bring you home rejoicing : once again into our doors.

✸ August 7

O Lord, let my soul rise up to meet you
as the day rises to meet the sun.

Glory to the Father, and to the Son, and to the Holy Spirit,
as it was in the beginning, is now, and will be forever. Amen.

Come, let us sing to the LORD : let us shout for joy to the Rock of our salvation.

Song "It Is Well with My Soul"

Teach us to trust in you, O Lord : and follow your way to the end.

Psalm 37:1–6
Do not fret yourself because of evildoers : **do not be jealous of those who do wrong.**
For they shall soon wither like the grass : **and like the green grass fade away.**
Put your trust in the LORD and do good : **dwell in the land and feed on its riches.**
Take delight in the LORD : **and he shall give you your heart's desire.**
Commit your way to the LORD and put your trust in him : **and he will bring it to pass.**
He will make your righteousness as clear as the light : **and your just dealing as the noonday.**

Teach us to trust in you, O Lord : and follow your way to the end.

1 Samuel 15:1–3, 7–23   Matthew 26:26–35

Teach us to trust in you, O Lord : and follow your way to the end.

Hear these words of church father Augustine of Hippo: "Our pilgrimage on earth cannot be exempt from trial. We actually progress by means of trial. We do not know ourselves except through trial, or receive a crown except after victory."

Prayers for Others

Our Father

Lord, we take comfort in knowing that you have shared in our trials. You know pain and betrayal, and you are familiar with suffering. Strengthen us in hard times and remind us that you have overcome the evil of this world. Amen.

May the peace of the Lord Christ go with you : wherever he may send you; may he guide you through the wilderness : protect you through the storm; may he bring you home rejoicing : at the wonders he has shown you; may he bring you home rejoicing : once again into our doors.

✠ August 8

O Lord, let my soul rise up to meet you
as the day rises to meet the sun.

Glory to the Father, and to the Son, and to the Holy Spirit, as it was in the beginning, is now, and will be forever. Amen.

Come, let us sing to the LORD : **let us shout for joy to the Rock of our salvation.**

Song "Go, Tell It on the Mountain"

Help us to watch and pray, Jesus : prepare our hearts to wonder.

Psalm 40:1–6
I waited patiently upon the LORD : **he stooped to me and heard my cry.**
He lifted me out of the desolate pit, out of the mire and clay : **he set my feet upon a high cliff and made my footing sure.**
He put a new song in my mouth, a song of praise to our God : **many shall see, and stand in awe, and put their trust in the LORD.**
Happy are they who trust in the LORD! : **they do not resort to evil spirits or turn to false gods.**
Great things are they that you have done, O LORD my God! how great your wonders and your plans for us! : **there is none who can be compared with you.**
Oh, that I could make them known and tell them! : **but they are more than I can count.**

Help us to watch and pray, Jesus : prepare our hearts to wonder.

1 Samuel 15:24–35   Matthew 26:36–46

Help us to watch and pray, Jesus : prepare our hearts to wonder.

These are the words of thirteenth-century poet and mystic Hadewijch of Antwerp:

> The madness of love
> is a blessed fate;
> and if we understood this
> we would seek no other:
> it brings into unity
> what was divided,
> and this is the truth:
> bitterness it makes sweet,
> it makes the stranger a neighbor,
> and what was lowly it raises on high.

Prayers for Others

Our Father

Lord, train us to hear your voice. When it is time to grieve, help us to grieve. When it is time to rejoice, help us to rejoice. When we grow weary, be the strength in our weakness. And may your most beautiful and perfect will, not ours, be done. Amen.

May the peace of the Lord Christ go with you : wherever he may send you; may he guide you through the wilderness : protect you through the storm; may he bring you home rejoicing : at the wonders he has shown you; may he bring you home rejoicing : once again into our doors.

August 9

Franz Jägerstätter (1907 – 1943)

Franz Jägerstätter was a humble Catholic peasant born to a poor German farm maid in the small town of Radegund, Upper Austria. He was baptized, married, and worked as a sexton in the same small parish. Though he was never part of any formal resistance groups, Franz was his village's sole conscientious objector to the annexation of Austria to Germany under Hitler. He felt deeply that his Christian faith could not permit him to fight in Hitler's army. Even under pressure by local priests and bishops to conform and serve in the military, Franz refused. He was imprisoned and beheaded for his refusal to serve in the Nazi army.

O Lord, let my soul rise up to meet you
as the day rises to meet the sun.

Glory to the Father, and to the Son, and to the Holy Spirit,
as it was in the beginning, is now, and will be forever. Amen.

Come, let us sing to the LORD : let us shout for joy to the Rock of our salvation.

Song "When the Saints Go Marching In"

Give us courage to confess your name : and go with you against the grain.

Psalm 46:5–10
There is a river whose streams make glad the city of God : **the holy habitation of the Most High.**
God is in the midst of her; she shall not be overthrown : **God shall help her at the break of day.**
The nations make much ado, and the kingdoms are shaken : **God has spoken, and the earth shall melt away.**
The LORD of hosts is with us : **the God of Jacob is our stronghold.**
Come now and look upon the works of the LORD : **what awesome things he has done on earth.**
It is he who makes war to cease in all the world : **he breaks the bow, and shatters the spear, and burns the shields with fire.**

Give us courage to confess your name : and go with you against the grain.

1 Samuel 16:1–13   Matthew 26:47–56

Give us courage to confess your name : and go with you against the grain.

A quote from Franz Jägerstätter: "Through his bitter suffering and death, Christ freed us only from eternal death, not from temporal suffering and mortal death. But Christ, too, demands a public confession of our faith, just as the Führer, Adolf Hitler, does from his followers."

Prayers for Others

Our Father

Sovereign Lord, forgive us for choosing violence instead of grace. Give us the courage to trust that the cross is more powerful than the sword. We thank you for the assurance that, in the end, love wins. Help us to live without fear in the light of your promise. Amen.

May the peace of the Lord Christ go with you : wherever he may send you; may he guide you through the wilderness : protect you through the storm; may he bring you home rejoicing : at the wonders he has shown you; may he bring you home rejoicing : once again into our doors.

August 10

O Lord, let my soul rise up to meet you
as the day rises to meet the sun.

**Glory to the Father, and to the Son, and to the Holy Spirit,
as it was in the beginning, is now, and will be forever. Amen.**

Come, let us bow down and the bend the knee : let us kneel before the LORD our Maker.

Song "I Want Jesus to Walk with Me"

Help us, God, by your power : to trust you now and every hour.

Psalm 54
Save me, O God, by your name : **in your might, defend my cause.**
Hear my prayer, O God : **give ear to the words of my mouth.**
For the arrogant have risen up against me, and the ruthless have sought my life : **those who have no regard for God.**
Behold, God is my helper : **it is the Lord who sustains my life.**
Render evil to those who spy on me : **in your faithfulness, destroy them.**
I will offer you a freewill sacrifice : **and praise your name, O LORD, for it is good.**
For you have rescued me from every trouble : **and my eye has seen the ruin of my foes.**

Help us, God, by your power : to trust you now and every hour.

1 Samuel 16:14–17:11   Matthew 26:57–68

Help us, God, by your power : to trust you now and every hour.

Listen to these words of Starets Zosima in Fyodor Dostoyevsky's novel *The Brothers Karamazov*: "At some thoughts one stands perplexed, above all at the sight of human sin, and wonders whether to combat it by force or by humble love. Always decide 'I will combat it by humble love.' If you resolve on that once and for all, you can conquer the whole world. Loving humility is a terrible force: it is the strongest of all things, and there is nothing else like it."

Prayers for Others

Our Father

God of love and Prince of Peace, give us courage in the face of trouble. Walk with us and give us a power that is not like that of chariots or armies. Arm us with grace. Make our tongues sharp with truth. Walk with us amid the principalities and powers of this dark world. Amen.

May the peace of the Lord Christ go with you : wherever he may send you;
may he guide you through the wilderness : protect you through the storm;
may he bring you home rejoicing : at the wonders he has shown you;
may he bring you home rejoicing : once again into our doors.

✻ August 11

Clare of Assisi (1194–1255)

Clare Offreduccio was born into Italian nobility in 1194. She ran away from home at the age of eighteen after hearing St. Francis preach on the streets of Assisi. She chose to wed Christ instead of the man her parents wanted her to marry. With Francis' help, she founded the Franciscan monastic community of the Order of Poor Ladies (The Poor Clares) at San Damiano. Clare became abbess of the order in 1216 and led the sisters in their commitment to poverty and manual labor. Her own mother and sisters later joined the order. As abbess she fought hard to resist any papal orders that the Poor Clares establish a rule of life. She is often depicted holding a monstrance, symbolizing her use of the blessed sacrament to defend her convent from invaders.

O Lord, let my soul rise up to meet you
as the day rises to meet the sun.

**Glory to the Father, and to the Son, and to the Holy Spirit,
as it was in the beginning, is now, and will be forever. Amen.**

Come, let us bow down and the bend the knee : let us kneel before the LORD our Maker.

Song "O Lord, Have Mercy"

In your mercy, receive us, Lord : and give us grace to cling to you.

Psalm 57:1–5
Be merciful to me, O God, be merciful, for I have taken refuge in you : **in the shadow of your wings will I take refuge until this time of trouble has gone by.**
I will call upon the Most High God : **the God who maintains my cause.**
He will send from heaven and save me; he will confound those who trample upon me : **God will send forth his love and his faithfulness.**
I lie in the midst of lions that devour the people : **their teeth are spears and arrows, their tongue a sharp sword.**
They have laid a net for my feet, and I am bowed low : **they have dug a pit before me, but have fallen into it themselves.**

In your mercy, receive us, Lord : and give us grace to cling to you.

1 Samuel 17:17–30   Matthew 26:69–75

In your mercy, receive us, Lord : and give us grace to cling to you.

When the pope offered to absolve Clare from her rigorous vow of poverty, she answered, "Absolve me from my sins, Holy Father, but not from my wish to follow Christ."

Prayers for Others

Our Father

Lord, help us to be faithful, even when we face our own fears. Remind us that we are your children, even when we feel inadequate. We know that you have overcome giants and crosses and all things evil. Help our unbelief. Amen.

May the peace of the Lord Christ go with you : wherever he may send you;
may he guide you through the wilderness : protect you through the storm;
may he bring you home rejoicing : at the wonders he has shown you;
may he bring you home rejoicing : once again into our doors.

✺ August 12

O Lord, let my soul rise up to meet you
as the day rises to meet the sun.

Glory to the Father, and to the Son, and to the Holy Spirit,
as it was in the beginning, is now, and will be forever. Amen.

Come, let us sing to the LORD : let us shout for joy to the Rock of our salvation.

Song   "Holy, Holy, Holy"

Heaven and earth are full of your glory : Hosanna in the highest!

Psalm 66:1–4
Be joyful in God, all you lands : **sing the glory of his name; sing the glory of his praise.**
Say to God, "How awesome are your deeds! : **because of your great strength your enemies cringe before you.**
All the earth bows down before you : **sings to you, sings out your name."**
Come now and see the works of God : **how wonderful he is in his doing toward all people.**

Heaven and earth are full of your glory : Hosanna in the highest!

1 Samuel 17:31–49   Matthew 27:1–10

Heaven and earth are full of your glory : Hosanna in the highest!

Dorothy Day, co-founder of the Catholic Worker Movement, said, "Neither revolutions nor faith can be won without keen suffering. For me Christ was not to be bought for thirty pieces of silver but with my heart's blood. We buy not cheap in this market."

Prayers for Others

Our Father

Loving God, your goodness is all around us. But sometimes it seems overshadowed by pain, death, and suffering. Assure us in times of doubt that you are the God of resurrection. May our lips sing your praise, and may our lives be a living sacrifice to you. Amen.

May the peace of the Lord Christ go with you : wherever he may send you; may he guide you through the wilderness : protect you through the storm; may he bring you home rejoicing : at the wonders he has shown you; may he bring you home rejoicing : once again into our doors.

August 13

In 1959, following the Supreme Court's decision against racial segregation in *Brown v. Board of Education*, African-American students in Arkansas were admitted to Little Rock High School for the first time.

O Lord, let my soul rise up to meet you
as the day rises to meet the sun.

Glory to the Father, and to the Son, and to the Holy Spirit, as it was in the beginning, is now, and will be forever. Amen.

Come, let us sing to the Lord : let us shout for joy to the Rock of our salvation.

Song "Freedom Train"

I will praise the name of God in song : I will proclaim his greatness with thanksgiving.

Psalm 69:34–38
The afflicted shall see and be glad : **you who seek God, your heart shall live.**
For the Lord listens to the needy : **and his prisoners he does not despise.**
Let the heavens and the earth praise him : **the seas and all that moves in them;**
for God will save Zion and rebuild the cities of Judah : **they shall live there and have it in possession.**

The children of his servants will inherit it : **and those who love his name will dwell therein.**

I will praise the name of God in song : I will proclaim his greatness with thanksgiving.

1 Samuel 20:1–23   Matthew 27:11–23

I will praise the name of God in song : I will proclaim his greatness with thanksgiving.

This is a prayer of Charles de Foucauld: "Father, I abandon myself into your hands. Do with me what you will. Whatever you may do, I will thank you. I am ready for all; I accept all. Let only your will be done in me, as in all your creatures. And I'll ask nothing else, my Lord."

Prayers for Others

Our Father

Lord, you came as a child to lead us toward your kingdom. We thank you for the dreams of the young. Fill us with wonder and give us a childlike audacity, even in the face of trials and persecution, to believe in another world despite the evidence around us, and to watch the evidence change. Amen.

May the peace of the Lord Christ go with you : wherever he may send you; may he guide you through the wilderness : protect you through the storm; may he bring you home rejoicing : at the wonders he has shown you; may he bring you home rejoicing : once again into our doors.

✸ August 14

Maximilian Kolbe (1894–1941)

Maximilian Kolbe was a Polish priest who provided shelter for thousands of Jews in his friary and was an active voice against the Nazi violence. He was arrested by the German Gestapo and imprisoned at Auschwitz. When a fellow prisoner escaped from the camp, the Nazis selected ten other prisoners to be killed in reprisal. As they were lined up to die, one of the ten began to cry, "My wife! My children! I will never see them again!" At this, Maximilian stepped forward and asked to die in his place. His request was granted, and he led the other men in song and prayer as they awaited their deaths. Maximilian had also lived in Japan and founded a monastery on the outskirts of Nagasaki. Four years after his martyrdom, on August 9, 1945, the atomic bomb was dropped on Nagasaki, but his monastery miraculously survived. Maximilian's feast day, when Christians around the world celebrate his life and sainthood as a hero of the church, falls one week after Nagasaki Day. Each year, we spend the week reflecting on the best and the worst that human beings are capable of.

O Lord, let my soul rise up to meet you
as the day rises to meet the sun.

**Glory to the Father, and to the Son, and to the Holy Spirit,
as it was in the beginning, is now, and will be forever. Amen.**

Come, let us bow down and bend the knee : let us kneel before the LORD our Maker.

Song "O Lord, Hear My Prayer"

In you, O God, have we taken refuge : let us never be put to shame.

Psalm 71:4–8
Deliver me, my God, from the hand of the wicked : **from the clutches of the evildoer and the oppressor.**
For you are my hope, O Lord GOD : **my confidence since I was young.**
I have been sustained by you ever since I was born; from my mother's womb you have been my strength : **my praise shall be always of you.**
I have become a portent to many : **but you are my refuge and my strength.**
Let my mouth be full of your praise : **and your glory all the day long.**

In you, O God, have we taken refuge : let us never be put to shame.

1 Samuel 20:24–42   Matthew 27:24–31

In you, O God, have we taken refuge : let us never be put to shame.

Maximilian Kolbe had this to say: "These Nazis will not kill our souls, since we prisoners certainly distinguish ourselves quite definitely from our tormentors; they will not be able to deprive us of the dignity of our Catholic belief. We will not give up. And when we die, then we die pure and peaceful, resigned to God in our hearts."

Prayers for Others

Our Father

Lord, we know that you often answer our prayers in mysterious and stunning ways. Make us sensitive to your Spirit that we might recognize your gentle nudge. And help us cultivate lives that are always ready to respond to your call. Form us into people who are truly ready to become the change we want to see. Amen.

May the peace of the Lord Christ go with you : wherever he may send you; may he guide you through the wilderness : protect you through the storm;

may he bring you home rejoicing : at the wonders he has shown you;
may he bring you home rejoicing : once again into our doors.

✺ August 15

O Lord, let my soul rise up to meet you
as the day rises to meet the sun.

**Glory to the Father, and to the Son, and to the Holy Spirit,
as it was in the beginning, is now, and will be forever. Amen.**

Come, let us bow down and bend the knee : let us kneel before the LORD our Maker.

Song "Were You There?"

Hear us when we cannot cry : troubled, trembling before your cross.

Psalm 77:1–4
I will cry aloud to God : **I will cry aloud, and he will hear me.**
In the day of my trouble I sought the Lord : **my hands were stretched out by night and did not tire; I refused to be comforted.**
I think of God, I am restless : **I ponder, and my spirit faints.**
You will not let my eyelids close : **I am troubled and I cannot speak.**

Hear us when we cannot cry : troubled, trembling before your cross.

1 Samuel 24:1–22   Matthew 27:32–44

Hear us when we cannot cry : troubled, trembling before your cross.

Francis of Assisi said, "We have no right to glory in ourselves because of any extraordinary gifts, since these do not belong to us but to God. But we may glory in crosses, afflictions and tribulations, because these are our own."

Prayers for Others

Our Father

Give us the courage to follow the way of your cross, and to trust that though it confounds the logic of the world, your way interrupts the patterns of sin and death, both now and forever. Amen.

**May the peace of the Lord Christ go with you : wherever he may send you;
may he guide you through the wilderness : protect you through the storm;
may he bring you home rejoicing : at the wonders he has shown you;
may he bring you home rejoicing : once again into our doors.**

✺ August 16

In 1989, a Solidarity-led government was elected in Poland, marking the beginning of a nonviolent victory over communism in Eastern Europe.

O Lord, let my soul rise up to meet you
as the day rises to meet the sun.

**Glory to the Father, and to the Son, and to the Holy Spirit,
as it was in the beginning, is now, and will be forever. Amen.**

Come, let us sing to the Lord : let us shout for joy to the Rock of our salvation.

Song "We Shall Overcome"

Expose our broken systems, Lord : save us by the power of your cross.

Psalm 80:1–3
Hear, O Shepherd of Israel, leading Joseph like a flock : **shine forth, you that are enthroned upon the cherubim.**
In the presence of Ephraim, Benjamin, and Manasseh : **stir up your strength and come to help us.**
Restore us, O God of hosts : **show the light of your countenance, and we shall be saved.**

Expose our broken systems, Lord : save us by the power of your cross.

1 Samuel 25:1–22   Matthew 27:45–54

Expose our broken systems, Lord : save us by the power of your cross.

A quote from Dietrich Bonhoeffer: "The church's task is not simply to bind the wounds of the victim beneath the wheel, but also to put a spoke in the wheel itself."

Prayers for Others

Our Father

Lord, use us to heal the broken systems. Equip us with wisdom and foresight. May our lives interrupt injustice with your grace. Amen.

**May the peace of the Lord Christ go with you : wherever he may send you;
may he guide you through the wilderness : protect you through the storm;
may he bring you home rejoicing : at the wonders he has shown you;
may he bring you home rejoicing : once again into our doors.**

✣ August 17

O Lord, let my soul rise up to meet you
as the day rises to meet the sun.

**Glory to the Father, and to the Son, and to the Holy Spirit,
as it was in the beginning, is now, and will be forever. Amen.**

Come, let us bow down and bend the knee : let us kneel before the Lord our Maker.

Song "Let All Mortal Flesh Keep Silence"

As for me, O Lord, I cry to you for help : in the morning my prayer comes before you.

Psalm 88:1–6
O Lord, my God, my Savior, : **by day and night I cry to you.**
Let my prayer enter into your presence : **incline your ear to my lamentation.**
For I am full of trouble : **my life is at the brink of the grave.**
I am counted among those who go down to the Pit : **I have become like one who has no strength;**
lost among the dead : **like the slain who lie in the grave,**
whom you remember no more : **for they are cut off from your hand.**

As for me, O Lord, I cry to you for help : in the morning my prayer comes before you.

1 Samuel 25:23–44   Matthew 27:55–66

As for me, O Lord, I cry to you for help : in the morning my prayer comes before you.

Ignatius of Lyon said this in the second century: "Christianity is not a matter of persuasive words. It is a matter of true greatness as long as it is hated by the world."

Prayers for Others

Our Father

God of the living and the dead, let our lives sing your praise. Make us the fragrance of your love. Rise in us, and awaken us from our slumber that we might live in your light. Amen.

**May the peace of the Lord Christ go with you : wherever he may send you;
may he guide you through the wilderness : protect you through the storm;
may he bring you home rejoicing : at the wonders he has shown you;
may he bring you home rejoicing : once again into our doors.**

Offering a Sacrifice of Praise

There is an old saying many Christians use: "Offer the Lord a sacrifice of praise," referring to Hebrews 13:15. In many circles this notion of a "sacrifice of praise" almost becomes cliché. (Perhaps because worship does not often come at much cost, especially compared with the sacrifices of saints who've gone before us.) But when we worship with folks of various traditions, there are times when we may hear a prayer that uses language we might not naturally use or sing a song that isn't really our style. That is part of what it means to be a member of a community as diverse as the church is. And perhaps that also helps shed some light on why it might require some sacrifice for us to give up ourselves.

When a song isn't working for you, consider praising God, because that probably means it is working for someone else who is very different from you. Offer your worship as a sacrifice rather than requiring others to sacrifice for your pleasure or contentment. There is something to the notion of becoming one as God is one; it doesn't mean that we are the same; it just means that we are united by one Spirit. After all, we can become one only if there are many of us to begin with.

Liturgy puts a brake on narcissism. Certainly, there is something beautiful about contemporary worship, where we can take old things and add a little spice to them, like singing hymns to rock tunes or reciting creeds as spoken word rhymes. But liturgy protects us from simply making worship into a self-pleasing act. So if a song or prayer doesn't quite work for you, be thankful that it is probably really resonating with someone who is different from you, and offer a sacrifice of praise.

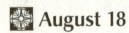
August 18

O Lord, let my soul rise up to meet you
as the day rises to meet the sun.

**Glory to the Father, and to the Son, and to the Holy Spirit,
as it was in the beginning, is now, and will be forever. Amen.**

Come, let us sing to the Lord : let us shout for joy to the Rock of our salvation.

Song   "Great Is Thy Faithfulness"

Root us in your word, O Lord : in the good soil of your field.

Psalm 92:5 – 8
Lord, how great are your works! : **your thoughts are very deep.**
The dullard does not know, nor does the fool understand : **that though the wicked grow like weeds, and all the workers of iniquity flourish,**
they flourish only to be destroyed for ever : **but you, O Lord, are exalted for evermore.**

For lo, your enemies, O Lord, lo, your enemies shall perish : **and all the workers of iniquity shall be scattered.**

Root us in your word, O Lord : in the good soil of your field.

1 Samuel 28:3–20   Matthew 28:1–10

Root us in your word, O Lord : in the good soil of your field.

Ambrose, bishop of Milan and a doctor of the church, said this in the fourth century: "Death comes to every person. You must keep facing it with perseverance. Death is a passover from corruption to incorruption, from mortality to immortality, from rough seas to a calm harbor. The word 'death' must not trouble us; the blessings that come from a safe journey should bring us joy. What is death, but the burial of sin and the resurrection of goodness? Scripture says: *Let my soul die among the souls of the just*; that is, let me be buried with the just, so that I may cast off my sins and put on the grace of the just, of those who bear the death of Christ with them, in their bodies and in their souls."

Prayers for Others

Our Father

Lord, you have conquered death and triumphed over evil. There is nothing left for us to fear. Put us to work on this earth, striving for the kingdom in everything we do. Let us die to ourselves each day that we might find ourselves made new in you. Amen.

May the peace of the Lord Christ go with you : wherever he may send you; may he guide you through the wilderness : protect you through the storm; may he bring you home rejoicing : at the wonders he has shown you; may he bring you home rejoicing : once again into our doors.

✹ August 19

O Lord, let my soul rise up to meet you
as the day rises to meet the sun.

**Glory to the Father, and to the Son, and to the Holy Spirit,
as it was in the beginning, is now, and will be forever. Amen.**

Come, let us sing to the Lord : let us shout for joy to the Rock of our salvation.

Song   "Sing, O Sky (Gaao Re)"

You are exalted, Lord Most High : Christ, be exalted in this humble place.

Psalm 97:5–9
The mountains melt like wax at the presence of the Lord : **at the presence of the Lord of the whole earth.**
The heavens declare his righteousness : **and all the peoples see his glory.**
Confounded be all who worship carved images and delight in false gods! : **Bow down before him, all you gods.**
Zion hears and is glad, and the cities of Judah rejoice : **because of your judgments, O Lord.**
For you are the Lord, most high over all the earth : **you are exalted far above all gods.**

You are exalted, Lord Most High : Christ, be exalted in this humble place.

1 Samuel 31:1–13   Matthew 28:11–20

You are exalted, Lord Most High : Christ, be exalted in this humble place.

Gregory the Great, the sixth-century monk-become-pope, said, "The dawn intimates that the night is over, but it does not yet proclaim the full light of day. Are not all of us who follow the truth in this life both daybreak and dawn? We do some things which already belong to the light, but we are not free from the remnants of darkness. It will be fully day for the church when she is no longer darkened by the shadow of sin. It will be fully day for her when she shines with the perfect brilliance of interior light. This dawn is an ongoing process. When the dawn has come, the day will retain nothing belonging to the darkness of night."

Prayers for Others

Our Father

Thank you, Lord, for working through us despite our sinfulness. By the power of your glorious resurrection, give us grace to love sinners like ourselves. We ask this in the name of our Lord Jesus, who lives and reigns with you and the Holy Spirit, one God now and forever. Amen.

**May the peace of the Lord Christ go with you : wherever he may send you;
may he guide you through the wilderness : protect you through the storm;
may he bring you home rejoicing : at the wonders he has shown you;
may he bring you home rejoicing : once again into our doors.**

✸ August 20

O Lord, let my soul rise up to meet you
as the day rises to meet the sun.

**Glory to the Father, and to the Son, and to the Holy Spirit,
as it was in the beginning, is now, and will be forever. Amen.**

Come, let us sing to the LORD : let us shout for joy to the Rock of our salvation.

Song "Vamos Todos al Banquete"

O Lord, you stretched out the heavens : make room for us at your banquet table.

Psalm 102:25–28
"In the beginning, O LORD, you laid the foundations of the earth : **and the heavens are the work of your hands;**
they shall perish, but you will endure; they all shall wear out like a garment : **as clothing you will change them, and they shall be changed;**
but you are always the same : **and your years will never end.**
The children of your servants shall continue : **and their offspring shall stand fast in your sight."**

O Lord, you stretched out the heavens : make room for us at your banquet table.

2 Samuel 1:1–16   Romans 8:1–11

O Lord, you stretched out the heavens : make room for us at your banquet table.

Contemporary writer and ragamuffin Brennan Manning has said, "The outstretched arms of Jesus exclude no one, not the drunk in the doorway, the panhandler on the street, gays and lesbians in their isolation, the most selfish and ungrateful in their cocoons, the most unjust of employers and the most overweening of snobs. The love of Christ embraces all without exception."

Prayers for Others

Our Father

Holy God, there is always room for one more at your banquet table. We pray to live in such a way that each person we meet knows they are welcome among your people. We welcome you as we welcome others this day. Amen.

**May the peace of the Lord Christ go with you : wherever he may send you;
may he guide you through the wilderness : protect you through the storm;
may he bring you home rejoicing : at the wonders he has shown you;
may he bring you home rejoicing : once again into our doors.**

✸ August 21

In 1831, Nat Turner led a slave revolt in Southhampton County, Virginia, killing fifty-five whites on his march to the county seat of Jerusalem, where he declared that the "great day of judgment" was at hand.

O Lord, let my soul rise up to meet you
as the day rises to meet the sun.

**Glory to the Father, and to the Son, and to the Holy Spirit,
as it was in the beginning, is now, and will be forever. Amen.**

Come, let us bow down and bend the knee : let us kneel before the LORD our Maker.

Song "We Shall Not Be Moved"

Judge us in your mercy, Lord : that we may live together in peace.

Psalm 105:3–7
Glory in his holy name : **let the hearts of those who seek the LORD rejoice.**
Search for the LORD and his strength : **continually seek his face.**
Remember the marvels he has done : **his wonders and the judgments of his mouth,**
O offspring of Abraham his servant : **O children of Jacob his chosen.**
He is the LORD our God : **his judgments prevail in all the world.**

Judge us in your mercy, Lord : that we may live together in peace.

2 Samuel 2:1–11   Romans 8:12–25

Judge us in your mercy, Lord : that we may live together in peace.

Martin Luther King Jr. said this: "There was a time when the church was very powerful. In those days the church was not merely a thermometer that recorded the ideas and principles of popular opinion; it was a thermostat that transformed the mores of society. Whenever the early Christians entered a town, the power structure got disturbed and immediately sought to convict them for being 'disturbers of the peace' and 'outside agitators.' But they went on with the conviction that they were 'a colony of heaven,' and had to obey God rather than man. They were small in number but big in commitment. They were too God-intoxicated to be 'astronomically intimidated.' They brought an end to such ancient evils as infanticide and gladiatorial contest."

Prayers for Others

Our Father

Lord God, help us to live out your gospel in the world. We pray for those who do not know your love, that they would be wooed by your goodness and seduced by your beauty. Form us into a family that runs deeper than biology or nationality or ethnicity, a family that is born again in you. May we be creators of holy mischief and agitators of comfort ... people who do not accept the world as it is but insist on its becoming what you want it to be. Let us groan as in the pains of childbirth for your kingdom to come on earth as it is in heaven. Help us to be midwives of that kingdom. Amen.

May the peace of the Lord Christ go with you : wherever he may send you; may he guide you through the wilderness : protect you through the storm; may he bring you home rejoicing : at the wonders he has shown you; may he bring you home rejoicing : once again into our doors.

✣ August 22

O Lord, let my soul rise up to meet you
as the day rises to meet the sun.

Glory to the Father, and to the Son, and to the Holy Spirit, as it was in the beginning, is now, and will be forever. Amen.

Come, let us sing to the LORD : let us shout for joy to the Rock of our salvation.

Song "O Mary, Don't You Weep"

Let your justice flow down like waters, Lord : and shower us with your mercy.

Psalm 107:33–35, 41–43
The LORD changed rivers into deserts : **and water springs into thirsty ground,**
a fruitful land into salt flats : **because of the wickedness of those who dwell there.**
He changed deserts into pools of water : **and dry land into water springs.**
He lifted up the poor out of misery : **and multiplied their families like flocks of sheep.**
The upright will see this and rejoice : **but all wickedness will shut its mouth.**
Whoever is wise will ponder these things : **and consider well the mercies of the LORD.**

Let your justice flow down like waters, Lord : and shower us with your mercy.

2 Samuel 5:1–12   Romans 8:26–30

Let your justice flow down like waters, Lord : and shower us with your mercy.

Hear these words from the desert fathers: "A brother came to Abba Theodore and began to converse with him about things which he had never put into practice. So the old man said to him, 'You have not yet found a ship nor put your cargo aboard it and before you have sailed, you have already arrived at the city. Do the work first; then you will have the speed you are making now.'"

Prayers for Others

Our Father

O God our deliverer, we thank you that you have not left us alone. Thank you for the Spirit who intercedes for us. Give us wisdom beyond ourselves that we might see the path you have set before us. Grant us words that bring life to the broken, the suffering, the addicted, the lonely, and those who long for the fulfillment of your kingdom. Amen.

May the peace of the Lord Christ go with you : wherever he may send you; may he guide you through the wilderness : protect you through the storm; may he bring you home rejoicing : at the wonders he has shown you; may he bring you home rejoicing : once again into our doors.

August 23

O Lord, let my soul rise up to meet you
as the day rises to meet the sun.

**Glory to the Father, and to the Son, and to the Holy Spirit,
as it was in the beginning, is now, and will be forever. Amen.**

Come, let us bow down and the bend the knee : let us kneel before the L ORD our Maker.

Song "Magnificat"

You lift the lowly and humble the proud : to feed us together at your table.

Psalm 113:4–7
The L ORD is high above all nations : **and his glory above the heavens.**
Who is like the L ORD our God, who sits enthroned on high : **but stoops to behold the heavens and the earth?**
He takes up the weak out of the dust : **and lifts up the poor from the ashes.**
He sets them with the princes : **with the princes of his people.**

You lift the lowly and humble the proud : to feed us together at your table.

2 Samuel 7:1–17   Romans 8:31–39

You lift the lowly and humble the proud : to feed us together at your table.

Mother Teresa said, "We are called to be contemplatives in the heart of the world — by seeking the face of God in everything, everyone, everywhere, all the time, and his hand in every happening; seeing and adoring the presence of Jesus, especially in the lowly appearance of bread, and in the distressing disguise of the poor."

Prayers for Others

Our Father

God of mercy, you cast the mighty from their thrones and lift up the lowly. Free us from the ghettoes of poverty and the ghettoes of wealth that we might meet on the level ground at the foot of the cross. Amen.

May the peace of the Lord Christ go with you : wherever he may send you; may he guide you through the wilderness : protect you through the storm; may he bring you home rejoicing : at the wonders he has shown you; may he bring you home rejoicing : once again into our doors.

Confession

The Scriptures have much to say about not coming to the altar if we are holding something against a sister or brother. We are told that we will be forgiven inasmuch as we forgive. The early church was known for its public confessions of sins. Many traditions of Christianity have practiced public confession, and many great revivals have been sparked by folks beating their breasts and confessing sins to one another.

Consider ways of creating a space for confession to happen. We have built in some space for confession in each evening prayer office, but there may be other community rituals you want to practice. One practice used in some communities is "prouds and sorries," where each person is given the space to share something they are proud of and something they are sorry about. Just as we confess things that are wrong, we also need to be reminded that we are better than the worst things we do. Reconciliation is one of the fruits of confession, and it is worth thinking about ways of speaking into each other's lives as we hope to restore whatever may have been broken or lost. (Some communities respond to confessions by saying together, "We proclaim to you God's forgiveness and ours.")

Confessional prayer assumes that our worship takes place in a deeply flawed community. The church has always been a worrisome and dysfunctional place. But by grace we can take small steps to restore trust. Maybe it is writing a note to someone we have offended or calling up someone we have murmured to (or about) and asking for their forgiveness. Maybe it means each week choosing to do something nice for someone it's hard for you to like. Sometimes we call this "doing penance." It's not that we have to do an act of penance to earn God's grace; it's the opposite — because we have experienced God's grace, we can't help but do some act of grace toward another person.

August 24

O Lord, let my soul rise up to meet you
as the day rises to meet the sun.

**Glory to the Father, and to the Son, and to the Holy Spirit,
as it was in the beginning, is now, and will be forever. Amen.**

Come, let us bow down and bend the knee : let us kneel before the LORD our Maker.

Song "Servant Song"

Lord, give us grace to serve you : as we wash one another's dishes.

Psalm 116:14–17
O LORD, I am your servant : **I am your servant and the child of your handmaid; you have freed me from my bonds.**
I will offer you the sacrifice of thanksgiving : **and call upon the name of the LORD.**
I will fulfill my vows to the LORD : **in the presence of all his people,**
in the courts of the LORD's house : **in the midst of you, O Jerusalem. Hallelujah!**

Lord, give us grace to serve you : as we wash one another's dishes.

2 Samuel 7:18–29 Romans 9:1–18

Lord, give us grace to serve you : as we wash one another's dishes.

Dorotheus of Gaza, monk and abbot of the sixth century, penned these words: "Each one according to his means should take care to be at one with everyone else, for the more one is united to his neighbor, the more he is united with God."

Prayers for Others

Our Father

King of Kings, King David was not ashamed to call himself your servant. Open our eyes to discover the joy of serving others. Let us do small things with great love today. Amen.

**May the peace of the Lord Christ go with you : wherever he may send you;
may he guide you through the wilderness : protect you through the storm;
may he bring you home rejoicing : at the wonders he has shown you;
may he bring you home rejoicing : once again into our doors.**

✸ August 25

O Lord, let my soul rise up to meet you
as the day rises to meet the sun.

**Glory to the Father, and to the Son, and to the Holy Spirit,
as it was in the beginning, is now, and will be forever. Amen.**

Come, let us bow down and bend the knee : let us kneel before the LORD our Maker.

Song "Take My Life and Let It Be"

O God, you are my God : I will serve you my whole life long.

Psalm 119:49–52
Remember your word to your servant : **because you have given me hope.**
This is my comfort in my trouble : **that your promise gives me life.**
The proud have derided me cruelly : **but I have not turned from your law.**
When I remember your judgments of old : **O LORD, I take great comfort.**

O God, you are my God : I will serve you my whole life long.

2 Samuel 9:1–13   Romans 9:19–33

O God, you are my God : I will serve you my whole life long.

Church father and "golden-mouthed" preacher John Chrysostom said this in the fourth century: "Our spirit should be quick to reach out toward God, not only when it is engaged in meditation; at other times also, when it is carrying out its duties, caring for the needy, performing works of charity, or giving generously in the service of others. Our spirit should long for God and call him to mind, so that these works may be seasoned with the salt of God's love, and so make a pleasing offering to the Lord of the universe."

Prayers for Others

Our Father

God, help us to show kindness and unrivaled hospitality as the natural extension of our commitment to you. Use us to bring hope and comfort to the abandoned and forsaken corners of your creation. Amen.

**May the peace of the Lord Christ go with you : wherever he may send you;
may he guide you through the wilderness : protect you through the storm;
may he bring you home rejoicing : at the wonders he has shown you;
may he bring you home rejoicing : once again into our doors.**

August 26

In 1920, the United States Congress ratified its nineteenth amendment to the Constitution, guaranteeing women the right to vote.

O Lord, let my soul rise up to meet you
as the day rises to meet the sun.

**Glory to the Father, and to the Son, and to the Holy Spirit,
as it was in the beginning, is now, and will be forever. Amen.**

Come, let us sing to the LORD : let us shout for joy to the Rock of our salvation.

Song "Be Thou My Vision"

Help us, Lord, to see as you see : and to change what is into what ought to be.

Psalm 119:137–38, 142–44
You are righteous, O LORD : **and upright are your judgments.**
You have issued your decrees : **with justice and in perfect faithfulness.**
Your justice is an everlasting justice : **and your law is the truth.**
Trouble and distress have come upon me : **yet your commandments are my delight.**
The righteousness of your decrees is everlasting : **grant me understanding, that I may live.**

Help us, Lord, to see as you see : and to change what is into what ought to be.

2 Samuel 11:1–27   Romans 10:1–13

Help us, Lord, to see as you see : and to change what is into what ought to be.

A reading from Paul's letter to the Galatians: "You are all children of God through faith, for all of you who were baptized into Christ have clothed yourselves with Christ. There is neither Jew nor Greek, neither slave nor free, neither male nor female, for you are all one in Christ Jesus."

Prayers for Others

Our Father

Creator God, with joy and thanksgiving we celebrate that you made humans in your image, both male and female. We thank you especially today for those women in our lives through whom we have caught glimpses of your love. Amen.

May the peace of the Lord Christ go with you : wherever he may send you;
may he guide you through the wilderness : protect you through the storm;
may he bring you home rejoicing : at the wonders he has shown you;
may he bring you home rejoicing : once again into our doors.

✸ August 27

O Lord, let my soul rise up to meet you
as the day rises to meet the sun.

**Glory to the Father, and to the Son, and to the Holy Spirit,
as it was in the beginning, is now, and will be forever. Amen.**

Come, let us bow down and bend the knee : let us kneel before the LORD our Maker.

Song "When the Saints Go Marching In"

May we become the church we pray for : and glimpse the New Jerusalem now.

Psalm 122:6–9
Pray for the peace of Jerusalem : "May they prosper who love you.
Peace be within your walls : **and quietness within your towers.**
For my brethren and companions' sake : **I pray for your prosperity.**
Because of the house of the LORD our God : **I will seek to do you good."**

May we become the church we pray for : and glimpse the New Jerusalem now.

2 Samuel 12:1–14   Romans 10:14–21

May we become the church we pray for : and glimpse the New Jerusalem now.

In his book *City of God*, Augustine of Hippo wrote, "The heavenly city, while it sojourns on earth, calls citizens out of all nations and gathers together a society of pilgrims of all languages. In its pilgrim state the heavenly city possesses peace by faith; and by this faith it lives."

Prayers for Others

Our Father

Steadfast God, perhaps one of the greatest mysteries is why you continue to entrust the work of your kingdom into our clumsy hands. But we are forever grateful that you do not want to change the world without us. May we become the church you dream of. Amen.

May the peace of the Lord Christ go with you : wherever he may send you;
may he guide you through the wilderness : protect you through the storm;
may he bring you home rejoicing : at the wonders he has shown you;
may he bring you home rejoicing : once again into our doors.

✸ August 28

Augustine of Hippo (354–430)

One of the greatest influences on the theology of Western Christianity, Augustine wanted from a young age to understand the meaning of life and the nature of good and evil. As a teacher, he sought answers to these questions through the best philosophy of his day. Although his mother, Monica, had instructed him in the Christian faith, he was not originally drawn to the tradition, but later found a depth and wisdom in Christianity to explain the question of evil and good. The famous story of Augustine's conversion involves an experience in a garden in Milan. Torn between living a life of chastity and remembering his former life of sin, he prayed for forgiveness and immediately heard the voice of a child singing from a neighboring house, "Take up and read!" He picked up a book of St. Paul's epistles left nearby, and the words he found there changed him forever. After his baptism, Augustine moved to North Africa to pursue a monastic life, but he was urged by the church to become ordained and was later made bishop of Hippo, where he served for thirty-five years. Augustine has rightly been criticized for silencing some important voices in his own day and passing on a harmful view of the body. He was not perfect, but he himself insisted that grace is the heart of our faith.

O Lord, let my soul rise up to meet you
as the day rises to meet the sun.

**Glory to the Father, and to the Son, and to the Holy Spirit,
as it was in the beginning, is now, and will be forever. Amen.**

Come, let us sing to the LORD : let us shout for joy to the Rock of our salvation.

Song "It Is Well with My Soul"

Late have I loved you, O Beauty ever ancient, ever new : late have I loved you!

Psalm 132:14–19
For the LORD has chosen Zion : **he has desired her for his habitation:**
"This shall be my resting place for ever : **here will I dwell, for I delight in her.**
I will surely bless her provisions : **and satisfy her poor with bread.**
I will clothe her priests with salvation : **and her faithful people will rejoice and sing.**

416 *Morning Prayer*

There will I make the horn of David flourish : **I have prepared a lamp for my Anointed.**
As for his enemies, I will clothe them with shame : **but as for him, his crown will shine."**

Late have I loved you, O Beauty ever ancient, ever new : late have I loved you!

2 Samuel 12:15–31   Romans 11:1–12

Late have I loved you, O Beauty ever ancient, ever new : late have I loved you!

Augustine of Hippo said, "Let us leave a little room for reflection in our lives, room too for silence. Let us look within ourselves and see whether there is some delightful hidden place inside where we can be free of noise and argument. Let us hear the Word of God in stillness and perhaps we will then come to understand it."

Prayers for Others

Our Father

Teach us to listen, Lord. Quiet the noise of our lives so we can hear your voice. Amen.

May the peace of the Lord Christ go with you : wherever he may send you; may he guide you through the wilderness : protect you through the storm; may he bring you home rejoicing : at the wonders he has shown you; may he bring you home rejoicing : once again into our doors.

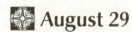 # August 29

John the Baptist (c. 30)

John the Baptist was the son of Zechariah, a priest in the Jerusalem temple, and Elizabeth, a cousin of Mary the mother of Jesus. John's parents were advanced in years and had prayed to have a child, yet had not conceived. But an angel of the Lord appeared to Zechariah and told him his wife would bear a son named John, "great in the sight of the Lord" and "filled with the Holy Spirit." Five months later, the same angel appeared to Mary and told her of the coming birth of Jesus. When Mary visited her cousin Elizabeth, Elizabeth's baby "leaped in her womb" a prophetic sign that John would be filled with the Holy Spirit all of his life. John lived in the wilderness of Judea until he was thirty, then began his public career preaching repentance. When Jesus came to him to be baptized, John recognized him as the Messiah and said, "It is I who need baptism from you." John often is referred to as the Precursor to Jesus; he foretold the coming of the Messiah and prepared the way for Jesus. His preaching encouraged many believers to follow Christ; in fact, Andrew and John learned of Christ through John's ministry.

O Lord, let my soul rise up to meet you
as the day rises to meet the sun.

**Glory to the Father, and to the Son, and to the Holy Spirit,
as it was in the beginning, is now, and will be forever. Amen.**

Come, let us bow down and bend the knee : let us kneel before the LORD our Maker.

Song "Come, Ye Sinners"

Forgive me, Lord, where I have gone astray : guide me on the King's highway.

Psalm 143:4–8
My spirit faints within me : **my heart within me is desolate.**
I remember the time past; I muse upon all your deeds : **I consider the works of your hands.**
I spread out my hands to you : **my soul gasps to you like a thirsty land.**
O LORD, make haste to answer me; my spirit fails me : **do not hide your face from me or I shall be like those who go down to the Pit.**
Let me hear of your loving-kindness in the morning, for I put my trust in you : **show me the road that I must walk, for I lift up my soul to you.**

Forgive me, Lord, where I have gone astray : guide me on the King's highway.

2 Samuel 18:9–33   Romans 11:13–24

Forgive me, Lord, where I have gone astray : guide me on the King's highway.

A reading from the gospel according to John: "Now this was John's testimony when the Jewish leaders in Jerusalem sent priests and Levites to ask him who he was. He did not fail to confess, but confessed freely, 'I am not the Messiah.' They asked him, 'Then who are you? Are you Elijah?' He said, 'I am not.' 'Are you the Prophet?' He answered, 'No.' Finally they said, 'Who are you? Give us an answer to take back to those who sent us. What do you say about yourself?' John replied in the words of Isaiah the prophet, 'I am the voice of one calling in the desert, "Make straight the way for the Lord."'"

Prayers for Others

Our Father

Merciful God, you must grieve over our broken earth as King David mourned the death of his disobedient son, Absalom. Break our own hearts with the things that break yours. Make us voices in the wilderness that cry out for your kingdom to come on earth. Amen.

May the peace of the Lord Christ go with you : wherever he may send you;
may he guide you through the wilderness : protect you through the storm;
may he bring you home rejoicing : at the wonders he has shown you;
may he bring you home rejoicing : once again into our doors.

❈ August 30

In 1964, Fannie Lou Hamer and Ruby D. Robinson led the Mississippi Freedom Democratic Party in their campaign to be seated at the Democratic National Convention, saying that they and thousands of African-Americans like them were "sick and tired of being sick and tired."

O Lord, let my soul rise up to meet you
as the day rises to meet the sun.

**Glory to the Father, and to the Son, and to the Holy Spirit,
as it was in the beginning, is now, and will be forever. Amen.**

Come, let us sing to the Lord : let us shout for joy to the Rock of our salvation.

Song "This Little Light of Mine"

We look to you in hope, O Lord : rain down your justice on us all.

Psalm 145:14–18
The Lord is faithful in all his words : **and merciful in all his deeds.**
The Lord upholds all those who fall : **he lifts up those who are bowed down.**
The eyes of all wait upon you, O Lord : **and you give them their food in due season.**
You open wide your hand : **and satisfy the needs of every living creature.**
The Lord is righteous in all his ways : **and loving in all his works.**

We look to you in hope, O Lord : rain down your justice on us all.

2 Samuel 23:1–7, 13–17   Romans 11:25–36

We look to you in hope, O Lord : rain down your justice on us all.

Listen to the words of Fannie Lou Hamer in the midst of the civil rights struggle: "We have to realize just how grave the problem is in the United States today, and I think the sixth chapter of Ephesians, the eleventh and twelfth verses help us to know what it is we are up against. It says, 'Put on the whole armor of God, that ye may be able to stand against the wiles of the devil. For we wrestle not against flesh and blood but against principalities, against powers, and against the rulers of the darkness of this world, against spiritual wickedness in high places.' This is what I think about when I think of my own work in the fight for freedom."

Prayers for Others

Our Father

Sweet Lord, save us. Heal all that is broken in our lives, in our streets, and in our world. Amen.

**May the peace of the Lord Christ go with you : wherever he may send you;
may he guide you through the wilderness : protect you through the storm;
may he bring you home rejoicing : at the wonders he has shown you;
may he bring you home rejoicing : once again into our doors.**

✣ August 31

O Lord, let my soul rise up to meet you
as the day rises to meet the sun.

Glory to the Father, and to the Son, and to the Holy Spirit,
as it was in the beginning, is now, and will be forever. Amen.

Come, let us sing to the Lord : let us shout for joy to the Rock of our salvation.

Song "I Will Trust in the Lord"

In our words and in our lives : may your will be done.

Psalm 146:1–3
Hallelujah! Praise the Lord, O my soul! : **I will praise the Lord as long as I live; I will sing praises to my God while I have my being.**
Put not your trust in rulers, nor in any child of earth : **for there is no help in them.**
When they breathe their last, they return to earth : **and in that day their thoughts perish.**

In our words and in our lives : may your will be done.

2 Samuel 24:1–2, 10–25   Romans 12:1–8

In our words and in our lives : may your will be done.

Salvadoran Archbishop Oscar Romero said this shortly before his assassination: "I am going to speak to you simply as a pastor, as one who, together with his people, has been learning the beautiful but harsh truth that the Christian faith does not cut us off from the world but immerses us in it; the church is not a fortress set apart from the city. The church follows Jesus, who lived, worked, struggled and died in the midst of a city, in the polis."

Prayers for Others

Our Father

Lord, help us not to conform to the patterns of this world but to be transformed by the renewing of our minds. Give us a new imagination so that we might live in ways that do not compute to the logic of materialism and militarism. Make us into holy nonconformists so that we might see the kingdoms of this world transformed into your glorious kingdom. Amen.

May the peace of the Lord Christ go with you : wherever he may send you; may he guide you through the wilderness : protect you through the storm; may he bring you home rejoicing : at the wonders he has shown you; may he bring you home rejoicing : once again into our doors.

> **Becoming the Answer to Our Prayers: A Few Ideas**
> 1. Build a little chapel or prayer room in your home or in the woods and start using it.
> 2. Do something that doesn't fit the status quo.
> 3. Forgive a politician, pastor, parent, or friend who wronged you.
> 4. Serve at a free clinic for persons who are uninsured.
> 5. Let your yes be yes and your no be no.

SEPTEMBER — THE SAN DAMIANO CROSS

SEPTEMBER

Marks of New Monasticism
Contemplative Prayer

Over and over Scripture invites us to abide in God. To rest in God. To dwell in God. More than fifty times, Paul repeats the phrase "in Christ." Contemplative prayer is not just about activity and speaking but also about listening and resting in God. Many of us have grown up thinking of prayer as a checklist of requests to God, like giving a grocery list to someone headed to the supermarket. As one kid said, "I'm heading off to pray — does anyone need anything?" Prayer is certainly about sharing our concerns and frustrations with God. God is personal enough to come down and wrestle in the dirt with Jacob or answer Abraham's pleading on behalf of Sodom and Gomorrah. Still, contemplative prayer goes deeper.

A primary purpose of prayer is to impress on us the personality and character of Christ. We want to become like Jesus, so the life that we live is no longer ours but Christ living in us and through us.

Prayer is less about trying to get God to do something we want God to do and more about getting ourselves to do what God wants us to do and to become who God wants us to become. There are times when we speak, weep, groan, and shout at God. But there are also times when we simply sit in silence and are held by our Beloved. We remember the character of God, the fruit of the Spirit, and the incarnation of Jesus as he reveals to us what God is like with flesh on. And we pray that God's character will become our character. The monks have been known to say, "If your speaking doesn't add something beautiful to the silence, don't speak." For many of us in the high-paced, cluttered world of materialism and noise, silence is a way we can free up the space to listen to God.

> **Suggested Reading for the Month**
> *Contemplation in a World of Action*
>   by Thomas Merton
> *Selected Works of Teresa of Avila*
> *Resistance and Contemplation*
>   by James Douglass

In most of our lives, silence gets interrupted pretty quickly. Whether it's a knock at the door, a cry from the nursery, or thoughts in our own heads, something almost always breaks the silence we long for in contemplative prayer. It is tempting to give up — to say that silence is not possible in our context or "I'm not cut out for this." But the wisdom of those who've gone before is helpful here. Teresa of Avila, who was distracted by her own thoughts in prayer, said she learned not to fight them but to let them come and go like waves in the sea, trusting that God was an anchor who could hold her through any storm.

Contemplation is about tending to the lines that anchor us in Christ. For Francis of Assisi, the San Damiano cross was one of those lines, serving as an icon to focus his prayer on Christ's love. It was in hours of prayer before this cross that he heard Jesus say, "Rebuild my church, which is in ruins," then he got up to start the most radical renewal movement of the Middle Ages. Activism that matters to the kingdom is always rooted in prayer. If we want to join God in changing the world, the place to begin is on our knees before the cross.

❈ September 1

O Lord, let my soul rise up to meet you
as the day rises to meet the sun.

**Glory to the Father, and to the Son, and to the Holy Spirit,
as it was in the beginning, is now, and will be forever. Amen.**

Come, let us bow down and bend the knee : let us kneel before the Lord our Maker.

Song "Swing Low, Sweet Chariot"

Broken, we kneel; humbled, we cry : help, Jesus! Raise us gently on high.

Psalm 6:1–4
Lord, do not rebuke me in your anger : **do not punish me in your wrath.**
Have pity on me, Lord, for I am weak : **heal me, Lord, for my bones are racked.**
My spirit shakes with terror : **how long, O Lord, how long?**
Turn, O Lord, and deliver me : **save me for your mercy's sake.**

Broken, we kneel; humbled, we cry : help, Jesus! Raise us gently on high.

Esther 1:1–4, 10–19   Matthew 4:18–25

Broken, we kneel; humbled, we cry : help, Jesus! Raise us gently on high.

Seventh-century monk and bishop Isaac of Syria said, "Do not fall into despair because of your stumblings, for you should not consider them incurable. There is indeed a healer: he who on the cross asked for mercy on those who were crucifying him, who pardoned murderers as he hung on the cross. Christ came on behalf of sinners, to heal the brokenhearted and to bind up their wounds."

Prayers for Others

Our Father

Lord, you are a God who heals and calls forth life. Keep us from the pitfalls of self-pity and despair, lest we ridicule your grace and power, and forsake our own healing. Amen.

**May the peace of the Lord Christ go with you : wherever he may send you;
may he guide you through the wilderness : protect you through the storm;
may he bring you home rejoicing : at the wonders he has shown you;
may he bring you home rejoicing : once again into our doors.**

September 2

O Lord, let my soul rise up to meet you
as the day rises to meet the sun.

**Glory to the Father, and to the Son, and to the Holy Spirit,
as it was in the beginning, is now, and will be forever. Amen.**

Come, let us bow down and bend the knee : let us kneel before the LORD our Maker.

Song "Let All Mortal Flesh Keep Silence"

Let your justice roll down like waters, Lord : but float us on your grace.

Psalm 9:13–15, 19–20
Have pity on me, O LORD : **see the misery I suffer from those who hate me, O you who lift me up from the gate of death;**
so that I may tell of all your praises and rejoice in your salvation : **in the gates of the city of Zion.**
The ungodly have fallen into the pit they dug : **and in the snare they set is their own foot caught.**
Rise up, O LORD, let not the ungodly have the upper hand : **let them be judged before you.**
Put fear upon them, O LORD : **let the ungodly know they are but mortal.**

Let your justice roll down like waters, Lord : but float us on your grace.

Esther 2:5–8, 15–23   Matthew 5:1–10

Let your justice roll down like waters, Lord : but float us on your grace.

Jean Vanier, founder of the L'Arche communities, said, "Jesus came to bring the good news to the poor, not to those who serve the poor! I think we can only truly experience the presence of God, meet Jesus, receive the good news, in and through our own poverty, because the kingdom of God belongs to the poor, the poor in spirit, the poor who are crying out for love."

Prayers for Others

Our Father

Lord, even the seraphim and cherubim hide their faces in your presence as they declare your praise. Help us mere mortals to humbly dethrone ourselves and bow before you, that in our weakness we might know your good news and forever sing your glory. Amen.

Morning Prayer

May the peace of the Lord Christ go with you : wherever he may send you;
may he guide you through the wilderness : protect you through the storm;
may he bring you home rejoicing : at the wonders he has shown you;
may he bring you home rejoicing : once again into our doors.

✺ September 3

O Lord, let my soul rise up to meet you
as the day rises to meet the sun.

**Glory to the Father, and to the Son, and to the Holy Spirit,
as it was in the beginning, is now, and will be forever. Amen.**

Come, let us sing to the LORD : let us shout for joy to the Rock of our salvation.

Song "Praise to the Lord, the Almighty"

You, and you alone, are Lord : our good above all others.

Psalm 16:1–4
Protect me, O God, for I take refuge in you : **I have said to the LORD, "You are my Lord, my good above all other."**
All my delight is upon the godly that are in the land : **upon those who are noble among the people.**
But those who run after other gods : **shall have their troubles multiplied.**
Their libations of blood I will not offer : **nor take the names of their gods upon my lips.**

You, and you alone, are Lord : our good above all others.

Esther 3:1–4:3   Matthew 5:11–16

You, and you alone, are Lord : our good above all others.

Alphonsus Liguori, eighteenth-century founder of the Redemptorists, wrote, "Persecutions are to the works of God what the frosts of the winter are to plants; far from destroying them, they help them to strike their roots deep in the soil and make them more full of life."

Prayers for Others

Our Father

Lord, where your church is weak through comfort, strengthen us through the necessary trials. Where your church is invisible through fear, make your word known through the boldness of prophets and through the courage of ordinary people like us. Amen.

May the peace of the Lord Christ go with you : wherever he may send you;
may he guide you through the wilderness : protect you through the storm;
may he bring you home rejoicing : at the wonders he has shown you;
may he bring you home rejoicing : once again into our doors.

✺ September 4

O Lord, let my soul rise up to meet you
as the day rises to meet the sun.

**Glory to the Father, and to the Son, and to the Holy Spirit,
as it was in the beginning, is now, and will be forever. Amen.**

Come, let us sing to the LORD : let us shout for joy to the Rock of our salvation.

Song "Come, Thou Fount"

Open our lives wide : to taste and see that you are good.

Psalm 19:7–10
The law of the LORD is perfect and revives the soul : **the testimony of the LORD is sure and gives wisdom to the innocent.**
The statutes of the LORD are just and rejoice the heart : **the commandment of the LORD is clear and gives light to the eyes.**
The fear of the LORD is clean and endures for ever : **the judgments of the LORD are true and righteous altogether.**
More to be desired are they than gold, more than much fine gold : **sweeter far than honey, than honey in the comb.**

Open our lives wide : to taste and see that you are good.

Esther 4:4–17   Matthew 5:17–20

Open our lives wide : to taste and see that you are good.

In his book *Life Together*, Dietrich Bonhoeffer says this to us: "Innumerable times a whole Christian community has broken down because it had sprung from a wish dream. The serious Christian, set down for the first time in a Christian community, is likely to bring with him a very definite idea of what Christian life together should be and to try to realize it. But God's grace speedily shatters such dreams. By sheer grace, God will not permit us to live even for a brief period in a dream world. The sooner this shock of disillusionment comes to an individual and to a community, the better for both."

Prayers for Others

Our Father

Lord, give us the imagination to dream and catch glimpses of the life you intend for us to live. Show us how our individual lives are entwined with those around us, and help us to live so truly together that we embody your good news in this world. Amen.

May the peace of the Lord Christ go with you : wherever he may send you;
may he guide you through the wilderness : protect you through the storm;
may he bring you home rejoicing : at the wonders he has shown you;
may he bring you home rejoicing : once again into our doors.

September 5

O Lord, let my soul rise up to meet you
as the day rises to meet the sun.

**Glory to the Father, and to the Son, and to the Holy Spirit,
as it was in the beginning, is now, and will be forever. Amen.**

Come, let us sing to the LORD : let us shout for joy to the Rock of our salvation.

Song "We Are Marching in the Light of God"

Open wide the doors of our homes: that we may embrace you with joy.

Psalm 24:7–10
Lift up your heads, O gates; lift them high, O everlasting doors : **and the King of glory shall come in.**
"Who is this King of glory?" : **"The LORD, strong and mighty, the LORD, mighty in battle."**
Lift up your heads, O gates; lift them high, O everlasting doors : **and the King of glory shall come in.**
"Who is he, this King of glory?" : **"The LORD of hosts, he is the King of glory."**

Open wide the doors of our homes: that we may embrace you with joy.

Esther 5:1–14   Matthew 5:21–26

Open wide the doors of our homes: that we may embrace you with joy.

In his book *With Open Hands*, Henri Nouwen wrote, "In another's eyes I see my plea for forgiveness, and in a hardened frown I see my refusal. When someone murders, I know that I too could have done that, and when someone gives birth, I know that I am capable of that as well. In the depths of my being, I meet my fellow humans with whom I share love and have life and death."

Prayers for Others

Our Father

Thank you, Lord, for the witness of women, like Esther, who understood themselves only in relation to their communities of faith. Grant us such a heart, and a similar mindset! Strengthen us with the joy of all those saints who have gone before us, that like them we might stand up to the powers that threaten your kingdom. Amen.

May the peace of the Lord Christ go with you : wherever he may send you; may he guide you through the wilderness : protect you through the storm; may he bring you home rejoicing : at the wonders he has shown you; may he bring you home rejoicing : once again into our doors.

 # September 6

O Lord, let my soul rise up to meet you
as the day rises to meet the sun.

Glory to the Father, and to the Son, and to the Holy Spirit,
as it was in the beginning, is now, and will be forever. Amen.

Come, let us sing to the LORD : let us shout for joy to the Rock of our salvation.

Song "Nothin' but the Blood"

To the faithful you show yourself faithful : may we keep faith when trust is broken.

Psalm 31:21–24
Blessed be the LORD! : **for he has shown me the wonders of his love in a besieged city.**
Yet I said in my alarm, "I have been cut off from the sight of your eyes." : **Nevertheless, you heard the sound of my entreaty when I cried out to you.**
Love the LORD, all you who worship him : **the LORD protects the faithful, but repays to the full those who act haughtily.**
Be strong and let your heart take courage : **all you who wait for the LORD.**

To the faithful you show yourself faithful : may we keep faith when trust is broken.

Esther 6:1–14   Matthew 5:27–37

To the faithful you show yourself faithful : may we keep faith when trust is broken.

English priest C. F. Andrews, who was called Deenabandhu (Friend of the Poor) by the Indians among whom he served, said this: "Christ seeks from us deeds not words. Devotion to him is in the first place not sentimental but practical. If the Christian faith has no power to restore or recreate the human will, leading one to deeds of unselfish service, then it stands self-condemned."

Prayers for Others

Our Father

Lord, keep us from following a faith that awaits peace in heaven. You are our peace, and you are always with us. May your peace come and your will be done on earth, as indeed it is in heaven. Amen.

**May the peace of the Lord Christ go with you : wherever he may send you;
may he guide you through the wilderness : protect you through the storm;
may he bring you home rejoicing : at the wonders he has shown you;
may he bring you home rejoicing : once again into our doors.**

 September 7

O Lord, let my soul rise up to meet you
as the day rises to meet the sun.

**Glory to the Father, and to the Son, and to the Holy Spirit,
as it was in the beginning, is now, and will be forever. Amen.**

Come, let us sing to the Lord : let us shout for joy to the Rock of our salvation.

Song "Glory, Glory, Hallelujah"

Humble us in your presence, Lord : that we may delight in abundance of peace.

Psalm 37:11–14
In a little while the wicked shall be no more : **you shall search out their place, but they will not be there.**
But the lowly shall possess the land : **they will delight in abundance of peace.**
The wicked plot against the righteous : **and gnash at them with their teeth.**
The Lord laughs at the wicked : **because he sees that their day will come.**

Humble us in your presence, Lord : that we may delight in abundance of peace.

Esther 7:1–10   Matthew 5:38–48

Humble us in your presence, Lord : that we may delight in abundance of peace.

Mechthild of Magdeburg, a thirteenth-century mystic, wrote, "What hinders spiritual people most of all from complete perfection is that they pay so little attention to small sins. I tell you in truth: when I hold back a smile which would harm no one, or have a sourness in my heart which I tell to no one, or feel some impatience with my own pain, then my soul becomes so dark and my heart so cold that I must weep greatly and lament pitiably and yearn greatly and humbly confess all my lack of virtue."

Prayers for Others

Our Father

Thank you, Lord, that no sin is too small to bring the conviction of heart that may lead us to repentance and more faithful living. Convict us of our smallest sins so we might learn to delight in your ways. Amen.

**May the peace of the Lord Christ go with you : wherever he may send you;
may he guide you through the wilderness : protect you through the storm;
may he bring you home rejoicing : at the wonders he has shown you;
may he bring you home rejoicing : once again into our doors.**

✦ September 8

In 1965, Filipino and Mexican farmworkers in Delano, California, went on strike, leading to the founding of the United Farm Workers Union.

O Lord, let my soul rise up to meet you
as the day rises to meet the sun.

**Glory to the Father, and to the Son, and to the Holy Spirit,
as it was in the beginning, is now, and will be forever. Amen.**

Come, let us bow down and bend the knee : let us kneel before the LORD our Maker.

Song "The Kingdom of God"

Send your light to guide us : may we follow wherever it leads.

Psalm 43:1–4
Give judgment for me, O God, and defend my cause against an ungodly people : **deliver me from the deceitful and the wicked.**
For you are the God of my strength; why have you put me from you? : **and why do I go so heavily while the enemy oppresses me?**

Morning Prayer

Send out your light and your truth, that they may lead me : **and bring me to your holy hill and to your dwelling;**
that I may go to the altar of God, to the God of my joy and gladness : **and on the harp I will give thanks to you, O God my God.**

Send your light to guide us : may we follow wherever it leads.

Esther 8:1–8, 15–17   Matthew 6:1–6, 16–18

Send your light to guide us : may we follow wherever it leads.

American activist and labor organizer Cesar Chavez said, "When we are really honest with ourselves, we must admit that our lives are all that really belong to us. So it is how we use our lives that determines what kind of men we are. It is my deepest belief that only by giving our lives do we find life. I am convinced that the truest act of courage, the strongest act of manliness is to sacrifice ourselves for others in totally nonviolent struggle for justice."

Prayers for Others

Our Father

Lord, we know the importance of doing for others. Teach us the importance of being for others, that we might take time to fast and pray and dwell with you in order to see more clearly how your light illuminates the faces of those we struggle alongside for justice. Amen.

May the peace of the Lord Christ go with you : wherever he may send you; may he guide you through the wilderness : protect you through the storm; may he bring you home rejoicing : at the wonders he has shown you; may he bring you home rejoicing : once again into our doors.

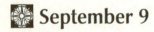 September 9

Peter Claver (1580–1654)

The patron saint of slaves and African-Americans, Peter Claver was a Jesuit priest who served the church in seventeenth-century Cartagena, Colombia. During his ministry, as many as ten thousand African slaves came through the port of Cartagena each year. Recognizing the blasphemy of human slavery, Claver worked tirelessly in ministry among the slaves, baptizing and preaching to as many as three hundred thousand in his lifetime. After welcoming them into the church in a society that considered itself Christian, Claver advocated for slaves' legal rights as fellow Christians.

O Lord, let my soul rise up to meet you
as the day rises to meet the sun.

Glory to the Father, and to the Son, and to the Holy Spirit,
as it was in the beginning, is now, and will be forever. Amen.

Come, let us bow down and bend the knee : let us kneel before the LORD our Maker.

Song "Guide My Feet"

Free us, Lord, from every chain : except the love that binds us to your way.

Psalm 44:15–18
My humiliation is daily before me : **and shame has covered my face;**
because of the taunts of the mockers and blasphemers : **because of the enemy and avenger.**
All this has come upon us : **yet we have not forgotten you, nor have we betrayed your covenant.**
Our heart never turned back : **nor did our footsteps stray from your path.**

Free us, Lord, from every chain : except the love that binds us to your way.

Hosea 1:1–2:1   Matthew 6:7–15

Free us, Lord, from every chain : except the love that binds us to your way.

Peter Claver liked to say, "Deeds come first, then the words."

Prayers for Others

Our Father

Lord, open our eyes to see that the fruit of life comes when we plant seeds of hope among those whom the world rejects. Amen.

**May the peace of the Lord Christ go with you : wherever he may send you;
may he guide you through the wilderness : protect you through the storm;
may he bring you home rejoicing : at the wonders he has shown you;
may he bring you home rejoicing : once again into our doors.**

 September 10

Mother Teresa of Calcutta (1910–1997)

Mother Teresa was born Agnesë Gonxhe Bojaxhiu in Albania. She joined the Sisters of Loreto, a Catholic religious order, at eighteen. After years of prayer and monastic discipline, she heard a "call within the call" to minister to Christ among the poorest of the poor in Calcutta, India. Moved with compassion for people who were dying in the streets, Mother Teresa took them in and gave them basic care. With no resources or established programs, she begged for food and supplies to care for those she welcomed. When others came to help her, she started the Missionaries of Charity in 1950. For nearly half a century, she committed herself, and the movement she led, to serving Christ in his most distressing disguise among the poor, the sick, the orphaned, and the dying.

O Lord, let my soul rise up to meet you
as the day rises to meet the sun.

**Glory to the Father, and to the Son, and to the Holy Spirit,
as it was in the beginning, is now, and will be forever. Amen.**

Come, let us sing to the Lord : let us shout for joy to the Rock of our salvation.

Song "Ubi Caritas"

Give us grace to be poor with your poor : and to love you among the dejected.

Psalm 51:16–20
Open my lips, O Lord : **and my mouth shall proclaim your praise.**
Had you desired it, I would have offered sacrifice : **but you take no delight in burnt offerings.**
The sacrifice of God is a troubled spirit : **a broken and contrite heart, O God, you will not despise.**
Be favorable and gracious to Zion : **and rebuild the walls of Jerusalem.**
Then you will be pleased with the appointed sacrifices, with burnt offerings and oblations : **then shall they offer young bullocks upon your altar.**

Give us grace to be poor with your poor : and to love you among the dejected.

Hosea 2:2–14   Matthew 6:19–24

Give us grace to be poor with your poor : and to love you among the dejected.

Mother Teresa said, "We can do not great things, only small things with great love. What is important is not how much you do, but how much love you put into doing it."

Prayers for Others

Our Father

Lord, teach us the distinction between the brokenness that leads us to squander our gifts and the brokenness that leads us to seek and find you, even in the most desolate places. Amen.

**May the peace of the Lord Christ go with you : wherever he may send you;
may he guide you through the wilderness : protect you through the storm;
may he bring you home rejoicing : at the wonders he has shown you;
may he bring you home rejoicing : once again into our doors.**

✤ September 11

On this day in 1973, the democratically elected government of Salvador Allende was overthrown in Chile by a CIA-backed coup. On the same day in 2001, terrorist attacks on the World Trade Center and the United States Pentagon killed twenty-eight hundred people.

O Lord, let my soul rise up to meet you
as the day rises to meet the sun.

**Glory to the Father, and to the Son, and to the Holy Spirit,
as it was in the beginning, is now, and will be forever. Amen.**

Come, let us bow down and bend the knee : let us kneel before the LORD our Maker.

Song "Waters of Babylon"

In God the LORD, whose word I praise : in God I trust and will not be afraid.

Psalm 56:3–7
Whenever I am afraid : **I will put my trust in you.**
In God, whose word I praise, in God I trust and will not be afraid : **for what can flesh do to me?**
All day long they damage my cause : **their only thought is to do me evil.**
They band together; they lie in wait : **they spy upon my footsteps; because they seek my life.**
Shall they escape despite their wickedness? : **O God, in your anger, cast down the peoples.**

In God the LORD, whose word I praise : in God I trust and will not be afraid.

Hosea 2:14–23   Matthew 6:25–34

In God the LORD, whose word I praise : in God I trust and will not be afraid.

Theophilus of Antioch, a second-century bishop, wrote, "Say to those that hate and curse you, 'You are our brothers!'"

Prayers for Others

Our Father

You who prayed from the cross for your Father to forgive those who were killing you, grant us the courage to forgive those who harm us in our families, in our communities, and in our world. Help us recognize our own need to seek the forgiveness of others. Amen.

May the peace of the Lord Christ go with you : wherever he may send you;
may he guide you through the wilderness : protect you through the storm;
may he bring you home rejoicing : at the wonders he has shown you;
may he bring you home rejoicing : once again into our doors.

✹ September 12

In 1915, the genocide of Armenians began in Turkey, marking the first of four acts of genocide that would plague the twentieth century.

O Lord, let my soul rise up to meet you
as the day rises to meet the sun.

Glory to the Father, and to the Son, and to the Holy Spirit,
as it was in the beginning, is now, and will be forever. Amen.

Come, let us bow down and bend the knee : let us kneel before the Lord our Maker.

Song "Lamb of God"

Save us, God, from the clutches of death : and bring forth life from our hands.

Psalm 64:1, 5–7
Hear my voice, O God, when I complain : **protect my life from fear of the enemy.**
They hold fast to their evil course : **they plan how they may hide their snares.**
They say, "Who will see us? who will find out our crimes? : **we have thought out a perfect plot."**
The human mind and heart are a mystery : **but God will loose an arrow at them, and suddenly they will be wounded.**

Save us, God, from the clutches of death : and bring forth life from our hands.

Hosea 3:1–5   Matthew 7:1–12

Save us, God, from the clutches of death : and bring forth life from our hands.

Tatian the Assyrian, a second-century theologian, wrote, "Die to the world by renouncing the madness of its stir and bustle. God created nothing evil. It is we who brought forth wickedness. Those who brought it about can also do away with it again."

Prayers for Others

Our Father

Lord, stir up the remnants of your goodness in us so that together we might proclaim, "Another world is possible — indeed, it is already here in Christ!" Amen.

**May the peace of the Lord Christ go with you : wherever he may send you;
may he guide you through the wilderness : protect you through the storm;
may he bring you home rejoicing : at the wonders he has shown you;
may he bring you home rejoicing : once again into our doors.**

✺ September 13

In 1971, inmates at Attica Prison in New York revolted and took control of their facility, presenting a list of demands to the governor of New York that included removal of the warden, better living conditions, and amnesty for those who had participated in the uprising. On September 13, a combined military and police force stormed the prison. By the end of the day, thirty-one prisoners and nine prison guards were dead. As we remember the prisoners and guards who died at Attica, we are also mindful of the fact that more than 1 percent of the US population is incarcerated today. Also noteworthy are the Oslo Accords signed on September 13, 1993, a milestone in the ongoing conflict in the Middle East. They were the first direct, face-to-face agreements between the government of Israel and the Palestine Liberation Organization, and were intended to be a framework for ongoing relations and negotiations in this troubled area of the Holy Land.

O Lord, let my soul rise up to meet you
as the day rises to meet the sun.

**Glory to the Father, and to the Son, and to the Holy Spirit,
as it was in the beginning, is now, and will be forever. Amen.**

Come, let us bow down and bend the knee : let us kneel before the LORD our Maker.

Song "Steal Away to Jesus"

You who died a criminal's death : raise us with you to freedom.

Psalm 69:16–17, 21–23
Save me from the mire; do not let me sink : **let me be rescued from those who hate me and out of the deep waters.**
Let not the torrent of waters wash over me, neither let the deep swallow me up : **do not let the Pit shut its mouth upon me.**

Morning Prayer

"You know my reproach, my shame, and my dishonor : **my adversaries are all in your sight.**"
Reproach has broken my heart, and it cannot be healed : **I looked for sympathy, but there was none, for comforters, but I could find no one.**
They gave me gall to eat : **and when I was thirsty, they gave me vinegar to drink.**

You who died a criminal's death : raise us with you to freedom.

Hosea 4:1–10   Matthew 7:13–21

You who died a criminal's death : raise us with you to freedom.

Clarence Jordan, co-founder of Koinonia Farm, wrote, "The Good News of the resurrection is not that we shall die and go home with him, but that he is risen and comes home with us, bringing all his hungry, naked, thirsty, sick, prisoner brothers with him."

Prayers for Others

Our Father

Lord, help us see that prison takes many forms in all nations, from the steel bars of injustice and unforgiveness to the open fields of consumerism and spirit-killing entertainment. Equip us by your Spirit's power to free one another from the various prisons in which we find ourselves. Amen.

May the peace of the Lord Christ go with you : wherever he may send you;
may he guide you through the wilderness : protect you through the storm;
may he bring you home rejoicing : at the wonders he has shown you;
may he bring you home rejoicing : once again into our doors.

 September 14

John Chrysostom (c. 347–407)

As a young man, John Chrysostom tried to be a desert monk, but he was deterred by poor health. So he decided to give his whole life to God in the city. He eventually became archbishop of Constantinople, but always insisted on a life of simplicity. John is remembered for his eloquence in preaching, especially against abuses of authority by both ecclesiastical and political leaders. After his death he was given the Greek surname *Chrysostomos*, meaning "golden-mouthed," because of his eloquence with words. In a time filled with so many words, John reminds us that words of truth have power to convict and transform.

O Lord, let my soul rise up to meet you

as the day rises to meet the sun.

**Glory to the Father, and to the Son, and to the Holy Spirit,
as it was in the beginning, is now, and will be forever. Amen.**

Come, let us sing to the LORD : let us shout for joy to the Rock of our salvation.

Song "All Creatures of Our God and King"

O Word made flesh, speak through us : words that bring new life.

Psalm 71:19–23
Your righteousness, O God, reaches to the heavens : **you have done great things; who is like you, O God?**
You have showed me great troubles and adversities : **but you will restore my life and bring me up again from the deep places of the earth.**
You strengthen me more and more : **you enfold and comfort me,**
therefore I will praise you upon the lyre for your faithfulness, O my God : **I will sing to you with the harp, O Holy One of Israel.**
My lips will sing with joy when I play to you : **and so will my soul, which you have redeemed.**

O Word made flesh, speak through us : words that bring new life.

Hosea 4:11–19   Matthew 7:22–29

O Word made flesh, speak through us : words that bring new life.

John Chrysostom said, "Prayer is the light of the spirit, and the spirit, raised up to heaven by prayer, clings to God with the utmost tenderness. Like a child crying tearfully for its mother, it craves the milk that God provides. Prayer also stands before God as an honored ambassador. It gives joy to the spirit, peace to the heart. I speak of prayer, not words. It is the longing for God, love too deep for words, a gift not given by humans, but by God's grace."

Prayers for Others

Our Father

Lord Jesus, you taught us to pray. Now help us pray for our daily bread while laboring with love for those who hunger. Show us how to hallow your name while striving for justice in our relationships and in society. May our whole lives become a prayer, ever to your glory. Amen.

**May the peace of the Lord Christ go with you : wherever he may send you;
may he guide you through the wilderness : protect you through the storm;
may he bring you home rejoicing : at the wonders he has shown you;
may he bring you home rejoicing : once again into our doors.**

✳ September 15

On September 15, 1963, a man later identified as Robert Chambliss placed a bomb under the steps of Sixteenth Street Baptist Church in Birmingham, Alabama. Addie Mae Collins (14), Carole Robertson (14), Cynthia Wesley (14), and Denise McNair (11) were killed by the explosion, and twenty-two others were injured. The girls were attending Sunday school classes at the church. Chambliss was found not guilty of murder, but was given a hundred-dollar fine and six months in jail for having dynamite. He was retried in 1973 and received a life sentence for the bombing.

O Lord, let my soul rise up to meet you
as the day rises to meet the sun.

**Glory to the Father, and to the Son, and to the Holy Spirit,
as it was in the beginning, is now, and will be forever. Amen.**

Come, let us bow down and bend the knee : let us kneel before the LORD our Maker.

Song "Poor Wayfaring Stranger"

How long, O Lord, will evildoers : harm your little ones?

Psalm 77:5–10
I consider the days of old : **I remember the years long past;**
I commune with my heart in the night : **I ponder and search my mind.**
Will the Lord cast me off for ever? : **will he no more show his favor?**
Has his loving-kindness come to an end for ever? : **has his promise failed for evermore?**
Has God forgotten to be gracious? : **has he, in his anger, withheld his compassion?**
And I said, "My grief is this : **the right hand of the Most High has lost its power."**

How long, O Lord, will evildoers : harm your little ones?

Hosea 5:1–7   Matthew 8:1–17

How long, O Lord, will evildoers : harm your little ones?

A reading from the gospel according to Matthew:
> A voice is heard in Ramah,
> weeping and great mourning,
> Rachel weeping for her children
> and refusing to be comforted,
> because they are no more.

Prayers for Others

Our Father

Lord, we weep with those who weep and refuse to be consoled. May our tears mix with yours in a river of justice, flowing down like mighty waters, transforming the world that is into the one that ought to be. Amen.

**May the peace of the Lord Christ go with you : wherever he may send you;
may he guide you through the wilderness : protect you through the storm;
may he bring you home rejoicing : at the wonders he has shown you;
may he bring you home rejoicing : once again into our doors.**

September 16

O Lord, let my soul rise up to meet you
as the day rises to meet the sun.

**Glory to the Father, and to the Son, and to the Holy Spirit,
as it was in the beginning, is now, and will be forever. Amen.**

Come, let us bow down and bend the knee : let us kneel before the Lord our Maker.

Song "Oh the Deep, Deep Love of Jesus"

Show us the light of your countenance, Lord : and we shall be saved.

Psalm 80:14–17
Turn now, O God of hosts, look down from heaven; behold and tend this vine : **preserve what your right hand has planted.**
They burn it with fire like rubbish : **at the rebuke of your countenance let them perish.**
Let your hand be upon the man of your right hand : **the son of man you have made so strong for yourself.**
And so will we never turn away from you : **give us life, that we may call upon your name.**

Show us the light of your countenance, Lord : and we shall be saved.

Hosea 5:8–6:6   Matthew 8:18–27

Show us the light of your countenance, Lord : and we shall be saved.

Ignatius of Loyola, founder of the Society of Jesus, wrote, "The most wonderful thing is unity with Jesus and with the Father. In him we shall partake in God if we firmly resist and flee all the arrogant attacks of the prince of this world. Unity of prayer, unity of supplication, unity of mind, unity of expectancy in love and in blameless joy: this is Jesus Christ and there is nothing greater than he. Flock together, all of you, as to one temple of God, as to one altar, to one Jesus Christ, who proceeded from the one Father, who is in the one and returned to the one."

Prayers for Others

Our Father

Bind us to you, O Lord, even when we are tempted to fall away, so we might witness to your faithfulness in your Spirit's power. Amen.

**May the peace of the Lord Christ go with you : wherever he may send you;
may he guide you through the wilderness : protect you through the storm;
may he bring you home rejoicing : at the wonders he has shown you;
may he bring you home rejoicing : once again into our doors.**

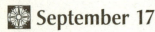 September 17

Hildegard of Bingen (1098 – 1179)

Hildegard was sent to the convent at the age of eight, where she learned to read Scripture, pray, and chant. Even as a child, she experienced supernatural religious visions in which she saw things invisible to others, foretold the future, and was filled with a luminosity she later called "the reflection of the Living Light." At age thirty-eight, she became abbess of the Benedictine community in which she was raised and, five years later, received her call to prophesy when she saw a fiery light that infused her heart and mind with knowledge. She finally was able to understand her visions as a means of divine revelation and began to write extensively about them. Her term for the grace of God inherent in all living things was *viriditas*, or greenness, endearing her in our generation to followers of creation spirituality. Hildegard's holistic approach to God and humanity is relevant today, particularly to those longing for wholeness and healing for all of creation.

O Lord, let my soul rise up to meet you
as the day rises to meet the sun.

**Glory to the Father, and to the Son, and to the Holy Spirit,
as it was in the beginning, is now, and will be forever. Amen.**

Come, let us sing to the Lord : let us shout for joy to the Rock of our salvation.

Song "We Are Marching in the Light of God"

Your word is in all the world : it flashes out in every creature.

Psalm 89:5–8
The heavens bear witness to your wonders, O Lord : **and to your faithfulness in the assembly of the holy ones;**
for who in the skies can be compared to the Lord? : **who is like the Lord among the gods?**
God is much to be feared in the council of the holy ones : **great and terrible to all those round about him.**
Who is like you, Lord God of hosts? : **O mighty Lord, your faithfulness is all around you.**

Your word is in all the world : it flashes out in every creature.

Hosea 10:1–15   Matthew 8:28–34

Your word is in all the world : it flashes out in every creature.

Hildegard of Bingen wrote, "We shall awaken from our dullness and rise vigorously toward justice. If we fall in love with creation deeper and deeper, we will respond to its endangerment with passion."

Prayers for Others

Our Father

Lord, when you invited Adam to name the animals, you invited us all to participate in your creative work. Teach us to rejoice in your creation and assist in its care, that we, your humble creatures, may in all things give you praise. Amen.

**May the peace of the Lord Christ go with you : wherever he may send you;
may he guide you through the wilderness : protect you through the storm;
may he bring you home rejoicing : at the wonders he has shown you;
may he bring you home rejoicing : once again into our doors.**

✶ September 18

O Lord, let my soul rise up to meet you
as the day rises to meet the sun.

Glory to the Father, and to the Son, and to the Holy Spirit,
as it was in the beginning, is now, and will be forever. Amen.

Come, let us sing to the Lord : **let us shout for joy to the Rock of our salvation.**

Song   "Fairest Lord Jesus"

We lift our hands in praise : to say these hands are yours.

Psalm 90:14–17
Satisfy us by your loving-kindness in the morning : **so shall we rejoice and be glad all the days of our life.**
Make us glad by the measure of the days that you afflicted us : **and the years in which we suffered adversity.**
Show your servants your works : **and your splendor to their children.**
May the graciousness of the LORD our God be upon us : **prosper the work of our hands; prosper our handiwork.**

We lift our hands in praise : to say these hands are yours.

Hosea 11:1–19   Matthew 9:1–8

We lift our hands in praise : to say these hands are yours.

Teresa of Avila, a sixteenth-century Spanish mystic, wrote, "Christ has no body now on earth but yours, no hands but yours, no feet but yours. Yours are the eyes through which Christ's compassion is to look out to the world; yours are the feet with which he is to go about doing good; yours are the hands with which God is to bless people now."

Prayers for Others

Our Father

Lord, give us the audacity to live as though we believe our hands and feet are instruments of prayer. Amen.

May the peace of the Lord Christ go with you : wherever he may send you; may he guide you through the wilderness : protect you through the storm; may he bring you home rejoicing : at the wonders he has shown you; may he bring you home rejoicing : once again into our doors.

✣ September 19

O Lord, let my soul rise up to meet you
as the day rises to meet the sun.

Glory to the Father, and to the Son, and to the Holy Spirit, as it was in the beginning, is now, and will be forever. Amen.

Come, let us bow down and bend the knee : let us kneel before the LORD our Maker.

Song   "Woke Up This Mornin'"

Call us with the voice we know : and give us grace to listen.

Psalm 95:8–11
Harden not your hearts, as your forebears did in the wilderness : **at Meribah, and on that day at Massah, when they tempted me.**
They put me to the test : **though they had seen my works.**
Forty years long I detested that generation and said : **"This people are wayward in their hearts; they do not know my ways."**
So I swore in my wrath : **"They shall not enter into my rest."**

Call us with the voice we know : and give us grace to listen.

Hosea 13:4–14   Matthew 9:9–17

Call us with the voice we know : and give us grace to listen.

Oscar Romero, martyr of the church in El Salvador, said, "A church that suffers no persecution but enjoys the privileges and support of the things of the earth — beware! — is not the true church of Jesus Christ. A preaching that does not point out sin is not the preaching of the gospel. A preaching that makes sinners feel good, so that they are secured in their sinful state, betrays the gospel's call."

Prayers for Others

Our Father

Lord, grant that in my earthly pilgrimage I may ever be supported by the love and prayer of your beloved community, and may know myself to be surrounded by their witness to your power and mercy. Amen.

May the peace of the Lord Christ go with you : wherever he may send you; may he guide you through the wilderness : protect you through the storm; may he bring you home rejoicing : at the wonders he has shown you; may he bring you home rejoicing : once again into our doors.

 # September 20

Paul Chong Hasang (1794?–1839) and the Korean Martyrs

Paul Chong Hasang was the son of Augustine Chong Yakjong, one of Korea's first converts to Christianity. Yakjong was martyred with Paul's older brother, but Yakjong's wife and their remaining children, including seven-year-old Paul, were spared. Paul became a government interpreter, which allowed him to travel and eventually meet a bishop in Beijing whom he entreated to send priests as missionaries to Korea. Years later, Paul learned Latin and theology, and he was about to be ordained when persecution broke out in 1839. Refusing to renounce his faith, Paul was bound to a cross on a cart. We remember him on this day, along with Andrew Kim Tae-gon, the first Korean-born Catholic priest, and 103 other Korean Christians who were martyred.

O Lord, let my soul rise up to meet you
as the day rises to meet the sun.

**Glory to the Father, and to the Son, and to the Holy Spirit,
as it was in the beginning, is now, and will be forever. Amen.**

Come, let us bow down and bend the knee : let us kneel before the LORD our Maker.

Song "What Wondrous Love"

Listen, Lord, to our hearts' cry : teach us how to pray.

Psalm 103:8–13
The LORD is full of compassion and mercy : **slow to anger and of great kindness.**
He will not always accuse us : **nor will he keep his anger for ever.**
He has not dealt with us according to our sins : **nor rewarded us according to our wickedness.**
For as the heavens are high above the earth : **so is his mercy great upon those who fear him.**
As far as the east is from the west : **so far has he removed our sins from us.**
As a father cares for his children : **so does the LORD care for those who fear him.**

Listen, Lord, to our hearts' cry : teach us how to pray.

Hosea 14:1–9   Matthew 9:18–26

Listen, Lord, to our hearts' cry : teach us how to pray.

When a judge told Paul Chong Hasang that the king had forbidden Christianity and that it was his duty as a loyal subject to renounce the faith, Paul replied, "I have told you that I am a Christian, and will be one until my death."

Prayers for Others

Our Father

Thank you, Lord, for the witness of those who have counted their relationship with you more important than their very lives. Draw us to you in constant prayer, that we might grow in the intimacy that makes your passion ours. Amen.

448 *Morning Prayer*

May the peace of the Lord Christ go with you : wherever he may send you;
may he guide you through the wilderness : protect you through the storm;
may he bring you home rejoicing : at the wonders he has shown you;
may he bring you home rejoicing : once again into our doors.

✷ September 21

Henri Nouwen (1932–1996)
Henri Nouwen was a Dutch Catholic priest who became an esteemed professor at both Yale and Harvard, but then followed the path of "downward mobility" in his pursuit of Jesus. He left the public eye to work among those struggling to survive in Latin America and then joined the work of L'Arche Daybreak Community in Canada. He was a "wounded healer" whose restless seeking for God has left a legacy to the world through prolific writings on the spirituality of brokenness and vulnerability. He died suddenly on this day in 1996.

O Lord, let my soul rise up to meet you
as the day rises to meet the sun.

**Glory to the Father, and to the Son, and to the Holy Spirit,
as it was in the beginning, is now, and will be forever. Amen.**

Come, let us sing to the LORD : let us shout for joy to the Rock of our salvation.

Song "Solid Rock"

Sing to the Lord, sing praises : make known his deeds among the nations.

Psalm 105:12–15
When they were few in number : **of little account, and sojourners in the land,**
wandering from nation to nation : **and from one kingdom to another,**
he let no one oppress them : **and rebuked kings for their sake,**
saying, "Do not touch my anointed : **and do my prophets no harm."**

Sing to the Lord, sing praises : make known his deeds among the nations.

Micah 1:1–9   Matthew 9:27–34

Sing to the Lord, sing praises : make known his deeds among the nations.

Henri Nouwen wrote, "Praying is no easy matter. It demands a relationship in which you allow someone other than yourself to enter into the very center of your person, to see there what you would rather leave in darkness, and to touch there what you would rather leave untouched."

Prayers for Others

Our Father

Lord, we bring to you our vulnerability, our wounds, our pain, and our growth. By the power of your forgiving love, help us also to become wounded healers. Amen.

May the peace of the Lord Christ go with you : wherever he may send you; may he guide you through the wilderness : protect you through the storm; may he bring you home rejoicing : at the wonders he has shown you; may he bring you home rejoicing : once again into our doors.

 September 22

O Lord, let my soul rise up to meet you
as the day rises to meet the sun.

Glory to the Father, and to the Son, and to the Holy Spirit, as it was in the beginning, is now, and will be forever. Amen.

Come, let us sing to the LORD : let us shout for joy to the Rock of our salvation.

Song "Great Is Thy Faithfulness"

Lord, you satisfy the thirsty : and fill the hungry with good things.

Psalm 107:4–8
Some wandered in desert wastes : **they found no way to a city where they might dwell.**
They were hungry and thirsty : **their spirits languished within them.**
Then they cried to the LORD in their trouble : **and he delivered them from their distress.**
He put their feet on a straight path : **to go to a city where they might dwell.**
Let them give thanks to the LORD for his mercy : **and the wonders he does for his children.**

Lord, you satisfy the thirsty : and fill the hungry with good things.

Micah 2:1–13   Matthew 9:35–10:15

Lord, you satisfy the thirsty : and fill the hungry with good things.

Dom Helder Camara, a twentieth-century bishop in Brazil, said, "When I feed the poor, they call me a saint, but when I ask why the poor are hungry, they call me a Communist."

Prayers for Others

Our Father

Lord, your good news brings healing to our bodies, minds, and spirits. Teach us the necessity and power of asking the right questions, and help us live the answers as living members of that new social order which is your body. Amen.

May the peace of the Lord Christ go with you : wherever he may send you; may he guide you through the wilderness : protect you through the storm; may he bring you home rejoicing : at the wonders he has shown you; may he bring you home rejoicing : once again into our doors.

✹ September 23

O Lord, let my soul rise up to meet you
as the day rises to meet the sun.

Glory to the Father, and to the Son, and to the Holy Spirit, as it was in the beginning, is now, and will be forever. Amen.

Come, let us sing to the LORD : let us shout for joy to the Rock of our salvation.

Song "We Are Marching in the Light of God"

Establish our hearts in your mercy, Lord : and establish your mercy in our hearts.

Psalm 112:4–8
Light shines in the darkness for the upright : **the righteous are merciful and full of compassion.**
It is good for them to be generous in lending : **and to manage their affairs with justice.**
For they will never be shaken : **the righteous will be kept in everlasting remembrance.**
They will not be afraid of any evil rumors : **their heart is right; they put their trust in the Lord.**
Their heart is established and will not shrink : **until they see their desire upon their enemies.**

Establish our hearts in your mercy, Lord : and establish your mercy in our hearts.

Micah 3:1–8   Matthew 10:16–42

Establish our hearts in your mercy, Lord : and establish your mercy in our hearts.

Gregory Palamas, a fourteenth-century monk of Mount Athos, said, "This is the nature of prayer: that it raises one from earth to heaven, higher than every heavenly name and dignity, and brings one before the very God of all."

Prayers for Others

Our Father

Lift our hearts to you, Lord Jesus, that we might by your Spirit's power be instruments of your mercy, to the glory of God the Father. Amen.

May the peace of the Lord Christ go with you : wherever he may send you; may he guide you through the wilderness : protect you through the storm; may he bring you home rejoicing : at the wonders he has shown you; may he bring you home rejoicing : once again into our doors.

 September 24

O Lord, let my soul rise up to meet you
as the day rises to meet the sun.

Glory to the Father, and to the Son, and to the Holy Spirit, as it was in the beginning, is now, and will be forever. Amen.

Come, let us bow down and bend the knee : let us kneel before the LORD our Maker.

Song "It Is Well with My Soul"

Be tender with your little ones : steady our souls as we learn to live.

Psalm 116:5–8
The LORD watches over the innocent : **I was brought very low, and he helped me.**
Turn again to your rest, O my soul : **for the LORD has treated you well.**
For you have rescued my life from death : **my eyes from tears, and my feet from stumbling.**
I will walk in the presence of the LORD : **in the land of the living.**

Be tender with your little ones : steady our souls as we learn to live.

Micah 3:9–4:5   Matthew 11:1–15

Be tender with your little ones : steady our souls as we learn to live.

A seventeenth-century French monk known as Brother Lawrence wrote of his experience with God: "I began to live as if there were not one in the world but Him and me. I adored Him as often as I could, keeping my mind in his holy presence and recalling it as often as it wandered. I had no little difficulty in this exercise, but I kept on despite all the difficulties and was not worried or distressed when I was involuntarily distracted. I did this during the day as often as I did it during the formal time specifically set aside for prayer; for at all times, at every hour, at every moment, even in the busiest times of my work, I banished and put away from my mind everything capable of diverting me from the thought of God."

Prayers for Others

Our Father

Lord, you have brought us in safety to this new day. Preserve us by your mighty power that we may not fall into sin nor be overcome by adversity, and in all that we do, direct us to the fulfilling of your purpose, through Jesus Christ our Lord. Amen.

May the peace of the Lord Christ go with you : wherever he may send you; may he guide you through the wilderness : protect you through the storm; may he bring you home rejoicing : at the wonders he has shown you; may he bring you home rejoicing : once again into our doors.

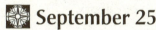 # September 25

O Lord, let my soul rise up to meet you
as the day rises to meet the sun.

Glory to the Father, and to the Son, and to the Holy Spirit, as it was in the beginning, is now, and will be forever. Amen.

Come, let us sing to the LORD : let us shout for joy to the Rock of our salvation.

Song "Be Thou My Vision"

The earth, O Lord, is full of your love : instruct us in your statutes.

Psalm 119:57–63
You only are my portion, O LORD : **I have promised to keep your words.**
I entreat you with all my heart : **be merciful to me according to your promise.**
I have considered my ways : **and turned my feet toward your decrees.**
I hasten and do not tarry : **to keep your commandments.**
Though the cords of the wicked entangle me : **I do not forget your law.**
At midnight I will rise to give you thanks : **because of your righteous judgments.**
I am a companion of all who fear you : **and of those who keep your commandments.**

The earth, O Lord, is full of your love : instruct us in your statutes.

Micah 5:1–4, 10–15   Matthew 11:16–30

The earth, O Lord, is full of your love : instruct us in your statutes.

God spoke to fourteenth-century mystic Catherine of Siena, saying, "I did not intend my creatures to make themselves servants and slaves to the world's pleasures. They owe their first love to me. Everything else they should love and possess, as I told you, not as if they owned it but as something lent them."

Prayers for Others

Our Father

Thank you, Lord, for the abundance of blessings you shower upon us. Forgive us for the many ways we have turned your gifts into our achievements and so forgotten your generosity. Open our eyes to see that everything is a gift, and that every gift is to be shared for your glory. Amen.

**May the peace of the Lord Christ go with you : wherever he may send you;
may he guide you through the wilderness : protect you through the storm;
may he bring you home rejoicing : at the wonders he has shown you;
may he bring you home rejoicing : once again into our doors.**

✺ September 26

O Lord, let my soul rise up to meet you
as the day rises to meet the sun.

**Glory to the Father, and to the Son, and to the Holy Spirit,
as it was in the beginning, is now, and will be forever. Amen.**

Come, let us bow down and bend the knee : let us kneel before the LORD our Maker.

Song   "I Want Jesus to Walk with Me"

I call with my whole heart : your word will give me life.

Psalm 119:146–52
I call to you; oh, that you would save me! : **I will keep your decrees.**
Early in the morning I cry out to you : **for in your word is my trust.**
My eyes are open in the night watches : **that I may meditate upon your promise.**
Hear my voice, O LORD, according to your loving-kindness : **according to your judgments, give me life.**

They draw near who in malice persecute me : **they are very far from your law.**
You, O LORD, are near at hand : **and all your commandments are true.**
Long have I known from your decrees : **that you have established them for ever.**

I call with my whole heart : your word will give me life.

Micah 6:1–8   Matthew 12:1–14

I call with my whole heart : your word will give me life.

We have these verses from John of the Cross:

> I will mourn my death already,
> lament the life I live, as long
> as misdeed, sin and wrong
> detain it in captivity.
> O my God, when will it be?
> The time when I can say for sure,
> at last I live: I die no more.

Prayers for Others

Our Father

Save us, Lord, from the grip of death that so often controls our lives. Help us each to say with the psalmist, "I shall not die, but live, and declare the works of the Lord!" Amen.

May the peace of the Lord Christ go with you : wherever he may send you;
may he guide you through the wilderness : protect you through the storm;
may he bring you home rejoicing : at the wonders he has shown you;
may he bring you home rejoicing : once again into our doors.

September 27

Vincent de Paul (1581 – 1660)

The son of French peasants, Vincent de Paul studied for the priesthood and was ordained in 1600. While serving the church, he was kidnapped by Turkish pirates and sold into slavery. After converting his master, Vincent escaped and returned to France, where he ministered to the poor and imprisoned, and invited others to join him, founding the Vincentians and the Daughters of Charity with Louise de Marillac. He prayed, "May the poor forgive me the bread that I give them."

O Lord, let my soul rise up to meet you
as the day rises to meet the sun.

**Glory to the Father, and to the Son, and to the Holy Spirit,
as it was in the beginning, is now, and will be forever. Amen.**

Come, let us bow down and bend the knee : let us kneel before the Lord our Maker.

Song "Oh the Deep, Deep Love of Jesus"

Let every deed we do today : rise up as a prayer of love.

Psalm 128:1–6
Happy are they all who fear the Lord : **and who follow in his ways!**
You shall eat the fruit of your labor : **happiness and prosperity shall be yours.**
Your wife shall be like a fruitful vine within your house : **your children like olive shoots round about your table.**
The man who fears the Lord : **shall thus indeed be blessed.**
The Lord bless you from Zion : **and may you see the prosperity of Jerusalem all the days of your life.**
May you live to see your children's children : **may peace be upon Israel.**

Let every deed we do today : rise up as a prayer of love.

Micah 7:1–7   Matthew 12:15–21

Let every deed we do today : rise up as a prayer of love.

Vincent de Paul said, "We must love God, but let it be in the work of our bodies, in the sweat of our brows. For very often many acts of love for God, of kindness, of good will, and other similar inclinations and interior practices of a tender heart, although good and very desirable, are yet very suspect when they do not lead to the practice of effective love."

Prayers for Others

Our Father

Lord, you have shown us what love looks like. Help us through acts of forgiveness and reconciliation to so love one another that our neighbors know we are your disciples and know that to be good news. Amen.

**May the peace of the Lord Christ go with you : wherever he may send you;
may he guide you through the wilderness : protect you through the storm;
may he bring you home rejoicing : at the wonders he has shown you;
may he bring you home rejoicing : once again into our doors.**

September 28

O Lord, let my soul rise up to meet you
as the day rises to meet the sun.

**Glory to the Father, and to the Son, and to the Holy Spirit,
as it was in the beginning, is now, and will be forever. Amen.**

Come, let us sing to the LORD : let us shout for joy to the Rock of our salvation.

Song "Woke Up This Mornin'"

You give your people justice : and show compassion to your servants.

Psalm 135:3–7
Praise the LORD, for the LORD is good : **sing praises to his name, for it is lovely.**
For the LORD has chosen Jacob for himself : **and Israel for his own possession.**
For I know that the LORD is great : **and that our Lord is above all gods.**
The LORD does whatever pleases him, in heaven and on earth : **in the seas and all the deeps.**
He brings up rain clouds from the ends of the earth : **he sends out lightning with the rain, and brings the winds out of his storehouse.**

You give your people justice : and show compassion to your servants.

Jonah 1:1–17a   Matthew 12:22–32

You give your people justice : and show compassion to your servants.

In his *Rule* for monastic communities, Benedict of Nursia wrote, "Indeed, obedience must be given with genuine good will, because God loves a cheerful giver. If obedience is given with a bad will and with murmuring not only in words but even in bitterness of heart, then even though the command may be externally fulfilled it will not be accepted by God, for he can see the resistance in the heart of a murmurer. One who behaves in such a way not only fails to receive the reward of grace but actually incurs the punishment deserved by murmurers. Only repentance and reparation can save such a one from this punishment."

Prayers for Others

Our Father

Lord, teach us to listen not only with our ears but with spirits that are eager to hear your will and do it. Amen.

May the peace of the Lord Christ go with you : wherever he may send you;
may he guide you through the wilderness : protect you through the storm;
may he bring you home rejoicing : at the wonders he has shown you;
may he bring you home rejoicing : once again into our doors.

✦ September 29

O Lord, let my soul rise up to meet you
as the day rises to meet the sun.

**Glory to the Father, and to the Son, and to the Holy Spirit,
as it was in the beginning, is now, and will be forever. Amen.**

Come, let us sing to the LORD : let us shout for joy to the Rock of our salvation.

Song "Guide My Feet"

Bury us in wonder, Lord : and raise us to sing your praise.

Psalm 139:2–5
You trace my journeys and my resting places : **and are acquainted with all my ways.**
Indeed, there is not a word on my lips : **but you, O LORD, know it altogether.**
You press upon me behind and before : **and lay your hand upon me.**
Such knowledge is too wonderful for me : **it is so high that I cannot attain to it.**

Bury us in wonder, Lord : and raise us to sing your praise.

Jonah 1:17–2:10   Matthew 12:33–42

Bury us in wonder, Lord : and raise us to sing your praise.

In his last sermon before being assassinated, Martin Luther King Jr. said, "Well, I don't know what will happen now. We've got some difficult days ahead. But it doesn't matter with me now. Because I've been to the mountaintop. And I don't mind. Like anybody, I would like to live a long life. Longevity has its place. But I'm not concerned about that now. I just want to do God's will. And he's allowed me to go up to the mountain. And I've looked over. And I've seen the Promised Land. I may not get there with you. But I want you to know tonight that we, as a people, will get to the Promised Land. And I'm happy tonight. I'm not worried about anything. I'm not fearing any man. Mine eyes have seen the glory of the coming of the Lord."

Prayers for Others

Our Father

Lord, we thank you for the cloud of witnesses who remind us that loving you is a perpetual call to active duty. Grant us both passion and courage to answer the call to peace and justice, no matter where it might lead us. Amen.

**May the peace of the Lord Christ go with you : wherever he may send you;
may he guide you through the wilderness : protect you through the storm;
may he bring you home rejoicing : at the wonders he has shown you;
may he bring you home rejoicing : once again into our doors.**

✸ September 30

O Lord, let my soul rise up to meet you
as the day rises to meet the sun.

Glory to the Father, and to the Son, and to the Holy Spirit,
as it was in the beginning, is now, and will be forever. Amen.

Come, let us sing to the Lord : let us shout for joy to the Rock of our salvation.

Song "Magnificat"

Through our lives and by our prayers : your kingdom come!

Psalm 145:10–13
All your works praise you, O Lord : **and your faithful servants bless you.**
They make known the glory of your kingdom : **and speak of your power;**
that the peoples may know of your power : **and the glorious splendor of your kingdom.**
Your kingdom is an everlasting kingdom : **your dominion endures throughout all ages.**

Through our lives and by our prayers : your kingdom come!

Jonah 3:1–4:11   Matthew 12:43–50

Through our lives and by our prayers : your kingdom come!

Sadhu Sundar Singh, an early-twentieth-century Indian missionary, wrote, "Diamonds do not dazzle with beauty unless they are cut. When cut, the rays of the sun fall on them and make them shine with wonderful colors. So when we are cut by the cross, we shall shine as jewels in the kingdom of God."

Prayers for Others

Our Father

Lord, keep us from making crosses out of the splinters of discomfort in our lives. Help us recognize the true crosses you call us to bear, those whose weight lends to the freedom and provision of others. Amen.

May the peace of the Lord Christ go with you : wherever he may send you;
may he guide you through the wilderness : protect you through the storm;
may he bring you home rejoicing : at the wonders he has shown you;
may he bring you home rejoicing : once again into our doors.

> **Becoming the Answer to Our Prayers: A Few Ideas**
> 1. Track down old teachers and mentors. Let them know the influence they have had on your life.
> 2. Hold a ritual of prayerfully cutting up credit cards.
> 3. Move to a place that makes you uncomfortable, or visit a place where you will be a minority.
> 4. Ask your pastor to remove the US flag from the altar, or to include the flags from the other 195 countries of the world.
> 5. Babysit for someone free of charge, especially someone who might really need a night off and not be able to afford a sitter.

OCTOBER — SAINT FRANCIS

OCTOBER

Marks of New Monasticism
Formation in the Way of Christ

For many of us, the judgmental, arrogant, legalistic Christianity we knew growing up has created a suspicion of discipline and order that can lead to a pretty sloppy spirituality. Reacting against the institution's sickness, we easily find ourselves with little to help us heal from our own wounds, create new disciplines, and carve out a space where goodness triumphs. People who are afraid of spiritual discipline will not produce very good disciples.

Community is pretty hip these days. The longing for community is in all of us. We long to love and to be loved. But if community doesn't exist for something beyond us, it will atrophy, suffocate, die. *Discipline* and *disciple* share the same roots, and without discipline, we become little more than hippie communes or frat houses. We easily fall short of God's dream to form a new humanity with distinct practices that offer hope and good news to the world. Like any culture, we who follow the way of Jesus have distinct ways of eating and partying, different from the culture of consumption, homogeneity, and hedonism. Our homes, our living rooms, even our parties can become places of solace and hospitality for those with addictions and struggles. But it doesn't happen without intentionality. Dorothy Day said, "We have to create an environment where it is easier to be good."

Suggested Reading for the Month
Celebration of Discipline by Richard Foster
The Spiritual Exercises of St. Ignatius of Loyola
The Rule of St. Benedict

St. Francis of Assisi is a model for us not only of what it looks like to follow hard after Jesus but also how we can celebrate the disciplines that have been passed down to us and become the church that we long for, even among people who've given up on "church." Our communities should be places where people can detox, whether that be from alcohol, tobacco, gluttony, shopping, or gossip. We long for a space that tips us toward goodness rather than away from it, where we can pick up new habits — holy habits — as we are formed into a new creation, transformed by God.

October 1

Therese of Lisieux (1873 – 1897)

Therese was born to a middle-class family in Lisieux, France. When she was fifteen, she got special permission to join her two older sisters at the Carmelite monastery in their hometown. When she died of tuberculosis nine years later at the age of twenty-four, she was little known outside her community. At the request of her spiritual director, however, Therese had written a memoir of her spiritual journey, titled *The Story of a Soul*. It became a spiritual classic almost immediately for its powerfully clear articulation of one ordinary person's desire to give her whole life to Christ by following every moment in the "Little Way" of love and service to one's neighbors. "After my death," Therese wrote, "I will let fall a shower of roses. I will spend my heaven in doing good upon earth."

O Lord, let my soul rise up to meet you
as the day rises to meet the sun.

**Glory to the Father, and to the Son, and to the Holy Spirit,
as it was in the beginning, is now, and will be forever. Amen.**

Come, let us bow down and bend the knee : let us kneel before the LORD our Maker.

Song "Ubi Caritas"

I am only a very little soul : bringing little things to you, O Lord.

Psalm 4:4 – 8
Tremble, then, and do not sin : **speak to your heart in silence upon your bed.**
Offer the appointed sacrifices : **and put your trust in the LORD.**
Many are saying, "Oh, that we might see better times!" : **Lift up the light of your countenance upon us, O LORD.**
You have put gladness in my heart : **more than when grain and wine and oil increase.**
I lie down in peace; at once I fall asleep : **for only you, LORD, make me dwell in safety.**

I am only a very little soul : bringing little things to you, O Lord.

Jeremiah 35:1 – 19   James 1:1 – 15

I am only a very little soul : bringing little things to you, O Lord.

Therese of Lisieux wrote, "My vocation is love! In the heart of the Church, who is my Mother, I will be love. So I shall be everything and so my dreams will be fulfilled — to make Love loved."

Prayers for Others

Our Father

Lord, strengthen our will to heed your commandments. We pray to be found faithful in the smallest things, that you might deem us worthy of more opportunities to serve you. Amen.

May the peace of the Lord Christ go with you : wherever he may send you; may he guide you through the wilderness : protect you through the storm; may he bring you home rejoicing : at the wonders he has shown you; may he bring you home rejoicing : once again into our doors.

✶ October 2

O Lord, let my soul rise up to meet you
as the day rises to meet the sun.

Glory to the Father, and to the Son, and to the Holy Spirit, as it was in the beginning, is now, and will be forever. Amen.

Come, let us bow down and bend the knee : let us kneel before the LORD our Maker.

Song "The Kingdom of God"

Give justice, Lord, to the orphan : and free us from terror's power.

Psalm 10:12–19
Rise up, O LORD; lift up your hand, O God : **do not forget the afflicted.**
Why should the wicked revile God? : **why should they say in their heart, "You do not care"?**
Surely, you behold trouble and misery : **you see it and take it into your own hand.**
The helpless commit themselves to you : **for you are the helper of orphans.**
Break the power of the wicked and evil : **search out their wickedness until you find none.**
The LORD is King for ever and ever : **the ungodly shall perish from his land.**
The LORD will hear the desire of the humble : **you will strengthen their heart and your ears shall hear;**
to give justice to the orphan and oppressed : **so that mere mortals may strike terror no more.**

Give justice, Lord, to the orphan : and free us from terror's power.

Jeremiah 36:1–10   James 1:16–27

Give justice, Lord, to the orphan : and free us from terror's power.

Ignacio Ellacuria, a Jesuit martyr of San Salvador, asked, "What is it to be a companion of Jesus today? It is to engage, under the standard of the cross, in the crucial struggle of our time: the struggle for faith and that struggle for justice which it includes."

Prayers for Others

Our Father

Lord, enable us to live so that others can truly say, "They engaged in the crucial struggle of our time." Amen.

May the peace of the Lord Christ go with you : wherever he may send you; may he guide you through the wilderness : protect you through the storm; may he bring you home rejoicing : at the wonders he has shown you; may he bring you home rejoicing : once again into our doors.

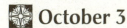 October 3

O Lord, let my soul rise up to meet you
as the day rises to meet the sun.

**Glory to the Father, and to the Son, and to the Holy Spirit,
as it was in the beginning, is now, and will be forever. Amen.**

Come, let us bow down and bend the knee : let us kneel before the LORD our Maker.

Song "Swing Low, Sweet Chariot"

Deliver us, Lord, from our troubles : and remake us in your image.

Psalm 17:13–16
Arise, O LORD; confront them and bring them down : **deliver me from the wicked by your sword.**
Deliver me, O LORD, by your hand : **from those whose portion in life is this world;**
whose bellies you fill with your treasure : **who are well supplied with children and leave their wealth to their little ones.**
But at my vindication I shall see your face : **when I awake, I shall be satisfied, beholding your likeness.**

Deliver us, Lord, from our troubles : and remake us in your image.

Jeremiah 36:11–26   James 2:1–13

Deliver us, Lord, from our troubles : and remake us in your image.

Church father Augustine of Hippo wrote, "'The times are bad! The times are troublesome!' This is what humans say. But we are our times. Let us live well and our times will be good. Such as we are, such are our times."

Prayers for Others

Our Father

Lord, grant that our actions hold a mirror to our prayers. Amen.

May the peace of the Lord Christ go with you : wherever he may send you; may he guide you through the wilderness : protect you through the storm; may he bring you home rejoicing : at the wonders he has shown you; may he bring you home rejoicing : once again into our doors.

 ## October 4

Francis of Assisi (1182 – 1226)

Francis was born to a merchant family in the Italian city of Assisi. As a young man, he was attracted to adventure and moved by romantic tales of knights. When he himself became a knight, Francis met a leper while riding through the countryside. Overwhelmed by a divine impulse, Francis dismounted his horse, shared his coat with the leper, and kissed the man's diseased face. Captivated by the experience, Francis began to re-imagine his life in light of the gospel, renouncing his selfish desires and his father's wealth. A beggar for Christ's sake, Francis inspired thousands to walk away from worldly success and join his movement of friars who sought to renew the church in their day.

O Lord, let my soul rise up to meet you
as the day rises to meet the sun.

Glory to the Father, and to the Son, and to the Holy Spirit, as it was in the beginning, is now, and will be forever. Amen.

Come, let us sing to the Lord : let us shout for joy to the Rock of our salvation.

Song "All Creatures of Our God and King"

Take my voice and let me sing : always only for my king!

Psalm 22:26 – 30
All the ends of the earth shall remember and turn to the Lord : **and all the families of the nations shall bow before him.**
For kingship belongs to the Lord : **he rules over the nations.**

To him alone all who sleep in the earth bow down in worship : **all who go down to the dust fall before him.**
My soul shall live for him; my descendants shall serve him : **they shall be known as the Lord's for ever.**
They shall come and make known to a people yet unborn : **the saving deeds that he has done.**

Take my voice and let me sing : always only for my king!

Jeremiah 36:27–37:2   James 2:14–26

Take my voice and let me sing : always only for my king!

While praying before a crucifix in the dilapidated chapel of San Damiano, Francis of Assisi heard a voice speak to him: "Francis, repair my church, which has fallen into disrepair, as you can see."

Prayers for Others

Our Father

Lord, your church is such that when one member of the body fails, the whole body suffers. Help us encourage one another in faith so that working together we might become a unified body that goes forth into the world to proclaim good news. Amen.

May the peace of the Lord Christ go with you : wherever he may send you; may he guide you through the wilderness : protect you through the storm; may he bring you home rejoicing : at the wonders he has shown you; may he bring you home rejoicing : once again into our doors.

❈ October 5

O Lord, let my soul rise up to meet you
as the day rises to meet the sun.

**Glory to the Father, and to the Son, and to the Holy Spirit,
as it was in the beginning, is now, and will be forever. Amen.**

Come, let us bow down and bend the knee : let us kneel before the Lord our Maker.

Song   "Nothin' but the Blood"

Lord Jesus Christ, Son of God : have mercy on me, a sinner.

Psalm 25:6–10
Remember not the sins of my youth and my transgressions : **remember me according to your love and for the sake of your goodness, O Lord.**
Gracious and upright is the Lord : **therefore he teaches sinners in his way.**
He guides the humble in doing right : **and teaches his way to the lowly.**
All the paths of the Lord are love and faithfulness : **to those who keep his covenant and his testimonies.**
For your name's sake, O Lord : **forgive my sin, for it is great.**

Lord Jesus Christ, Son of God : have mercy on me, a sinner.

Jeremiah 37:3–21   James 3:1–12

Lord Jesus Christ, Son of God : have mercy on me, a sinner.

In the anonymously authored *Way of the Pilgrim*, we find these words: "My whole desire was fixed upon one thing only — to say the Prayer of Jesus, and as soon as I went on with it I was filled with joy and relief. It was as though my lips and my tongue pronounced the words entirely of themselves without any urging from me. I spent the whole day in a state of the greatest contentment. I lived as though in another world."

Prayers for Others

Our Father

Lord, teach us to pray without ceasing, even when words escape us, and to work toward your kingdom, even when we cannot see it. Amen.

May the peace of the Lord Christ go with you : wherever he may send you;
may he guide you through the wilderness : protect you through the storm;
may he bring you home rejoicing : at the wonders he has shown you;
may he bring you home rejoicing : once again into our doors.

# October 6

Fannie Lou Hamer (1917–1977)

Fannie Lou Hamer was born the daughter of sharecroppers in Mississippi, a poor black woman in the poorest region of America at the time. She rose up from obscurity to challenge the principalities and powers of her day. A fiery and eloquent voice for freedom, she helped to guide and inspire the struggle for freedom. In Hamer's later years, her concerns grew beyond civil rights to include opposition to the Vietnam War and efforts to unite poor people of all shades of skin in a movement to end poverty. She was known for her line, "I am sick and tired of being sick and tired."

O Lord, let my soul rise up to meet you
as the day rises to meet the sun.

**Glory to the Father, and to the Son, and to the Holy Spirit,
as it was in the beginning, is now, and will be forever. Amen.**

Come, let us sing to the LORD : let us shout for joy to the Rock of our salvation.

Song "Freedom Train"

Let your wondrous love be upon us : for in you alone have we put our trust.

Psalm 33:1–5
Rejoice in the LORD, you righteous : **it is good for the just to sing praises.**
Praise the LORD with the harp : **play to him upon the psaltery and lyre.**
Sing for him a new song : **sound a fanfare with all your skill upon the trumpet.**
For the word of the LORD is right : **and all his works are sure.**
He loves righteousness and justice : **the loving-kindness of the LORD fills the whole earth.**

Let your wondrous love be upon us : for in you alone have we put our trust.

Jeremiah 38:1–13   James 3:13–4:12

Let your wondrous love be upon us : for in you alone have we put our trust.

Russian novelist Fyodor Dostoyevsky wrote, "Love in action is a harsh and dreadful thing compared to love in dreams."

Prayers for Others

Our Father

Loving God, even in the midst of the world's pain and sorrow, we can encounter your joy. Show us that such joy comes when we are caught up in works of mercy and find ourselves unable to distinguish between our blessings and those of our brothers and sisters. Amen.

**May the peace of the Lord Christ go with you : wherever he may send you;
may he guide you through the wilderness : protect you through the storm;
may he bring you home rejoicing : at the wonders he has shown you;
may he bring you home rejoicing : once again into our doors.**

Morning Prayer

❂ October 7

In 2001, a US-led coalition began bombing Afghanistan in response to the September 11 terrorist attacks.

O Lord, let my soul rise up to meet you
as the day rises to meet the sun.

**Glory to the Father, and to the Son, and to the Holy Spirit,
as it was in the beginning, is now, and will be forever. Amen.**

Come, let us bow down and bend the knee : let us kneel before the LORD our Maker.

Song "Waters of Babylon"

You see the violence of the wicked, Lord : rise up and defend your children.

Psalm 35:17–23
O Lord, how long will you look on? : **rescue me from the roaring beasts, and my life from the young lions.**
I will give you thanks in the great congregation : **I will praise you in the mighty throng.**
Do not let my treacherous foes rejoice over me : **nor let those who hate me without a cause wink at each other.**
For they do not plan for peace : **but invent deceitful schemes against the quiet in the land.**
They opened their mouths at me and said : **"Aha! we saw it with our own eyes."**
You saw it, O LORD; do not be silent : **O Lord, be not far from me.**
Awake, arise, to my cause! : **to my defense, my God and my Lord!**

You see the violence of the wicked, Lord : rise up and defend your children.

Jeremiah 38:14–28   James 4:13–5:6

You see the violence of the wicked, Lord : rise up and defend your children.

Origen of Alexandria wrote in the third century, "We will not raise arms against any other nation, we will not practice the art of war, because through Jesus Christ we have become the children of peace."

Prayers for Others

Our Father

God of peace, dawn reminds us that your mercies are new every morning. You have been merciful to us despite our sin. Teach us such mercy. Open our eyes to see the violence we condone with our silences and with our consumption. We give thanks that repentance is the beginning of true conversion. Amen.

May the peace of the Lord Christ go with you : wherever he may send you;
may he guide you through the wilderness : protect you through the storm;
may he bring you home rejoicing : at the wonders he has shown you;
may he bring you home rejoicing : once again into our doors.

✦ October 8

O Lord, let my soul rise up to meet you
as the day rises to meet the sun.

Glory to the Father, and to the Son, and to the Holy Spirit,
as it was in the beginning, is now, and will be forever. Amen.

Come, let us bow down and bend the knee : let us kneel before the LORD our Maker.

Song "I Will Trust in the Lord"

You are my helper and my deliverer : do not tarry, O my God.

Psalm 40:12–14
You are the LORD; do not withhold your compassion from me : **let your love and your faithfulness keep me safe for ever,**
for innumerable troubles have crowded upon me; my sins have overtaken me, and I cannot see : **they are more in number than the hairs of my head, and my heart fails me.**
Be pleased, O LORD, to deliver me : **O LORD, make haste to help me.**

You are my helper and my deliverer : do not tarry, O my God.

2 Kings 25:8–12, 22–26   James 5:7–12

You are my helper and my deliverer : do not tarry, O my God.

Andy Raine of the Northumbria Community has written, "Do not hurry as you walk with grief; it does not help the journey. Walk slowly, pausing often: do not hurry as you walk with grief. Be not disturbed by memories that come unbidden. Swiftly forgive; and let Christ speak for you unspoken words. Unfinished conversation will be resolved in him. Be not disturbed. Be gentle with the one who walks with grief. If it is you, be gentle with yourself. Swiftly forgive; walk slowly, pausing often. Take time, be gentle as you walk with grief."

Prayers for Others

Our Father

Lord, as the seasons turn, creation teaches us of grief, patience, and renewal. Make us good students of these rhythms that we might not hurry the work of grief but receive the gift of your presence in our time of need. Amen.

**May the peace of the Lord Christ go with you : wherever he may send you;
may he guide you through the wilderness : protect you through the storm;
may he bring you home rejoicing : at the wonders he has shown you;
may he bring you home rejoicing : once again into our doors.**

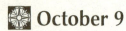
October 9

Oskar Schindler (1908–1974)

Oskar Schindler was a German living in Czechoslovakia when he joined the Nazi party in 1939. When Germany invaded Poland later that same year, he moved to Krakow and took over two manufacturing companies and, like many other businessmen there, made his fortune using cheap labor — Jews from the Krakow ghetto. When he began to witness the Germans killing and deporting Jews in the ghetto, Oskar was moved to transfer the Jewish workers from his factory to a safe place. Later, he received permission from the Germans to move not only his workers but other Jews as well to his native land of Czechoslovakia. Over time, Schindler's occupation changed, until ultimately the rescue of the Jews became his top priority. Using the factory as cover, he saved more and more Jews, putting his own life in danger to ensure the safety of those in his protection. At one point, when a train carrying more than one thousand Jews was on its way to a new factory site in Czechoslovakia, it was accidentally diverted to Auschwitz. Schindler offered the Nazis diamonds and gold to make sure those in his care reached safety. Ultimately, Schindler saved twelve hundred Jews from extermination, and today there are more than seven thousand descendants of the Schindler Jews living all over the world. Through his actions, Schindler was a living example of the reality of human decency, love, goodness, and compassion in the face of unspeakable horror. He has been called an unlikely hero, not only because nothing in his prior life suggested the extent of his heroic deeds but also because he was an ordinary man who did extraordinary things. His life is a testament to the fact that we are all called to put our faith into action, sometimes in the most unexpected, bold, and courageous ways.

O Lord, let my soul rise up to meet you
as the day rises to meet the sun.

**Glory to the Father, and to the Son, and to the Holy Spirit,
as it was in the beginning, is now, and will be forever. Amen.**

Come, let us sing to the Lord : let us shout for joy to the Rock of our salvation.

Song "Praise to the Lord, the Almighty"

Overwhelm us with wonder, Lord : that our souls might rest in awe.

Psalm 46:9–12
Come now and look upon the works of the Lord : **what awesome things he has done on earth.**
It is he who makes war to cease in all the world : **he breaks the bow, and shatters the spear, and burns the shields with fire.**
"Be still, then, and know that I am God : **I will be exalted among the nations; I will be exalted in the earth."**
The Lord of hosts is with us : **the God of Jacob is our stronghold.**

Overwhelm us with wonder, Lord : that our souls might rest in awe.

Jeremiah 29:1, 4–14   James 5:13–20

Overwhelm us with wonder, Lord : that our souls might rest in awe.

Oskar Schindler said, "He who saves one life saves the entire world."

Prayers for Others

Our Father

God, you never fail to dazzle us with your grace and mercy. We pray for the boldness to await the fulfillment of life that you promise, through Jesus Christ our Lord. Amen.

**May the peace of the Lord Christ go with you : wherever he may send you;
may he guide you through the wilderness : protect you through the storm;
may he bring you home rejoicing : at the wonders he has shown you;
may he bring you home rejoicing : once again into our doors.**

✹ October 10

In 1991, the Women in Black began their regular Wednesday vigil against war in Belgrade, Serbia.

O Lord, let my soul rise up to meet you
as the day rises to meet the sun.

Glory to the Father, and to the Son, and to the Holy Spirit,
as it was in the beginning, is now, and will be forever. Amen.

Come, let us bow down and bend the knee : let us kneel before the LORD our Maker.

Song "Were You There?"

To you we cry in anguish, Lord : listen to our plea and help us.

Psalm 55:18–20, 24–26
In the evening, in the morning, and at noonday, I will complain and lament : **and he will hear my voice.**
He will bring me safely back from the battle waged against me : **for there are many who fight me.**
God, who is enthroned of old, will hear me and bring them down : **they never change; they do not fear God.**
Cast your burden upon the LORD, and he will sustain you : **he will never let the righteous stumble.**
For you will bring the bloodthirsty and deceitful : **down to the pit of destruction, O God.**
They shall not live out half their days : **but I will put my trust in you.**

To you we cry in anguish, Lord : listen to our plea and help us.

Jeremiah 44:1–14   2 Corinthians 1:1–11

To you we cry in anguish, Lord : listen to our plea and help us.

English poet and cleric John Donne wrote, "There we leave you in that blessed dependency, to hang upon him that hangs upon the cross, there bathe in his tears, there suck at his wounds, and lie down in peace in his grave, till he vouchsafe you a resurrection, and an ascension into that Kingdom, which he has purchased for you with the inestimable price of his incorruptible blood."

Prayers for Others

Our Father

Jesus, keep us near your cross, and reveal to us your glory. Amen.

**May the peace of the Lord Christ go with you : wherever he may send you;
may he guide you through the wilderness : protect you through the storm;
may he bring you home rejoicing : at the wonders he has shown you;
may he bring you home rejoicing : once again into our doors.**

✺ October 11

O Lord, let my soul rise up to meet you
as the day rises to meet the sun.

**Glory to the Father, and to the Son, and to the Holy Spirit,
as it was in the beginning, is now, and will be forever. Amen.**

Come, let us bow down and bend the knee : let us kneel before the LORD our Maker.

Song "Come, Ye Sinners"

Rise up, O Lord, come and see : save us from the enemy.

Psalm 59:1–5
Rescue me from my enemies, O God : **protect me from those who rise up against me.**
Rescue me from evildoers : **and save me from those who thirst for my blood.**
See how they lie in wait for my life, how the mighty gather together against me : **not for any offense or fault of mine, O LORD.**
Not because of any guilt of mine : **they run and prepare themselves for battle.**
Rouse yourself, come to my side, and see : **for you, LORD God of hosts, are Israel's God.**

Rise up, O Lord, come and see : save us from the enemy.

Lamentations 1:1–12   2 Corinthians 1:12–22

Rise up, O Lord, come and see : save us from the enemy.

Early church apologist Minucius Felix wrote, "What a beautiful sight it is for God when a Christian mocks at the clatter of the tools of death and the horror of the executioner; when he defends and upholds his liberty in the face of kings and princes, obeying God alone to whom he belongs. Among us, boys and frail women laugh to scorn torture and the gallows cross, the wild beasts and all the other horrors of execution!"

Prayers for Others

Our Father

Lord, we pray against fear of persecution and death, knowing we are always walking toward eternal life as we follow the path you have set for us. Amen.

**May the peace of the Lord Christ go with you : wherever he may send you;
may he guide you through the wilderness : protect you through the storm;
may he bring you home rejoicing : at the wonders he has shown you;
may he bring you home rejoicing : once again into our doors.**

✵ October 12

In 1492, the indigenous peoples of the Americas discovered Christopher Columbus.

O Lord, let my soul rise up to meet you
as the day rises to meet the sun.

**Glory to the Father, and to the Son, and to the Holy Spirit,
as it was in the beginning, is now, and will be forever. Amen.**

Come, let us bow down and bend the knee : let us kneel before the Lord our Maker.

Song "Come, Ye Sinners"

Born to sin, we inherit stolen land : heal us with justice from your hand.

Psalm 62:6–9
For God alone my soul in silence waits : **truly, my hope is in him.**
He alone is my rock and my salvation : **my stronghold, so that I shall not be shaken.**
In God is my safety and my honor : **God is my strong rock and my refuge.**
Put your trust in him always, O people : **pour out your hearts before him, for God is our refuge.**

Born to sin, we inherit stolen land : heal us with justice from your hand.

Lamentations 2:8–15   2 Corinthians 1:23–2:17

Born to sin, we inherit stolen land : heal us with justice from your hand.

Lakota Sioux holy man Black Elk said, "A good nation I will make live."

Prayers for Others

Our Father

Lord, help us not to shy away from our own transgressions, neither to hold the sins of others against them, but to name sin with confidence that your forgiveness has the power to effect a just reconciliation in our world. Amen.

**May the peace of the Lord Christ go with you : wherever he may send you;
may he guide you through the wilderness : protect you through the storm;
may he bring you home rejoicing : at the wonders he has shown you;
may he bring you home rejoicing : once again into our doors.**

Note for Columbus Day: We Need New Heroes

Many thoughtful authors have helped correct our revisionist history and our amnesia about the past. For instance, in his book *Lies My Teacher Told Me*, James W. Loewen points out that Columbus and the Spaniard conquerors approached the Native Americans and read aloud what came to be called "The Requirement," which went like this: "I implore you to recognize the Church as a lady and in the name of the Pope take the King as lord of this land and obey his mandates. If you do not do it, I tell you that with the help of God I will enter powerfully against you all. I will make war everywhere and every way that I can. I will subject you to the yoke and obedience to the Church and to his majesty. I will take your women and children and make them slaves.... The deaths and injuries that you will recieve from here on will be your own fault and not that of his majesty nor of the gentlemen that accompany me." Part of what we hope to do in this book, rather than read the Bible with imperial eyes, is to read the empire with biblical eyes.

In the church, we celebrate martyrs and saints, not warriors and conquistadors. The church has a rich history of celebrating particular people. While the United States might celebrate Christopher Columbus, the church celebrates the lives of saints on feast days. We need to be about discovering lost relatives and forgotten ancestors.

History is filled with subversive "holy heroes," such as Oskar Schindler and Harriet Tubman, and even Hollywood tells their stories in moving films like *Schindler's List* and *Hotel Rwanda*. Sometimes we just have to discover the stories that we are in danger of losing, stories that don't always make the news. Sure, it's easier to build a memorial than to build a movement, and we're always better at sculpting our saints than following them. But we have to remember the stories of people who have lived and died well.

Who are your heroes? Take a few minutes to say their names out loud and thank God for them. For bonus points, sing "When the Saints Go Marching In" when you are finished.

 October 13

O Lord, let my soul rise up to meet you
as the day rises to meet the sun.

**Glory to the Father, and to the Son, and to the Holy Spirit,
as it was in the beginning, is now, and will be forever. Amen.**

Come, let us sing to the L ORD : let us shout for joy to the Rock of our salvation.

Song "Glory, Glory, Hallelujah"

Blessed be the Lord, day by day : the God who bears our burdens.

Psalm 68:7–10
O God, when you went forth before your people : **when you marched through the wilderness,**
the earth shook, and the skies poured down rain, at the presence of God, the God of Sinai : **at the presence of God, the God of Israel.**
You sent a gracious rain, O God, upon your inheritance : **you refreshed the land when it was weary.**
Your people found their home in it : **in your goodness, O God, you have made provision for the poor.**

Blessed be the Lord, day by day : the God who bears our burdens.

Ezra 1:1–11   2 Corinthians 3:1–18

Blessed be the Lord, day by day : the God who bears our burdens.

In his *Rule* for monastic communities, Benedict of Nursia wrote, "With all this in mind, what we mean to establish is a school for the Lord's service. In the guidance we lay down to achieve this, we hope to impose nothing harsh or burdensome. If, however, you find in it anything which seems rather strict, but which is demanded reasonably for the correction of vice or the preservation of love, do not let that frighten you into fleeing from the way of salvation; it is a way which is bound to seem narrow to start with. But, as we progress in this monastic way of life and in faith, our hearts will warm to its vision, and with eager love and delight that defies expression, we shall go forward on the way of God's commandments. Then we shall never think of deserting his guidance; we shall persevere in fidelity to his teaching in the monastery until death so that through our patience we may be granted some part in Christ's own passion and thus in the end receive a share in his kingdom. Amen."

Prayers for Others

Our Father

Lord, it is a privilege to abide by your word and to discipline ourselves in the Spirit. Present us with ample opportunities today to water the seeds of discipline in our lives that they might in time bear fruit, to the glory of your name. Amen.

May the peace of the Lord Christ go with you : wherever he may send you;
may he guide you through the wilderness : protect you through the storm;
may he bring you home rejoicing : at the wonders he has shown you;
may he bring you home rejoicing : once again into our doors.

October 14

O Lord, let my soul rise up to meet you
as the day rises to meet the sun.

**Glory to the Father, and to the Son, and to the Holy Spirit,
as it was in the beginning, is now, and will be forever. Amen.**

Come, let us sing to the LORD : let us shout for joy to the Rock of our salvation.

Song "Come, Thou Fount"

Blessed be the God of Israel : who alone is just and righteous.

Psalm 72:1–7
Give the King your justice, O God : **and your righteousness to the King's Son;**
that he may rule your people righteously : **and the poor with justice;**
that the mountains may bring prosperity to the people : **and the little hills bring righteousness.**
He shall defend the needy among the people : **he shall rescue the poor and crush the oppressor.**
He shall live as long as the sun and moon endure : **from one generation to another.**
He shall come down like rain upon the mown field : **like showers that water the earth.**
In his time shall the righteous flourish : **there shall be abundance of peace till the moon shall be no more.**

Blessed be the God of Israel : who alone is just and righteous.

Ezra 3:1–13   2 Corinthians 4:1–12

Blessed be the God of Israel : who alone is just and righteous.

American abolitionist Frederick Douglass said, "If there is no struggle, there is no progress. Those who profess to favor freedom yet deprecate agitation are men who want crops without plowing up the ground; they want rain without thunder and lightning. They want the ocean without the awful roar of its many waters. Power concedes nothing without demand. It never did and it never will. Find out just what any people will quietly submit to and you have found out the exact measure of injustice and wrong which will be imposed upon them, and these will continue till they are resisted with either words or blows, or with both. The limits of tyrants are prescribed by the endurance of those whom they oppress."

Prayers for Others

Our Father

Morning Prayer

God of peace, keep us from confusing peace with submission in the face of injustice. Keep us from confusing patience with tolerance in the face of oppression. Grant us true discernment for the sake of your kingdom. Amen.

**May the peace of the Lord Christ go with you : wherever he may send you;
may he guide you through the wilderness : protect you through the storm;
may he bring you home rejoicing : at the wonders he has shown you;
may he bring you home rejoicing : once again into our doors.**

 October 15

Teresa of Avila (1515–1582)

In sixteenth-century Spain, where women had little voice, Teresa of Avila stood out as a spiritual giant, reforming her Carmelite order, founding seventeen new communities, writing four books, and challenging countless men and women to grow in the life of prayer. As attested to by her writings and by her friends and disciples (including John of the Cross), Teresa's own prayer life was perhaps her most important gift to the church. "Prayer," she wrote, "is nothing but friendly intercourse, and frequent solitary converse, with Him who we know loves us."

O Lord, let my soul rise up to meet you
as the day rises to meet the sun.

**Glory to the Father, and to the Son, and to the Holy Spirit,
as it was in the beginning, is now, and will be forever. Amen.**

Come, let us sing to the Lord : let us shout for joy to the Rock of our salvation.

Song "O Mary, Don't You Weep"

Let nothing disturb you, nothing dismay : All things are possible. God does not change.

Psalm 81:13–16
Oh, that my people would listen to me! : **that Israel would walk in my ways!**
I should soon subdue their enemies : **and turn my hand against their foes.**
Those who hate the Lord would cringe before him : **and their punishment would last for ever.**
But Israel would I feed with the finest wheat : **and satisfy him with honey from the rock.**

Let nothing disturb you, nothing dismay : All things are possible. God does not change.

Ezra 4:7, 11–24   2 Corinthians 4:13–5:10

Let nothing disturb you, nothing dismay : All things are possible. God does not change.

Teresa of Avila said, "Remember that you have only one soul; that you have only one death to die; that you have only one life, which is short and has to be lived by you alone; and that there is only one glory, which is eternal. If you do this, there will be many things about which you care nothing."

Prayers for Others

Our Father

Purify our hearts, O Lord, to long for the one true thing and be distracted by nothing. Amen.

May the peace of the Lord Christ go with you : wherever he may send you; may he guide you through the wilderness : protect you through the storm; may he bring you home rejoicing : at the wonders he has shown you; may he bring you home rejoicing : once again into our doors.

✦ October 16

The Soviet Union and Cuba made an agreement in 1962 to allow the storage of nuclear missiles on the island of Cuba. Once the United States discovered the plan, the US Navy surrounded the island on October 16. Tensions were high as the Cold War enemies faced off ninety miles from US soil. The Soviet Union agreed to remove the missiles if the US removed its own missiles from southern Italy and Turkey and did not attack Cuba.

O Lord, let my soul rise up to meet you
as the day rises to meet the sun.

Glory to the Father, and to the Son, and to the Holy Spirit, as it was in the beginning, is now, and will be forever. Amen.

Come, let us bow down and bend the knee : let us kneel before the Lord our Maker.

Song "Lamb of God"

You have been gracious to your land, O Lord : preserve us from self-destruction.

Psalm 85:7–11
Show us your mercy, O Lord : **and grant us your salvation.**
I will listen to what the Lord God is saying : **for he is speaking peace to his faithful people and to those who turn their hearts to him.**

Morning Prayer

Truly, his salvation is very near to those who fear him : **that his glory may dwell in our land.**
Mercy and truth have met together : **righteousness and peace have kissed each other.**
Truth shall spring up from the earth : **and righteousness shall look down from heaven.**

You have been gracious to your land, O Lord : preserve us from self-destruction.

Haggai 1:1–2:9   2 Corinthians 5:11–6:2

You have been gracious to your land, O Lord : preserve us from self-destruction.

Catholic peace activist Jim Douglass has written, "The Cold War has been followed by its twin, the War on Terror. We are engaged in another apocalyptic struggle against an enemy seen as absolute evil. Terrorism has replaced Communism as the enemy. We are told we can be safe only through the threat of escalating violence. Yet the redemptive means John Kennedy turned to, in a similar struggle, was dialogue with the enemy. When the enemy is seen as human, everything changes."

Prayers for Others

Our Father

Lord, you have brought us in safety to this new day. Preserve us now by your mighty power that we might not fall into sin nor be overcome by adversity, and in all that we do, direct us to the fulfilling of your purpose, through Jesus Christ our Lord. Amen.

May the peace of the Lord Christ go with you : wherever he may send you; may he guide you through the wilderness : protect you through the storm; may he bring you home rejoicing : at the wonders he has shown you; may he bring you home rejoicing : once again into our doors.

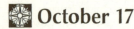 October 17

Ignatius of Antioch (c. 107)

Ignatius, whose surname was Theophorus ("God-bearer"), may have been a disciple of John the Evangelist. Little is known about his early life, but he took charge of the church at Antioch around the year 69 and was condemned to death during the time of Trajan's persecution. While in transit to Rome, the boat carrying him to his death made stops along the shores of Asia Minor, and he was able to preach in the churches along the way. Faithful Christians met Ignatius upon his arrival in Rome, both to celebrate his presence and mourn his impending death. Praying with the believers, he asked for an end to persecution, blessings on the church, and charity for the faithful. He was taken to the amphitheater in Rome, where it is reported two lions were set upon him.

O Lord, let my soul rise up to meet you
as the day rises to meet the sun.

**Glory to the Father, and to the Son, and to the Holy Spirit,
as it was in the beginning, is now, and will be forever. Amen.**

Come, let us sing to the LORD : let us shout for joy to the Rock of our salvation.

Song "Steal Away to Jesus"

Dying, we rise to you, O Lord : come, be our light.

Psalm 89:11–15
Yours are the heavens; the earth also is yours : **you laid the foundations of the world and all that is in it.**
You have made the north and the south : **Tabor and Hermon rejoice in your name.**
You have a mighty arm : **strong is your hand and high is your right hand.**
Righteousness and justice are the foundations of your throne : **love and truth go before your face.**
Happy are the people who know the festal shout! : **they walk, O LORD, in the light of your presence.**

Dying, we rise to you, O Lord : come, be our light.

Zechariah 1:7–17   2 Corinthians 6:3–13

Dying, we rise to you, O Lord : come, be our light.

Ignatius of Antioch wrote, "The delights of this world and all its kingdoms will not profit me. I would prefer to die in Jesus Christ than to rule over all the earth. I seek him who died for us; I desire him who rose for us. I am in the throes of being born again. Bear with me, my brothers and sisters. Let me see the pure light; when I am there, I shall be truly a human being at last. Let me imitate the sufferings of my God."

Prayers for Others

Our Father

Lord God, instill in us such a fervor for you that we cannot help but preach your love and reconciliation in times of sorrow and joy. Amen.

May the peace of the Lord Christ go with you : wherever he may send you;
may he guide you through the wilderness : protect you through the storm;
may he bring you home rejoicing : at the wonders he has shown you;
may he bring you home rejoicing : once again into our doors.

✣ October 18

O Lord, let my soul rise up to meet you
as the day rises to meet the sun.

Glory to the Father, and to the Son, and to the Holy Spirit,
as it was in the beginning, is now, and will be forever. Amen.

Come, let us sing to the LORD : let us shout for joy to the Rock of our salvation.

Song "We Shall Not Be Moved"

Shelter us not with walls that exclude : but with your widespread wing.

Psalm 91:9–13
Because you have made the LORD your refuge : **and the Most High your habitation,**
there shall no evil happen to you : **neither shall any plague come near your dwelling.**
For he shall give his angels charge over you : **to keep you in all your ways.**
They shall bear you in their hands : **lest you dash your foot against a stone.**
You shall tread upon the lion and adder : **you shall trample the young lion and the serpent under your feet.**

Shelter us not with walls that exclude : but with your widespread wing.

Ezra 5:1–17   2 Corinthians 6:14–7:1

Shelter us not with walls that exclude : but with your widespread wing.

Origen of Alexandria wrote, "Once the people of God had surrounded the city Jericho, it had to be stormed. How then was Jericho stormed? No sword was drawn against it, no battering ram was aimed at it, no javelins were hurled. The priests merely sounded their trumpets, and the walls of Jericho collapsed. Jericho will fall, then; this world will perish. How will the world be brought to an end, and by what means will it be destroyed? The answer of Scripture is, by the sound of trumpets. If you ask what trumpets, then let Paul reveal the secret: *The trumpet will sound, and the dead who are in Christ will rise incorruptible.*"

Prayers for Others

Our Father

Lord, may your trumpet sound in the songs we sing, in the prayer we pray, in the lives we live, and in the bread we break. Come, Lord Jesus, come. Amen.

**May the peace of the Lord Christ go with you : wherever he may send you;
may he guide you through the wilderness : protect you through the storm;
may he bring you home rejoicing : at the wonders he has shown you;
may he bring you home rejoicing : once again into our doors.**

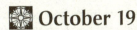 October 19

John Woolman (1720–1772)

John Woolman was born October 19, 1720. After refusing as a young man to write a bill of sale for a slave, Woolman went on to play a key role in challenging Quakers to give up slavery and recognize it as unchristian. Thanks to the active faith of Woolman and others, Quakers played an important role in the abolition movement throughout the nineteenth century.

O Lord, let my soul rise up to meet you
as the day rises to meet the sun.

Glory to the Father, and to the Son, and to the Holy Spirit,
as it was in the beginning, is now, and will be forever. Amen.

Come, let us sing to the LORD : let us shout for joy to the Rock of our salvation.

Song "Freedom Train"

You order your kingdom with justice : and establish the world in peace.

Psalm 96:7–10
Ascribe to the LORD, you families of the peoples : **ascribe to the LORD honor and power.**
Ascribe to the LORD the honor due his name : **bring offerings and come into his courts.**
Worship the LORD in the beauty of holiness : **let the whole earth tremble before him.**
Tell it out among the nations: "The LORD is King! : **he has made the world so firm that it cannot be moved; he will judge the peoples with equity."**

You order your kingdom with justice : and establish the world in peace.

Ezra 6:1–22   2 Corinthians 7:2–16

You order your kingdom with justice : and establish the world in peace.

John Woolman said, "The only Christian way to treat a slave is to set him free."

Prayers for Others

Our Father

Lord, within your community we are strengthened to persevere, empowered to proclaim your truth, and shaped to wait on you. Teach us anew what we can learn from other faithful brothers and sisters who serve you in their particular ways of worship and proclamation. Amen.

May the peace of the Lord Christ go with you : wherever he may send you; may he guide you through the wilderness : protect you through the storm; may he bring you home rejoicing : at the wonders he has shown you; may he bring you home rejoicing : once again into our doors.

✹ October 20

O Lord, let my soul rise up to meet you
as the day rises to meet the sun.

Glory to the Father, and to the Son, and to the Holy Spirit,
as it was in the beginning, is now, and will be forever. Amen.

Come, let us sing to the LORD : let us shout for joy to the Rock of our salvation.

Song "Servant Song"

Show us your glory, O Lord : and teach us to rise by descending.

Psalm 102:13–16
You will arise and have compassion on Zion, for it is time to have mercy upon her : **indeed, the appointed time has come.**
For your servants love her very rubble : **and are moved to pity even for her dust.**
The nations shall fear your name, O LORD : **and all the kings of the earth your glory.**
For the LORD will build up Zion : **and his glory will appear.**

Show us your glory, O Lord : and teach us to rise by descending.

Nehemiah 1:1–11   2 Corinthians 8:1–16

Show us your glory, O Lord : and teach us to rise by descending.

Twentieth-century Catholic journalist Penny Lernoux said, "You can look at a slum or peasant village, but it is only by entering into the world — by living in it — that you begin to understand what it is like to be powerless, to be like Christ."

Prayers for Others

Our Father

Lord, you descended into the mire of this world to raise us up. Enable us to descend as you descended that we might rise with you to the beloved community of your resurrected life. Amen.

**May the peace of the Lord Christ go with you : wherever he may send you;
may he guide you through the wilderness : protect you through the storm;
may he bring you home rejoicing : at the wonders he has shown you;
may he bring you home rejoicing : once again into our doors.**

❈ October 21

O Lord, let my soul rise up to meet you
as the day rises to meet the sun.

**Glory to the Father, and to the Son, and to the Holy Spirit,
as it was in the beginning, is now, and will be forever. Amen.**

Come, let us sing to the LORD : let us shout for joy to the Rock of our salvation.

Song "Vamos Todos al Banquete"

Save us that we might give thanks : and glory in your praise.

Psalm 106:1–5
Hallelujah! Give thanks to the LORD, for he is good : **for his mercy endures for ever.**
Who can declare the mighty acts of the LORD : **or show forth all his praise?**
Happy are those who act with justice : **and always do what is right!**
Remember me, O LORD, with the favor you have for your people : **and visit me with your saving help;**
that I may see the prosperity of your elect and be glad with the gladness of your people : **that I may glory with your inheritance.**

Save us that we might give thanks : and glory in your praise.

Nehemiah 2:1–20   2 Corinthians 8:16–24

Save us that we might give thanks : and glory in your praise.

Clement of Alexandria said, "One purchases immortality through generosity; and, by giving the perishing things of the world, receives in exchange for these an eternal mansion in the heavens! Rush to this market, if you are wise, O rich man! If need be, sail around the whole world."

Prayers for Others

Our Father

Lord, teach us the power of a generosity that interrupts the logic of scarcity with the extravagant self-giving of divine love. Amen.

May the peace of the Lord Christ go with you : wherever he may send you; may he guide you through the wilderness : protect you through the storm; may he bring you home rejoicing : at the wonders he has shown you; may he bring you home rejoicing : once again into our doors.

October 22

O Lord, let my soul rise up to meet you
as the day rises to meet the sun.

Glory to the Father, and to the Son, and to the Holy Spirit, as it was in the beginning, is now, and will be forever. Amen.

Come, let us sing to the LORD : let us shout for joy to the Rock of our salvation.

Song "We Shall Overcome"

Bring an end to evil, Lord : and save us from our enemies.

Psalm 109:28–30
Let my accusers be clothed with disgrace : **and wrap themselves in their shame as in a cloak.**
I will give great thanks to the LORD with my mouth : **in the midst of the multitude will I praise him;**
because he stands at the right hand of the needy : **to save his life from those who would condemn him.**

Bring an end to evil, Lord : and save us from our enemies.

Nehemiah 4:1–23   2 Corinthians 9:1–15

Bring an end to evil, Lord : and save us from our enemies.

Twentieth-century martyrs Felipe and Mary Barreda wrote, "We discovered that faith is not expecting that the Lord will miraculously give us whatever we ask, or feeling the security that we will not be killed and that everything will turn out as we want. We learned that faith is putting ourselves in His hands, whatever happens, good or bad. He will help us somehow."

Prayers for Others

Our Father

Lord, our lives are in your hands. Do not let our enemies triumph over us. Teach us how to love even those who intend us harm. Amen.

May the peace of the Lord Christ go with you : wherever he may send you; may he guide you through the wilderness : protect you through the storm; may he bring you home rejoicing : at the wonders he has shown you; may he bring you home rejoicing : once again into our doors.

 October 23

O Lord, let my soul rise up to meet you
as the day rises to meet the sun.

Glory to the Father, and to the Son, and to the Holy Spirit, as it was in the beginning, is now, and will be forever. Amen.

Come, let us sing to the LORD : let us shout for joy to the Rock of our salvation.

Song "Sing, O Sky (Gaao Re)"

Not to us, not to us : but to your name give glory.

Psalm 115:12–18
The LORD has been mindful of us, and he will bless us : **he will bless the house of Israel; he will bless the house of Aaron;**
he will bless those who fear the LORD : **both small and great together.**
May the LORD increase you more and more : **you and your children after you.**
May you be blessed by the LORD : **the maker of heaven and earth.**
The heaven of heavens is the LORD's : **but he entrusted the earth to its peoples.**
The dead do not praise the LORD : **nor all those who go down into silence;**
but we will bless the LORD : **from this time forth for evermore. Hallelujah!**

Not to us, not to us : but to your name give glory.

Nehemiah 5:1–19   2 Corinthians 10:1–18

Not to us, not to us : but to your name give glory.

Second-century bishop Melito of Sardis wrote, "Nature trembled and said with astonishment: What new mystery is this? The Judge is judged and remains silent; the Invisible One is seen and does not hide himself; the Incomprehensible One is comprehended and does not resist; the Unmeasurable One is measured and does not struggle; the One beyond suffering suffers and does not avenge himself; the Immortal One dies and does not refuse death. What new mystery is this?"

Prayers for Others

Our Father

In the light of the morning, Lord, we glorify your name. May the mystery of your incarnation shine through the complexities of this day so that in all we do, your name might be praised. Amen.

**May the peace of the Lord Christ go with you : wherever he may send you;
may he guide you through the wilderness : protect you through the storm;
may he bring you home rejoicing : at the wonders he has shown you;
may he bring you home rejoicing : once again into our doors.**

✣ October 24

O Lord, let my soul rise up to meet you
as the day rises to meet the sun.

Glory to the Father, and to the Son, and to the Holy Spirit,
as it was in the beginning, is now, and will be forever. Amen.

Come, let us sing to the Lord : let us shout for joy to the Rock of our salvation.

Song "This Little Light of Mine"

I shall not die but live : and declare the works of the Lord.

Psalm 118:6–9
The Lord is at my side, therefore I will not fear : **what can anyone do to me?**
The Lord is at my side to help me : **I will triumph over those who hate me.**
It is better to rely on the Lord : **than to put any trust in flesh.**
It is better to rely on the Lord : **than to put any trust in rulers.**

I shall not die but live : and declare the works of the Lord.

Nehemiah 6:1–19   2 Corinthians 11:1–21a

I shall not die but live : and declare the works of the Lord.

Paul Miki, a martyr of Japan, said, "My religion teaches me to pardon my enemies and all who have offended me. I do gladly pardon the emperor and all who have sought my death. I beg them to seek baptism and be Christians themselves."

Prayers for Others

Our Father

Lord, help us not to take offense at those who question and judge our works of mercy. Rather, enable us to pray that they too might receive the merciful calling to new life with which you have blessed us. Amen.

May the peace of the Lord Christ go with you : wherever he may send you; may he guide you through the wilderness : protect you through the storm; may he bring you home rejoicing : at the wonders he has shown you; may he bring you home rejoicing : once again into our doors.

 ## October 25

O Lord, let my soul rise up to meet you
as the day rises to meet the sun.

Glory to the Father, and to the Son, and to the Holy Spirit, as it was in the beginning, is now, and will be forever. Amen.

Come, let us bow down and bend the knee : let us kneel before the LORD our Maker.

Song "Take My Life and Let It Be"

Let my heart be sound in your statutes : that I may not be put to shame.

Psalm 119:73–77
Your hands have made me and fashioned me : **give me understanding, that I may learn your commandments.**
Those who fear you will be glad when they see me : **because I trust in your word.**
I know, O LORD, that your judgments are right : **and that in faithfulness you have afflicted me.**
Let your loving-kindness be my comfort : **as you have promised to your servant.**
Let your compassion come to me, that I may live : **for your law is my delight.**

Let my heart be sound in your statutes : that I may not be put to shame.

Nehemiah 12:27–31a, 42b–47   2 Corinthians 11:21b–33

Let my heart be sound in your statutes : that I may not be put to shame.

Andre Trocmé, who pastored the remarkable Le Chambon community during World War II, said, "Nonviolence was not a theory superimposed upon reality; it was an itinerary that we explored day after day in communal prayer and in obedience to the commands of the Spirit."

Prayers for Others

Our Father

Lord, teach us that spiritual formation takes time and discipline just as a seed must be watered, nurtured, and pruned as it grows. Deepen our roots in spiritual growth even as we are extended in our passion for peace and justice. Amen.

May the peace of the Lord Christ go with you : wherever he may send you; may he guide you through the wilderness : protect you through the storm; may he bring you home rejoicing : at the wonders he has shown you; may he bring you home rejoicing : once again into our doors.

✣ October 26

O Lord, let my soul rise up to meet you
as the day rises to meet the sun.

Glory to the Father, and to the Son, and to the Holy Spirit, as it was in the beginning, is now, and will be forever. Amen.

Come, let us bow down and bend the knee : let us kneel before the LORD our Maker.

Song "O Lord, Have Mercy"

We delight to walk in your way : lead us in your mercy.

Psalm 119:153–56
Behold my affliction and deliver me : **for I do not forget your law.**
Plead my cause and redeem me : **according to your promise, give me life.**
Deliverance is far from the wicked : **for they do not study your statutes.**
Great is your compassion, O LORD : **preserve my life, according to your judgments.**

We delight to walk in your way : lead us in your mercy.

Nehemiah 13:4–22   2 Corinthians 12:1–10

We delight to walk in your way : lead us in your mercy.

Clement of Rome wrote, "Let our whole body, then, be preserved in Christ Jesus; and let everyone be subject to his neighbor. Let the strong not despise the weak, and let the weak show respect to the strong. Let the rich man provide for the wants of the poor; and let the poor man bless God, because he has given him a community that can provide for his needs. Let us consider then, brothers, the matter out of which we were made, how we came into the world, from utter darkness, as if emerging from a grave. He who made us and fashioned us, prepared his bountiful gifts for us before we were born, and introduced us into his world. Since, therefore, we receive all these things from him, we ought to give him thanks for everything; to whom be glory forever and ever. Amen."

Prayers for Others

Our Father

Lord, when we weary of the journey, strengthen us by your Spirit to imagine new heavens and a new earth. Amen.

**May the peace of the Lord Christ go with you : wherever he may send you;
may he guide you through the wilderness : protect you through the storm;
may he bring you home rejoicing : at the wonders he has shown you;
may he bring you home rejoicing : once again into our doors.**

✺ October 27

O Lord, let my soul rise up to meet you
as the day rises to meet the sun.

**Glory to the Father, and to the Son, and to the Holy Spirit,
as it was in the beginning, is now, and will be forever. Amen.**

Come, let us sing to the LORD : let us shout for joy to the Rock of our salvation.

Song "Solid Rock"

If it had not been for the Lord on our side : tell me, where would we be?

Psalm 124:1–5
If the LORD had not been on our side : **let Israel now say;**
if the LORD had not been on our side : **when enemies rose up against us;**
then would they have swallowed us up alive : **in their fierce anger toward us;**
then would the waters have overwhelmed us : **and the torrent gone over us;**
then would the raging waters : **have gone right over us.**

If it had not been for the Lord on our side : tell me, where would we be?

Morning Prayer 493

Ezra 7:1–26   2 Corinthians 12:11–21

If it had not been for the Lord on our side : tell me, where would we be?

The ancient *Letter to Diognetus* records these observations about the early church: "The Christians are distinguished from other men neither by country, nor by language, nor by the customs that they observe; for they neither inhabit cities of their own, nor employ a peculiar form of speech. They dwell in their own countries, but simply as sojourners. They marry, as do all others; they beget children; but they do not destroy their offspring. They have a common table, but not a common bed. They are in the flesh, but they do not live after the flesh. They pass their days on earth, but they are citizens of heaven. They obey the prescribed laws, and at the same time surpass the laws by their lives. They love all men, and are persecuted by all. They are unknown and condemned; they are put to death, and restored to life. They are poor, yet they make many rich; they are lacking all things, and yet abound in all; they are dishonored, and yet in their very dishonor are glorified. They are spoken of as evil, and yet are justified; they are reviled, and bless; they are insulted and repay the insult with honor; they do good, yet are punished as evildoers."

Prayers for Others

Our Father

With each new morning, Lord, we praise you and delight that our lives are in your hand. Your goodness sustains us. Your calling gives us purpose. Your victory ensures that our times are in your hands. Amen.

May the peace of the Lord Christ go with you : wherever he may send you;
may he guide you through the wilderness : protect you through the storm;
may he bring you home rejoicing : at the wonders he has shown you;
may he bring you home rejoicing : once again into our doors.

October 28

O Lord, let my soul rise up to meet you
as the day rises to meet the sun.

Glory to the Father, and to the Son, and to the Holy Spirit,
as it was in the beginning, is now, and will be forever. Amen.

Come, let us sing to the L{\sc ord} : let us shout for joy to the Rock of our salvation.

Song   "Fairest Lord Jesus"

O Jesus, how I love your name : its power is every day the same.

Psalm 135:13–14, 19–21
O LORD, your name is everlasting : **your renown, O LORD, endures from age to age.**
For the LORD gives his people justice : **and shows compassion to his servants.**
Bless the LORD, O house of Israel : **O house of Aaron, bless the LORD.**
Bless the LORD, O house of Levi : **you who fear the LORD, bless the LORD.**
Blessed be the LORD out of Zion : **who dwells in Jerusalem. Hallelujah!**

O Jesus, how I love your name : its power is every day the same.

Ezra 9:1–15   2 Corinthians 13:1–14

O Jesus, how I love your name : its power is every day the same.

In his *Rule* for monastic communities, Benedict of Nursia wrote, "Such a follower of Christ lives in reverence of him and does not take the credit for a good life but, believing that all the good we do comes from the Lord, gives him the credit and thanksgiving for what his gift brings about in our hearts. In that spirit our prayer from the psalm should be: Not to us, O Lord, not to us give the glory but to your own name. That is St Paul's example, for he took no credit to himself for his preaching when he said: It is by God's grace that I am what I am. And again he says: Let anyone who wants to boast, boast in the Lord."

Prayers for Others

Our Father

You, who led Israel through the waters, plant us by streams of living water. Root us in your love and grow us up to bear the fruit of your Spirit: love, joy, peace, patience, kindness, goodness, faithfulness, gentleness, and self-control. Amen.

**May the peace of the Lord Christ go with you : wherever he may send you;
may he guide you through the wilderness : protect you through the storm;
may he bring you home rejoicing : at the wonders he has shown you;
may he bring you home rejoicing : once again into our doors.**

 October 29

Clarence Jordan (1912–1969)

A son of the American South, Clarence Jordan was troubled by his people's comfortable embrace of both Jesus and racism. After studying for a doctorate in New Testament at the Southern Baptist Seminary, Jordan and his family returned to Georgia in 1942 to start Koinonia Farm, an interracial community in the heart of the Jim Crow South. Greeted by Ku Klux Klan members who told him, "We don't let the sun set on people like you around here," Jordan smiled and replied, "Pleased to meet y'all. I've been waiting all my life to meet someone who could make the sun stand still."

O Lord, let my soul rise up to meet you
as the day rises to meet the sun.

**Glory to the Father, and to the Son, and to the Holy Spirit,
as it was in the beginning, is now, and will be forever. Amen.**

Come, let us sing to the LORD : let us shout for joy to the Rock of our salvation.

Song "Amazing Grace"

May a great move of God spread : through earth, as through the heavens.

Psalm 140:1–3, 7–9
Deliver me, O LORD, from evildoers : **protect me from the violent,**
who devise evil in their hearts : **and stir up strife all day long.**
They have sharpened their tongues like a serpent : **adder's poison is under their lips.**
O Lord GOD, the strength of my salvation : **you have covered my head in the day of battle.**
Do not grant the desires of the wicked, O LORD : **nor let their evil plans prosper.**
Let not those who surround me lift up their heads : **let the evil of their lips overwhelm them.**

May a great move of God spread : through earth, as through the heavens.

Ezra 10:1–17   Titus 1:1–16

May a great move of God spread : through earth, as through the heavens.

Clarence Jordan wrote, "Jesus has been so zealously worshiped, his deity so vehemently affirmed, his halo so brightly illumined, and his cross so beautifully polished that in the minds of many he no longer exists as a man. By thus glorifying him we more effectively rid ourselves of him than did those who tried to do so by crudely crucifying him."

Prayers for Others

Our Father

God, keep us from the temptation to so polish your image that those who most need your love feel too dirty to approach you. Amen.

**May the peace of the Lord Christ go with you : wherever he may send you;
may he guide you through the wilderness : protect you through the storm;**

may he bring you home rejoicing : at the wonders he has shown you;
may he bring you home rejoicing : once again into our doors.

✶ October 30

O Lord, let my soul rise up to meet you
as the day rises to meet the sun.

**Glory to the Father, and to the Son, and to the Holy Spirit,
as it was in the beginning, is now, and will be forever. Amen.**

Come, let us bow down and bend the knee : let us kneel before the LORD our Maker.

Song "O Lord, Hear My Prayer"

Tune our spirits, Lord : to sing out with the sky.

Psalm 145:19–22
The LORD is near to those who call upon him : **to all who call upon him faithfully.**
He fulfills the desire of those who fear him : **he hears their cry and helps them.**
The LORD preserves all those who love him : **but he destroys all the wicked.**
My mouth shall speak the praise of the LORD : **let all flesh bless his holy name for ever and ever.**

Tune our spirits, Lord : to sing out with the sky.

Nehemiah 9:1–38   Titus 2:1–3:15

Tune our spirits, Lord : to sing out with the sky.

Russian novelist Fyodor Dostoyevsky said, "The world will be saved by beauty."

Prayers for Others

Our Father

Go before us, God, that we may follow in your steps. Go behind us, God, to steer us when we stray. Go beside us, God, as our strength and our joy for the journey. Amen.

**May the peace of the Lord Christ go with you : wherever he may send you;
may he guide you through the wilderness : protect you through the storm;
may he bring you home rejoicing : at the wonders he has shown you;
may he bring you home rejoicing : once again into our doors.**

October 31

O Lord, let my soul rise up to meet you
as the day rises to meet the sun.

**Glory to the Father, and to the Son, and to the Holy Spirit,
as it was in the beginning, is now, and will be forever. Amen.**

Come, let us bow down and bend the knee : let us kneel before the Lord our Maker.

Song "Jesus, Help Us Live in Peace"

I bind unto myself today : the strong name of the Trinity.

Psalm 146:4–9
Happy are they who have the God of Jacob for their help! : **whose hope is in the Lord their God;**
who made heaven and earth, the seas, and all that is in them : **who keeps his promise for ever;**
who gives justice to those who are oppressed : **and food to those who hunger.**
The Lord sets the prisoners free; the Lord opens the eyes of the blind : **the Lord lifts up those who are bowed down;**
the Lord loves the righteous; the Lord cares for the stranger : **he sustains the orphan and widow, but frustrates the way of the wicked.**
The Lord shall reign for ever : **your God, O Zion, throughout all generations. Hallelujah!**

I bind unto myself today : the strong name of the Trinity.

Nehemiah 7:73b–8:3, 5–18   Philemon 1–25

I bind unto myself today : the strong name of the Trinity.

Patrick of Ireland prayed this prayer:

> Against all Satan's spells and wiles
> against false words of heresy,
> against the knowledge that defiles,
> against the heart's idolatry,
> against the wizard's evil craft,
> against the death-wound and the burning,
> the choking wave and poisoned shaft,
> protect me, Christ, till thy returning.

Prayers for Others

Our Father

Draw us ever closer into your community, Father, Son, and Holy Spirit, that we might love one another and work with one another in ways that mirror your care and unending love. Amen.

May the peace of the Lord Christ go with you : wherever he may send you;
may he guide you through the wilderness : protect you through the storm;
may he bring you home rejoicing : at the wonders he has shown you;
may he bring you home rejoicing : once again into our doors.

> **Becoming the Answer to Our Prayers: A Few Ideas**
> 1. Start setting aside 10 percent of your income to give away to folks in need.
> 2. Write letters (by hand on paper) for a month. Try writing to someone who needs encouragement or to whom you should say, "I'm sorry."
> 3. Contact your local crisis pregnancy center and invite a pregnant woman to live with your family.
> 4. Go without food for one day to remember the two billion people who live on less than a dollar a day.
> 5. Find a piece of land and care for it. Create a little guerilla garden, and participate with God to help it bear food and flowers. Have kids help out or get a school or youth group involved.

NOVEMBER — DOROTHY DAY

NOVEMBER

Marks of New Monasticism
Nurturing a Common Life

Independence is a value of our culture, but it is not a gospel value. Jesus lived in community and was part of a village culture. Remember the incident in his youth when his parents lost track of him for several days during the Passover festival (Luke 2)? Don't you sort of wonder how you lose your kid, especially when you are raising the Messiah? They were part of a village, traveling together, and probably trusting that he was in the good hands of some friend or family member. Jesus' culture was more like the Bedouins than the burbs.

The Scriptures teach us to value interdependence and community more highly than independence, and tell us that we are to lose our lives if we want to find them. Forming our lives around something other than our own desires, jobs, and goals is radically countercultural. Even our architecture is built around individual families, not around community. But for many Native Americans and tribal cultures, society and architecture are built around a village. Individual dwellings, like the tepee, are very small, and they are built around a central common space where people eat, dance, sing, and tell stories. The rampant individualism of Western society is a relatively new thing, and its emptiness is increasingly evident. We are wealthy and lonely. But God invites us into a common life with others.

Rather than build our lives around the individualistic dream of a house with a white picket fence, we can build our lives around God's vision for community.

We dream of a holy village in the middle of the urban desert, with a little cluster of row homes sprinkled about and a neighborhood where folks are committed to God and to each other. Some folks are indigenous to the neighborhood. Some are missional relocators. Some have gone off to school, trained as doctors, lawyers, social workers, or business folk, and then returned to the neighborhood to offer their gifts to the work of restoration. The houses are small, but that is all we need — a place to lay our heads — because most of our lives are lived on the streets, on the stoop, sweating in the practice of resurrection. Village life begins by greeting the day in morning prayer, and in the evenings we share a meal or grill out on the street. Maybe there is a village center where folks can cook healthy breakfasts

> **Suggested Reading for the Month**
> *Life Together* by Dietrich Bonhoeffer
> *Why We Live in Community* by Eberhard Arnold
> *Community and Growth* by Jean Vanier

for the kids as they head off to school. Perhaps in that center there are laundry machines that we can all share and a game library where kids can borrow a game for the afternoon. Maybe there's a tool library so folks can check out a saw or a drill for the day; maybe there's an exercise space for lifting weights or taking an aerobics class to keep our bodies healthy. It's a dream for a village that shares things in common, a space that makes sure possessions and privileges are available for all, a place on earth where there truly is a "common wealth."

Shaping a life together sometimes begins simply by creating a space for community. For many intentional communities, that means that we work only part-time so that we free up time for things we don't get paid to do, like welcoming homeless folks for a meal, helping neighborhood kids with homework, planting gardens on abandoned lots, or praying together each day. Sometimes we have to remove some of the clutter that is occupying our time and energy, like getting rid of the television. But then, as we say no to some things, we say yes to others — cooking meals, painting murals, playing games. And most people don't miss the old life much anyway. A reporter once told Mother Teresa, "I wouldn't do what you do for a million dollars." She responded, "Me neither." We live in community and among the suffering because it is what we are made for. Not only does it give life to others, but it gives us life as well.

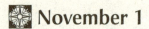 **November 1**

All Saints

Since its earliest centuries, the church has set aside a day to remember the great cloud of witnesses who have gone before us in the faith, stretching across the centuries and around the globe. However hard it might seem to follow the way of Jesus in our own time and place, this is a day to remember that we may be crazy, but we are not alone.

O Lord, let my soul rise up to meet you
as the day rises to meet the sun.

**Glory to the Father, and to the Son, and to the Holy Spirit,
as it was in the beginning, is now, and will be forever. Amen.**

Come, let us sing to the LORD : let us shout for joy to the Rock of our salvation.

Song "When the Saints Go Marching In"

Heaven and earth are full of your glory : Hosanna in the highest!

Psalm 8
O LORD our Governor : **how exalted is your name in all the world!**
Out of the mouths of infants and children : **your majesty is praised above the heavens.**
You have set up a stronghold against your adversaries : **to quell the enemy and the avenger.**
When I consider your heavens, the work of your fingers : **the moon and the stars you have set in their courses,**
what is man that you should be mindful of him? : **the son of man that you should seek him out?**
you have made him but little lower than the angels : **you adorn him with glory and honor;**
you give him mastery over the works of your hands : **you put all things under his feet:**
all sheep and oxen : **even the wild beasts of the field,**
the birds of the air, the fish of the sea : **and whatsoever walks in the paths of the sea.**
O LORD our Governor : **how exalted is your name in all the world!**

Revelation 7:2–4, 9–17   Matthew 5:1–12

Heaven and earth are full of your glory : Hosanna in the highest!

Fourteenth-century mystic Meister Eckhart said, "Do not think that saintliness comes from occupation; it depends rather on what one is. The kind of work we do does not make us holy, but we may make it holy."

Heaven and earth are full of your glory : Hosanna in the highest!

Prayer for Others

Our Father

Lord, your saints come from every nation and every tribe. Such is the beauty of your kingdom, where every race and people are honored and recognized as being made in your image. Help us live lives of peace and reconciliation that pay homage to the diversity of your great cloud of witnesses. Amen.

May the peace of the Lord Christ go with you : wherever he may send you; may he guide you through the wilderness : protect you through the storm; may he bring you home rejoicing : at the wonders he has shown you; may he bring you home rejoicing : once again into our doors.

> For centuries, many traditions have sung a simple Alleluia chorus before and after the reading of the Gospel. Feel free to do that throughout the year as you pray. *Alleluia* means "praise God." When Lent comes around and we spend forty days fasting and preparing ourselves for Easter, we omit the Alleluia. Then, on Easter morning, we let it burst out again—like Jesus coming out of the grave. So every Alleluia is a little celebration that our God is stronger than death. Alleluia!

✦ November 2

In 1996, the first World Christian Gathering of Indigenous People took place in Rotorua, New Zealand. Founded by a Maori couple, Monte and Linda Ohia, the World Christian Gathering is a coming together of the world's indigenous peoples to worship the Creator and celebrate their traditional cultures.

O Lord, let my soul rise up to meet you
as the day rises to meet the sun.

Glory to the Father, and to the Son, and to the Holy Spirit,
as it was in the beginning, is now, and will be forever. Amen.

Come, let us bow down and bend the knee : let us kneel before the Lord our Maker.

Song "Let All Mortal Flesh Keep Silence"

Pardon, Lord, what we ask in ignorance : but hear our cry for justice.

Morning Prayer

Psalm 9:16–20
The LORD is known by his acts of justice : **the wicked are trapped in the works of their own hands.**
The wicked shall be given over to the grave : **and also all the peoples that forget God.**
For the needy shall not always be forgotten : **and the hope of the poor shall not perish for ever.**
Rise up, O LORD, let not the ungodly have the upper hand : **let them be judged before you.**
Put fear upon them, O LORD : **let the ungodly know they are but mortal.**

Pardon, Lord, what we ask in ignorance : but hear our cry for justice.

Joel 1:1–13   Revelation 8:1–13

Pardon, Lord, what we ask in ignorance : but hear our cry for justice.

Great preacher and civil rights leader Martin Luther King Jr. said, "Injustice anywhere is a threat to justice everywhere. We are caught in an inescapable network of mutuality, tied in a single garment of destiny. Whatever affects one directly affects all indirectly."

Prayers for Others

Our Father

God, we are so used to seeing ourselves as individuals with personal destinies. Remind us that we are made in your image, the image of community. Help us to love each other and be made one as you are one. Whisper your love to us and let us whisper your love to the world today. Amen.

May the peace of the Lord Christ go with you : wherever he may send you;
may he guide you through the wilderness : protect you through the storm;
may he bring you home rejoicing : at the wonders he has shown you;
may he bring you home rejoicing : once again into our doors.

November 3

Martin de Porres
The illegitimate son of a Spanish nobleman in sixteenth-century Peru, Martin de Porres bore the complexion of his black mother. He presented himself at fifteen as someone who could sweep the floors at a Dominican monastery, but his talents, especially in the art of healing, were soon recognized. As head of the monastery's infirmary, Martin not only treated the brothers but went out into the streets of Peru and brought in the poor, even offering his own bed for them to sleep in. When Martin was made a saint in 1962, Pope John XXIII named him patron of all who work for social justice.

O Lord, let my soul rise up to meet you
as the day rises to meet the sun.

**Glory to the Father, and to the Son, and to the Holy Spirit,
as it was in the beginning, is now, and will be forever. Amen.**

Come, let us sing to the LORD : let us shout for joy to the Rock of our salvation.

Song "Ubi Caritas"

You, O LORD, are my lamp : my God, you make my darkness bright.

Psalm 18:21–25
The LORD rewarded me because of my righteous dealing : **because my hands were clean he rewarded me;**
for I have kept the ways of the LORD : **and have not offended against my God;**
for all his judgments are before my eyes : **and his decrees I have not put away from me;**
for I have been blameless with him : **and have kept myself from iniquity;**
therefore the LORD rewarded me according to my righteous dealing : **because of the cleanness of my hands in his sight.**

You, O LORD, are my lamp : my God, you make my darkness bright.

Joel 1:15–20   Revelation 9:1–12

You, O LORD, are my lamp : my God, you make my darkness bright.

A contemporary of Martin de Porres testified, "He was a man of great charity, who being in charge of the infirmary not only healed his brother religious when they were sick but also assisted in the larger duty of spreading the Great Love of the world. For this they knew him as their father and consolation, calling him father of the poor."

Prayers for Others

Our Father

Lord, when we open our hands and hearts to the poor, your kingdom is at hand. Remind us that there is always enough to give to those who are in need. Make us generous today with the goods you have entrusted to us. Amen.

**May the peace of the Lord Christ go with you : wherever he may send you;
may he guide you through the wilderness : protect you through the storm;
may he bring you home rejoicing : at the wonders he has shown you;
may he bring you home rejoicing : once again into our doors.**

✤ November 4

Watchman Nee (1903–1972)

Watchman Nee was a Chinese church leader in the early twentieth century. He was born into a Methodist family on November 4, 1903. Nee was a courageous pastor and writer who saw a great revival in China. He had no formal theological training, but with a deep commitment, he undertook thirty years of ministry in the underground church in China. Eventually he was imprisoned for his faith and remained in prison for two decades until his death in 1972.

O Lord, let my soul rise up to meet you
as the day rises to meet the sun.

**Glory to the Father, and to the Son, and to the Holy Spirit,
as it was in the beginning, is now, and will be forever. Amen.**

Come, let us bow down and bend the knee : let us kneel before the Lord our Maker.

Song "Poor Wayfaring Stranger"

Be not far away, O Lord : you are my strength; hasten to help me.

Psalm 22:12–17
Many young bulls encircle me : **strong bulls of Bashan surround me.**
They open wide their jaws at me : **like a ravening and a roaring lion.**
I am poured out like water; all my bones are out of joint : **my heart within my breast is melting wax.**
My mouth is dried out like a pot-sherd; my tongue sticks to the roof of my mouth : **and you have laid me in the dust of the grave.**
Packs of dogs close me in, and gangs of evildoers circle around me : **they pierce my hands and my feet; I can count all my bones.**
They stare and gloat over me : **they divide my garments among them; they cast lots for my clothing.**

Be not far away, O Lord : you are my strength; hasten to help me.

Joel 2:1–11   Revelation 9:13–21

Be not far away, O Lord : you are my strength; hasten to help me.

Salvadoran martyr Rutilio Grande said, "It is a dangerous thing to be a Christian in our world."

Prayers for Others

Our Father

Lord, remind us that we are resident aliens, called to be in the world but not of it. Show us today what it means to live as though your kingdom has come, while trusting that it is still coming. Amen.

May the peace of the Lord Christ go with you : wherever he may send you; may he guide you through the wilderness : protect you through the storm; may he bring you home rejoicing : at the wonders he has shown you; may he bring you home rejoicing : once again into our doors.

 # November 5

O Lord, let my soul rise up to meet you
as the day rises to meet the sun.

Glory to the Father, and to the Son, and to the Holy Spirit, as it was in the beginning, is now, and will be forever. Amen.

Come, let us bow down and bend the knee : let us kneel before the LORD our Maker.

Song "Fairest Lord Jesus"

Teach us the fear that leads to wisdom : and the love that drives out fear.

Psalm 25:11–14
Who are they who fear the LORD? : **he will teach them the way that they should choose.**
They shall dwell in prosperity : **and their offspring shall inherit the land.**
The LORD is a friend to those who fear him : **and will show them his covenant.**
My eyes are ever looking to the LORD : **for he shall pluck my feet out of the net.**

Teach us the fear that leads to wisdom : and the love that drives out fear.

Joel 2:12–19   Revelation 10:1–11

Teach us the fear that leads to wisdom : and the love that drives out fear.

Desert father Anthony of Egypt said, "I no longer fear God, but I love him."

Prayers for Others

Our Father

Lord, if we are to be afraid of anything, let it be the fear of not committing ourselves fully to you. Let us fear that the day will pass without our having lightened the load of another. Let us fear that someone will come looking for you and find only us. Amen.

May the peace of the Lord Christ go with you : wherever he may send you; may he guide you through the wilderness : protect you through the storm; may he bring you home rejoicing : at the wonders he has shown you; may he bring you home rejoicing : once again into our doors.

 # November 6

O Lord, let my soul rise up to meet you
as the day rises to meet the sun.

Glory to the Father, and to the Son, and to the Holy Spirit, as it was in the beginning, is now, and will be forever. Amen.

Come, let us bow down and bend the knee : let us kneel before the Lord our Maker.

Song "O Lord, Have Mercy"

Rescue me from the hand of my enemy : and from thoughts that trouble me.

Psalm 31:9–12
Have mercy on me, O Lord, for I am in trouble : **my eye is consumed with sorrow, and also my throat and my belly.**
For my life is wasted with grief, and my years with sighing : **my strength fails me because of affliction, and my bones are consumed.**
I have become a reproach to all my enemies and even to my neighbors, a dismay to those of my acquaintance : **when they see me in the street they avoid me.**
I am forgotten like a dead man, out of mind : **I am as useless as a broken pot.**

Rescue me from the hand of my enemy : and from thoughts that trouble me.

Joel 2:21–27   Revelation 11:1–14

Rescue me from the hand of my enemy : and from thoughts that trouble me.

Desert mother Amma Theodora said, "There was a monk, who, because of the great number of his temptations, said, 'I will go away from here.' As he was putting on his sandals, he saw another man who was also putting on his sandals and this other monk said to him, 'Is it on my account that you are going away? Because I go before you wherever you are going.'"

Prayers for Others

Our Father

Lord, show us when the enemy we fear is to be found within ourselves. Equip us, then, with the sword of your word and the shield of faith that we might stand our ground in this place where you have called us to dwell together in unity. Amen.

May the peace of the Lord Christ go with you : wherever he may send you; may he guide you through the wilderness : protect you through the storm; may he bring you home rejoicing : at the wonders he has shown you; may he bring you home rejoicing : once again into our doors.

 November 7

O Lord, let my soul rise up to meet you
as the day rises to meet the sun.

Glory to the Father, and to the Son, and to the Holy Spirit, as it was in the beginning, is now, and will be forever. Amen.

Come, let us sing to the LORD : let us shout for joy to the Rock of our salvation.

Song "The Kingdom of God"

Establish our works in justice, Lord : and make us anew out of the stuff that lasts.

Psalm 37:19–21, 28–29
The LORD cares for the lives of the godly : **and their inheritance shall last for ever.**
They shall not be ashamed in bad times : **and in days of famine they shall have enough.**
As for the wicked, they shall perish : **and the enemies of the LORD, like the glory of the meadows, shall vanish; they shall vanish like smoke.**
Turn from evil, and do good : **and dwell in the land for ever.**
For the LORD loves justice : **he does not forsake his faithful ones.**

Establish our works in justice, Lord : and make us anew out of the stuff that lasts.

Joel 2:28–3:8   Revelation 11:14–19

Establish our works in justice, Lord : and make us anew out of the stuff that lasts.

A reading from Paul's letter to the Romans: "Therefore, I urge you, brothers and sisters, in view of God's mercy, to offer your bodies as a living sacrifice, holy and pleasing to God — this is true worship. Do not conform to the pattern of this world, but be transformed by the renewing of your mind. Then you will be able to test and approve what God's will is — his good, pleasing and perfect will."

Prayers for Others

Our Father

Lord, save us from times of trial, strengthen us to stand firm in the faith, and fill us with joy at your coming. Amen.

**May the peace of the Lord Christ go with you : wherever he may send you;
may he guide you through the wilderness : protect you through the storm;
may he bring you home rejoicing : at the wonders he has shown you;
may he bring you home rejoicing : once again into our doors.**

 # November 8

O Lord, let my soul rise up to meet you
as the day rises to meet the sun.

Glory to the Father, and to the Son, and to the Holy Spirit,
as it was in the beginning, is now, and will be forever. Amen.

Come, let us sing to the Lord : let us shout for joy to the Rock of our salvation.

Song "Great Is Thy Faithfulness"

If it had not been for the Lord on my side : tell me, where would I be?

Psalm 40:7–11
In sacrifice and offering you take no pleasure : **(you have given me ears to hear you);**
burnt offering and sin offering you have not required : **and so I said, "Behold, I come.**
In the roll of the book it is written concerning me : **'I love to do your will, O my God; your law is deep in my heart.'"**
I proclaimed righteousness in the great congregation : **behold, I did not restrain my lips; and that, O Lord, you know.**
Your righteousness have I not hidden in my heart; I have spoken of your faithfulness and your deliverance : **I have not concealed your love and faithfulness from the great congregation.**

If it had not been for the Lord on my side : tell me, where would I be?

Joel 3:9–17   Revelation 12:1–6

If it had not been for the Lord on my side : tell me, where would I be?

Dorothy Day, co-founder of the Catholic Worker Movement, wrote, "Whatever I had read as a child about the saints had thrilled me. I could see the nobility of giving one's life for the sick, the maimed, the leper. But there was another question in my mind. Why was so much done in remedying the evil instead of avoiding it in the first place? Where were the saints to try to change the social order, not just to minister to the slaves, but to do away with slavery?"

Prayers for Others

Our Father

Lord, we are slow to come to our senses. Often our feeble offerings are merely extensions of our sin. Quicken your Spirit within us and move us to offer up that which is pleasing to you: justice, kindness, and humility of heart. Amen.

**May the peace of the Lord Christ go with you : wherever he may send you;
may he guide you through the wilderness : protect you through the storm;
may he bring you home rejoicing : at the wonders he has shown you;
may he bring you home rejoicing : once again into our doors.**

 # November 9

In 1989, the Berlin Wall fell, signaling an end to the Cold War and a victory for the long nonviolent resistance to communism in Eastern Europe.

O Lord, let my soul rise up to meet you
as the day rises to meet the sun.

**Glory to the Father, and to the Son, and to the Holy Spirit,
as it was in the beginning, is now, and will be forever. Amen.**

Come, let us sing to the LORD : let us shout for joy to the Rock of our salvation.

Song   "This Little Light of Mine"

You have conquered, O Lamb of God : lead us on to victory.

Psalm 44:3–7
For they did not take the land by their sword, nor did their arm win the victory for them : **but your right hand, your arm, and the light of your countenance, because you favored them.**
You are my King and my God : **you command victories for Jacob.**

Through you we pushed back our adversaries : **through your name we trampled on those who rose up against us.**
For I do not rely on my bow : **and my sword does not give me the victory.**
Surely, you gave us victory over our adversaries : **and put those who hate us to shame.**

You have conquered, O Lamb of God : lead us on to victory.

Habakkuk 1:1–2:1   Revelation 12:7–17

You have conquered, O Lamb of God : lead us on to victory.

Twentieth-century peace activist A. J. Muste often said, "There is no way to peace, peace itself being the way."

Prayers for Others

Our Father

Lord, any good thing that comes today is of your doing. Any victory over injustice, poverty, hunger, sickness, loneliness, displacement, and greed is by your might. We are merely channels for your work. Use us as you see fit and help us stand back when necessary. Amen.

May the peace of the Lord Christ go with you : wherever he may send you;
may he guide you through the wilderness : protect you through the storm;
may he bring you home rejoicing : at the wonders he has shown you;
may he bring you home rejoicing : once again into our doors.

✺ November 10

On November 10, 1938, Jewish men and women in Germany were beaten and murdered by Nazi troops. Jewish shops were destroyed and hundreds of synagogues were burned, their broken windows giving the evening its name — Kristallnacht, "the night of glass." Some twenty-five thousand Jewish men were sent to concentration camps. Following the brutality, Jewish people were forced to clean up the debris and were banned from all hospitals.

O Lord, let my soul rise up to meet you
as the day rises to meet the sun.

Glory to the Father, and to the Son, and to the Holy Spirit,
as it was in the beginning, is now, and will be forever. Amen.

Come, let us bow down and bend the knee : let us kneel before the Lord our Maker.

Song "Come, Ye Sinners"

Jesus Christ, Son of God : have mercy on me, a sinner.

Psalm 51:1–4
Have mercy on me, O God, according to your loving-kindness : **in your great compassion blot out my offenses.**
Wash me through and through from my wickedness : **and cleanse me from my sin.**
For I know my transgressions : **and my sin is ever before me.**
Against you only have I sinned : **and done what is evil in your sight.**

Jesus Christ, Son of God : have mercy on me, a sinner.

Habakkuk 2:1–4, 9–20   Revelation 13:1–10

Jesus Christ, Son of God : have mercy on me, a sinner.

Desert father John Cassian wrote, "If we go into the desert with our faults still hidden within us, they no longer hurt others, but our love of them remains. Of every sin not eradicated, the root is still growing secretly within. If we compare our own strict discipline with the lax practices of another and feel the slightest temptation to puff ourselves up, it proves that the terrible plague of pride is still infecting us. If we still see these signs within, we know that it is not the desire to sin but the opportunity to sin which has vanished."

Prayers for Others

Our Father

How merciful you are, Lord, that you forgive us our sins, all our sins. Teach us the merciful art of public and private confession, not for our shame but for the cleansing of our sins and the fallowing of our rough hearts. Amen.

**May the peace of the Lord Christ go with you : wherever he may send you;
may he guide you through the wilderness : protect you through the storm;
may he bring you home rejoicing : at the wonders he has shown you;
may he bring you home rejoicing : once again into our doors.**

✺ November 11

Originally called Armistice Day, November 11 is set aside to remember the 24.9 million military veterans in the United States.

O Lord, let my soul rise up to meet you
as the day rises to meet the sun.

**Glory to the Father, and to the Son, and to the Holy Spirit,
as it was in the beginning, is now, and will be forever. Amen.**

Come, let us bow down and bend the knee : let us kneel before the Lord our Maker.

Song "O Lord, Hear My Prayer"

Listen, Lord, listen : not to our words but to our prayer.

Psalm 60:1–5
O God, you have cast us off and broken us : **you have been angry; oh, take us back to you again.**
You have shaken the earth and split it open : **repair the cracks in it, for it totters.**
You have made your people know hardship : **you have given us wine that makes us stagger.**
You have set up a banner for those who fear you : **to be a refuge from the power of the bow.**
Save us by your right hand and answer us : **that those who are dear to you may be delivered.**

Listen, Lord, listen : not to our words but to our prayer.

Habakkuk 3:1–18   Revelation 13:11–18

Listen, Lord, listen : not to our words but to our prayer.

Charles Péguy said, "We must be saved together. We cannot go to God alone; else he would ask, 'Where are the others?'"

Prayers for Others

Our Father

Lord, whether we face it or not, we do not live in isolation. Our words and our actions impact our communities. Help us to learn to speak after appropriate silence and reflection. Help us to recognize the work we can put our hands to so we are able to engage with it prayerfully and patiently. Amen.

**May the peace of the Lord Christ go with you : wherever he may send you;
may he guide you through the wilderness : protect you through the storm;
may he bring you home rejoicing : at the wonders he has shown you;
may he bring you home rejoicing : once again into our doors.**

November 12

O Lord, let my soul rise up to meet you
as the day rises to meet the sun.

**Glory to the Father, and to the Son, and to the Holy Spirit,
as it was in the beginning, is now, and will be forever. Amen.**

Come, let us sing to the LORD : **let us shout for joy to the Rock of our salvation.**

Song "Oh the Deep, Deep Love of Jesus"

Jesus, you've been better to me : than I have been to myself.

Psalm 66:14–18
Come and listen, all you who fear God : **and I will tell you what he has done for me.**
I called out to him with my mouth : **and his praise was on my tongue.**
If I had found evil in my heart : **the Lord would not have heard me;**
but in truth God has heard me : **he has attended to the voice of my prayer.**
Blessed be God, who has not rejected my prayer : **nor withheld his love from me.**

Jesus, you've been better to me : than I have been to myself.

Malachi 1:1, 6–14   Revelation 14:1–13

Jesus, you've been better to me : than I have been to myself.

Hymn writer Thomas Chisholm wrote these words:
> Great is thy faithfulness, Lord God our Father.
> There is no shadow of turning with thee.
> All I have needed thy hand hath provided.
> Great is thy faithfulness, Lord unto me.

Prayers for Others

Our Father

Thank you, God, that each morning you provide a new opportunity for us to follow you. We offer you the best of what we have, what already belongs to you. Let your tender mercies come to us that we might live. Amen.

**May the peace of the Lord Christ go with you : wherever he may send you;
may he guide you through the wilderness : protect you through the storm;
may he bring you home rejoicing : at the wonders he has shown you;
may he bring you home rejoicing : once again into our doors.**

November 13

O Lord, let my soul rise up to meet you
as the day rises to meet the sun.

**Glory to the Father, and to the Son, and to the Holy Spirit,
as it was in the beginning, is now, and will be forever. Amen.**

Come, let us sing to the LORD : **let us shout for joy to the Rock of our salvation.**

Song "Sing, O Sky (Gaao Re)"

Your majesty is over Israel, Lord : your strength is in the sky.

Psalm 68:28–34
Send forth your strength, O God : **establish, O God, what you have wrought for us.**
Kings shall bring gifts to you : **for your temple's sake at Jerusalem.**
Rebuke the wild beast of the reeds : **and the peoples, a herd of wild bulls with its calves.**
Trample down those who lust after silver : **scatter the peoples that delight in war.**
Let tribute be brought out of Egypt : **let Ethiopia stretch out her hands to God.**
Sing to God, O kingdoms of the earth : **sing praises to the Lord.**
He rides in the heavens, the ancient heavens : **he sends forth his voice, his mighty voice.**

Your majesty is over Israel, Lord : your strength is in the sky.

Malachi 2:1–16   Revelation 14:14–15:8

Your majesty is over Israel, Lord : your strength is in the sky.

John Scotus Eriugena, a ninth-century Irish monk, wrote, "Christ wears 'two shoes' in the world: Scripture and nature. Both are necessary to understand the Lord, and at no stage can creation be seen as a separation of things from God."

Prayers for Others

Our Father

Thank you, Lord, for the endless ways you reveal yourself to us. We are so quick to separate heaven from earth, but you shine forth in all things created by your hand. Teach us that to delight in the beauty of the earth is another way of praising you. Amen.

May the peace of the Lord Christ go with you : wherever he may send you;
may he guide you through the wilderness : protect you through the storm;
may he bring you home rejoicing : at the wonders he has shown you;
may he bring you home rejoicing : once again into our doors.

✹ November 14

O Lord, let my soul rise up to meet you
as the day rises to meet the sun.

**Glory to the Father, and to the Son, and to the Holy Spirit,
as it was in the beginning, is now, and will be forever. Amen.**

Come, let us bow down and bend the knee : let us kneel before the LORD our Maker.

Song "Guide My Feet"

Dispel our illusions, Jesus : that we might see the wisdom of your way.

Psalm 73:12–18
So then, these are the wicked : **always at ease, they increase their wealth.**
In vain have I kept my heart clean : **and washed my hands in innocence.**
I have been afflicted all day long : **and punished every morning.**
Had I gone on speaking this way : **I should have betrayed the generation of your children.**
When I tried to understand these things : **it was too hard for me;**
until I entered the sanctuary of God : **and discerned the end of the wicked.**
Surely, you set them in slippery places : **you cast them down in ruin.**

Dispel our illusions, Jesus : that we might see the wisdom of your way.

Malachi 3:1–12   Revelation 16:1–11

Dispel our illusions, Jesus : that we might see the wisdom of your way.

Fifth-century monk Nilus of Ancyra wrote, "We should remain within the limits imposed by our basic needs and strive with all our power not to exceed them. For once we are carried a little beyond these limits in our desire for the pleasures of life, there is then no criterion by which to check our onward movement, since no bounds can be set to that which exceeds the necessary."

Prayers for Others

Our Father

Lord, your refiner's fire peels away the dross of our self-making. Grant us the discipline and desire to be purified by you. Amen.

May the peace of the Lord Christ go with you : wherever he may send you;
may he guide you through the wilderness : protect you through the storm;
may he bring you home rejoicing : at the wonders he has shown you;
may he bring you home rejoicing : once again into our doors.

✣ November 15

O Lord, let my soul rise up to meet you
as the day rises to meet the sun.

Glory to the Father, and to the Son, and to the Holy Spirit,
as it was in the beginning, is now, and will be forever. Amen.

Come, let us sing to the LORD : let us shout for joy to the Rock of our salvation.

Song "I Will Trust in the Lord"

Risen Lord, teach us to trust : the power of your cross.

Psalm 78:18–22
They tested God in their hearts : **demanding food for their craving.**
They railed against God and said : **"Can God set a table in the wilderness?**
True, he struck the rock, the waters gushed out, and the gullies overflowed :
    but is he able to give bread or to provide meat for his people?"
When the LORD heard this, he was full of wrath : **a fire was kindled against**
    Jacob, and his anger mounted against Israel;
for they had no faith in God : **nor did they put their trust in his saving**
    power.

Risen Lord, teach us to trust : the power of your cross.

Malachi 3:13–4:6   Revelation 16:12–21

Risen Lord, teach us to trust : the power of your cross.

Death-row inmate Mumia Abu-Jamal has asked, "Isn't it odd that Christendom — that huge body of humankind that claims spiritual descent from the Jewish carpenter of Nazareth — claims to pray to and adore a being who was a prisoner of Roman power, an inmate of the empire's death row? That the one it considers the personification of the Creator of the Universe was tortured, humiliated, beaten, and crucified on a barren scrap of land on the imperial periphery, at Golgotha, the place of the skull? That the majority of its adherents strenuously support the state's execution of thousands of imprisoned citizens? That the overwhelming majority of its judges, prosecutors, and lawyers — those who condemn, prosecute, and sell out the condemned — claim to be followers of the fettered, spat-upon, naked God?"

Prayers for Others

Our Father

Lord, to know you, we must dwell on the reality of your life, not just your death and resurrection. Remind us of our roots in Nazareth, in Galilee, in Capernaum, in Judea, and on Golgotha. Remind us that a servant is no greater than their Master. Amen.

May the peace of the Lord Christ go with you : wherever he may send you; may he guide you through the wilderness : protect you through the storm; may he bring you home rejoicing : at the wonders he has shown you; may he bring you home rejoicing : once again into our doors.

 November 16

O Lord, let my soul rise up to meet you
as the day rises to meet the sun.

Glory to the Father, and to the Son, and to the Holy Spirit, as it was in the beginning, is now, and will be forever. Amen.

Come, let us bow down and bend the knee : let us kneel before the LORD our Maker.

Song "I Want Jesus to Walk with Me"

Teach us to proclaim with our lives : that we have no God but you.

Psalm 81:8–12
Hear, O my people, and I will admonish you : **O Israel, if you would but listen to me!**
There shall be no strange god among you : **you shall not worship a foreign god.**
I am the LORD your God, who brought you out of the land of Egypt and said : **"Open your mouth wide, and I will fill it."**
And yet my people did not hear my voice : **and Israel would not obey me.**
So I gave them over to the stubbornness of their hearts : **to follow their own devices.**

Teach us to proclaim with our lives : that we have no God but you.

Zechariah 9:9–16   Revelation 17:1–18

Teach us to proclaim with our lives : that we have no God but you.

Athenagoras said of the early church, "They charge us on two points: that we do not sacrifice and that we do not believe in the same gods as the State."

Prayers for Others

Our Father

Lord, keep us from following the gods of pride, stubbornness, vanity, sloth, greed, and comfort that beckon for our allegiance every day. You brought us through the night watches, you who neither slumber nor sleep. We pray to follow you along the path of generosity, humility, and love throughout this day. Amen.

May the peace of the Lord Christ go with you : wherever he may send you; may he guide you through the wilderness : protect you through the storm; may he bring you home rejoicing : at the wonders he has shown you; may he bring you home rejoicing : once again into our doors.

 # November 17

O Lord, let my soul rise up to meet you
as the day rises to meet the sun.

Glory to the Father, and to the Son, and to the Holy Spirit,
as it was in the beginning, is now, and will be forever. Amen.

Come, let us bow down and bend the knee : let us kneel before the LORD our Maker.

Song "Steal Away to Jesus"

Hide us, your anxious children : under the shadow of your wing.

Psalm 86:14–17
The arrogant rise up against me, O God, and a band of violent men seeks my life : **they have not set you before their eyes.**
But you, O LORD, are gracious and full of compassion : **slow to anger, and full of kindness and truth.**
Turn to me and have mercy upon me : **give your strength to your servant; and save the child of your handmaid.**
Show me a sign of your favor, so that those who hate me may see it and be ashamed : **because you, O LORD, have helped me and comforted me.**

Hide us, your anxious children : under the shadow of your wing.

Zechariah 10:1–12   Revelation 18:1–14

Hide us, your anxious children : under the shadow of your wing.

A passage from *Forgotten among the Lilies* by Ronald Rolheiser: "If the Catholicism that I was raised in had a fault, and it did, it was precisely that it did not allow for mistakes. It demanded that you get it right the first time. There was supposed to be no need for a second chance. If you made a mistake, you lived with it and, like the rich young man, were doomed to be sad, at least for the rest of your life. A serious mistake was a permanent stigmatization, a mark that you wore like Cain. I have seen that mark on all kinds of people: divorcees, ex-priests, ex-religious, people who have had abortions, married people who have had affairs, people who have had children outside of marriage, parents who have made serious mistakes with their children, and countless others who have made serious mistakes. There is too little around to help them. We need a theology of brokenness. We need a theology which teaches us that even though we cannot unscramble an egg, God's grace lets us live happily and with renewed innocence far beyond any egg we may have scrambled. We need a theology that teaches us that God does not just give us one chance, but that every time we close a door, he opens another one for us."

Prayers for Others

Our Father

Thank you, Lord, for the many ways you watch over and protect us in the course of the day. As you shelter us, show us also how to provide physical and spiritual shelter for those we encounter today. Amen.

May the peace of the Lord Christ go with you : wherever he may send you;
may he guide you through the wilderness : protect you through the storm;
may he bring you home rejoicing : at the wonders he has shown you;
may he bring you home rejoicing : once again into our doors.

✹ November 18

O Lord, let my soul rise up to meet you
as the day rises to meet the sun.

Glory to the Father, and to the Son, and to the Holy Spirit,
as it was in the beginning, is now, and will be forever. Amen.

Come, let us bow down and bend the knee : let us kneel before the Lord our Maker.

Song   "Be Thou My Vision"

Give us rest, O God : that we might delight in the work you are doing.

Psalm 94:12–15
Happy are they whom you instruct, O Lord! : **whom you teach out of your law;**
to give them rest in evil days : **until a pit is dug for the wicked.**
For the LORD will not abandon his people : **nor will he forsake his own.**
For judgment will again be just : **and all the true of heart will follow it.**

Give us rest, O God : that we might delight in the work you are doing.

Zechariah 11:4–17   Revelation 18:15–24

Give us rest, O God : that we might delight in the work you are doing.

Pope Clement said in the first century, "If we review the various ages of history, we will see that in every generation the Lord has offered the opportunity of repentance to any who were willing to turn to him. When Noah preached God's message of repentance, all who listened to him were saved. Jonah told the Ninevites they were going to be destroyed, but when they repented, their prayers gained God's forgiveness for their sins, and they were saved, even though they were not of God's people. We should be suppliant before him and turn to his compassion, rejecting empty works and quarreling and jealousy, which only lead to death."

Prayers for Others

Our Father

Lord, you always provide a way for us to turn back to you. Remind us that there is always hope for the weary, the wounded, the lost, and the contrite of heart. Help us receive this good news and share it with others. Amen.

May the peace of the Lord Christ go with you : wherever he may send you;
may he guide you through the wilderness : protect you through the storm;
may he bring you home rejoicing : at the wonders he has shown you;
may he bring you home rejoicing : once again into our doors.

November 19

O Lord, let my soul rise up to meet you
as the day rises to meet the sun.

Glory to the Father, and to the Son, and to the Holy Spirit,
as it was in the beginning, is now, and will be forever. Amen.

Come, let us sing to the LORD : let us shout for joy to the Rock of our salvation.

Song "Sing and Rejoice"

God is good all the time : all the time, God is good.

Psalm 98:1–5
Sing to the LORD a new song : **for he has done marvelous things.**
With his right hand and his holy arm : **has he won for himself the victory.**
The LORD has made known his victory : **his righteousness has he openly shown in the sight of the nations.**
He remembers his mercy and faithfulness to the house of Israel : **and all the ends of the earth have seen the victory of our God.**
Shout with joy to the LORD, all you lands : **lift up your voice, rejoice, and sing.**

God is good all the time : all the time, God is good.

Zechariah 12:1–10   Revelation 19:1–10

God is good all the time : all the time, God is good.

A reading from *The Cloud of Unknowing*: "For I tell you this: one loving, blind desire for God alone is more valuable in itself, more pleasing to God and to the saints, more beneficial to your own growth, and more helpful to your friends, both living and dead, than anything else you could do."

Prayers for Others

Our Father

Lord, we boldly and unabashedly declare our love for you and our faith in your precepts. You are the Lord of life, the light in the darkness, the salvation for the world, the God who was and is and is to come. We pray to make this day one of celebration simply because you are God. Amen.

May the peace of the Lord Christ go with you : wherever he may send you; may he guide you through the wilderness : protect you through the storm; may he bring you home rejoicing : at the wonders he has shown you; may he bring you home rejoicing : once again into our doors.

✣ November 20

O Lord, let my soul rise up to meet you
as the day rises to meet the sun.

**Glory to the Father, and to the Son, and to the Holy Spirit,
as it was in the beginning, is now, and will be forever. Amen.**

Come, let us sing to the Lord : let us shout for joy to the Rock of our salvation.

Song "We Shall Not Be Moved"

Root us in a place, Lord : that we might find our home in you.

Psalm 102:17–22
He will look with favor on the prayer of the homeless : **he will not despise their plea.**
Let this be written for a future generation : **so that a people yet unborn may praise the Lord.**
For the Lord looked down from his holy place on high : **from the heavens he beheld the earth;**
that he might hear the groan of the captive : **and set free those condemned to die;**
that they may declare in Zion the name of the Lord : **and his praise in Jerusalem;**
when the peoples are gathered together : **and the kingdoms also, to serve the Lord.**

Root us in a place, Lord : that we might find our home in you.

Zechariah 13:1–9   Revelation 19:11–21

Root us in a place, Lord : that we might find our home in you.

Gregory of Nyssa wrote in the fourth century, "This is the most marvelous thing of all: how the same thing is both a standing still and a moving. I mean by this that the firmer and the more immovable someone remains in the Good, the more he progresses in the course of the virtues. It is like using the standing still as if it were a wing while the heart flies upward through its stability in the Good."

Prayers for Others

Our Father

Lord, to be rooted in place takes commitment to land, to people, to friends and family, to transients in our community, and to the plight of our neighborhoods. Being rooted is no easy task, but you demonstrated such rootedness in your incarnation. Give us courage to take up the hard task of knowing you while standing in place. Amen.

**May the peace of the Lord Christ go with you : wherever he may send you;
may he guide you through the wilderness : protect you through the storm;
may he bring you home rejoicing : at the wonders he has shown you;
may he bring you home rejoicing : once again into our doors.**

✹ November 21

O Lord, let my soul rise up to meet you
as the day rises to meet the sun.

**Glory to the Father, and to the Son, and to the Holy Spirit,
as it was in the beginning, is now, and will be forever. Amen.**

Come, let us bow down and bend the knee : let us kneel before the LORD our Maker.

Song "Were You There?"

Jesus, remember me : when you come into your kingdom.

Psalm 106:43–46
Many a time did he deliver them, but they rebelled through their own devices : **and were brought down in their iniquity.**
Nevertheless, he saw their distress : **when he heard their lamentation.**
He remembered his covenant with them : **and relented in accordance with his great mercy.**
He caused them to be pitied : **by those who held them captive.**

Jesus, remember me : when you come into your kingdom.

Zechariah 14:1–11   Revelation 20:1–6

Jesus, remember me : when you come into your kingdom.

A prayer of Catherine of Siena: "My sweet Lord, look with mercy upon your people and especially upon the mystical body of your church. It would be no consolation for me to enjoy your life if your holy people stood in death. For I see that sin darkens the life of your bride the church — my sin and the sins of others."

Prayers for Others

Our Father

Jesus, please remember us, and that will strengthen us to turn again to you, to choose life, to work for justice and peace, to practice hospitality, to love our neighbors, and to trust that you will strengthen and equip us for the task. Thanks be to God. Amen.

**May the peace of the Lord Christ go with you : wherever he may send you;
may he guide you through the wilderness : protect you through the storm;
may he bring you home rejoicing : at the wonders he has shown you;
may he bring you home rejoicing : once again into our doors.**

November 22

Eberhard and Emmy Arnold (1883–1935; 1884–1980)

During the Reformation, there were those who believed that Luther and Calvin did not go far enough in recovering the radical spirit of Christianity, namely in regard to the Christian attitude toward violence and personal property. These Radical Reformers stressed community, simplicity, and an uncompromising commitment to gospel nonviolence. They suffered persecution from Protestants and Catholics alike, and their spirit took root in such communities as the Hutterites and Mennonites, which continue to this day. Eberhard and Emmy Arnold drew on this tradition centuries later in the midst of Nazi Germany. They started a community called the Bruderhof ("house of brothers"), whose ethic was the Sermon on the Mount. Their presence was a prophetic critique of the nationalism and militarism of Nazi Germany and of the Christianity that was silent amid such evil. In November 1933, their community was taken over by the Gestapo and they fled. Eberhard died in 1935 and Emmy lived on for forty-five more years, helping to start many other communities. Their lives and writings have inspired many communities, and their witness has touched people around the world.

O Lord, let my soul rise up to meet you
as the day rises to meet the sun.

**Glory to the Father, and to the Son, and to the Holy Spirit,
as it was in the beginning, is now, and will be forever. Amen.**

Come, let us sing to the Lord : let us shout for joy to the Rock of our salvation.

Song   "Freedom Train"

Just when I thought I was lost : my dungeon shook and the chains fell off.

Psalm 107:10–16
Some sat in darkness and deep gloom : **bound fast in misery and iron;**
because they rebelled against the words of God : **and despised the counsel of the Most High.**
So he humbled their spirits with hard labor : **they stumbled, and there was none to help.**
Then they cried to the Lord in their trouble : **and he delivered them from their distress.**
He led them out of darkness and deep gloom : **and broke their bonds asunder.**
Let them give thanks to the Lord for his mercy : **and the wonders he does for his children.**
For he shatters the doors of bronze : **and breaks in two the iron bars.**

Just when I thought I was lost : my dungeon shook and the chains fell off.

Zechariah 14:12–21   Revelation 20:7–15

Just when I thought I was lost : my dungeon shook and the chains fell off.

Eberhard Arnold said, "Life in community is no less than a necessity for us — it is an inescapable 'must' that determines everything we do and think. Yet it is not our good intentions or efforts that have been decisive in our choosing this way of life. Rather, we have been overwhelmed by a certainty — a certainty that has its origin and power in the Source of everything that exists. We acknowledge God as this Source. We must live in community because all life created by God exists in a communal order and works toward community."

Albert Luthuli, who struggled nonviolently against apartheid in South Africa, said, "It is inevitable that in working for freedom some individuals and some families must take the lead and suffer: the road to freedom is via the cross."

Prayers for Others

Our Father

Father, Son, and Holy Spirit, our journey with you shapes our journey with one another. Let your tender mercies come to us that we may live again. Amen.
May the peace of the Lord Christ go with you : wherever he may send you; may he guide you through the wilderness : protect you through the storm; may he bring you home rejoicing : at the wonders he has shown you; may he bring you home rejoicing : once again into our doors.

✶ November 23

O Lord, let my soul rise up to meet you
as the day rises to meet the sun.

Glory to the Father, and to the Son, and to the Holy Spirit, as it was in the beginning, is now, and will be forever. Amen.

Come, let us sing to the LORD : let us shout for joy to the Rock of our salvation.

Song   "Glory, Glory, Hallelujah"

Glory to your name, O Lord : you are our help and our shield.

Psalm 115:1–3, 9–11
Not to us, O LORD, not to us, but to your name give glory : **because of your love and because of your faithfulness.**
Why should the heathen say : **"Where then is their God?"**
Our God is in heaven : **whatever he wills to do he does.**
O Israel, trust in the LORD : **he is their help and their shield.**
O house of Aaron, trust in the LORD : **he is their help and their shield.**
You who fear the LORD, trust in the LORD : **he is their help and their shield.**

Glory to your name, O Lord : you are our help and our shield.

Isaiah 65:17–25   Revelation 21:1–8

Glory to your name, O Lord : you are our help and our shield.

Ignatius of Antioch said in the first century, "Our Lord was nailed on the cross so that through his resurrection he might set up a banner of victory throughout all ages."

Prayers for Others

Our Father

Lord, help us remember that no matter what things look like today, there is always a new dawn, a new morning, a new creation on the horizon. Your mercies are new every morning. Great is your faithfulness, Lord. Amen.

May the peace of the Lord Christ go with you : wherever he may send you;
may he guide you through the wilderness : protect you through the storm;
may he bring you home rejoicing : at the wonders he has shown you;
may he bring you home rejoicing : once again into our doors.

✳ November 24

O Lord, let my soul rise up to meet you
as the day rises to meet the sun.

Glory to the Father, and to the Son, and to the Holy Spirit,
as it was in the beginning, is now, and will be forever. Amen.

Come, let us sing to the LORD : let us shout for joy to the Rock of our salvation.

Song   "Woke Up This Mornin' "

Your mercies are new each morning, Lord : your faithful love lasts forever.

Psalm 118:1–5
Give thanks to the L ORD, for he is good : **his mercy endures for ever.**
Let Israel now proclaim : **"His mercy endures for ever."**
Let the house of Aaron now proclaim : **"His mercy endures for ever."**
Let those who fear the L ORD now proclaim : **"His mercy endures for ever."**
I called to the L ORD in my distress : **the L ORD answered by setting me free.**

Your mercies are new each morning, Lord : your faithful love lasts forever.

Isaiah 19:19–25   Revelation 21:22–22:5

Your mercies are new each morning, Lord : your faithful love lasts forever.

A prayer of Irish monk Columbanus: "Loving Savior, be pleased to show yourself to us who knock, so that in knowing you, we may love only you, love you alone, desire you alone, contemplate only you day and night, and always think of you. Inspire in us the depth of love that is fitting for you to receive as God. May our love be so great that the many waters of sky, land and sea cannot extinguish it in us."

Prayers for Others

Our Father

Lord, you've brought us safely to this new day. Help us to live it with joy, and in simple acts of kindness. Amen.

May the peace of the Lord Christ go with you : wherever he may send you;
may he guide you through the wilderness : protect you through the storm;
may he bring you home rejoicing : at the wonders he has shown you;
may he bring you home rejoicing : once again into our doors.

✦ November 25

O Lord, let my soul rise up to meet you
as the day rises to meet the sun.

Glory to the Father, and to the Son, and to the Holy Spirit,
as it was in the beginning, is now, and will be forever. Amen.

Come, let us sing to the L ORD : let us shout for joy to the Rock of our salvation.

Song   "It Is Well with My Soul"

Wake us to your presence, Lord : that we might not waste our times of trial.

Psalm 119:65–68
O LORD, you have dealt graciously with your servant : **according to your word.**
Teach me discernment and knowledge : **for I have believed in your commandments.**
Before I was afflicted I went astray : **but now I keep your word.**
You are good and you bring forth good : **instruct me in your statutes.**

Wake us to your presence, Lord : that we might not waste our times of trial.

Nahum 1:1–13   Revelation 22:6–13

Wake us to your presence, Lord : that we might not waste our times of trial.

Twentieth-century mystic Simone Weil wrote, "Affliction compels us to recognize as real what we do not think possible."

Prayers for Others

Our Father

What would you teach us today in our trials, Lord? Make us receptive! Help us see your victory and compassion rather than look for easy answers to our troubles. So make us expectant, Lord, and patient. Amen.

**May the peace of the Lord Christ go with you : wherever he may send you;
may he guide you through the wilderness : protect you through the storm;
may he bring you home rejoicing : at the wonders he has shown you;
may he bring you home rejoicing : once again into our doors.**

November 26

Sojourner Truth

Sojourner Truth, named Isabella by her master, escaped from slavery to freedom in 1826 and worked for several years as a domestic in New York City. But when she heard a call to travel, going "up and down the land, showing the people their sins and being a sign unto them," Isabella changed her name and became an itinerant evangelist for the causes of abolition and women's rights. In 1864, she traveled to Washington, D.C., to encourage Abraham Lincoln in his struggle against the Confederacy, staying on to minister to the ex-slaves who had gathered in refugee camps. She was still there on December 12, 1865, when Congress ratified its thirteenth amendment to the Constitution, abolishing slavery in the United States.

O Lord, let my soul rise up to meet you
as the day rises to meet the sun.

**Glory to the Father, and to the Son, and to the Holy Spirit,
as it was in the beginning, is now, and will be forever. Amen.**

Come, let us bow down and bend the knee : let us kneel before the LORD our Maker.

Song "Swing Low, Sweet Chariot"

Free us from the chains, Lord : that bind us as slaves and masters.

Psalm 119:169–74
Let my cry come before you, O LORD : **give me understanding, according to your word.**
Let my supplication come before you : **deliver me, according to your promise.**
My lips shall pour forth your praise : **when you teach me your statutes.**
My tongue shall sing of your promise : **for all your commandments are righteous.**
Let your hand be ready to help me : **for I have chosen your commandments.**
I long for your salvation, O LORD : **and your law is my delight.**

Free us from the chains, Lord : that bind us as slaves and masters.

Obadiah 15–21   Revelation 22:14–21

Free us from the chains, Lord : that bind us as slaves and masters.

Sojourner Truth said, "What we give the poor, we lend to the Lord."

Prayers for Others

Our Father

Lord, please make it so that we would rather choose death than partake in evils against humanity. Make it so that we would rather risk our reputation and security than deny your call to work for freedom for the oppressed. Amen.

**May the peace of the Lord Christ go with you : wherever he may send you;
may he guide you through the wilderness : protect you through the storm;
may he bring you home rejoicing : at the wonders he has shown you;
may he bring you home rejoicing : once again into our doors.**

November 27

O Lord, let my soul rise up to meet you
as the day rises to meet the sun.

**Glory to the Father, and to the Son, and to the Holy Spirit,
as it was in the beginning, is now, and will be forever. Amen.**

Come, let us sing to the LORD : **let us shout for joy to the Rock of our salvation.**

Song "Solid Rock"

Show us your goodness, Lord : and steady our hearts in you.

Psalm 125
Those who trust in the LORD are like Mount Zion : **which cannot be moved, but stands fast for ever.**
The hills stand about Jerusalem : **so does the LORD stand round about his people, from this time forth for evermore.**
The scepter of the wicked shall not hold sway over the land allotted to the just : **so that the just shall not put their hands to evil.**
Show your goodness, O LORD, to those who are good : **and to those who are true of heart.**
As for those who turn aside to crooked ways, the LORD will lead them away with the evildoers : **but peace be upon Israel.**

Show us your goodness, Lord : and steady our hearts in you.

Zephaniah 3:1 – 13   Mark 13:1 – 8

Show us your goodness, Lord : and steady our hearts in you.

Genesius the Actor had a conversion experience while mocking Christians before Emperor Diocletian and was martyred for his faith. He said, "There is no other Lord beside him whom I have seen. Him I worship and serve, and to him I will cling, though I should suffer a thousand deaths."

Prayers for Others

Our Father

Lord, steady our feet when the world tries to rock and shake our faith. When materialism beckons with coy hands, steady our feet. When lust sashays within us, steady our feet. When fear tugs at our knees, steady our faith. Show us your goodness, and steady our hearts in you. Amen.

May the peace of the Lord Christ go with you : wherever he may send you;
may he guide you through the wilderness : protect you through the storm;
may he bring you home rejoicing : at the wonders he has shown you;
may he bring you home rejoicing : once again into our doors.

✸ November 28

O Lord, let my soul rise up to meet you
as the day rises to meet the sun.

**Glory to the Father, and to the Son, and to the Holy Spirit,
as it was in the beginning, is now, and will be forever. Amen.**

Come, let us sing to the LORD : let us shout for joy to the Rock of our salvation.

Song "Vamos Todos al Banquete"

We thank you for your goodness, Lord : we praise you for your mercy.

Psalm 136:1–3, 7–9
Give thanks to the LORD, for he is good : **for his mercy endures for ever.**
Give thanks to the God of gods : **for his mercy endures for ever.**
Give thanks to the Lord of lords : **for his mercy endures for ever.**
Who created great lights : **for his mercy endures for ever;**
the sun to rule the day : **for his mercy endures for ever;**
the moon and the stars to govern the night : **for his mercy endures for ever.**

We thank you for your goodness, Lord : we praise you for your mercy.

Isaiah 24:14–23   Mark 13:9–23

We thank you for your goodness, Lord : we praise you for your mercy.

Erasmus of Rotterdam, a sixteenth-century priest who was committed to reforming the church from within, said, "When faith came to be in writings rather than in hearts, contention grew hot and love grew cold. That which is forced cannot be sincere, and that which is not voluntary cannot please Christ."

Prayers for Others

Our Father

Lord, just as your love knows no bounds and finds endless ways to reveal itself, so help us to express a gratitude too deep for words. Help us to learn to reveal our thanksgiving in the countless ways there are to love others, to provide for those in need, to serve where service is rare. Amen.

May the peace of the Lord Christ go with you : wherever he may send you;
may he guide you through the wilderness : protect you through the storm;
may he bring you home rejoicing : at the wonders he has shown you;
may he bring you home rejoicing : once again into our doors.

✸ November 29

Dorothy Day (1897 – 1980)
Dorothy Day was born in Brooklyn in 1897. She worked as a journalist for radical newspapers in the 1920s and found most of her friends in the bohemian crowds that gathered in Greenwich Village. While living with a man she loved in 1926, she became pregnant and experienced a mysterious conversion to Jesus. As a Roman Catholic, she struggled to unite her personal faith with passion for social justice until she met Peter Maurin, with whom she founded the Catholic Worker Movement in 1933. Through hospitality houses in the city, agronomic universities on the land, and roundtable discussions for the clarification of thought, they aimed to "create a new society within the shell of the old," offering American Christianity the witness of a new monasticism that combines piety and practice, charity and justice.

O Lord, let my soul rise up to meet you
as the day rises to meet the sun.

**Glory to the Father, and to the Son, and to the Holy Spirit,
as it was in the beginning, is now, and will be forever. Amen.**

Come, let us sing to the LORD : let us shout for joy to the Rock of our salvation.

Song "Come, Thou Fount"

Teach us, Lord, every day : the duty of delight.

Psalm 139:10 – 16
If I say, "Surely the darkness will cover me : **and the light around me turn to night,"**
darkness is not dark to you; the night is as bright as the day : **darkness and light to you are both alike.**
For you yourself created my inmost parts : **you knit me together in my mother's womb.**
I will thank you because I am marvelously made : **your works are wonderful, and I know it well.**
My body was not hidden from you : **while I was being made in secret and woven in the depths of the earth.**
Your eyes beheld my limbs, yet unfinished in the womb; all of them were

written in your book : **they were fashioned day by day, when as yet there was none of them.**
How deep I find your thoughts, O God! : **how great is the sum of them!**

Teach us, Lord, every day : the duty of delight.

Micah 7:1–10   Mark 13:24–31

Teach us, Lord, every day : the duty of delight.

Dorothy Day said, "The greatest challenge of the day is how to bring about a revolution of the heart, a revolution which has to start with each one of us."

Prayers for Others

Our Father

Lord, you show us the same compassion and commitment that a mother has for her tiny child. Teach us to care so completely. Show us how to delight in serving with the same joy you show in nurturing your creation. Amen.

**May the peace of the Lord Christ go with you : wherever he may send you;
may he guide you through the wilderness : protect you through the storm;
may he bring you home rejoicing : at the wonders he has shown you;
may he bring you home rejoicing : once again into our doors.**

 November 30

O Lord, let my soul rise up to meet you
as the day rises to meet the sun.

**Glory to the Father, and to the Son, and to the Holy Spirit,
as it was in the beginning, is now, and will be forever. Amen.**

Come, let us sing to the LORD : **let us shout for joy to the Rock of our salvation.**

Song   "We Are Marching in the Light of God"

If we are in the light as you are in the light : we can find our way together.

Psalm 147:1–5
Hallelujah! How good it is to sing praises to our God! : **how pleasant it is to honor him with praise!**
The LORD rebuilds Jerusalem : **he gathers the exiles of Israel.**
He heals the brokenhearted : **and binds up their wounds.**
He counts the number of the stars : **and calls them all by their names.**
Great is our LORD and mighty in power : **there is no limit to his wisdom.**

If we are in the light as you are in the light : we can find our way together.

Micah 7:11–20   Mark 13:32–37

If we are in the light as you are in the light : we can find our way together.

American farmer and poet Wendell Berry has written, "Sabbath observance invites us to stop. It invites us to rest. It asks us to notice that while we rest, the world continues without our help. It invites us to delight in the world's beauty and abundance."

Prayers for Others

Our Father

Lord, the morning sings of your beauty and lightness of heart. There is always fresh hope in the morning if we stop to receive it. The new possibilities of morning are like a glimpse of Sabbath, when we are reminded that everything happens because you permit it and that the end of history is in your hands. Thanks be to God. Amen.

**May the peace of the Lord Christ go with you : wherever he may send you;
may he guide you through the wilderness : protect you through the storm;
may he bring you home rejoicing : at the wonders he has shown you;
may he bring you home rejoicing : once again into our doors.**

> **A Note on Christ the King Sunday**
>
> The last day of the Christian calendar is Christ the King Sunday. This day was established very late in the life of the church (1925), in the face of rising violence and racism in the world. On this final Sunday we remember that our first and foremost allegiance is to Jesus, not to nation, tribe, or biological family. The next day marks the beginning of Advent, and we'll do it all again (for another two thousand years).

Becoming the Answer to Our Prayers: A Few Ideas

1. Spend the day baking cookies or bread. Give them away to the person who delivers your mail or picks up your trash next time you see them.
2. Host a rain barrel party and teach neighbors how to capture water to use in the garden or for doing laundry.
3. Spend a day hiking in the woods. Consider how God cares for the lilies and the sparrows—and you.
4. Gather some neighbors and plant a tree in your neighborhood together.
5. Hold a knowledge exchange, in which you gather friends or neighbors to share a skill or something they are learning.

MIDDAY PRAYER

Draw us into your love, Christ Jesus : **and deliver us from fear.**

**Lord, make me an instrument of your peace.
Where there is hatred, let me bring love;
where there is injury, pardon;
where there is doubt, faith;
where there is despair, hope;
where there is darkness, light;
where there is sadness, joy.
O Divine Master, grant that I may not
so much seek to be consoled as to console,
to be understood as to understand,
to be loved as to love.
For it is in giving that we receive,
it is in pardoning that we are pardoned,
and it is in dying that we are born to eternal life.**

**Glory to the Father, and to the Son, and to the Holy Spirit,
as it was in the beginning, is now, and will be forever. Amen.**

Silence for meditation

Our Father

Make us worthy, Lord, to serve our brothers and sisters throughout the world, who live and die in poverty and pain. Give them today, through our hands, their daily bread and, through our understanding, love; give peace and joy. Amen.

Blessed are the poor,
for theirs is the kingdom of God.
Blessed are the hungry,
for they shall be filled.
Blessed are the meek,
for they shall inherit the earth.
Blessed are the pure in heart,
for they shall see God.
Blessed are those who mourn,
for they shall be comforted.
Blessed are the merciful,
for they shall be shown mercy.

Blessed are the peacemakers,
for they are the children of God.
Blessed are those who are persecuted for righteousness and justice,
for great is their reward.

Come, Holy Spirit. We pray that your fruit would be in us : love, joy, peace, patience, kindness, goodness, faithfulness, gentleness, and self-control.

Dear Jesus, help us to spread your fragrance everywhere we go.

Soul of Christ, sanctify me;
body of Christ, save me;
blood of Christ, inebriate me;
water from the side of Christ, wash me;
passion of Christ, strengthen me.
O good Jesus, hear me;
within your wounds hide me;
suffer me not to be separated from you;
from the malicious enemy defend me;
in the hour of my death call me,
and bid me come to you
that with your saints I may praise you
forever and ever. Amen.

Through our lives and by our prayers : may your kingdom come!

In the name of the Father, and of the Son, and of the Holy Spirit. Amen.

Passing the Peace

> **Passing the Peace**
>
> "Passing the peace" is an ancient tradition whereby brothers and sisters in Christ share a hug or handshake, or a "holy kiss," as a sign of our love. (Perhaps try starting with a holy hug.) Often the embrace is accompanied by a wish for the "peace of Christ" to be with another. (This is often said out loud as hugs are exchanged.) It is also a sign that we have reconciled wrongs with one another and with anyone who might be holding something against us (Rom. 16:16; 1 Cor. 16:20; 2 Cor. 13:12; 1 Thess. 5:26; 1 Peter 5:14). Even if you say your midday prayer alone, take a moment to think of the people you need to connect with to share a joy, a confession, or a burden.

OCCASIONAL PRAYERS

These prayers for special occasions have been gathered from communities around the globe. Some of them are new, and some are ancient. They are offered here as tools, and you are invited to use them or adapt them so that they fit your community and the occasion. Many other prayers are available on the website www.commonprayer.net.

✠ House Blessing

At the Doorway

May God give a blessing to this house.
God bless this house from roof to floor,
from wall to wall,
from end to end,
from its foundation and in its covering.
In the strong name of the triune God,
all disturbance cease,
captive spirits freed,
God's Spirit alone
dwell within these walls.

**We call upon the Sacred Three
to save, shield, and surround
this house, this home,
this day, this night,
and every night.**

In the Entrance or Foyer

May all be welcomed here,
friend and stranger, from near and far.
May each be blessed and honored
as they enter.
There is a friend's love
in the gentle heart of the Savior.
For love of him we offer friendship
and welcome every guest.

**We call upon the Sacred Three
to save, shield, and surround
this house, this home,
this day, this night,
and every night.**

In the Living Room

There is a friend's love
in the gentle heart of the Savior.
For love of him we offer friendship
and welcome every guest.
Lord, kindle in our hearts
a flame of love for our neighbor,
for our enemies, our friends, our kindred all,
from the lowliest thing that liveth
to the name that is highest of all.

**We call upon the Sacred Three
to save, shield, and surround
this house, this home,
this day, this night,
and every night.**

At a Warm Place (or the Furnace)

There is a fiery power
in the gentle heart of the Spirit.
Our hearts are agreed
as we kneel by the hearth,
and call on the Sacred Three
to save, shield, and surround
us and our kin,
this house, this home,
this day, this night,
and every night.

**We call upon the Sacred Three
to save, shield, and surround
this house, this home,
this day, this night,
and every night.**

In the Kitchen

May we welcome the poor and honor them.
May we welcome the sick and care for them,
in the presence of angels,
and we ask you, God, to bless and embrace us all.
Seeing a stranger approach,
may we put food in the eating place,
drink in the drinking place,

music in the listening place,
and look with joy for the blessing of God,
who often comes to our homes
in the blessing of a stranger.

**We call upon the Sacred Three
to save, shield, and surround
this house, this home,
this day, this night,
and every night.**

For a Bedroom

Peace be here in the name of the King of life;
the peace of Christ above all peace,
the Lord's blessing over you.

**We call upon the Sacred Three
to save, shield, and surround
this house, this home,
this day, this night,
and every night.**

For the Bedroom of a Single Person

Peace be here in the name of the King of life;
the peace of Christ above all peace,
the Lord's blessing over you.

May God the Father be the guardian of this place
and bring his peace,
that fear may find no entry here.
May Christ be a chosen companion and friend.
May loneliness be banished.
May the Spirit bring lightness and laughter,
and be the comforter of tears.
Courage be at each going out;
rest be present at each return;
each day, each night,
each going out and each returning.

For the Bedroom of a Married Couple

Peace be here in the name of the King of life;
the peace of Christ above all peace,
the Lord's blessing over you.

Peace between person and person;
peace between husband and wife.
The peace of Christ above all peace,
peace between lovers
in love of the King of life.

For a Guest Room

**Peace be here in the name of the King of life;
the peace of Christ above all peace,
the Lord's blessing over you.**

May all be welcomed here
as the Christ child at the stable:
in simplicity and joy,
and as saints before us have welcomed the poor,
may the smile of the Son of Peace
be found here
whenever the door is opened.

For the Room of a Young Child

To be said by the parent(s) if possible:
**Peace be here in the name of the King of life;
the peace of Christ above all peace,
the Lord's blessing over you.**

They say nothing is given birth without pain.
I have a secret joy in thee, my God,
for if thou art my Father,
thou art my Mother too,
and of thy tenderness, healing, and patience
there is no end at all.
I pray for (*name*).
(*Name*), may the joy and peace of heaven
be with you.
The Lord bless you.

For the Room of an Older Son or Daughter, Present or Absent

To be said by the parent(s) if possible:
**Peace be here in the name of the King of life;
the peace of Christ above all peace,
the Lord's blessing over you.**

Son of my breast/daughter of my heart,
the joy of God be in thy face,
joy to all who see thee,
the circle of God around thee,
angels of God shielding thee.
Joy of night and day be thine;
joy of sun and moon be thine;
joy of men and women be thine;
each land and sea thou goest,
be every season happy for thee;
be every season bright for thee;
be every season glad for thee.
Be thine the compassing of the God of life;
be thine the compassing of the Christ of love;
be thine the compassing of the Spirit of grace:
to befriend thee and to aid thee,
(*Name*), thou beloved son of my breast/
thou beloved daughter of my heart.

At the Door (or at a Cross)

Christ, in our coming
and in our leaving,
the Door and the Keeper;
for us and our dear ones,
this day and every day,
blessing for always. Amen.

**We call upon the Sacred Three
to save, shield, and surround
this house, this home,
this day, this night,
and every night.
Amen.**

✣ Prayers for a Workplace

Outside the Doorway

May God give a blessing on this place.
God bless it from roof to floor,
from wall to wall, from end to end,
from its foundation and in its covering.
In the strong name of the triune God:
all evil be banished,
all disturbance cease,
captive spirits freed.
God's Spirit alone
dwell within these walls.

**We call upon the Sacred Three
to save, shield, and surround
this house, this home,
this day, this night,
and every night.**

In Each Room and Work Area

**Peace be here in the name of the King of life;
the peace of Christ above all peace,
the Lord's blessing over all.**

May God the Father
be guardian of this place
and bring his peace.
May God's love be shared here,
may God's will be found here,
and may there be peace between all people who work here.

**We call upon the Sacred Three
to save, shield, and surround
this house, this home,
this day, this night,
and every night.**

At the Door

Christ, in our coming
and in our leaving,
be the Door and the Keeper
for us

and for all who work within this place,
this day and every day,
forever and always.
Amen.

We call upon the Sacred Three
to save, shield, and surround
this house, this home,
this day, this night,
and every night.
Amen.

Major Life Transition

Lord, help me now to unclutter my life, to organize myself in the direction of simplicity. Lord, teach me to listen to my heart; teach me to welcome change, instead of fearing it. Lord, I give you these stirrings inside me. I give you my discontent. I give you my restlessness. I give you my doubt. I give you my despair. I give you all the longings I hold inside. Help me to listen to these signs of change, of growth; help me to listen seriously and follow where they lead through the breathtaking empty space of an open door.

✠ Before or After a Meal

Lord God, Creator of all,
in your wisdom,
you have bound us together so that we must depend on others
for the food we eat,
the resources we use,
the gifts of your creation that bring life, health, and joy.

Creator God, we give thanks.

Holy be the hands that sew our clothes so that we do not have to go naked;
sacred be the hands that build our homes so that we do not have to be cold;
blessed be the hands that work the land so that we do not have to go hungry.

Creator God, we give thanks.

Holy be the feet of all who labor so that we might have rest;
sacred be the feet of all who run swiftly to stand with the oppressed;
blessed be the feet of all whose bodies are too broken or weary to stand.

Creator God, we give thanks.

Holy be the sound of children laughing to take away our sorrow;
sacred be the sound of water falling to take away our thirst;
blessed be the sound of your people singing to heal our troubled hearts.

Creator God, we give thanks.

Holy be the bodies of those who know hunger;
sacred be the bodies of those who are broken;
blessed be the bodies of those who suffer.
In your mercy and grace,
soften our callous hearts and
fill us with gratitude for all the gifts you have given us.
In your love,
break down the walls that separate us
and guide us along your path of peace,
that we might humbly worship you in Spirit and in truth.
Amen.

✠ Prayer to Welcome the Sabbath

Lord of Creation,
create in us a new rhythm of life
composed of hours that sustain rather than stress,
of days that deliver rather than destroy,
of time that tickles rather than tackles.

Lord of Liberation,
by the rhythm of your truth, set us free
from the bondage and baggage that break us,
from the Pharaohs and fellows who fail us,
from the plans and pursuits that prey upon us.

Lord of Resurrection,
may we be raised into the rhythm of your new life,
dead to deceitful calendars,
dead to fleeting friend requests,
dead to the empty peace of our accomplishments.

To our packed-full planners, we bid, "Peace!"
To our over-caffeinated consciences, we say, "Cease!"
To our suffocating selves, Lord, grant release.

Drowning in a sea of deadlines and death chimes,
we rest in you, our lifeline.

By your ever-restful grace,
allow us to enter your Sabbath rest
as your Sabbath rest enters into us.

In the name of our Creator,
our Liberator,
our Resurrection and Life,
we pray.
Amen.

✠ Death of Someone Killed in the Neighborhood

Lamb of God,
you take away the sins of the world.
Have mercy on us.
Grant us peace.

For the unbearable toil of our sinful world,
we plead for remission.
For the terror of absence from our beloved,
we plead for your comfort.
For the scandalous presence of death in your creation,
we plead for the resurrection.

Lamb of God,
you take away the sins of the world.
Have mercy on us.
Grant us peace.
Come, Holy Spirit, and heal all that is broken in our lives, in our streets, and in our world. In the name of the Father, and of the Son, and of the Holy Spirit. Amen.

✠ For Healing

In the name of the Father, and of the Son, and of the Holy Spirit,
we enjoin your divine mercies.
Lord, why do we suffer?
Why do we hurt?
Shall our only answer
be the eternal abyss of the cosmos?
Shall our only answer be the whirlwind of unknowing
which engulfed Job?
Why do the wicked flourish,
while the righteous waste away?
I am left speechless, left with the words,
"I will trust in you, my God."

God, we ask for the sending of your healing Spirit,
who came to us through Jesus, as he breathed upon his disciples.
This Spirit gathered your people,
to be warmed by the fire of divine presence.
By this warmth, may (*name of sick person*)
be healed and taken into your care.

Like the blind man whom Jesus healed,
may (*name of sick person*) become a sign
of your glory, calling you the Anointed One,
the one who also anoints us and points us to the love of God.
Grants us your healing peace. Amen.

✠ A Prayer for Adoption

Generous and divine Trinity,
we give thanks for the presence
of our holy brothers and sisters.

We give thanks that you created the world,
though it turned from your ways.
We give thanks that you began a people
to bless this world,
though it did not always bless.
We give thanks, with greatest reverence,
for the gift of your Son, Jesus Christ,
who indeed blessed the world.
Thanks be to you for the signs and glory of
the Lamb of God.

In him, we are all adopted children of God.
We are brought into the divine redemption,
which now subsists in each embrace,
each extension of love.
Each sacrament,
each kiss and act of service.

May the adoption of this beloved child (*name of adopted*)
be blessed.
Almighty God, you adopted your people in Egypt,
and they came out into the wilderness to pitch a tent.
May (we) the family of this beloved child
enjoy the presence of God
in the tent of life together
as they (we) look toward the pillar of fire by day —
a sign of your coming glorious redemption;
and the pillar of cloud by night —
a sign of your presence amid our trials and darkness.

In Christ, the Son of God,
there is neither adoptive nor natural parents and children.

We are all born again in the Spirit of God.
This Spirit redeems us with the substance of faith, hope, and love.
May this child be blessed by the mysterious presence, mercy, and grace of the Trinity,
Father, Son, and Holy Spirit.
Amen.

✠ Baby Dedication

Celebrant:

The blessing of Christ
comes to you in this child.
God's blessing is mercy
and kindness and joy.
Blessing comes to home
and to family.

Welcome, *(name of child)*,
child of love.
God is here to bless you.
And blessed are you,
beyond telling,
to be born to parents
who love you
and love each other.

Grow gently, *(name of child)*,
in love of God.
We bless you,
and pray
Christ be near you,
now and each hour
of your life.

All:

**God be with you
in this your day,
every day and every way,
with you and for you
in this your day,
and the love
and affection
of heaven
be toward you.**

Celebrant:
As a tiny baby
your parents cover
and clothe you
in their love
and with their faith.

As you grow
may faith grow with you.
May you find the presence
of Christ your clothing
and protection.
And year by year may the
knowledge of his presence
be greater for you,
that daily you may put on Christ
and walk as his own in the world.

Parents:
May God make clear to you each road;
may God make safe to you each step;
should you stumble, hold you;
if you fall, lift you up;
when you are hard pressed with evil,
deliver you,
and bring you at last to God's glory.

Celebrant, facing the parents:
The blessing of Christ
comes to you in your (*name of child*);
this blessing is mercy
and kindness and joy.
Blessing comes to home
and to family.

✠ Commissioning/Sending Out

In the name of the divine Trinity,
let us pray.
God, you have called us into being
through love.
You have joined us to one another
in love.
How good and pleasant it is
when your people dwell together in unity.

Shine your light upon your people
that we can see the glory of eternal life.
Grant (*name of commissioned*) the strength
to carry your blessing from this place to the next.
May he/she be at home in any land,
for all the earth is yours.
And, with his/her hopes set on your coming glory in the world,
live also an alien in all lands.
May the lamp of your word
guide his/her feet on the unsure paths of life.

Our lives are but a breath,
but our breaths are drawn from your divine Spirit.
You have created us as walking paradoxes.
Specks of dust and divine-image bearers.
We are constantly restless
until we rest in you.

Grant (*name of commissioned*) a deeper fullness
of being and spirit,
by carrying our memory with him/her
in the coming journey.
May his/her face be fuller in glory and joy,
now bearing new shape,
as our faces transform and supplement one another.

Go in the peace of Christ to love and serve the Lord.

Thanks be to God!

✠ Celibacy Commitment

Initiate: My Father,
I abandon myself to you.
Make of me what you will.
Whatever you make of me,
I thank you.
I am ready for everything.
I accept everything.
Provided that your will be done in me,
in all your creatures,
I desire nothing else, Lord.
I put my soul in your hands.
I give it to you, Lord,
with all the love in my heart,
because I love you,
and because it is for me a need of love
to give myself,
to put myself in your hands unreservedly,
with infinite trust.
For you are my Father!

Minister: What do you ask?
Initiate: The mercy of God and of the church.

Minister: The Lord Christ has chosen you to be in the church a sign of pure love.
Initiate: Uphold me, O God, according to your word, and I shall live; and do not disappoint me in my hope.

Minister: Do you commit to celibacy in the context of Christian community so long as you shall live?
Initiate: I do.

Minister: Do you give yourself fully to the church?
Initiate: I do.

Minister: Will you love her, comfort her, honor and keep her, in sickness and in health; and forsaking all others be faithful only unto her, so long as you shall live?
Initiate: I will.

Minister: Do you, (*name of initiate*), promise to love, rather than force your way; to give your life away, no longer living for yourself but for your sisters and brothers, loving them, humbly submitting to them, shepherding them, living with them?
Initiate: I do.

Minister: Do you, (*name of congregation/community*), promise to honor (*name of initiate*) as part of your family and not to take his/her offering lightly? Do you take (*name of initiate*) to be your brother/sister, to love him/her, comfort him/her, honor and keep him/her in sickness and in health?
Larger community: We do.

Minster: Family and friends, do you rejoice with (*name of initiate*) in his/her love for the church?
Family and friends: We do.

Minster: Are you willing, now and always, to support and encourage (*name of initiate*) in his/her promise to church community and celibacy?
Family and friends: We are.

Minister: God, receive this daughter/son
who has promised single-minded devotion to you.
Give him/her grace to keep these promises,
sustain him/her by the encouragement of this community,
and lead us together into eternal life,
through Jesus Christ, our Lord. Amen.

✢ Blessing of the Land or a Garden

God of the Universe,
you made the heavens and the earth,
so we do not call our home merely "planet earth."
We call it your creation, a divine mystery,
a gift from your most blessed hand.
The world itself is your miracle.
Bread and vegetables from earth are thus also from heaven.
Help us to see in our daily bread your presence.

Upon this garden
may your stars rain down their blessed dust.

May you send rain and sunshine upon our garden and us.
Grant us the humility to touch the humus,
that we might become more human,
that we might mend our rift from your creation,
that we might then know the sacredness of the gift of life,
that we might truly experience life from your hand.
For you planted humanity in a garden
and began our resurrection in a garden.
Our blessed memory and hope lie in a garden.

Thanks be to God,
who made the world teeming with variety,
of things on the earth, above the earth, and under the earth.
Thanks be to God
for the many kinds of plants, trees, and fruits
that we celebrate.
For the centipedes, ants, and worms,
for the mice, marmots, and bats,
for the cucumbers, tomatoes, and peppers,
we rejoice
that we find ourselves eclipsed by the magnitude
of generosity and mystery.
Thanks be to God.

A Litany to Honor Women

We walk in the company of the women who have gone before, mothers of the faith both named and unnamed,
testifying with ferocity and faith to the Spirit of wisdom and healing.
They are the judges, the prophets, the martyrs, the warriors, poets, lovers, and saints
who are near to us in the shadow of awareness, in the crevices of memory, in the landscape of our dreams.

We walk in the company of Deborah,
who judged the Israelites with authority and strength.

We walk in the company of Esther,
who used her position as queen to ensure the welfare of her people.

We walk in the company of you whose names have been lost and silenced,
who kept and cradled the wisdom of the ages.

We walk in the company of the woman with the flow of blood,
who audaciously sought her healing and release.

We walk in the company of Mary Magdalene,
who wept at the empty tomb until the risen Christ appeared.

We walk in the company of Phoebe,
who led an early church in the empire of Rome.

We walk in the company of Perpetua of Carthage,
whose witness in the third century led to her martyrdom.

We walk in the company of St. Christina the Astonishing,
who resisted death with persistence and wonder.

We walk in the company of Julian of Norwich,
who wed imagination and theology, proclaiming, "All shall be well."

We walk in the company of Sojourner Truth,
who stood against oppression, righteously declaring in 1852, "Ain't I a woman!"

We walk in the company of the Argentine mothers of the Plaza de Mayo,
who turned their grief to strength, standing together to remember "the disappeared" children of war with a holy indignation.

We walk in the company of Alice Walker,
who named the lavender hue of womanish strength.

We walk in the company of you mothers of the faith,
who teach us to resist evil with boldness, to lead with wisdom, and to heal.

Amen.

✠ Sanctus

Holy, holy, holy Lord,
God of power and might,
heaven and earth are full of your glory.
Hosanna in the highest.
Blessed is he who comes in the name of the Lord.
Hosanna in the highest.

✠ Prayer for Communion/Eucharist

Celebrant:
The table of bread is now to be made ready.
It is the table of company with Jesus,
and all who love him.
It is the table of sharing with the poor of the world,
with whom Jesus identified himself.
It is the table of communion with the earth,
in which Christ became incarnate.
So come to this table,
you who have much faith
and you who would like to have more;
you who have been here often
and you who have not been for a long time;
you who have tried to follow Jesus,
and you who have failed;
come.
It is Christ who invites us to meet him here.

All:
**Loving God,
through your goodness
we have this bread and wine/grape juice to offer,
which has come forth from the earth
and human hands have made.
May we know your presence
in the sharing,
so that we may know your touch
and presence in all things.
We celebrate the life that Jesus has shared
among his community through the centuries,
and shares with us now.
Made one in Christ
and one with each other,
we offer these gifts and with them ourselves,
a single, living act of praise.
Amen.**

SONGBOOK

All Creatures of Our God and King

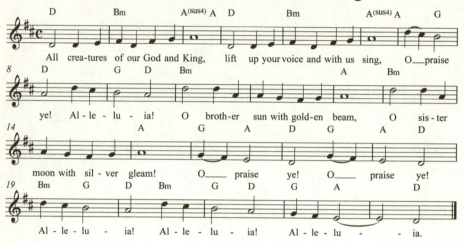

Amazing Grace

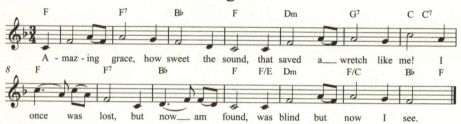

Be Thou My Vision

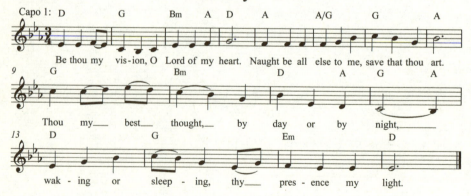

Come, Thou Fount

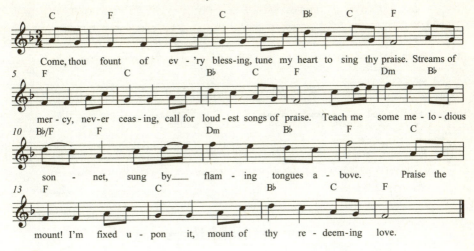

Come, Ye Sinners

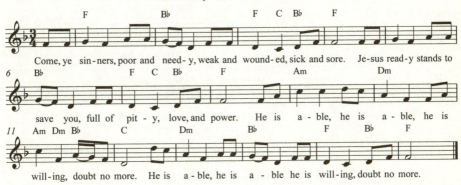

Doxology

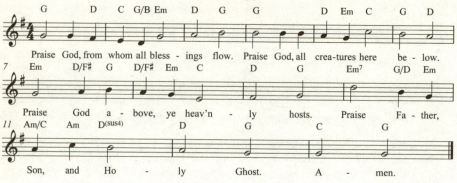

Fairest Lord Jesus

Freedom Train

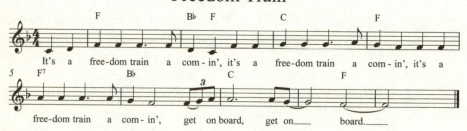

Gloria

Glory, Glory, Hallelujah

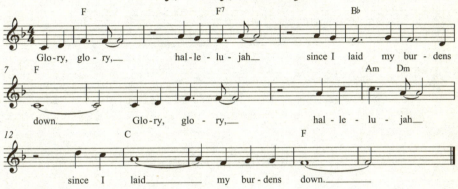

Go, Tell It on the Mountain

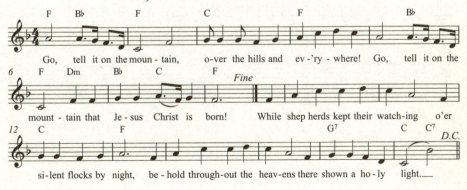

Great Is Thy Faithfulness

Guide My Feet

570 Songbook

Holy, Holy, Holy

It Is Well with My Soul

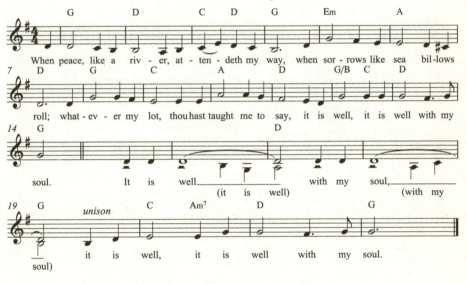

I Want Jesus to Walk with Me

I Will Trust in the Lord

Jesus, Help Us Live in Peace

The Kingdom of God

"The Kingdom of God," by Taizé
Copyright © 2007, Ateliers et Presses de Taizé,
Taizé Community, France
GIA Publications, Inc.
All rights reserved. Used by permission.

Lamb of God

"Lamb of God," by Tom Wuest
Used by permission.

Let All Mortal Flesh Keep Silence

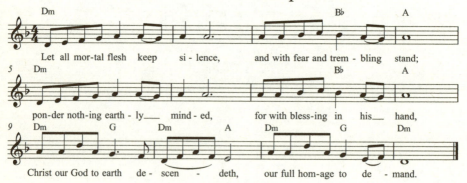

Magnificat

May the Peace of the Lord Christ Go with You

Nothin' but the Blood

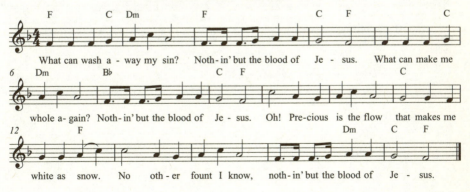

Oh the Deep, Deep Love of Jesus

O Lord, Have Mercy

"O Lord, Have Mercy," by Tom Wuest
Used by permission.

O Lord, Hear My Prayer

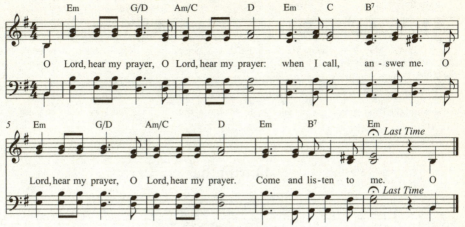

"O Lord, Hear My Prayer," by Taizé
Copyright © 1991, Ateliers et Presses de Taizé,
Taizé Community, France
GIA Publications, Inc.
All rights reserved. Used by permission.

O Lord, Let My Soul Rise Up to Meet You

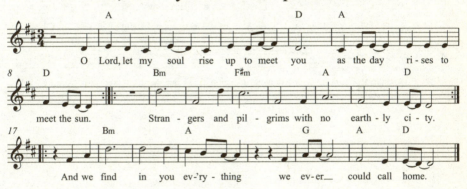

"O Lord, Let My Soul Rise Up to Meet You," by Jeremy Seigrist.
All rights reserved. Used by permission.

O Mary, Don't You Weep

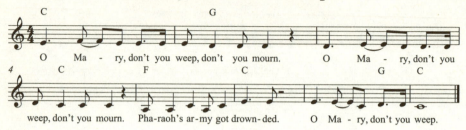

Our Father

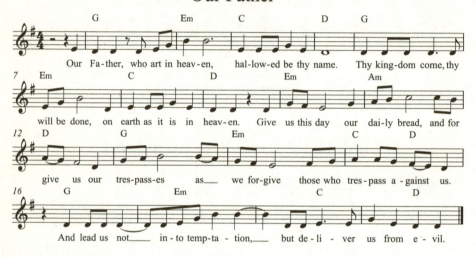

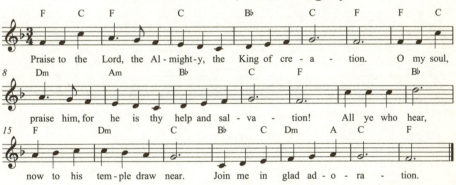

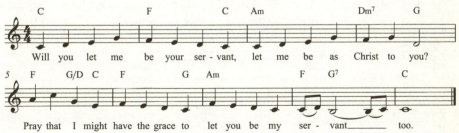

Composition/Song Title: THE SERVANT SONG
Writer Credits: Richard Gillard
Copyright: © 1977 Universal Music – Brentwood Benson Publishing (ASCAP).
All Rights Reserved. Used By Permission.

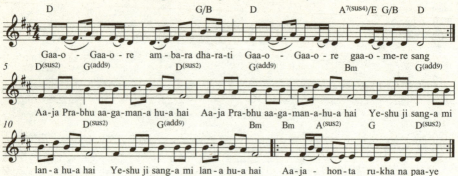
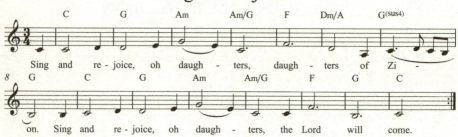
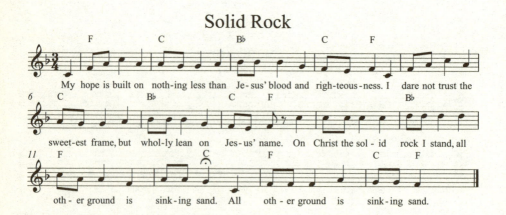

Steal Away to Jesus
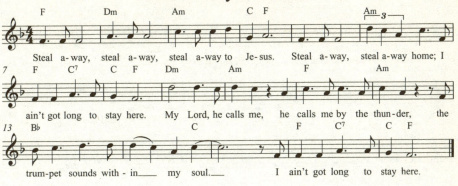

Swing Low, Sweet Chariot

Take My Life and Let It Be

This Little Light of Mine

Ubi Caritas

"Ubi Caritas," by Taizé
Copyright © 1978, 1980, 1981, Ateliers et Presses de Taizé,
Taizé Community, France
GIA Publications, Inc.
All rights reserved. Used by permission.

Vamos Todos al Banquete

Walk in the Light

Waters of Babylon

We Are Marching in the Light of God

Were You There?

We Shall Not Be Moved

We Shall Overcome

What Is This Place?

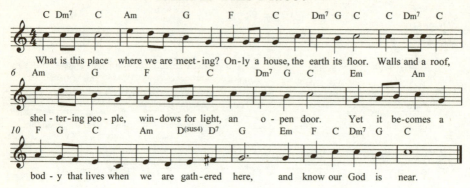

Text and Arrangement ©1967, Gooi En Sticht, Bv., Baarn, The Netherlands. All rights reserved.
Exclusive Agent for English-language Countries: OCP, 5536 NE Hassalo, Portland, OR 97213.
Music (c) 1983, OCP. Music, 5536 NE Hassalo, Portland, OR 97213.
All rights reserved. Used with permission.

What Wondrous Love

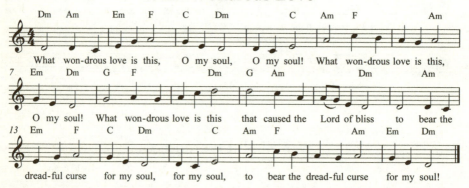

When the Saints Go Marching In

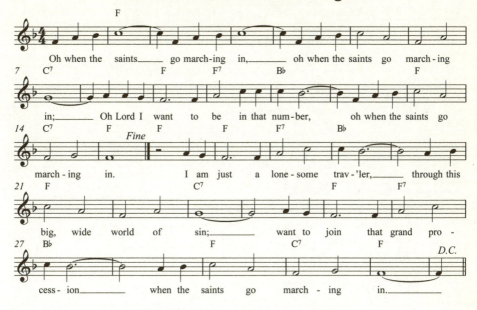

Woke Up This Mornin'

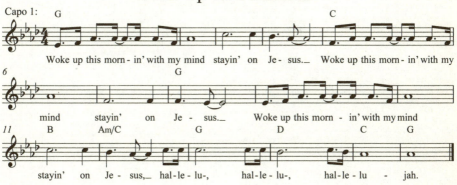

CREDITS

Common Prayer is something akin to a patchwork quilt of the prayers, quotes, songs, and Scriptures that are written on the hearts and on the walls of new monastics and their community houses. Much of what is here was gathered from elsewhere. The compilers acknowledge with thanks permission to reproduce the songs and poems listed below. Every effort has been made to trace copyright holders, and the compilers apologize to anyone whose rights have inadvertently not been acknowledged. This will be corrected in any future reprint.

"Jesus, Help Us Live in Peace," by JD Martin
    All rights reserved. Used by permission.

"The Kingdom of God," by Taizé
    Copyright © 2007, Ateliers et Presses de Taizé,
    Taizé Community, France
    GIA Publications, Inc., exclusive North American agent,
    7404 S. Mason Ave., Chicago, IL 60638
    www.giamusic.com 800.442.1358
    All rights reserved. Used by permission.

"Lamb of God," by Tom Wuest
    All rights reserved. Used by permission.

"Lord, Have Mercy," by Tom Wuest
    All rights reserved. Used by permission.

"May the Peace of the Lord Christ Go with You," by Peter Sutcliffe
    All rights reserved. Used by permission of the Northumbria Community.

"O Lord, Hear My Prayer," by Taizé
    Copyright © 1991, Ateliers et Presses de Taizé,
    Taizé Community, France
    GIA Publications, Inc., exclusive North American agent,
    7404 S. Mason Ave., Chicago, IL 60638
    www.giamusic.com 800.442.1358
    All rights reserved. Used by permission.

"O Lord, Let My Soul Rise Up to Meet You," by Jeremy Seigrist
All rights reserved. Used by permission.

"The Servant Song," by Richard Gillard
Copyright © 1977 Universal Music—Brentwood Benson Publishing (ASCAP).
All rights reserved. Used by permission.

"Sing, O Sky (Gaao Re)"
Melody by Pete Hicks and Chris Hale of Aradhna
Lyrics by Daisy Augustine
All rights reserved. Used by permission.

"Sing and Rejoice," by Tom Wuest
All rights reserved. Used by permission.

"Ubi Caritas," by Taizé
Copyright © 1978, 1980, 1981, Ateliers et Presses de Taizé,
Taizé Community, France
GIA Publications, Inc., exclusive North American agent,
7404 S. Mason Ave., Chicago, IL 60638
www.giamusic.com 800.442.1358
All rights reserved. Used by permission.

"What Is This Place?"
Text and Arrangement © 1967, Gooi En Sticht, Bv., Baarn, The Netherlands. All rights reserved. Exclusive Agent for English-language Countries: OCP, 5536 NE Hassalo, Portland, OR 97213. Music © 1983, OCP. Music, 5536 NE Hassalo, Portland, OR 97213. All rights reserved. Used with permission.

Excerpt from the poem "Manifesto: The Mad Farmer Liberation Front" from *The Collected Poems of Wendell Berry, 1957–1982*, © 1985 by Wendell Berry. Reprinted by permission of Counterpoint, 1919 Fifth Street, Berkeley, CA 94710.

The poem "Praying" from *Thirst* by Mary Oliver, copyright © 2006 by Mary Oliver. Reprinted by permission of Beacon Press.